W9-CGV-994

LIVING ABROAD IN
CHINA

BARBARA & STUART STROTHER

Contents

At Home in China

Welcome to the Middle Kingdom, as China calls itself. This is a land of ancient culture and modern progress, old ways and hip new styles, the proverbial yin and yang of contemporary Chinese life. This is a place where you'll still see fields being plowed by oxen, but the farmer may be chatting on his mobile phone as he works. Executives in Armani suits dash between high-powered business meetings, yet spend their holidays with Nai Nai (Grandma) at her village home, where she keeps ducks, grows plum trees, and cooks spicy tofu in her kitchen wok over an open fire.

When we were offered the opportunity to take jobs in China, we had a comfortable Midwestern American lifestyle: a big house in the country where our twin two-year-olds chased our fat black cat. But when we got that call, it didn't take much convincing to decide to trade the monotony of middle management for adventure in the Middle Kingdom.

Although we'd traveled in China on several occasions before, we were apprehensive about our move. We didn't know what our apartment would look like, what the job would be like, if we would love living there, or if we'd be tempted to beat a hasty retreat. We were fond of our American amenities: central air-conditioning, long hot showers, a Maytag washer and dryer, plush carpeted floors, a minivan, and a local Target store. Of all the modern conveniences we had come to rely on, how many would China be able to offer? And how would we get along without them? We didn't know if daily life in China would be as difficult to handle as we had always predicted, but we were willing to give it a try.

As we made our preparations for the big move, our excitement grew. The thrill of experiencing a new culture and the opportunity to expose our boys

to foreign worlds gradually overtook our fears of the unknown. We put our house on the market, got passports for the kids, and watched the movie *Big Bird in China* until we could sing along by heart.

We arrived in Shanghai on the eve of the Chinese New Year, watching exploding fireworks out the window of our new (and, thankfully, modern) apartment until we all drifted off to sleep. As we settled into our new life in China, we delightedly found that more often than not, life is actually easier in China. Without the hectic American do-all-you-can-do schedule, life slows down considerably. With this slower pace, we could make frequent forays beyond our city to discover China's innumerable fascinating spots. We've had dusty days in Kashgar chatting with locals over juicy lamb kebabs, muggy days drifting along Hangzhou's West Lake with icy green-tea Popsicles to cool us, and wintry days in Beijing laughing over snowball fights on the Great Wall.

Granted, life in China isn't all rosy. The language poses an especially difficult hurdle, and always getting the "foreigner's markup" in prices gets old quickly, as does being openly stared at and talked about. But in our opinion the rewards far outweigh the hardships.

It's from all these experiences that this book came about, and we hope that it will prepare you for what's in store and paint a vivid picture of what your life in China may look like. So go ahead and begin your joyful exploration of the Middle Kingdom. We'll get you started, but this is your adventure to create. Enjoy it!

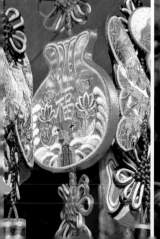

▶ WHAT WE LOVE ABOUT CHINA

- Street food that's convenient, cheap, and tasty. Stopping along the sidewalk for refreshing pineapple-on-a-stick in the summertime, hot roasted yams in the winter, and spicy lamb kabobs any time of the year

- The popularity of Chinese games like mahjong and *xiang qi* (Chinese chess), and the delight you bring to the Chinese when you know how to play

- Bicycles as a major form of transportation: good for the environment, good for the figure

- All the biking conveniences: wide bike lanes, parking lots for bikes, collapsible bike baskets, and even umbrella stands that attach to handlebars (sold in cities that get a lot of rain)

- The optimism, smiles, openness, and curiosity of the Chinese. Making new friends here is easy; chatting with strangers is always encouraged

- Amusing potato chip flavors like Strawberry Cheetos, Grilled-Steak Bugles, and Lay's chips in Finger Licking Braised Pork or Breezy Blueberry

- The teahouse culture: chillax with friends over a good cup o' *cha* (tea) in an environment oozing with traditional charm

- The celebrity status of foreigners. Being invited to participate in events or sought out by strangers for photos just because you're a *lao wai*

- Chinese hair salons. Professional haircuts for less than $10 including a full upper body massage for free. Or skip the cut: It's common to just get your hair washed, free massage included, for under $5

- Easy customization. Getting shoes, bikes, clothing, or bags repaired or modified by the nearest sidewalk tailor or mechanic

- Chinese menus, which are often giant tomes of dishes you've never tried before

- Discovering new delicacies. Learning to like (and in time to love and crave) foods that you once thought too strange to be palatable

- The challenge. The constant puzzle to figure out what's going on in a place where you can't read all the signs or understand everything that's been spoken. The complexity of everyday life in a culture so different from your own

- Each day is an adventure waiting to happen. No matter how long you've lived here, every day you can see, learn, or do something new

WELCOME TO CHINA

© TYLER CHRISTIAN

INTRODUCTION

China is a challenging land that is changing unbelievably fast. The poor have next to nothing, and the rich can have it all, yet both find their incomes rising every year. Futuristic skyscrapers tower over colorful old Buddhist temples, and bullet trains race past donkeys pulling their carts to market. China's mounting economy is taking the world by storm. Educators around the world are hailing Mandarin as the language that will best prepare our kids for their global future. Individuals and businesses from every corner of the globe are coming here to ride the economic wave of growing prosperity.

Despite their development and modernization, the Chinese are still often an enigma to Westerners. They wear dress shoes to go hiking and two-piece suits to do construction, but put on pajamas to go shopping. They open the windows on the coldest winter days. They'd rather eat chicken feet than boneless chicken breast. They tell jokes that seem to have no punch line. But it is just this sense of mystery, this impression that this place is so very different from anything you've ever known, that makes people fall in love with

© BARBARA STROTHER

China—and keeps them coming back for more.

Is China right for you? Life in China can be both richly rewarding and incredibly frustrating. To live here for an extended period of time takes a great deal of flexibility and fortitude. If you are adventurous, if you genuinely like engaging people of other cultures even when there is a language barrier, and if you can handle roughing it when you need to, you may find your time in China to be one of the best times of your life. After all, we're entering into what is being hailed as the China Century, and this might be a wave that you'll want to ride.

On the other hand, if you get

© BARBARA STROTHER

Surprise locals by challenging them to a *xiangqi* game.

stressed or angry when things don't meet your expectations, it would be better just to enjoy China as a short-term travel destination. If you are particular about ordering your life just the way you like it, China is simply not for you. You may have a rough time if you have special needs (such as wheelchair access, allergies, or a strict diet), if you have no intention of learning Chinese, or if you have high standards for cleanliness, service, and fairness. Don't underestimate how much you may miss easy access to English books and magazines, your favorite foods, ice, drinkable tap water, Western medicine, and above all, the simple ability to understand what's going on around you. One recent figure put the percentage of expats returning home early as high as 70 percent. These are people who come to China with grand expectations but leave disappointed and disillusioned.

Despite the difficulties, the good news is that you'll come away from your time in China enriched with the knowledge of a new culture and language, with amazing stories to tell and pictures to show. You can expect to have a lot of fun, a lot of laughs, and a lot of new friends. Nothing is as rewarding as the friendships. We'll never forget playing mahjong with coworkers until the wee hours of the morning. Or surprising the old men at the community park when we asked to join in their *xiangqi* (Chinese chess) games. Or spending countless hours on the basketball court with Kevin Garnett, Scotty Pippen, and Vince Carter . . . not the real stars, of course, just the chosen English names of our basketball-crazed students.

In the end, after living in China you can hold your head that much higher, knowing you've taken on the very difficult task of living in a new culture, and a complex one at that. As with so many difficulties life throws our way, the greater the challenge, the greater the reward.

The Lay of the Land

China is close to the same size as the United States, and is laid out in much the same way. Both have a cold rugged northeast, a humid south that speaks its own vernacular, a capital city close to the eastern seaboard, and an east coast lined with important cities. Both the western United States and western China have reputations as places for the independent-minded and the tough, places where you might ride your horse (or yak or motorcycle) to round up your herd. Both countries have important waterways along which key inland cities have sprung up.

The three most prominent economic areas are centered around the Bohai Sea to the north (Tianjin and nearby Beijing, Dalian, Qingdao), the Yangtze River Delta to the east (Shanghai, Suzhou, Nanjing, Hangzhou), and the Pearl River Delta in the south (Hong Kong, Shenzhen, Macau, Guangzhou, Zhuhai).

Northern China is marked by an ever-expanding desert, and northern cities struggle with sandstorms and dry, dusty conditions. Southern China, on the other hand, is a humid land of verdant greens and lush vegetation.

© BARBARA STROTHER

A river cuts through terraced land in southern China.

HOW DOES CHINA COMPARE TO THE UNITED STATES?

	United States of America	People's Republic of China
Arable land	18 percent	15 percent
Area	9.8 million sq. km	9.6 million sq. km
Ethnic mix	white 80 percent, black 13 percent, Asian 4 percent	Han 92 percent
GDP	$13.8 trillion	$3.3 trillion
GDP per capita	$45,800	$5,400
Infant mortality	6.3 deaths/ 1,000 live births	21 deaths/ 1,000 live births
Life expectancy	78 years	73.2 years
Literacy	99 percent	91 percent
Median age	36.7 years	33.6 years
People in poverty	12 percent	8 percent
Population	304 million	1,330 million

Source: CIA World Fact Book

Central China is graced with picturesque terraced hills of paddy fields and tea plantations. Eastern fields of neon-yellow rape flowers contrast with the barren lunar landscapes of the northwest. And in the southwest lie the piercing highlands of the Himalayas and the great Mt. Everest, the highest spot in the world. Though most people know the Himalayas have one foot in China, many don't realize just how hilly and mountainous the rest of the country can be, with mountains long considered sacred to the Taoists and Buddhists scattered throughout the land.

COUNTRY DIVISIONS

The People's Republic of China (PRC) is divided into 22 provinces, four independent municipalities (Beijing, Tianjin, Shanghai, Chongqing), five autonomous regions, and two Special Administrative Regions, or SARs (Hong Kong and Macau—although the central government is trying to work out an agreement with Taiwan to join this list). Within each province and autonomous region there is a capital city, and further governmental powers are given to each municipality and county. Cities are broken down into districts, and some neighborhoods within a district have their own additional governing body.

Though the central government of the PRC has a historic reputation of ruling over the country with a strong hand, each autonomous region is allowed to create its own laws, within limits, based on the needs of the unique minority cultures in their region. The two SARs, Macau and Hong Kong, are allowed to keep their own governments in all areas except diplomatic relations and national defense.

POPULATION DENSITY

China is the most populated country in the world, of course, with over 1.3 billion people, more than four times the population of the United States. Of the top 50 most populated cities around the globe, 20 percent are located in China. To grasp the density, imagine all 300 million Americans suddenly moving to Florida. The whole concept of population changes here. You'll find yourself referring to a city of one million residents as a small town, and so-called villages might have a few hundred thousand residents. There are times you'll feel the weight of this hefty city population, such as while you're trying to push your way through the masses who are all shopping for Spring Holiday, or when the rush-hour crowd carries you through the subway door like a helpless stick in a river.

Ironically, though China's cities are densely populated, the country as a whole is not. An estimated 56 percent of its people are considered rural, a number that has been slowly decreasing over the past two decades. In addition, vast tracts of land are uninhabited due to natural environments too harsh to support communities.

shopping among the masses at Yuyuan Bazaar in Shanghai

© JENNA HENLEY

Almost all of China's premier cities line the coast along the eastern to southern seaboard, causing population maps to look like a bright sliver of a crescent centered on its southeastern shore. There are only a handful of key cities that are farther than a couple of hours' drive from the sea. China's wealth tends to follow that same crescent. As a general rule, the farther from the sea you go, the poorer the areas are. In the eastern province of Zhejiang many farming families are living large with colorful and ornate Barbie-style houses four or five stories tall, while those that live off the land in the poorest hinterlands barely scrape by, some in homes made from handmade brick or retrofitted caves.

WEATHER

In a country this vast, the weather can vary extremely from one side of the country to another. Except for its extreme mountainous corners, though, one thing's for sure: When it's summer in China, it's *hot*. On the coast it's hot and muggy. In Beijing it's hot and dusty. Even in Tibet with its grand elevation, the sun beats down and will fry you to a crisp in no time if you're not expecting it.

Winters, on the other hand, provide more diversity across the nation. Northeastern lands stay frozen and sparkling white for many months while the south doesn't see a single snowflake. On tropical Hainan Island you can get a golden tan while blizzards rage across subarctic Inner Mongolia. Fall brings pleasant relief from summer's intensity, and spring brings blossoms to Chinese gardens throughout the land, making these seasons the most pleasant times to be in the Middle Kingdom.

FLORA AND FAUNA
Flora

China's vegetation is incredibly varied. Straight and narrow poplars and silvery aspens line the dusty roads of Xinjiang to the west, towering alpine firs cover snowy mountains in Heilongjiang to the north, and tropical palm trees sway in the breeze on the sunny beaches of the South China Sea. Bamboo forests, delicate orchids, and giant lotus floating on calm ponds uniquely symbolize China.

Agriculture and landscape play a leading role in Chinese culture. The peach and plum, strong symbols of Chinese mythology, bring out throngs of Chinese to walk the orchards when in spring bloom. Part of Chinese regionalism involves boasting of the agricultural products from your hometown, and the Chinese know what is grown where. Travel with a Chinese friend to the interior

WELCOME TO CHINA

of Hainan Island and they will insist you try the five-finger greens that can only be found growing wild here; a trip to Turpan won't be complete without sampling the dried apricots, mulberries, and raisins that prosper in this desert locale.

Gardens also play a very important role in Chinese history and culture. We're not talking about rows of lettuce and cucumbers, though there are plenty of those types too. Chinese gardens are ornate places filled with winding paths, arched bridges, rock sculptures, ponds with giant carp, and gorgeous flowers. Many of the Chinese gardens date back hundreds of years, though

© BARBARA STROTHER

A lotus blossom floats in a garden pond.

today the Chinese cultural priority for flowers and greenery is reflected in their amazing city landscaping. We were always amazed when a gorgeous design of annuals along Shanghai's public walkways was dug up and replaced with bright new blooms before the old flowers had any chance to wilt.

Fauna

What would China be without its most loveable native and most popular mascot, the panda? Each Chinese region has its own famous beasts: majestic reindeer in northeastern mountains, double-humped camels in northwestern deserts, giant pandas in central bamboo forests, the rare freshwater dolphins of the Yangtze River, long-haired yaks in Tibetan villages. You'll see China's creatures at rest in city zoos or at work in fields and on roads, especially if you travel off the beaten path. You might even see some served at your dinner table, like it or not.

Social Climate

For the most part, Chinese society is quite harmonious. With the help of the present economic boom, most of the population have a general contentment about their lives and a positive outlook on their future. You will find pockets, however, that are less than content. When bulldozers roll in to tear down old homes and overtake farmland in the name of economic development, residents and farmers get angry. And when a Chinese Muslim walks into the 1,000-year-old mosque where his ancestors prayed to Allah for generations and finds a typical Han Chinese repairman smoking and spitting inside, there's sure to be an ugly exchange. Although you're not likely to hear about protests and demonstrations in China's official media, they do happen all the time. The most famous recent incident involved mass protest by residents of the city of Xiamen concerning the location of a heavily polluting factory, which was one of the first times such protests proved successful.

The more time you spend in areas with high numbers of marginalized populations, such as minorities and some religious groups that resent government control, the more tension you'll see in the local social climate. Even in the most modern cities, you'll witness a subtle but ubiquitous disdain for migrant workers. For the most part, tensions in China's social climate don't play a significant role in the life of a foreigner in China unless you are in some way aligned with one of these less-accepted groups.

CHINA AND FOREIGNERS

China has a long history of being closed to outsiders, closely guarding its borders for centuries, uninterested in the outside world. In the years of colonialism and concessions, other nations courted China for a time before all were kicked

out and the doors locked shut. But things have changed over the years. In the 1980s China slowly cracked the door open for a trickle of outsiders, and now has pushed the doors wide open and put out the welcome mat: "Foreigners welcome and wanted" (as long as they bring their bank book with them).

In many ways the Chinese are enamored with all things Western. Their pop culture is now a strong blend of Chinese culture with a Western twist. American movies and music are hugely popular in China; it is not uncommon to meet a local who has a more extensive collection of American DVDs than any Westerner would dream

East meets West: over 1.3 billion served

© BARBARA STROTHER

of. McDonalds, KFC, Pizza Hut, and Starbucks are an ingrained part of life, as are U.S. sports heroes, especially NBA players. All of this adds to a general affinity for Westerners. While the attraction tends to be stronger toward Caucasian Westerners, the popularity of sports stars like Michael Jordan and Shaquille O'Neal has brought about a fascination for African Americans, especially tall male ones. Foreigners from other parts of the world will be treated well enough, although people from the Middle East, Latin America, or other Asian countries, especially the Japanese, might not get the same red-carpet treatment that Caucasians receive.

The Chinese are generally friendly and always very curious. They are often fascinated by foreigners, especially outside the key cities with high foreign populations. Strangers will want to take their picture with you, the foreigner. They'll watch what you do and what you buy when you shop; they'll have conversations with their friends about you right in front of you, examining you like a creature in a zoo. You'll be sought out for English practice and asked for clarification on grammar rules. On our first trip to Shanghai in 1993, large crowds gathered to watch us when we stopped on the Bund to take a group photo. Nowadays Shanghai is too inundated with foreigners for the locals to care all that much—unless your group happens to include a number of cute little foreign kids.

Foreign Population in China

Foreigners come to China for a number of reasons: some teach, some study, some do business, and some just roam. The number of foreigners living in China is difficult to determine, though some estimates put it higher than half a million. As an increasing number of firms open locations in China, the demand for expat professionals is on the rise. Foreign-student enrollment at China's colleges is at an all-time high, fueled by China's growing global importance as well as the relatively low cost of higher education. And foreign

DEFINING THE TERM *EXPAT*

The term *expat*, short for *expatriate*, simply refers to one who is residing away from his or her home country. This word can be used as a noun, as in "Will there be other expats at the karaoke bar?" or as an adjective, as in "This Irish pub is the main expat hangout in town." The Chinese equivalent is technically *waiguoren*, "people from outside countries," though you're more likely to hear the affectionate term *laowai*, "old outsider."

© BARBARA STROTHER

making friends on the Great Wall

English teachers, once relegated to the university classroom, now teach at all grade levels in all types of schools. Of course the number of foreigners in China is just a drop in the bucket compared to China's 1.3 billion, but in the few key cities where most foreign populations are concentrated, the ratio feels much higher. Many of China's smaller cities have no more than a handful of foreign residents, though you'll still see plenty of foreigners as you travel, attributed to the more than 130 million tourists who come every year.

HISTORY, GOVERNMENT, AND ECONOMY

To gain an understanding of modern China and its future, you first need to learn something about where this ancient nation has been. There are few countries in the world that have a history as long and rich as China's. The Middle Kingdom has played its part in world history with pomp and circumstance, flair and fervor, from the colorful courts of Kublai Khan to the triumphs and tragedies of Chairman Mao's communist revolution.

China's ancient dynastic history is a story of emperors and warlords competing for control of an ever-expanding geography. China's modern history is dominated by two stories: first, China's difficulty engaging foreigners who are eager to trade and quick on their triggers; second, China's painful rebuilding as an autonomous communist state free from foreign influence. Coming from a strongly totalitarian background, the Chinese government is showing more and more signs of political freedom, and red China is now in many ways one of the most capitalistic countries in the world.

© BARBARA STROTHER

History

Chinese history is typically organized according to dynastic periods. Like European historical eras (e.g. the Tudor period), Chinese dynasties are named after the royal family that ascended to power. This makes the study more memorable but paints a somewhat inaccurate picture of China as a single country ruled by a single emperor who passed leadership on to other strongmen once his dynastic clock had run out. In actuality, the geographic borders of China have varied across the centuries, as did the influence wielded by those in power.

THE CHINESE DYNASTIES
Xia and Shang Dynasties

The legendary birth of Chinese civilization begins with three mythological figures: Yan Di, the Fiery Emperor, ruler of the elements; Huang Di, the Yellow Emperor, ruler of the Yellow River valley; and Shang Di, the Heavenly Emperor, ruler of the spirit world. Together these three were responsible for human creation, and today some still consider them to be active in the affairs of humans. When Robert Morrison translated the Bible into Chinese in 1807 he chose the name Shang Di to refer to the Christian God.

© BARBARA STROTHER

China's past is riddled with tales of warlords and warriors.

The Xia Dynasty (20th–16th centuries B.C.) might be better regarded as mythology than history, because the Xia were believed to be direct descendants of Yan Di, Huang Di, and Shang Di. Textbooks describe the Xia Dynasty as the beginning of urban life in China, but little else is known about this era. Society was thought to be hierarchical with much of the population living in slavery, and the rulers were thought to practice human sacrifice as part of their worship.

The Shang Dynasty (16th–12th centuries B.C.) ruled a geographic area centered in modern-day Shandong Province. Archaeological evidence shows that they created a written pictographic language (the basis for modern Chinese characters) and developed organized religion based on communicating with dead ancestors. The Shang also had a wicked penchant for human sacrifice: When a king died, a hundred slaves (some beheaded, some still alive) would be buried with him. The technological development of bronze tools, weapons, and chariots empowered Shang warlords to extend their rule across an area about the size of five modern-day provinces.

Zhou Dynasty (1122-256 B.C.)

The Zhou family enlisted the support of neighboring tribes and eventually overthrew the Shang. They expanded geographically by conquering territory adjacent to the earlier Shang borders. These areas became more civilized, and the rule of law replaced the harsh rule of the Shang warlords. The Zhou developed a sophisticated bureaucracy that led to peaceful civilization and a rise in population. Consequently the Zhou Dynasty endured as the longest of all the dynasties. But with the development of iron came warfare, and the Zhou Dynasty eventually gave way to the Warring States period, characterized by small tyrant kingdoms fighting each other for over 200 years.

The warlords apparently had good military advice, because during this time Sun Tzu's book *The Art of War* was released. A traveling scholar named Confucius also emerged, and he taught that harsh legalistic rule should be replaced by humanitarian leadership. Although wars were not eliminated, Confucian ideals of benevolent intellectual leadership and filial piety were widely embraced and have since been the model of leadership throughout Asia.

Qin Dynasty (221-206 B.C.)

Emperor Qin Shihuang ended the Warring States period by winning the wars and uniting the various tribes into a single Chinese empire. It is from the name "Qin" that outsiders first began calling the country "China." Emperor Qin was not a big fan of Confucius's ideals regarding

terra-cotta warriors buried with Emperor Qin

© BARBARA STROTHER

scholarship and respect for authority, so he ordered the burning of all books and the execution of scholars. Paranoid about retribution in the afterlife, he constructed thousands of terra-cotta warriors to be buried with him. He was also worried about invaders from the north and started construction of the Great Wall. Although the Qin Dynasty was the shortest, no other dynasty did as much for modern-day tourism.

Han Dynasty (206 B.C.-A.D. 220)

In a trend later to be followed by Sun Yatsen and Mao Zedong, a peasant named Han grew angry at official abuses and incited a peasant uprising that dethroned the brutal Qin rulers. Han had the brilliant idea of replacing harsh rulers with intellectuals. He instituted a university system and selected bureaucrats based on their calligraphy skills, knowledge of Confucian texts, and other esoteric criteria. The Han made much progress in agriculture, textiles, paper, and warfare. Today the Han ethnic group comprises the majority of China's population.

The Han Dynasty eventually fragmented into the so-called Period of Division, which lasted about 400 years. It was during this time of relaxed government rule that Buddhism came along the Silk Road from India. In response to this foreign competition, Taoists and Confucians stepped up their recruiting efforts as well, resulting in a renaissance of religion throughout Chinese society.

© BARBARA STROTHER

reenacting a Tang Dynasty poetry and drinking game with floating shot glasses

Sui and Tang Dynasties (A.D. 580-907)

The Sui Dynasty (580–618) briefly reunited China, but it was uneventfully succeeded by one of the most significant of all dynasties, the Tang, who extended the rule of China as far south as modern-day Vietnam and as far west as modern-day Uzbekistan. The Tang Dynasty made many advances in transportation and culture. Through diplomacy and military might, Silk Road trade expanded, and the Grand

Canal emerged as a vibrant trade route between Beijing and Hangzhou. It is still used today by heavily laden sampan boats.

These transportation advances also facilitated cultural growth, especially in art, poetry, and music. Stringed musical instruments came along the Silk Road and have remained an important part of Chinese music ever since. Tang Dynasty art also reveals an improvement in women's rights, status, and contributions to the state that would unfortunately not last long. Tang art is filled with active women, and the plump ones were considered the most attractive. Empress Wu of the Tang was the only woman ever to bear the title of Chinese Empress.

Song Dynasty (960-1279)

After the Tang Dynasty slowly lost its central control, the Song stepped in to reunify the nation. The Song Dynasty was a time of great economic development in China. To protect themselves from raiders and to facilitate transport, large ships called junks filled the harbors of China's port cities. The junks functioned as floating Wal-Marts, and along with the advent of paper currency, rapid economic development and urbanization occurred. But women lost ground in the Song Dynasty as many were bought and sold as servants, concubines, and prostitutes. Ideas about female beauty changed, and men who preferred slender dainty women initiated the cruel practice of foot binding, which lasted until the Communist Revolution. Song Dynasty government officials allowed free commerce to flourish, focusing their attention on scholarly pursuits including literature and calligraphy. Even though the Chinese had just invented gunpowder, they were unprepared when the Mongols arrived at their door.

Yuan Dynasty (1279-1368)

China's neighbors to the north, the Mongols, decided to invade after centuries of fighting amongst themselves. In 1279 Kublai Khan conquered Beijing and added China to the empire that his grandfather, Genghis Khan, had already established, stretching from Siberia to Hungary. China's Empress Dowager Xie had built a large army, but they were no match for the Mongol hordes, and neither was the Great Wall, built to keep the Mongols out. Chinese historians named this era the Yuan Dynasty, which makes it sound like just another period of Chinese rule, taking away some of the sting of foreign occupation.

The Yuan Dynasty's administration used the Mongol language and employed not Chinese but Mongolians, Central Asians, Arabs, and even one famous Italian—Marco Polo. The Mongols turned out to be much better at

© BARBARA STROTHER

A man is not a man until he's climbed the Great Wall.

conquering than ruling, and they were eventually weakened by their own infighting. Perhaps they were too cozy in the Forbidden City that they built. After numerous attempts to overthrow the Mongols, a militia led by the Zhu family succeeded in driving them back to the northern steppes in 1368, thus establishing the Ming Dynasty.

Ming Dynasty (1368-1644)

During the Ming Dynasty, China's navy and merchant ships brought numerous technological innovations into the country. *Ming* literally means "bright" or "clear," which amply describes their cultural development. Movable type was invented, resulting in large-scale book production, including the classics *Peony Pavilion* and *Journey to the West.* Their fine arts renaissance is best represented by the famous Ming Dynasty blue-on-white porcelain. The Ming also took the good ideas of the Great Wall and the Forbidden City of previous dynasties and built them into the impressive structures that exist today (with a little help from reconstruction over the centuries). At this time China was the most advanced society on earth, but the inept leaders, known for being a bit lazy, crazy, and nasty, lacked the funds to finance a proper military. When foreign invaders from Manchuria attacked, the Chinese were once again conquered by outsiders.

Qing Dynasty (1644-1911)

During the Qing Dynasty, another period of rule by outsiders, Manchu rulers quickly imposed their will on the Chinese. Property was seized, and Chinese were prohibited from owning weapons and even bamboo, which could be fashioned into weaponry. Chinese men were required to adopt the Manchu hairstyle, the queue—the head shaved except for a long ponytail. Conservative values were enforced, and Qing rulers closed theaters and banned numerous books and dramas, although one of the most famous works of Chinese literature, *Dream of Red Mansions,* was written at this time. To pacify the powerful educated Chinese, the Qing restored the literati to an elevated position in society and encouraged educated men to serve in the imperial court, including foreign Jesuit missionaries. While Manchu rulers were busy extending the borders of the empire to include Xinjiang and Tibet, Western colonial powers had a keen eye on China's natural resources, especially tea.

IMPERIALISM, OPIUM WARS, AND REBELLIONS

Spanish, Portuguese, and Dutch trade ships had been visiting China's port cities since the Ming Dynasty. By the 19th century, trade was dominated by the British government–owned East India Company, which was impatient with the Ming rulers' reluctance to adopt European trading practices. By this time, Europeans had developed an appetite for Chinese silk, porcelain, and tea. To expand their trading operations, the Brits produced opium in India and imported it to China to trade for Chinese goods, especially tea.

Chinese officials weren't thrilled that their people were becoming addicted to the drug, so they complained to the Queen of England. The Portuguese also objected to British trade practices and banished them from their colony of Macau, forcing the Brits to settle in the uninhabited muddy islands of Hong Kong. The political situation deteriorated and resulted in the first Opium War (1840–1842). The Chinese were outgunned, and the war was resolved with the first of many aptly named Unequal Treaties. Among other things, the treaties required exorbitant silver payments from the Chinese and the establishment of foreign "concessions," geographic areas where foreigners were immune from Chinese law, in port cities like Shanghai, Guangzhou, Tianjin, and Qingdao.

The Taiping Rebellion

Qing Dynasty rulers also had their own internal threats to put up with, the most notorious of which was the Taiping Rebellion. A peasant named Hong Xiuquan believed he was the brother of Jesus Christ, and he thought he had been given a heavenly mandate to establish a kingdom on earth. Although Taiping literally means "heavenly peace," Hong's plan was to establish his kingdom through brute military force. From their base in Nanjing, Hong and his pals conquered territory in 16 provinces, resulting in the deaths of over 20 million people before the Qing rulers finally shut them down.

The Boxer Rebellion

From 1861 to 1911 the Manchu Dynasty was controlled by a wickedly selfish woman, the Empress Dowager Cixi. In 1898 she encouraged ignorant young men from the countryside to attack foreign businesses, missionaries, and locals who had converted to Christianity. In their spare time the young men practiced boxing and other martial arts, and this event was known as the Boxer Rebellion. The Boxers spread their violence beyond Beijing to other cities, and after two years the foreigners had had enough. In June 1900 an army of 20,000 troops was assembled from numerous Western powers, and within two months the Boxer Rebellion was squashed and China fell victim to another unfair treaty. With better equipment the Chinese military might have mounted a better defense, but Cixi had already squandered state resources. In one infamous incident, Cixi took funds that were allocated to build warships for the navy and instead spent them on the construction of an immobile marble ship (which you can still see today at the Summer Palace in Beijing) for her entertainment.

Rise of Nationalism

After decades of diplomatic failures and disillusionment with the Manchu rulers, the masses eventually backed a revolution led by a Western-trained doctor named Sun Yatsen. Sun recruited the help of military generals and secret societies who functioned like the Italian mafia. As seen in the movie *The Last Emperor,* the Qing Dynasty child emperor was dethroned, and power-hungry generals, warlords, and gangsters fought with each other, giving the masses little hope that the country would be improved. Consequently, the period from 1912 to 1928 is referred to as the Warlord Period. Although Sun failed to create a new society, his success in ending centuries of rule by aloof emperors earned him the nickname "the father of modern China"—a Chinese George Washington.

During this time the May 4th Movement occurred. In reaction to the failure of Allied Forces to make good on their treaty promise to return foreign concessions to the Chinese, 3,000 students gathered in Beijing to protest on May 4th, 1919. Under the former Qing rule, there was little patriotism among the

© RYAN SHAW

Sun Yatsen's mausoleum in Nanjing

people or unification of a spirit of being Chinese. This rallying event, therefore, remains significant as the inauguration of China's first nationalist movement.

When Sun Yatsen died of cancer, Chiang Kai-Shek took over Sun's Nationalist Party. This group, also known as the Kuomintang, successfully recruited urban factory workers who were tired of being exploited by the factory owners, many of whom were British or Japanese. Chiang also enlisted support from the underworld, including Shanghai's powerful Green Gang.

CIVIL WAR

In 1921 the Chinese Communist Party was founded and, with the bold leadership of Mao Zedong, quickly gained a wide following, especially among the rural peasants who were attracted by Mao's promises of equality, prosperity, and freedom from oppressive landlords. Although Sun Yatsen had initially forged an alliance with the fledgling communist group before he died, Chiang Kai-Shek turned on them and launched a massacre that started a long struggle for control of China's future between the Nationalists and the Communists.

In 1934 Nationalist troops encircled the out-gunned Communist troops around Hunan Province and nearly wiped them out before the Communists slipped away. In their legendary escape, known as the Long March, Communist troops traveled 6,000 miles on foot to a new base in Shaanxi. Of the 80,000 troops who began the arduous yearlong journey, only 6,000 made it to Shaanxi.

During this time Japan seized the territories of Taiwan and Manchuria from China. They tried provoking China into an all-out war in 1937 by launching a full-scale invasion and conquering major cities. Both Beijing and Shanghai were besieged, but no city suffered worse than Nanjing. The "Rape of Nanjing" lasted seven bitter weeks in the winter of 1937. Japanese soldiers committed every imaginable cruelty, including torture, more than 80,000 rapes, 300,000 murders, and horrific medical experiments. If you can stomach it, the Massacre Museum in Nanjing today serves as a sad reminder of this dark time.

© BARBARA STROTHER

Zhejiang University's towering Mao statue, one of the few remaining in eastern China

The saying that "there is no better bond of friendship than a common enemy" proved true in China as the Nationalists and Communists formed an alliance to drive out the Japanese. With the help of the American military, their efforts were successful, as the Japanese had no fight left in them after the atomic bombs were dropped on Japan in 1945.

After rousting the Japanese, the United States urged the Communists and Nationalists to put their guns down and start anew with a two-party system, but neither side liked the idea, and civil war broke out from 1947 to 1949. Despite being better armed, the Nationalists were disorganized and lost favor with the people due to corruption and infighting. Rather than suffer a certain military defeat, they fled the mainland and settled in Taiwan. Mao's Communists quickly filled the vacuum, marking October 1, 1949, as the official birth date of the People's Republic of China. To this day, the Republic of China (Taiwan) considers itself a sovereign nation, but Beijing sees it as a breakaway province that should be reunited with the mainland.

COMMUNIST RULE
The Great Leap Forward and the Cultural Revolution

The new government ended the opium trade, improved infrastructure, and advanced women's rights. But it also cut ties with foreign businesses, seized all land and buildings, ended diplomatic ties to the West, persecuted the

© BARBARA STROTHER

figurines from the Cultural Revolution

religious, and harshly punished those bold enough to oppose it. In Mao's Great Leap Forward all agriculture was organized into giant collectives, and millions of peasants were put to work building bridges, roads, and other worthy infrastructure projects. But the central planners in Beijing were incapable of managing the complexities of such a grand project, and the Great Leap ended with the Three Bitter Years (1959–1962) of famine, resulting in 30 million deaths.

Without a doubt the most infamous failure of communism under Mao was the Cultural Revolution (1966–1976). Fearing the loss of power to influential political rivals, Mao induced impressionable youths to join a new pseudomilitary group called the Red Guards. The Red Guards terrorized society's most productive members, especially doctors and intellectuals. Many were forced to work on farms and labor camps, while their jobs were filled by unskilled peasants. (Imagine having a serious medical problem and instead of seeing a trained professional being examined by the local turnip farmer!) Few people dared criticize Mao's policy failures, but as soon as he died in 1976, government officials quickly punished Mao's closest allies, the "Gang of Four," including Mao's wife, who was sentenced to death but instead committed suicide.

Reform, the Open Door, and Deng Xiaoping

Though Mao made considerable contributions by uniting China and freeing its citizens from foreign domination, much of what makes China great today should be attributed to the work of Mao's successor, Deng Xiaoping. Deng's sensible reforms transformed a backward agricultural country into a global superpower. Deng's success can be traced to his drive to liberalize government policies. After Deng took the reigns, China opened up to foreign businesses, foreign investment, and privatization of state-run business and industry.

Government

China is one of the five remaining communist states along with Laos, Vietnam, North Korea, and Cuba. Chinese political affairs are dominated by the Chinese Communist Party (CCP), the People's Liberation Army (PLA), and the national government headed by the president. In the past, there was little distinction between the party, the state, and the army, but in recent years they have grown independent of each other. Local government has considerably more impact on the average Chinese resident than the national government, in part because it is at the local level that the greatest amount of government corruption exists.

GOVERNMENT STRUCTURE

The Chinese Communist Party (CCP) determines all policy from the national down to the local level. A Party Congress is held every five years to elect new leaders. Unlike the glory days of the revolution when the masses eagerly joined the party, today a mere 5 percent of the population belongs to the party. Since China is moving further toward a market economy, the advantages of being

© BARBARA STROTHER

a PLA flag ceremony

a party member are diminishing. Eight other token political parties exist but exert no real influence. The national government is headed by the National People's Congress, which is the legislative body that meets once a year to enact the policies that have already been predetermined by the Party. Each province and city also has its own local government officials who form and enforce policies for their respective regions.

The People's Liberation Army (PLA) includes the army, navy, and air force. With well over 2 million members, it is the largest military in the world. Although historically the PLA has been used to defend China from invaders (i.e. Japanese), in many ways the PLA functions more as police than as soldiers. It is primarily the role of the PLA to restore peace in standoffs with separatists and unruly protest groups, as well as the more popular tasks of assisting with domestic emergency relief and economic construction.

To accommodate its minority groups, China has given some regions a level of self-rule. This applies to the Autonomous Regions of Xinjiang, Tibet, Ningxia Hui, Guangxi Zhuang, and Inner Mongolia. The Special Administrative Regions (SARs) of Macau and Hong Kong are also governed differently from the mainland. When the colonial powers returned these lands back to Chinese rule, much of the former political and economic systems were left intact. While both SARs are responsible for their own domestic affairs, Beijing holds the reigns of their national defense and diplomatic relations.

CHANGING EXPECTATIONS OF GOVERNMENT

Unlike other regimes that ruled China as a group of elites, the Communists desired to govern according to peasant values. The unequal distribution of wealth that plagued the dynasties was to be eliminated. People were to be kept safe from alien invaders and local gangs, but most importantly, people were to have equal incomes, property, housing, education, and daily needs. The "iron rice bowl" policy was instituted, which guaranteed lifetime employment.

Today the Chinese have lowered expectations of their government. Under the economic reforms instituted by Deng Xiaoping, much of the burden of providing for people's daily needs shifted to employers. Under the model of pure communism, these companies were state-owned, so the government was the employer. People now must take responsibility for their own needs, including housing, health care, and retirement, unless they work for the state or for large companies. In some ways, large companies have taken over the state's socialist role, providing generous benefits such as on-site housing and even schools for employees' children, although the law no longer requires it. Just as in the West, most residents of China have grown apathetic about government and see it as mostly irrelevant to their daily lives.

GOVERNMENT AND EXPATS

Every Westerner who has accepted a job in China faces interrogation—by his family members before he leaves! "What are you going to eat? Don't they eat dog there? What about your safety? Aren't you worried about living in a communist country?" In many stories about China that foreigners hear, the government is the villain. The reality is that unless you are an entrepreneur or a journalist, chances are you'll have little interaction with Chinese government officials. After the customs agent stamps your entry visa, and you register with your friendly neighborhood PSB, you may have no more interaction with your Big Red Brother. You probably won't file a Chinese tax return because your employer will handle that for you.

Economy

No country has ever experienced the level of economic growth that China is currently enjoying. After growing around 10 percent annually for 30 years, China has the second-largest national economy after the United States. It's currently the second-largest importer and exporter, and has by far the largest foreign exchange reserves and current account surplus. China now enjoys the

© BARBARA STROTHER

China's booming economy is fueled by its position as the workshop of the world.

status of one of the world's three global economic superpowers, along with the United States and the European Union.

In the past 20 years more than 250 million Chinese residents have been lifted out of poverty, a staggering accomplishment unheard of throughout world history. Today the middle and upper classes are growing by leaps and bounds, and although the income gap is getting wider, the underprivileged have considerable faith in greater prosperity for their future. The worldwide financial crisis of 2008 drastically impacted the Chinese economy, especially manufacturing for export, but rising domestic consumption has helped lessen the losses. Despite worldwide economic woes, China's economy is continuing to grow, albeit at a less fiery pace than before 2008.

IS IT REALLY COMMUNIST?

Within an hour of your arrival to "communist" China, you're bound to encounter capitalistic street vendors selling everything from mobile phones to haircuts to *chou doufu* (stinky tofu). In no time it will be obvious that the government can't possibly control such a vast economy. And when the big Hummer or shiny black Cadillac runs the stinky-tofu vendor's oversize tricycle off the road, it will be apparent that there is an unequal distribution of wealth. So, on a practical level, this whole "communist" label seems to be a misnomer.

The Chinese prefer to describe their system as a socialist market economy system, or more fondly, "socialism with Chinese characteristics." The socialist label means that all central government plans are designed with the best interests of the people as the focus, while the "market" label refers to increased freedom for businesses to produce the goods and services that are desired in the Chinese market and abroad. This blend of control and freedom is often called a "mixed economy," and compared to the massive government intervention in Western countries, the differences are not that great. The central government used to own all of the large companies, but most have been sold off to the highest bidder. Generally speaking, the only enterprises still owned by the government are in the heavy industries, media, telecommunications, tourism, and tobacco, and definitely not stinky-tofu vendors.

BLACK CAT, WHITE CAT

"Poverty is not socialism; to be rich is glorious," declared Deng Xiaoping as he broke from Mao's socialist ideals and implemented capitalistic reforms in 1970s China. He explained, "It doesn't matter if a cat is black or white, so long as it catches mice." Mao freed China's economy from the colonial powers and, looking to the Soviet Union for inspiration, started the country on the fast track to industrialization. The failures of the Great Leap Forward and the Cultural Revolution revealed the soft underbelly of communism, setting the stage for Deng Xiaoping's free market reforms in the 1970s and 1980s. Deng's policies changed the system from a centrally planned economy to a mixed economy, which helped China become the main economic powerhouse of the East. The reforms were incremental and can be thought of in three distinct eras: Opening Up, Rapid Development, and Deep Reforms.

In the Opening Up period, agricultural collectives were disbanded and farmers were freed to make their own decisions about what to produce. The "iron rice bowl" ended, and people went to work for private companies. Special Economic Zones (SEZ) were established in Shanghai, Shenzhen, Zhuhai, and Xiamen that attracted foreign companies with their tax breaks, cheap labor, and other incentives. Most of the foreign firms taking advantage of this new open-door policy entered into joint ventures with Chinese companies, many of them state-owned.

In the Rapid Development period of the 1980s, Deng privatized many of the large state-owned businesses and eliminated price and wage controls. Previously the government determined all price and wage rates, but now both were allowed to fluctuate based on supply and demand. In the Deep Reform period, from 1992 to the present, financial and educational systems have been modernized to follow standards in Western countries. Sustainable-development measures have been put in place in attempts to harmonize business interests with the environment. Significant efforts have also been made to continue development of the western regions, including Tibet and especially Xinjiang with its precious oil reserves. Significant land reforms were enacted in 2008, giving farmers greater control over land. Every year sees new reforms, making it difficult to stay up-to-date on ever-changing regulations but continually providing new opportunities for business.

GLOBAL BUSINESS

For decades, global businesses have set up manufacturing sites in China to take advantage of the cheap labor costs for exporting products abroad. Foreign manufacturing firms can be found in every major Chinese city, but Shanghai is the top location for foreign firms' headquarters as well as research and development sites. In addition to using China as a supply and manufacturing base, businesses from all over the globe have flocked to China believing the old marketing adage that if you could capture just 1 percent of the Chinese market, you'd be rich. Whether exporting their goods from abroad (such as the popular Washington State apples) or setting up production facilities within China (and avoiding Chinese import tariffs), sales to the exploding Chinese consumer market have been good. In fact, many transnational firms such as GM concede that their sales within China have kept their firms afloat during difficult financial times in their primary North American and European

© BARBARA STROTHER

Coca-Cola in China

markets. Many of the world's top businesses recognize the importance of the growing Chinese consumer market as a primary and central directive of their long-term global strategy.

ECONOMIC ISSUES

China's increased integration into the world economy has not been without struggles. Some of the major economic issues have included intellectual property violations, poor work conditions, income inequality, environmental pollution, currency manipulation, the underground economy, and tainted product manufacturing.

Intellectual Property Rights

Foreigners and locals flock to China's famous markets, which are loaded with counterfeit goods such as fake Gucci purses, Nike shoes, Microsoft software, and Hollywood DVDs. There will occasionally be a token crackdown by the police, but the penalties are not severe enough to keep the vendors off the streets—the next day after a bust you might see the same cops browsing the DVDs with you. Some companies such as Nintendo have opted out of the Chinese market altogether because they don't want to lose profit to the IPR pirates. Foreign companies who are not being compensated for their intellectual property just don't have enough influence to get the Chinese to effectively prosecute intellectual property violations. However, as Chinese businesses are gaining in the sophistication of their own products that are then being copied by their countrymen, more strict enforcement of the law is expected.

Poor Working Conditions

The Western media has been very critical of working conditions in Chinese factories, labeling them "sweatshops" and arguing that the employees are forced to work too many hours and are paid too little. The Chinese business managers counter that they are providing jobs for people who otherwise wouldn't have the opportunity to earn money. Young men and women from the countryside move to the cities in a desperate search for work, and choose employment in sweatshops to earn quick money. The more hours they work in a given week, the sooner they get home. Chinese managers also argue that they can't afford to pay higher wages because the foreign retailers they ship to (such as Wal-Mart, Target, and others) demand the low prices that are a result of cheap labor.

© BARBARA STROTHER

China's factories provide jobs that help millions pull themselves out of poverty.

Income Inequality

In a booming economy, incomes rise faster for the rich than for the lower classes. Many of China's nouveaux riches got that way because of *guanxi,* connections to government officials and/or investors. The opening-up policies have been very good to them, but those without connections or skills have not reaped as many rewards from China's economic boom. Most Chinese are experiencing rising standards of living, but when the income gap between rich and poor grows, the poor get restless. Every year the official number of recorded public demonstrations has increased, and many of these protests are prompted by the discontentment of the underprivileged. It is ironic that the unequal distribution of wealth that Mao attempted to eliminate through communism has rebounded, bringing the People's Republic of China in some ways right back to where it started in 1949.

The Environment

In the past most of China's considerable pollution has been caused by industrial effluence and coal-burning power plants, though in recent years the greenhouse gas emissions from the mounting number of cars on the road have become a significant source of concern. Damage to the environment is especially worrisome in China because only a small part of its land can be used productively. Geographically, China is the fourth-largest country in the world, but only

CHINA'S ONE-CHILD POLICY

Chinese officials aren't necessarily pleased that their country is the most populous nation in the world. Along with masses of people come the problems of providing for those masses. In an attempt to curb rapid population growth, the government enacted its infamous one-child policy back in 1979, allowing only one baby for each family. Abortions, forced birth control, and steep fines for subsequent pregnancies help to keep the Chinese in compliance, though most Chinese approach the law with a sense of patriotism and duty. A strong memory of ridiculously crowded train stations and the fierce competition for limited spots in good schools help bolster citizens' continued commitment to the policy.

You've probably heard about this policy already, but you may not be aware of just how many exceptions there are to the rule. Minorities of the autonomous regions are not required to follow the policy, and rural farmers have fewer rules concerning the number of children they're allowed. For wealthy families who can afford to pay the fines, having more than one child becomes something of a status symbol. Expensive private schools for China's upper-class citizens boast much higher numbers of siblings than the general population. Recent reforms to the policy allow two children for parents who were both only children in an attempt to save the lineages that would disappear if the third-generation child were to die young. On the other hand, couples that faithfully abide by the one-child policy get an extra stipend in their retirement years, and an even higher amount if their only child is a girl.

about 15 percent of the land is arable; the rest is dominated by the Himalayas, the Tibetan plateau, the Taklamakan Desert, and the Gobi Desert. It is typical for developing nations to pay greater attention to economic growth than environmental protection, but China is now reaching the point where environmental concerns are necessarily gaining momentum. Fortunately a sustainable-growth movement appears to be gaining considerable influence, and government regulations concerning pollution are becoming more stringent and more regularly enforced, though there's still quite a long way to go.

Currency Manipulation

The central government no longer manipulates prices, but they do manipulate the currency. Most countries allow their currency to "float" with an exchange rate that fluctuates based on market conditions around the world. For close to 10 years, China opted for a "pegged" system, where one U.S. dollar was worth 8.28 yuan regardless of conditions in international markets. In 2005 China pegged the yuan to a basket of foreign currencies, and the exchange rate dropped as low as 6.5. The result of this currency manipulation is that the yuan is kept artificially weak. This is bad news for foreign businesses whose products become too expensive for Chinese consumers, but good news for Chinese companies whose goods remain affordable for foreigners. This is also good news for expats living in China. A weak yuan means a strong dollar, so your dollars will buy more.

Tainted Products

In early 2007 tainted pet food manufactured in China caused the death of hundreds of pets worldwide. In late 2007 Mattel Inc. recalled nearly 20 million toys made in China due to dangerous lead-based paints and hazardous strong magnets. In 2008 Chinese baby formula tainted with melamine caused 300,000 infants to become sick, including six deaths. "Made in China" has gained a bad name due to these serious scares. Investigations often lead to a government official who was bribed to allow the tainted product to pass inspections. The Chinese central government does not take such infractions lightly; corrupt officials are often publicly executed. Time will tell if Chinese manufacturing can put these unethical practices behind them and rebuild worldwide trust among consumers.

PEOPLE AND CULTURE

There is arguably no country as culturally rich and diverse as China: ancient, colorful, and altogether different from the West. It's often the rich cultural experience that draws foreigners to want to live in China in the first place, and when the culture shock hits, it's what makes some rush home with a newfound appreciation for their native land. At times frustrating and at times utterly delightful, Chinese culture is nothing if not thoroughly unique.

China is well known for its cultural icons: chopsticks, painted opera faces, elegant scrolls of calligraphy, ornate temples, acrobatic martial arts. An elderly man puts on his old blue Mao suit to play mahjong at the park. A young businesswoman buttons the high collar of her *qi pao* (traditional dress) that's made from modern pinstriped suiting rather than shiny silk. A Buddhist monk tightens the sash around his mustard-colored robes as he rises from his prayers. A Mongolian couple puts on pointy felt boots to check on their herd of sheep.

© BARBARA STROTHER

Each of these people, in their own way, represents a tiny piece of the grand puzzle of Chinese culture.

The Chinese also have a unique social culture. Conformity is valued over independence; elders are to be treated with the utmost honor. Relationships are supreme, and preserving the social balance is more important than asserting one's rights. In China it's not what you know but whom you know and what you do to build those associations. It takes years to learn the intricacies of Chinese social culture, which means that no matter whether you stay in China for one month or one decade, you'll always be learning something new.

© BARBARA STROTHER

using cormorants to catch fish the traditional way

The People

ETHNICITY

What does it mean to be Chinese? The majority of the Chinese population, nearly 92 percent, belong to the Han ethnic group. When most people picture a Chinese person, they visualize a Han. But the remaining 8 percent of the population consists of 55 different national minorities that total well over 100 million people—more than the entire population of Mexico. Most have their own customs, costumes, architecture, arts, culinary specialties,

THE AVERAGE ZHOU

There are fewer than 450 family names in China, and 90 percent of the population shares the top 100 most common names, including Zhou (pronounced like "Joe"), Zhao, Sun, Li, Wang, Qian, and Zhang. *Lao bai xing*, literally "old hundred surnames," is a term that refers to the general population and is translated simply as "people." More individuals share the top three most popular Chinese names (Li, Wang, and Zhang) than the entire population of the United States.

BEING A LITTLE *DIFFERENT* IN CHINA

RACISM IN CHINA
You probably won't experience direct racism in China, but you may experience some discrimination if you're not Caucasian. Chinese employers are apt to choose the candidate with the fairest skin, especially if there are chances to feature a Western employee in the company's marketing materials.

HOMOSEXUALITY IN CHINA
Homosexuality is a sensitive issue in China, though it is very slowly gaining acceptance. In more cosmopolitan cities you will find a few bars and nightclubs that cater to the small gay and lesbian community in China. Beyond that, the subject is still mostly taboo, especially with older generations and in rural areas. Gays and lesbians in China may not find their lifestyle embraced by the Chinese, but it is unlikely they will experience rudeness or open aggression on the issue.

VEGETARIANISM IN CHINA
Despite the abundance of vegetables in every Chinese restaurant in the United States, very few places in China cook without meat. Larger cities will have places designated as vegetarian, though they are few and far between. Temples, and restaurants near them, often serve strictly vegetarian meals; some take their nonmeat dishes to an art form in replicating the real thing.

OBESITY IN CHINA
Westerners who are overweight need to be prepared for the comments they will receive in China, where it isn't taboo to openly talk about a person's size. You may have both strangers and friends ask you why you are so big or make jokes about your size that would be considered quite offensive back home. Take it in stride; with China's history of famines, being big has traditionally been associated with wealth and power.

RELIGION IN CHINA
China grants a fair amount of religious freedom to its foreign residents, as long as you abide by their laws not to evangelize the locals. You can bring in your own personal religious reading material, but not bulk materials meant for the masses. A private conversation between friends about beliefs won't be punished, but stronger evangelistic efforts will be. For Christians, most major cities offer at least one worship service for foreigners conducted in English, though typically only foreigners are allowed to attend in an effort to protect the services from being overrun by curious locals or beggars. However, foreigners are also free to attend Chinese religious services.

© BARBARA STROTHER

Zhu, the character for Lord, adorns a Chinese church.

religion, and language. Social customs are often the most distinguishing feature of minorities because differences in physical attributes from the Han are not often discernible. Most of these minorities live along China's borders, such as the Mongolians in the north, the Uighurs of the northwest, the Tibetans of the Himalayas, and a large and diverse variety of groups along the southwestern borderlands. Increasingly you'll find them working in China's major cities; it is no longer unusual to see Muslim Chinese, with pillbox hats or headscarves, walking down the cosmopolitan streets of Shanghai.

Chinese minority groups are given a fair amount of autonomy, including exclusion from the one-child policy. Five of China's "provinces" are actually "autonomous regions" (Guangxi, Tibet, Ningxia, Xinjiang, and Inner Mongolia) where the minority residents are allowed self-governance, with limits. As for their religions, such as Tibetan Buddhism, the same rules apply as any other worship in the nation—no foreign leadership, no secret meetings, and every gathering must be registered with the government.

Although the customs of some nationalities have suffered persecution under Communist rule, the PRC has also helped to preserve their heritage, such as creating writing systems for groups that previously only had a spoken language. Today the government even grants affirmative-action perks for minority individuals, such as preference for government positions and university placement.

CLASS

China has the bright distinction of bringing more of its people out of poverty than any other nation in the history of the world. A new middle class is emerging across China. In fact, the majority of city dwellers consider themselves middle class even if their income doesn't meet the official mark. While the growing economy continues to raise the standard of living for all Chinese, unfortunately the gap is getting larger between the haves and the have-nots. In other words, what Communism originally tried so hard to eradicate—class distinction—is coming back with a vengeance. To make matters worse, the newly wealthy tend to flaunt their wealth, driving luxury cars, sending their kids to prestigious private schools, and filling their closets with Gucci and Versace (the real kind, not knockoffs). On the other hand, China's poor are still very poor, with many migrant workers and farmers making barely enough to scrape by.

PATRIOTISM, REGIONALISM, AND DISCRIMINATION

On average the people of China tend to be quite patriotic, vehemently defending the actions of their government against the accusations and rebuffs of outsiders. In their patriotism, they have a tendency to consider themselves a little better than other Asian nations (especially the Japanese), although these attitudes don't often show up in personal relationships. Due to this patriotism the Chinese typically shun conversations that involve government criticism or other disparaging remarks about their homeland. Open dialogues about national issues must, therefore, be approached with great sensitivity.

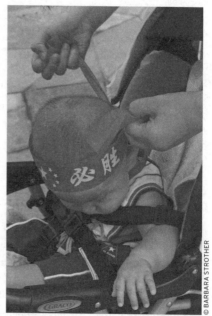
Patriotism comes in all shapes and sizes in China.

There is also a strong focus on regionalism within China. The Chinese have always strongly identified with the province, and even the village, they originally hail from, which is intensified by the many local dialects and cuisines that distinguish one area from another. This regionalism is due in part to the historical belief in ancestor worship, which tied a person to their ancestral hometown where the spirits, who could bring both pleasure and pain if not properly worshipped, dwelled. Like patriotism, regionalism in China can lead to an attitude of superiority toward those from other areas within the country. In addition, some Han Chinese are quick to stereotype minorities as troublemakers and criminals.

Social Values

ETIQUETTE

While it's always important to avoid offending one's hosts when abroad, in China you might frequently find yourself feeling offended as well. Many Western etiquette principles—such as don't stare, don't point, don't talk with your mouth full, don't spit, don't pee in public places, don't push, don't cut in line, don't take so much for yourself that those after you won't get any, don't ask inappropriate questions—aren't valued in China. You'll have to have a flexible attitude to take the Western taboo-breaking in stride, and before long you'll hardly notice when your business partner in her designer suit dribbles shrimp shells out of the side of her mouth as she talks during lunch.

While the Chinese may not follow the same etiquette rules that Westerners do, there are a few things that they find incredibly rude that we are often unaware of. For example, you should use both hands to receive a business card. Showing respect to elders and superiors is also very important to the Chinese. You should always allow them (insist, even) to enter or exit a door before you, and be sure to address them with the correct term of respect depending on their age in relation to yours. Touching the rim of your glass below theirs during a toast shows respect as well. Chinese people will expect these gestures and feel slighted when ignorant Westerners fail to show proper respect.

At banquets the most honored seat is the one that faces the door, followed by the seat on either side of the most honored. You should always wait for your host to tell you where to sit. Always offer to fill others' beverage glasses before you fill your own, and wait for the honored guest or the host to start the special dishes before you fill your plate. If you've been invited to someone's home, always remember to remove your shoes before entering the home; many hosts will provide slippers for their guests' use.

© BARBARA STROTHER

Dining out in China is always family-style.

GIFT-GIVING

While some Chinese customs will confound you, others may delight you, like the tradition of gift-giving. We were always particularly fond of the custom of giving away wedding chocolates; our kids appreciate the custom of giving children *hong bao* (red envelopes) full of cash on the holidays. Gift-giving is a central part of social life in Chinese culture, and it is one area where it is easy to offend if you don't know what's expected of you.

Hong bao are colorful red and gold packets filled with cash and given at holidays and special occasions. The amount inside is typically an even number but never a 4, which is a homonym for death. *Hong bao* are given at weddings to the happy couple, at Chinese New Year to kids of all ages, as an extra token of security for good service to doctors, and on the negative side, as bribery to government officials. Older generations give them to the younger, the married to the unmarried, and unless you're attending a wedding, don't give one to a peer or you'll risk offending them. If your child gets a red envelope from an adult who has their own children, you must give a similar gift to the original giver's kids to keep things even between the families.

All gifts, invitations, and the like should be refused at least twice before you accept. Presents that are wrapped should be opened later in private unless the giver insists you open it immediately. A token gift of fresh flowers, fresh fruit, an item from your hometown, or a tin of high-quality tea is an appropriate gesture for a host, regardless of where you are meeting or for what purpose (a formal business visit, a meal with someone you haven't seen in some time, staying at someone's home overnight, etc.).

DINING CUSTOMS

The best way to look more like a local is to learn how to act like one at a restaurant. When you are seated, your table will be given just one menu for the entire group. If you are the host of a large group that covers more than one table, it is customary for whatever you order to be multiplied by the number of tables in your group, so that every table gets exactly the same dishes.

You'll be expected to pick one starch, or what the Chinese would refer to as a main food, which includes rice, dumplings, steamed buns, savory pancakes, or noodles. Although in the United States we can't imagine eating Chinese food that isn't piled on top of rice, the Chinese custom is to eat rice *after* you've finished all other dishes, just to fill up.

Many restaurants in China have aquariums and tubs filled with your potential dinner swimming and slithering about. If you order a meal with one

© BARBARA STROTHER

Don't let the heads scare you; these birds taste good!

of these delicacies, you may be required to either pick the one you want, or at the very least verify that the creature is still alive and healthy before the chef hacks into him. We found this out the hard way when we were encouraged to look into a plastic bag our waiter gingerly brought to our table and saw a very angry and very large snake hissing back at us. If they show you your critter before they cook him, control your urge to gasp and just give a quick nod to show your approval.

A shared meal in China is always very literally shared. All food will be delivered to the middle of the table and everyone will help themselves, using their own chopsticks to delve into the communal dishes time and again. If you are extremely cautious about the spread of germs, you can request serving spoons, although it is not the traditional Chinese way.

If you struggle with using chopsticks, it is perfectly acceptable to hold a bowl up close to your mouth as you eat from it. Similarly, soup can be drunk from the bowl. Chinese soup spoons are a ubiquitous option for the chopstick-impaired; few restaurants have forks, and knives are never used at the table. If the food comes too big to take in one bite, you are expected to hold it with your chopsticks and nibble off bite-size pieces. Gristle, bones, and shells can be quietly dropped onto the table next to your plate or into an unused bowl. Never leave your chopsticks sticking straight up in your food—this symbolizes death.

Concerning drinks, many restaurants provide a complimentary pot of hot tea before the meal. Tea is considered an appetite stimulator, not refreshment,

CHINA'S KITCHEN

China's many cuisines are categorized by the provinces and cities where the culinary style was first developed. Restaurants in China typically choose one regional cuisine to specialize in, though they will add some of the most common dishes from other regions as well. Here are a few broad categories that you will run across most frequently.

NORTH: BEIJING, MONGOLIAN, AND DONGBEI

Northern foods have a reputation for being bland but filling, based more on wheat-based breads, noodles, and dumplings than the rice-based diet of the south, and relying heavily on cabbage, garlic, leeks, and onions. The most famous foods from northern China are Beijing Duck (sliced roasted duck served on thin pancakes with spring onions and plum sauce) and Mongolian hot pot (order several raw ingredients and a pot of hot broth will be placed at your table; drop in the ingredients yourself, then fish them out when they are done). Dongbei (northeast) food has a Korean influence, including their taste for dog meat.

EAST: ZHEJIANG PROVINCE AND SHANGHAI

The fish of Hangzhou's West Lake, Shanghai's hairy crabs and *xiaolongbao* dumplings, Shaoxing's stinky tofu and yellow wine – these are just a few of the diverse dishes from the eastern coastlands. Known for fresh ingredients (especially seafood), simple seasonings, and fancy presentations, this regional cuisine is considered the oldest – and most refined – in China. Shanghai in particular is known for its sweet tooth, adding a little more sugar to its dishes than other cuisines.

© BARBARA STROTHER

spicy Sichuan-style duck heads

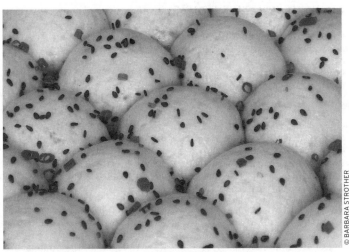

© BARBARA STROTHER

shengjian, Shanghai-style pan-fried dumplings

SOUTH: CANTONESE AND DIM SUM

The Cantonese (residents of Guangdong Province) are infamously known for "eating everything that has legs except the kitchen table." In the deep south you may be served rat, dog, insects, or even an endangered species, as well as lots of interesting animal parts that you never knew were edible. On a more palatable note, the Cantonese are also known for their dim sum. In traditional dim sum restaurants, carts are wheeled around for you to choose from their variety of small plates and bamboo steamers filled with shrimp dumplings, spring rolls, custards, and other two-bite delicacies.

SOUTHWEST: SICHUAN AND YUNNAN

The climate of the southwestern provinces, especially Sichuan, is particularly hospitable to growing chili peppers. Sichuan cuisine ("Szechwan" in the States) loads every dish with hundreds of chili-pepper pieces, making the predominant color a deep, intense red. Yunnanese restaurants, on the other hand, take their inspiration from neighboring Vietnam and Thailand with specialties like pineapple-fried rice, fried bananas, and exotic mushrooms.

XINJIANG AND THE NORTHWEST

At northwest-style restaurants (Xinjiang, Ningxia, and Lanzhou) you'll find Muslim-influenced cuisine of hand-pulled noodles, savory rice pilaf, round flat breads, and a predominance of lamb – by the leg, on a stick, grilled, fried, or roasted. You may also find dancers and musicians performing their art in Middle Eastern style, which makes for a very festive atmosphere.

SHARK'S FIN AND SICHUAN PEPPER

AN INTERVIEW WITH FOOD WRITER FUCHSIA DUNLOP

Fuchsia Dunlop, London-based cookbook author and restaurant consultant, specializes in authentic Chinese cuisine and spends much of her time in China doing food research and leading gastronomic tours. Her acclaimed autobiographical book, *Shark's Fin and Sichuan Pepper: A Sweet-Sour Memoir of Eating in China,* tells of her time as a culinary student in China and her subsequent travels in search of new Chinese culinary techniques, ingredients, and flavors.

What first inspired your passion for China and its regional cuisines?

I became fascinated by China while working as a sub-editor for the BBC and, after a thrilling trip to Hong Kong and the mainland, started taking Mandarin classes in London. Soon afterward I won a British Council scholarship to study in China and chose to go to Sichuan University in Chengdu, partly, I must admit, because of the reputation of Sichuanese cuisine and because I'd eaten so well there on my first visit to the city. I wasn't disappointed. The food in Chengdu was unlike any I'd encountered in Britain, and utterly delicious.

   I started begging friends and restaurant owners to let me into their kitchens and then, with a German friend, took a few private cooking classes at the famous Sichuan Institute of Higher Cuisine. A few months later, after the end of my scholarship, the cooking school invited me to enroll as a regular student on a professional course, which I did. It was a challenge being the only foreigner and one of only three women in a class of 50 young Sichuanese, but I loved my time there. And of course it completely changed the direction of my life.

What are your impressions of living in Chengdu?

Living in Chengdu in the mid-1990s was a constant pleasure. People were welcoming, the atmosphere of the city was laid-back and charming, and it didn't cost much to live extremely well. Chengdu at that time was an old city, where street vendors touted for business in the winding lanes, people sat around all day chatting in teahouses, and there was a bustling street market in every neighborhood. I just adored it, like most of my foreign classmates at Sichuan University. Of course the appearance of the city has dramatically altered since then, and I've been sad to see the destruction of all the old streets. But people there are as much fun as ever, and the atmosphere is as congenial.

so expect the teapot and the cups to disappear when your food arrives. At cafeterias, you are expected to use your soup as a drink. Glasses of water are not provided with meals, and ice is rare, although chilled soft drinks, beer, and bottled water are always readily available. The beer is often cheapest (unless it's imported), but you'll have to request it cold (*bing de*) if that's how you like it, since many Chinese still prefer their drinks at room temperature. If you order water, you may get a cup of hot water—a common drink in cold

In all your travels throughout China, is there a place you would call your favorite?

I'll always feel a very deep affection for Chengdu, which was my first love in terms of Chinese places, but I've also had unforgettable adventures in other parts of the country. The places that have particular resonance for me include the Tibetan and Uighur areas of the west and northwest, with their stunning scenery and distinctive cultures; western Hunan, where I traveled with my friend Sansan; inland Fujian, with its beautiful mountains and tea plantations; and more recently, Hangzhou and Yangzhou. But the thing that is so incredible about China is that there is always more to explore.

What do you most love about Chinese food?

I find the subject of Chinese food endlessly interesting. Chinese cuisines themselves are far more diverse and sophisticated than most people in the West realize; after more than a decade of research I'm still learning new things on a daily, if not hourly, basis whenever I'm in China. And Chinese culinary culture can be a lens for viewing China in general: its history, customs, social structures, philosophies, religious practices, medicinal tradition, and so on.

What drives me is the excitement of writing on a subject that has in the past been relatively unexplored and misunderstood by people in the West. It's such a rich territory, and I don't think I'd be able to write about any other cuisine that would give me the same kick, the same thrill of discovery. I hope that my work does something toward promoting appreciation of what is arguably the world's greatest culinary tradition. It's about time the outside world gave it the recognition it deserves.

COURTESY OF FUCHSIA DUNLOP

Fuchsia Dunlop

northern climates. Requesting *"bing de bai kai shui"* will get you a free glass of cold water that's safe to drink.

The cry of *gan bei!* is a toast that signifies everyone should drink down whatever alcohol is left in his or her glass. You can politely refuse to do so and just take a sip, though your companions may chide you. The Chinese find it incredibly funny to get a foreigner drunk, especially if you're their boss, so watch out—their *bai jiu* (hard liquor) is rather potent!

ALL THE TEA IN CHINA

In China, tea comes in a variety of forms, including loose leaves, tiny balls, and beautiful flowers. There are five main categories of tea in China.

GREEN

Green tea, the most common in China, keeps its color because it is not fermented before it is dried. The pride of all green teas is the Long Jing (dragon well) tea that hails from Hangzhou.

RED

Red tea is what is called black tea in the West. It is fermented before drying, making it black, but creates a reddish-brown liquid when steeped.

BLACK

Chinese black tea is hardened into compressed bricks, making it easy to transport to remote areas, where it is popular among minority groups. It is also referred to as brick tea due to its shape.

OOLONG

Because it is made after partial fermentation, the color of Oolong tea is between green and black. Oolong is grown in Taiwan and Fujian Province.

FLOWER

These teas are made from fragrant flowers such as jasmine or chrysanthemum, often creating a very beautiful presentation when served in a clear glass. The popular Eight Treasures Tea combines eight colorful ingredients such as chrysanthemum, jujube, Chinese wolfberries, lily buds, rock sugar, dates, longans, and green tea.

© BARBARA STROTHER

flower tea

Banquets are times to impress, and that means the most exotic foods. You may be treated to duck's tongue, baby pigeon, fish-head soup, chicken feet, cow's lung, pig intestines, scorpions, squid, and a whole lot more. Take only a very small amount of each dish, because you won't believe how much food they will keep bringing. You'll know the meal is over when the complimentary slices of fruit arrive. You will have to ask for the check (*mai dan*) when you are ready to leave.

In China, whoever does the inviting is the one who also does the ordering and the paying. Splitting the cost of a meal is rude by Chinese custom, though Chinese who are familiar with foreign ways may be open to it. Instead, the accounts are balanced when your guests later invite you out for a meal.

If it's your birthday, you're expected to treat your friends to a meal rather than being treated. We discovered this early on when we invited out a large group of Chinese coworkers to celebrate the birthday of a newly arrived fellow American, who was incidentally quite low on cash at the time. Lots of people came—and ate—without offering to pitch in a single *jiao* (dime), much to our unexpected chagrin.

SAVING FACE

It is of utmost importance to the Chinese never to cause another to look down on you, never to look ignorant or incompetent, and always to be completely respectable and respected. While Westerners also value not losing face, it is nowhere nearly as significant as it is to a typical Chinese person. For this reason, nine times out of 10 a Chinese individual would rather give you a wrong answer than admit he doesn't know the answer, or will avoid answering a question if the answer might upset you.

Saving face plays an important role in the nitty-gritty confrontations of everyday life. Direct confrontation and challenge is not the Chinese way and will deeply offend and humiliate, no matter how simple the issue is. This can be counterintuitive to us Westerners, who are used to demanding what we believe we deserve. A direct challenge may get you what you want, but in the end the damage to the relationship could prove to be insurmountable. Often the way the Chinese avoid this is to make up excuses or tell little white lies rather than being direct, in order to prevent a loss of face for either party.

There are times when you can use the Chinese value of "saving face" to your advantage. Foreign teachers find it the most productive way to discipline a young Chinese classroom. One round of the song "Lee and Lilly sitting in a tree, k-i-s-s-i-n-g . . ." will bring naughty little Lee and Lilly to tears—but they'll be better behaved than they ever have been before.

GUANXI

Guanxi, which means connection or network, signifies a relational system based on repaying favors between friends and family. It is the backbone of how many Chinese relationships function. If you have *guanxi* with an individual, they are going to do what they can to take care of you, and the same is expected of you. Whether helping your *guanxi* partner get a job, introducing them to your other "connections" in advantageous positions, or helping them out of a tough situation, building *guanxi* can someday benefit you when you are the one in need. The flip side of the *guanxi* system is that it can leave you feeling used when an acquaintance's previous generosity and hospitality later seem like down payments on the unduly large favor they eventually ask of you.

If you are concerned about what may be lurking behind someone's offer of generosity, don't accept it. Or if you accept it, be prepared to return the favor immediately to even the score. You will find that this is the way many

XIAO HUANG DI: LITTLE EMPERORS

One child, two parents, four grandparents: China's one-child policy has resulted in the unforeseen effect of creating spoiled kids doted on by six admiring adults. Many families in China are raising *xiao huang di,* or "little emperors" – a Chinese term to describe children who have never had to learn to share their toys with their brothers or sisters and never had to get along with their cousins. You'll notice the little emperors around you, mostly younger kids, screaming for their Häagen Dazs ice cream, shouting at their parents when they don't want to do what they are told, and sassing grandma when she asks her little queen not to climb so high on the playground.

This trend is having an impact on the social fiber of the nation as these young generations of emperors, who have become accustomed to the world revolving around them, grow older. Now that the first generation of *xiao huang di* are adults, more and more parents are complaining of the lack of respect from their grown children, even to the point of some parents suing their kids over the lack of care. On the other hand, the tendency of the younger generation toward instant gratification, though conflicting with the traditional Chinese value of thrift and saving money, has added fuel to the fire of the expanding Chinese economy.

Chinese people approach relationships. A cheap Christmas gift once given to our neighbor's son was immediately met with multiple gifts and cash for our sons. You often can't out-give the Chinese, nor should you always try. You may be putting an undue burden on a less-affluent Chinese family if you give them a considerably benevolent gift or favor.

Gender Roles

Mao's Communist Revolution may have done some serious damage to the nation during its worst years, but one thing it did quite well was to increase the status of women. The PRC has always treated women as equals, expecting them to labor in the fields alongside the men to achieve the Communist ideals of the glorious working class. Today most Chinese women have careers. Though the majority of the highest-ranking positions in business and government are still filled by men, women can and do play significant leadership roles across all private and public sectors. Staying home to raise a child and tend the house is not a common practice in China. Indeed, domestic helpers who cook and clean can be hired for cheap, and taking care of the baby is a duty that grandparents are expected to fulfill. For wealthy double-income Chinese families, prestigious boarding schools take little ones during the week and return them to their parents for the weekends.

Within a typical modern Chinese home, the division of labor between men and women is not so different from what you would expect in the Western world. Women tend to carry most of the domestic responsibility, but at friends' homes the men are often better cooks than their wives. Raising children also falls more heavily on the shoulders of the women, but modern Chinese men take very active roles in raising their kids. However, there is less of this sense of domestic equality in more rural and traditional families.

© BARBARA STROTHER

Chinese women through the ages

Religion

Communist China is officially an atheistic state. During the early days of communism and the Cultural Revolution, the state sought to eradicate all religious belief, but religion has deep roots in China, and their efforts were unsuccessful. In 1982 an amendment to the constitution allowed freedom of religion within certain boundaries. Today, China is experiencing a spiritual revival of all religions as temples, churches, and monasteries long vacant are being restored and returned to their original purposes. Buddhism, Taoism, ancestor worship, Confucianism, Lamaism, Islam, and Christianity are all flourishing, and often the Chinese mix and match many of these belief systems without feeling the need to delineate which, exactly, they adhere to.

© BARBARA STROTHER

Many churches and temples are being restored to their original purposes.

ANIMISM AND ANCESTOR WORSHIP

The earliest spiritual roots in China revolved around animism and ancestor worship, and these influences are evident in the prevalent superstitions and veneration of the dead that still exist. It is common in China to burn paper replicas of money, cars, and cell phones for one's ancestors, gifts for their use in the netherworld, in the hopes that these spirits will bring prosperity and blessing in return.

CONFUCIANISM AND TAOISM

Confucius taught an ethical code of social behavior, not a spiritual faith, yet many have made Confucianism

Confucius

© BARBARA STROTHER

into a pseudo-religion. Taoism, on the other hand, is China's only truly indigenous religion. The Tao, meaning "the way," has been described as the way of nature, or the spiritual operating force of the universe, though they claim that if you can describe the Tao, then you don't really know it. In Taoism all things have balance, a yin and yang, which can be achieved through a mystical sense of inaction and letting things develop as they may. Active Taoists today use the martial art tai chi to achieve an inner state of harmony with the Tao, as well as the worship and appeasement of a pantheon of good and evil spirits.

BUDDHISM

Buddhism infiltrated China from India by the 5th century and remains the most popular religion among the Chinese. In classical Buddhist belief, nirvana (a high state of enlightenment) is achieved when you can eradicate the suffering that desire creates using meditation, self-denial, and right conduct. After the massive destruction of the Cultural Revolution, it was rare to find any active Buddhist temples or monasteries, but today restored Buddhist temples and monasteries are busy with the activity of incense-burning and kowtowing constituents in prayer.

The Tibetans formed their own strain of Buddhism, essentially a marriage of Buddhist tenets with the shamanic religion that preceded them. Tibetan Buddhism, also known as Lamaism, focuses on the mystical practices of ritual postures, spoken mantras, and sacred art.

ISLAM

Islam was peacefully introduced to China through Arab traders at southern seaports, though today the religion is most prevalent in north-western provinces. In cities along the ancient Silk Road, the Muslim Ui-ghur and Hui minority populations have faithfully preserved their Islam-ic way of life, worshipping Allah and following the teachings of the proph-et Muhammad. The Chinese Mus-lims are not as rigid in their practices as other Muslim nations, which can most readily be seen in the Hui's free-dom to drink alcohol.

CHRISTIANITY

China's Christian history dates back to the 7th-century Nestorian Chris-tians, though a strong missionary presence didn't take hold until the 1800s. Christian missionaries fol-lowed in the footsteps of opium merchants, and although they did good works like running schools and orphanages, they were eventu-ally blamed for much of the nega-tive influence of the West at that time. All missionaries were forced to leave when the Communists es-tablished the PRC and have been forbidden since.

© BARBARA STROTHER

giant seated Buddha at Hangzhou's ancient Lingyin Temple

© BARBARA STROTHER

Chinese Madonna and child, Macau

China's regulations provide for one official Catholic organization, the Catholic Patriotic Association, and one official Protestant organization, the Three Self Patriotic Movement (TSPM). Chinese Christian churches must abide by laws requiring self-propagation, self-governance, and self-support, forbidding foreigners from leadership, financial support, and evangelism (although the Chinese can evangelize other Chinese). Chinese law also forbids unofficial assembly for any group, spiritual or otherwise, meaning all Christian gatherings must take place in a registered location.

While the government puts the official number of Protestants at 10 million and Catholics at 4 million, some estimate the true number to be as high as 100 million and 20 million respectively, due to the vast number who are part of the unofficial underground church. Many Chinese Christians, balking at the control of the church by an atheistic organization and fearing religious persecution, have taken to secretly meeting in people's homes rather than under the watchful eye of the government. It is primarily the crackdown on this illegal practice of secret meetings that results in what the rest of the world protests as religious persecution in China.

Arts

LITERATURE

The canon of Chinese literature reads like a list of golden oldies rock-and-roll bands: the Five Classics, the Three Character Classics, the Four Books, the Eight Great Literary Masters, and the beat goes on. Though it's too much to cover in detail here, there are a few titles every expat should be aware of due to their abiding presence in modern Chinese culture.

The earliest Chinese classic is the *I-Ching,* which teaches the ancient art of divination. The ancient philosophy of Laozi's *Tao Te Ching (The Book of the Way and Its Power)* expounds the spiritual teaching of the Tao. Confucius proposed self-sacrifice, personal morality, and social responsibility in his writings and became the most influential philosopher in Chinese history. The definitive text on military strategy, Sun Tzu's *The Art of War,* written over 2,500 years ago, is still popular today among strategists in business and board games.

Among Chinese novels there are four key classics. *The Dream of the Red Chamber,* also known as *A Dream of Red Mansions,* is a love tragedy considered by some to be one of the finest literary works of all time. *Water Margin* depicts the lives of 12th-century bandits, while *The Journey to the West* introduces the beloved Monkey King as he travels with a Buddhist monk, a pig-monster, and a water demon. *Romance of the Three Kingdoms* delves into the

Literary arts and scholarship have always been a key part of Chinese culture.

political turmoil of the fall of the Han Dynasty, immortalized in a popular PlayStation game of the same name.

Poetry plays an integral role in Chinese classical literary art. The Tang Dynasty produced the two most famous of all Chinese poets, Li Bai and Du Fu. While Du Fu wrote of deep grief, Li Bai and his poetic pals used wine-drinking games as impetus for creativity.

Although the Cultural Revolution and the widespread censorship that followed the 100 Flowers Movement put a damper on literary freedom for decades, modern Chinese literature is once again pushing the envelope of creativity and indulging in a newfound freedom.

VISUAL ARTS

Historically China's visual arts have focused on ink-wash landscapes and natural elements, such as birds and flowers, which grace traditional Chinese scrolls. Fine crafts include work in cloisonné, porcelain, lacquerware, embroidery, and jade carvings. Calligraphy, the marriage of visual and literary art, is the oldest art form in China. Through the centuries the Chinese have developed several different types of artistic scripts that take years to master. Sometimes what looks the sloppiest to untrained foreign eyes is actually the disciplined work of a master calligrapher. China's modern art, like its literature, tends to make shocking and bold visual statements with a newfound freedom of expression that would not have been tolerated just a few decades ago.

erhu player

© BARBARA STROTHER

MUSIC

Traditional Chinese music, with its preference for nasal voices and high-pitched tones, is often described by foreigners in terms of cats (cats fighting in a cymbal shop, cats being tortured, cats being murdered; you get the picture). While it's true that some Chinese music is an acquired taste, there is much out there that is entirely enjoyable, especially pieces using the traditional instruments of the violin-like *erhu,* the flute-like *dizi,* and the lute-like *pipa.*

China's popular music is a mixture of a heavy dose of Western pop stars and Asian ones, with a majority of Chinese music stars hailing from Hong Kong and Taiwan. China's popular music scene is still years behind the West but is fast gaining ground, and Chinese pop stars like Coco Lee, Jacky Cheung, Jay Chou, and Wei Wei enjoy demigod status just as much as their Western counterparts.

CHINESE OPERA

Chinese opera is a unique dramatic form that uses singing, dancing, acrobatics, mime, swordplay, and traditional music to tell its stories. The best known and most refined style of Chinese opera is Beijing Opera, though there are more than 300 individual forms named for the region where each developed. The Sichuan Opera is known for "face changes," a highly refined skill of suddenly changing an artist's look (with face paint or a facial screen mask), leaving the audience wondering, like a magician's show, "How'd he do that?" The Shaoxing Opera, one of the newest forms, breaks from the strong male tradition by primarily using female performers.

FILM

Modern films of the mainland, perhaps because they are still somewhat censored to safe subject matters, are often beautiful period pieces full of tragedy with a technical focus on skilled uses of color, texture, and light to create moods. The film industry of Hong Kong, on the other hand, tends toward violent, gory, and chaotic ghost stories and kung fu pieces or, on the lighter

WELCOME TO CHINA

side, slapstick. China has produced several film stars loved the world over, including Hong Kong's Jackie Chan, Chou Yun-Fat, and Jet Li, and the mainland's most famous actress, Gong Li.

ARCHITECTURE

Chinese traditional architecture has an elegant style dating back to ancient times. Characteristic traits include sloping tile roofs with up-turned eaves, elaborately decorated brackets and carved roof figures, and rooms built around open court-yards. The common raised thresh-olds were designed to keep less-in-telligent evil spirits, who apparently

© BARBARA STROTHER

Fist of Fury: Cao Chongen's sculpture of Bruce Lee in Hong Kong

do not know how to step over, at bay. Feng shui plays an important role in traditional architecture, determining details like which direction doors should face to maximize the inflow of good luck and keep evil spirits away.

Some regions within China have unique architectural styles, including the tan, boxy earthen homes of the Uighurs, the round felt tents of the Mongols, cave houses in the hills near Xi'an, and large, round communal wooden Hakka homes. Throughout China's modern cities, however, you'll find a variety of architectural styles, from the plain concrete boxes of Russian Communist influence to gaudy and elaborate classical European details, mixed in with the world's most futuristic and awe-inspiring skyscrapers.

Sports and Games

SPORTS

In the United States we have the right to free speech and assembly; in China they have the right to sports. The government of the PRC takes sports so seriously that they've written it into their law, guaranteeing the opportunity for every citizen to get physical. And due in part to their successful hosting of the 2008 Beijing Olympics (51 gold medals for China, compared to 36 for the United States), producing world-class athletes remains a top priority for the government.

© BARBARA STROTHER

Chinese and *laowai* shootin' hoops

The number-one sport in the country is soccer, which the Chinese claim to have invented. They also claim to have invented golf, which is quickly growing in popularity among Chinese yuppies. Table tennis has played an important role not only in recreation but also in modern politics: It was a ping pong tournament in 1971 that was the catalyst for opening diplomatic relations between the United States and the PRC. It will only take one good beating in table tennis by a seven-year-old for you to realize how important the game is to the culture. Basketball has gained a tremendous following in China; courts are filled at all hours with young men hoping to be the next Yao Ming.

GAMES

Among Chinese table games, the one that is most well known is mahjong, similar to the gin card game but using carved tiles instead of cards. Mahjong has a rough reputation among the Chinese since the game is used for gambling. The Chinese also have their own version of chess, *xiang qi*, with rules and characters that are similar to the Western version. *Xiang qi* typically uses wooden disks carved with the piece's title, so to play you'll have to learn to recognize about a dozen Chinese characters. Knowing how to play either—or both—of these popular games is one of the best ways to make friends with the locals, who are always delighted to discover a *laowai* (foreigner) who can play.

PLANNING YOUR FACT-FINDING TRIP

If you are considering a move to China and haven't been there yet, put this down and book your flight immediately. Reading about China, though vitally important to understanding the country, cannot paint a true picture of the real thing. You will never know if you will love or hate the unfamiliar foods, complex language, and overly friendly curiosity of the Chinese until you've spent time with them on their turf. And if you have a choice of living locations within China, roaming around the country is the best way to get a feel for which part of this vast nation best fits your style and your needs.

Planning a fact-finding trip to China is not quite the same as planning a vacation to China. The focus of your trip needs to be on doing the research that will make your move as smooth as possible, but you should be able to squeeze in a little fun along the way as well. The good news is, once you make

© BARBARA STROTHER

your move to China, you'll likely have enough travel opportunities to give your friends back home a serious case of travel envy.

Preparing to Leave

WHAT TO TAKE
Documents
A passport with a Chinese tourist visa is required for your arrival in mainland China, although North Americans and Europeans can stay in Hong Kong up to 90 days without a visa. (For more information, see the *Visas and Residence Permits* section of the *Making the Move* chapter.) If you have travel insurance, bring your documentation, including information on what to do if you should need an emergency medical evacuation. If you happen to be coming from a country where contracting yellow fever is a possibility, you'll be required to show proof of immunization when you arrive in China. You'll also want to make sure you are up-to-date on all of your other travel shots. (For detailed information on immunizations, see the *Health* chapter.)

Clothing
When it comes to clothing, we recommend traveling very light. It is easier to buy extra clothes there, should you need them, than bother with bulky luggage—unless you are very large or tall, in which case you may struggle to find clothes that fit in China. It's also perfectly acceptable in China to wear the same outfit for two or three days in a row. Bring a good pair of comfortable walking shoes because you will be putting them hard to work daily. You may want to pack a disposable poncho if traveling during the summer rainy season, although umbrella peddlers will suddenly appear as soon as the first drops start to fall.

Miscellaneous
Other items you may want to consider packing include a small calculator to help with bargaining and the exchange rate, a detailed travel guide, a pocket-size phrasebook, insect repellent, hand sanitizer, and a few tissue packs for toilet paper on the go. If you love to shop, consider bringing an empty extra suitcase nestled into your larger case in order to cart home all the treasures you're bound to pick up on the way. (You could also buy an extra suitcase there.)

Be sure to bring a journal for jotting down notes about your fact-finding research, and a thin plastic file holder can organize the magazines and materials you pick up along the way. A camera, whether still or video, is great for both remembering what you've seen and showing friends and family what your new life may look like, especially if you have kids back home who will be moving with you. If you're bringing a laptop, add a small travel surge protector that does double duty as a plug adaptor.

Business cards are an important part of both the business and social culture in China, so you'll want to have a small stack with you. If you don't already have business cards, get some simple name cards that include your email and other contact information printed before you go. Keep in mind that proper Chinese protocol requires you to give and receive business cards with two hands as a gesture of respect.

MONEY
How Much to Bring?

Just how much money will you need for your journey? This greatly depends on your itinerary and your standards. Smaller cities come quite cheap, but the main tourist drags of Beijing, Shanghai, and the like are not the bargains they once were. Comfortable but low-frills mid-range travel can be done for about $60–100 a day; serious budget travelers can get by in the mainland with $20–30 a day if they choose hostels, street food, trains instead of planes, and public transportation instead of taxis. But if you intend to stay at five-star international hotels, take multiple flights, and enjoy China's haute cuisine, your budget could be over $250 per day. Be sure to bring plenty of spending money on top of this. If your travel plans include pricey Hong Kong, you'll spend considerably more.

© BARBARA STROTHER

Eating cheap street food is a tasty way to go easy on the budget.

Currency and Exchange

Consider bringing a mixture of currency options, including credit cards, traveler's checks, and an ATM card, since you never know which will work best at the time you need money. The bulk of your money, however, should be in cash. Traveler's checks, though they do protect against loss and theft, are often a bigger hassle than they're worth: Not all banks and hotel exchange desks accept them. Credit cards are a fairly new idea in China, and only a handful of businesses, such as nice hotels and restaurants, are equipped to take them. You will, however, want to bring your ATM card, as ATMs have become very common in China. (It sometimes takes a try at several machines before you find one that will take your card, however.) Most bank locations, high-end department stores, and large supermarkets have ATMs that are both bilingual and dependable. To save money on ATM fees, find out which Chinese bank is partnered with your home bank before you go.

You can exchange your dollars for renminbi at the airport, which you'll need to do since you can't use U.S. dollars in China. The exchange rates at Chinese airports are usually not bad, but they tack on a fee unless you're exchanging a decent amount of cash. You'll get a better deal at a branch location of a local bank or at your hotel's exchange desk, so either only exchange enough at the airport to keep you going for a couple days or exchange a large enough amount to avoid the fees. When you do make it to a bank, the standard procedure is to take a number as you enter and watch the electronic signs above each teller for your turn. The simplest place to change money, though, is at your hotel; you'll need your room number to use their services. You'll always need your passport to exchange money regardless of where it's done, and be sure to keep your original exchange receipt if you want to change renminbi back into dollars at the end of your trip.

Precautionary Measures

Keep an eye on your money and bags at all times. Though China is far from being as crime-ridden as other international destinations, it is always better to be safe than sorry. Hotel rooms often provide a small safe, which is a good place to store your valuables when you're not in your room. Put your wallet in a buttoned pocket if possible, or fasten the pocket containing your wallet with a safety pin when going into crowded areas such as buses, subways, and popular markets. Petty theft is more prevalent in southern China (especially Guangzhou), at bus and train stations, and around the time of Chinese holidays, when migrant workers are expected to bring gifts home to their families even if they're cash-poor. Consider using a hidden money belt or pouch for extra protection.

WHEN TO GO

The best time to visit just about anywhere in China is either spring or fall. Northern winters are unbearably cold, and even the south can chill you to your bones since by law all public buildings south of the Yangtze River have no central heat. Summers are hot throughout the country, and many cities experience their rainy season during summer. Fall offers wonderfully mild temperatures and pleasant weather; springtime has the added benefit of the trees and gardens in bloom. But if the primary purpose of your trip is to consider a long-term move to a land of extreme temperatures, you may want to visit during their worst season. Don't try to imagine how it will feel to wait at a bus stop in the biting winter winds of Harbin or to walk to summer classes in a hot and wet Hong Kong monsoon; go experience it for yourself. See if Chengdu's winter grays depress you. After all, it is what you'll have to deal with if you move here, and firsthand experience is one of the best ways to prepare yourself mentally for your relocation.

Though Chinese holidays can be a delightfully colorful and fun time to travel, you'll struggle with the masses of Chinese that are also traveling during the holiday. Public transportation will be packed; tickets and hotel rooms will be hard to come by, with no room for the typical price bargaining. If you choose to travel during a major holiday, book everything well in advance, and try not to roam too much around the country until everyone is back at work again.

JOINING A TOUR GROUP

Some travelers to China prefer to join a package tour, especially on their maiden voyage. Although these trips can be expensive, a package tour will guarantee a certain level of quality in accommodations, food, and transportation, as well as the comfort of a bilingual guide making all your arrangements for you. If you want to cover a lot of territory, a package tour may end up being cheaper than what you could put together on your own. And if you want to visit a restricted area, such as Tibet, you'll have to be officially part of a tour group to get the necessary government permits.

On the other hand, if you forgo the group tour to set out on your own, you will get a richer experience of what life in China is really like. Package tours frequent the places that are most fit for big groups of foreigners, such as large restaurants with bland food and foreign hotels that tend to keep you distanced from the fascinating world outside their doors. Traveling on your own, however, will allow you to be flexible and spontaneous, making your own choices about when to splurge and when to save, when to rest and when

CHINESE FESTIVALS AND HOLIDAYS

A colorful time to travel, or more hassle than it's worth? Regardless of whether you want to join them or avoid them, here are the key events of the year:

- **Chinese New Year/Spring Festival:** This is China's most significant holiday. On the eve of the New Year, cities resemble war zones as fireworks fill the sky with bursts of color, sonic booms, and lingering smoke. It is customary to visit family and bring gifts during this holiday. Late January or early February.

- **Lantern Festival:** When dusk falls, people walk the streets with paper lanterns. Mid-late February.

- **Tomb Sweeping Festival:** This is a day dedicated to tending relatives' graves. Some people burn paper replicas of money for great grandpa to enjoy in the netherworld. First week of April.

- **Labor Day/May Day:** This international holiday celebrates the workers of the world. Many Chinese prefer to spend their vacation doing sightseeing travel. May 1.

- **Dragon Boat Festival:** For this festival, people watch dragon boat races and eat traditional *zongzi*, a triangular delicacy of sticky rice wrapped in a large leaf. Typically in June.

- **Mid-Autumn Festival/Moon Festival:** This romantic night may be meant for gazing at the moon, but it is perhaps most popularly celebrated by eating moon cakes. Late September or early October.

- **National Day:** This state holiday celebrates the creation of the People's Republic of China. October 1.

© BARBARA STROTHER

A dragon boat rests at the beach on Lantau Island, Hong Kong.

© BARBARA STROTHER

Traveling without a tour group: depressingly lonely or delightfully alone?

to go. You will also be able to customize your daily itinerary based on what to see in preparation for your move. Most tours won't give you enough spare time for exploring expat neighborhoods, international schools, or local grocery stores and shopping venues outside tourist zones.

Arriving in China

CUSTOMS

While it is possible to slip in one of China's backdoors by ship, train, or four-wheel drive, most likely you'll make your arrival via an international airport. Before your plane arrives, the flight attendants will hand out the forms you'll need to clear customs and immigration. Be sure to document any expensive equipment you are bringing into the country, or they may try to charge you duty on the item when you leave.

Although lines for customs and immigration can be long at some airports, the process is relatively easy. Just wait your turn to approach the window, hand over your passport and forms, and you'll be on your way within a matter of moments. Random individuals are chosen for bag searches; if you're not particularly suspicious-looking, they'll most likely wave you by.

Nothing pornographic, or even slightly risqué, will be allowed in. Large amounts of religious materials will be confiscated—anything that looks like it's meant for the masses—but there is no problem bringing in religious books for your own personal use. All medications should be in their original container; prescription drugs should have the original prescription. China takes drug offenses seriously; do not give them any reason to suspect you may be involved in illegal drug activity. Drug dealers are executed in China—even foreign ones.

TRANSPORTATION

When you've successfully made it through with bags in hand, it will be time to step out of the gray zone of the airport and into the hustle and bustle of modern-day China. Most airports are located a considerable distance from the city center, but you'll have several ways to get into town. Subway lines serve a few of the major airports. Inexpensive airport buses are common, although you will need to know the city fairly well to know which bus will take you to your destination. Only the luxury hotels offer airport shuttle buses. The easiest way out of all airport areas is simply to hop in a taxi. You'll have to find the taxi queue and take the next one in line. Fares to and from airports can be steep; you should budget as much as $50 to be safe. Make sure you agree on a price first and/or demand that they run the meter because airport taxi drivers are infamous for preying on ignorant first-time visitors. It's best to have a business card or a fax with the hotel's name in Chinese characters to show your driver; the majority of cabbies in China do not speak any English, and some even struggle to understand foreigners who speak Chinese.

Sample Itineraries

China is a big, big country. You can't experience all of China in one trip, but with enough cash for airfare and energy for an intense pace, you could cover quite a bit. We recommend, however, focusing your itinerary to just a handful of cities or a couple of parts of the country, leaving the discovery of the rest of China for future trips. The best itinerary will allow you to contrast the energy and modern amenities of big-city life with the cross-cultural appeal of life in a smaller city. It should give you a view of the countryside, if only through the window of a bus or train, and plenty of time to check out the local expat scene, housing options, and supermarkets. And don't forget to allow some time for a little fun.

If already have a job opportunity in China, you'll want to focus your itinerary on the location of the position. If your future is not bound to one particular city, the sample itineraries will give you a broad experience of the key highlights of China. If your trip is solely for the purpose of fact-finding, one week should give you plenty of time to do the research you need to do. If, however, you want to look at multiple areas around the nation, or if you want to include a fair amount of tourism and sightseeing, extend your trip to two weeks or even a full month.

THINGS TO DO
Daily Life Research

You'll want to make sure you experience as much of daily life in China as you can. For starters, spend some time wandering around grocery stores. Try a megamart like Carrefour as well as a little convenience store. Stop by an open-air wet market where vegetables still smell of dirt and tonight's dinner is still breathing (but stay away from the live-bird area in light of the possibility of avian flu). These places are also good environments for you

SQUAT POTS

If you have a weak stomach, you may not want to read further. Chinese squat toilets are a reality of living in China, and they can be truly nasty.

Squat toilets are so called because you don't sit on anything: You simply squat over an opening. The nicest ones are porcelain, have indented spots to show you exactly where to put your two feet, and have a flush handle. Typically they'll include a nearby trash can for disposing of used toilet paper in order to spare weak plumbing systems. You'll find this type in public places like restaurants, although more modern establishments may have Western toilets.

The worst squat pots don't even have a pot. You'll step up between stall walls (sorry, no doors) to a raised platform, and squat over a long trough that extends to all the stalls. There's no individual flush (so try not to look down or breathe through your nose); occasionally a flood of water will race violently down the trough to wash everything away. You may encounter these in places like older bus or train stations, and they are much more common in little towns and rural areas than in the cosmopolitan cities.

Using the squat system isn't too hard to master, although for a West-ern woman who never knew it was possible to take care of business without sitting on a toilet, it can be a bit daunting at first. You'll often need to provide your own toilet paper, which is why you'll find cheap little tissue packs sold everywhere you go. And don't get too excited if you find a Western-style toilet in a public place. Many Chinese people prefer to squat, so the seat may be marked with the footprints of those who've squatted where you are getting ready to sit.

© TYLER CHRISTIAN

to try communicating in Chinese, even if you don't know any—use that phrasebook!

Be sure you schedule some time to check out the housing scene if your employer won't be providing housing for you. This can be as simple as looking at the postings in the windows of the real estate agencies you pass, or as complex as arranging several days with an agent to visit numerous properties.

Other places you may want to visit include international schools for your kids, local health facilities, both upscale shopping malls and cheap clothing bazaars, and the city's restaurants and clubs where expats tend to gather. If you're thinking of attending university in China, check out the foreign student dorms and the cafeteria, and try to sit in on a class. If you already have a job or if you have an employer in mind, you'll want to tour the facilities and get to know the part of town where they are located since this may become your stomping ground in the near future.

Challenging Experiences

Challenge yourself to test out a few experiences that are quite different from what you may be used to. Use scary public restrooms. Order a meal in a tiny dive where no one speaks any English. Try the street food. Take as many modes of public transportation as possible rather than relying on the ease of taxis. Rent a bike, or simply buy a cheap temporary one, to pedal around the parts of town you wouldn't otherwise see. Hop on the subway, especially at rush hour. And *always* fit in at least one train journey; make it hard seat (for

© BARBARA STROTHER

You won't find many star-rated toilets in China.

short journeys) or hard sleeper (for long journeys). These are the best ways to interact with the locals, and it's the little interactions you have with the Chinese, and the new friendships you make along the way, that will give you the most satisfying journey in the end.

Tourist Stuff

Although setting your specific itinerary will depend on the areas you may live in, there are places that really shouldn't be missed. The list is endless, but here are a few options to get you started. Any visitor to China will want to see the Great Wall, which most tourists access via Beijing. Xi'an's terra-cotta warriors are also usually high on the list, as well as Shanghai's metropolis and historic Bund. The beauty of Hangzhou and Suzhou must be seen sometime, although these could be saved for future excursions; the same goes for the seaside resorts of Dalian, Qingdao, and Xiamen. Hong Kong and Macau are worlds unto themselves, Chinese at heart but in so many ways unlike the rest of the mainland—or anyplace else in the world, for that matter.

ONE WEEK

With just a week in China you could divide your time between two major cities, but we recommend you focus on just one region by making your base in one major city and taking day trips from there. We'll give you a one-week sample itinerary for Shanghai that includes short trips to Hangzhou and Suzhou, but you can use this example as a model for other places as well. For

© TYLER CHRISTIAN

Taking a horse to the Great Wall is an adventurous alternative to a tour bus.

example, one week based in Beijing can also include the Great Wall, Tianjin's antique market and European concessions, and Chengdu's odd mix of temples. A week based in Hong Kong could include a day trip to charming Macau and a two-day trip to Guangzhou for a feel of the "real" China.

Day 1

If you leave home on a Friday night, you can expect to arrive in Shanghai on Sunday morning local time. By the time you go through customs, exchange some money, and check in to your hotel, you'll have just enough time to grab a bite to eat and make your way to the Sunday afternoon expat service at the Shanghai Community Fellowship Church on Hengshan Road in the French Concession. Even if you're not a religious person, this is the place you'll find the most foreigners gathered together, so it's a great way to meet people that can tell you what it's really like to live here. From the church, make your way eastward by public bus down upscale Huai Hai Road. Feel free to hop off the bus and walk a little among the posh upscale stores, glamorous residences, and sidewalk crowds.

Xintiandi, toward the eastern end of Huai Hai Street, is a pleasant place to end your day. You'll have your choice of high-end restaurants, both Chinese and international, as well as trendy nightclubs where you may want to stay and play for a while if you're not too exhausted from all your travels. Before you head back to your hotel, be sure to pick up one of Shanghai's English-language magazines, such as *That's Shanghai* or *City Weekend,* given out free at area restaurants, for tons of great information about living in the city as well as classifieds with good leads for housing, job opportunities, and the like.

Days 2-3

Monday and Tuesday should be dedicated to your fact-finding research. Tour the local international schools, talk with potential employers, or tour the university campus if you are considering studying abroad. Schedule appointments with a realtor in advance to take you to see homes in the areas you are most interested in. Be sure you squeeze in time to check out the local shopping and dining areas in these neighborhoods; you may want to end the day at a mall or a megamart like Carrefour where you can both shop and grab dinner in the dining court. If you have numerous appointments scattered around the city, consider renting a car and driver for the day (just ask your hotel for help) or negotiating a day-rate with a taxi. Be sure you leave plenty of time between scheduled appointments, especially if they are located in different parts of the city.

Day 4

After two days of research, you can have a little fun on Wednesday. Start your day on the west end of the Nanjing Road pedestrian shopping area near People's Park, and make your way gradually east to its end at the Bund with stops for shopping and a lunch along the way. When you get to the waterfront, sign up for a river cruise for late in the evening before you enjoy the views of passing ships and Pudong's modern skyline. Take the Tourist Tunnel (with its oddly psychedelic light show) to get to the other side of the river. Ascend the futuristic Oriental Pearl TV Tower for a bird's-eye view of the city; if you're traveling with kids (or kids at heart), don't miss the roller coaster ride located in the lowest sphere. Dinner options all have great views; choose between a bistro right on the Pudong waterfront just steps from the water's edge, a restaurant with windows overlooking the Bund inside the Super Brand Mall (including what has to be one of the nicest Pizza Huts in the world), or a gourmet meal at one of the pricey places inside the Hyatt on the 54th floor of the nearby Jin Mao building, with its stunning views of the city far below (reservations strongly recommended).

After your meal, the Tourist Tunnel is the fastest way to get back to the Bund, just in time to board your evening river cruise up and down the Huang Pu.

Days 5-6

Thursday and Friday are good days to escape big-city Shanghai. Although you could spend these two days in Nanjing, Suzhou, Ningbo, or even Putuoshan Island, we recommend Hangzhou, arguably China's most beautiful city. A two-hour train ride in the morning will get you into Hangzhou with time to check into a hotel (preferably one close to the West Lake, such as the Hyatt on the high end or the Hangzhou International Youth Hostel on the budget end) and grab a bite to eat. If you are considering moving to Hangzhou, you'll want to make sure you see the things that most relate to you: for students, Zhejiang University; for parents, Hangzhou International school; for those in need of a place to live, a tour of housing options with a local real estate agent. If you have time to play, Hanghzou has tons to do. You'll definitely want to explore the lakefront area and take a boat to the islands in the middle of the lake. The silk museum or tea museum are educational options, or if you'd rather buy silk than learn about it, head straight for the Silk Market.

The downtown area to the east of the lake is loaded with great restaurants and shops, and the area is relatively easy to navigate by foot. Hefang Jie is a lively pedestrian shopping street in traditional old buildings; head up from the square to the Chenghuang teahouse on the hill that overlooks the city.

© BARBARA STROTHER

Schedule a few days to look at housing options; bringing the kids can help them visualize their upcoming move.

When the sun goes down, don't miss the outdoor night market on Wushan Road downtown for a fun bargaining experience. Night owls will enjoy the lively bar scene along Nan Shan Road, which is also a good spot to run into expats who live in Hangzhou. Return to Shanghai by train or bus on Friday night to get well rested for Saturday, your last full day in China.

Day 7

You'll want to take stock of your remaining questions to plan your time for this day. If there are places you couldn't see or people you didn't have a chance to meet with, now's the time. You may also want to explore the traditional Yuyuan Garden and the historic area surrounding it, including the iconic Huaxingtin Teahouse, or check out the museums around People's Square. Saturday could also be spent exploring Suzhou's historic gardens or wander the narrow paths of ancient Xitang, the beautiful old river town where parts of the movie *Mission Impossible III* were filmed. You can show up in the morning at the tourist bus station in the Shanghai stadium, and the helpful ladies there will show you which tourist buses are leaving next and where they are headed. Some trips have tour guides, and some do not; just be sure you also find out what time the bus returns to Shanghai so you don't miss it. You'll want to be well rested before your Sunday morning flight back home. With the time zone difference, you'll most likely leave China on Sunday morning and arrive back home before Sunday evening.

TWO WEEKS

If you have two weeks to spend in China, you can cover quite a bit more ground—and have a bit more fun on the way. Boarding a Friday night flight to China, you could start your tour on Sunday morning in Hong Kong, followed by travels through all the first-tier cities (Hong Kong, Shanghai, Beijing) as well as a few days in second-tier cities that double as destinations for both expats and tourists. If you have a strong interest in Shanghai or Beijing, you can simply skip Macau and the second-tier city excursion in order to have more days to explore these metropolitan giants.

Days 1-2

Once you get settled in to your hotel on Sunday, walk off your jet lag by meandering around the neighborhood to get the Hong Kong vibe. Wander into the shops, eat some local grub, and do a little people-watching along the way. After dinner head to the Tsim Sha Tsui Promenade on the harbor to watch the whole city turn into a laser show set to music, starting nightly at 8 P.M. If you're still full of energy, head up to the Temple Street Night Market by way of Nathan Road with its famously picturesque neon signs.

Hop a tram to Hong Kong's Central Market.

© BARBARA STROTHER

On Monday morning join the crowds of busy professionals among Central's impressive high-rises, navigating by foot and double-decker streetcar. Shop for bargains along the tiny alleys of Li Yuen Street East and West on your way up to Soho's outdoor escalator, and grab a lunch at one of the trendy spots nearby. Make your way up to the top of Victoria Peak in the afternoon on the historic Peak Tram. Stroll around the summit for its amazing views, and grab dinner at Café Deco or one of the restaurants overlooking the city.

Days 3-4
Start your fact-finding research on Tuesday. Consider taking a look at the housing situation in the areas you're interested in, schooling options for kids, or meeting with potential employers. Be sure you stop in a grocery store and a Watsons drugstore to get a feel for prices and what's available. Finish up your research on Wednesday by going a little farther afoot; choose either the charms of laid-back Stanley, with its beach-view homes and its open-air pubs along the waterfront, or the Chinese culture of the New Territories.

Day 5
Take a hovercraft ferry to Macau for an entertaining day trip. Wander Macau's cobblestone streets among colorful architecture left over from its Portuguese heritage. Gourmands will be delighted by the cuisine at Macau Tower's revolving restaurant, and thrill-seekers should head to the top of the tower to tackle the tallest bungee jump in the world. End your day at one of Macau's many gambling spots, such as the Venetian, the world's biggest casino.

Days 6-8
On Thursday morning say good-bye to the Hong Kong highlife and fly out to one of China's second-tier cities. The best destinations would be Chengdu, Xi'an, Xiamen, or Qingdao, where three days will give you ample time to explore the expat scene and take in famous tourist sites while you're there. But if you have a specific interest in another second-tier city, this is your opportunity to customize your trip. If you're on a tight budget, consider first taking the train from Hong Kong to Guangzhou, where you can get inexpensive flights and overnight trains to many destinations in China.

Days 9-11
Schedule a Monday morning flight to Shanghai. Three days in Shanghai will give you a feel for the Shanghai vibe (see the one-week itinerary for specific

suggestions). For a break from the big city bustle, hop on a train or bus for a short trip to neighboring Suzhou or Xitang. Take the overnight express train Wednesday night from Shanghai to Beijing.

Days 12-14

Arriving in Beijing on Thursday morning will give you just barely enough time to get to know this city. Start by visiting its most legendary historical sites, including the Forbidden City, Tiananmen Square, and the Temple of Heaven. Spend a day exploring the expat life in the city's neighborhoods, shops, and schools. Finish your journey with a climactic day trip to the Great Wall before you leave for home on Sunday morning.

ONE MONTH

If you can afford to take the time, a month will let you experience China the way it deserves to be seen. Even with this much time, you won't be able to see all of the country's highlights, but you will get a good introduction to the key locations. On a one-month tour, you can follow a path that will cover many of China's most prominent cities for expatriates. In any city that you may eventually move to, you'll want to schedule several extra days for specific fact-finding research—use the one-week itinerary as your guide. But even your time spent on tourism around the country will expose you to the highlights and the difficulties of living within the Chinese culture.

© BARBARA STROTHER

Week 1: Beijing and the North

Start from Beijing, where you can do the must-see sights of the Forbidden City, Tiananmen Square, and the Great Wall while you explore expat life in the "Jing." Consider passing through neighboring Tianjin, especially if you're moving with a family. There's not a lot for tourists here but plenty for the expatriate life, like

A firece beast guards the Forbidden City in Beijing.

good schools and pleasant neighborhoods. Head to one of the very pleasant northern sea towns, such as Qingdao or Dalian, which consistently rank high on the lists of the best places to live.

Week 2: Shanghai and the East

Following the eastern coastline, a couple of days is all you'll need to get a good introduction to Nanjing; be sure not to miss the melancholy museum of the Japanese massacre or the lively Confucius Temple area in your explorations. On the way to Shanghai, Suzhou is famous for its elegant ancient gardens and canals, though its suburban development zones with their high foreign concentration are making economic history. The energy of cosmopolitan Shanghai will keep you hopping for a few days between seeing the colorful sites and discovering the vibrant expat life; follow it with a few relaxing days in laid-back and beautiful Hangzhou.

Week 3: Inland

Heading inland, admire the ancient relics of Xi'an and get to know the layout of the city with a bike ride on the top of its city wall (rentals are available at the east and south gates). Or choose Wuhan instead, especially if you're considering teaching or studying at one of its many universities. Fly or take an overnight train to ancient and culturally rich Chengdu, which is one of the few places in the world you can hold a panda (for a small fee, of course, at the Panda Research Center on the northern outskirts of the city). Suffer your way through the spicy Sichuan hot-pot at one of the city's outdoor dining spots. If you have a few days to go exploring, Chengdu is the gateway to many gorgeous scenic destinations as well as Tibetan lands.

Week 4: Hong Kong and the South

On the southern coast you can enjoy Xiamen's charms with a lingering Mediterranean flair from its European concession days. Explore the island's eastern shore for foreigner-friendly residential communities right next to the beach. Next head to the Pearl River Delta, where you can spend some time in a number of prominent cities for business and manufacturing, including Guangzhou, Shenzhen, and Zhuhai. In Hong Kong, you'll want to spend a few days island-hopping, bargain shopping, and gourmet dining to experience local life. Across the water lies Macau with its unique mix of Portuguese and Chinese culture, an up-and-coming casino destination giving Las Vegas a run for its money.

Practicalities

Once upon a time not so long ago, foreigners were required to stay at lodgings that were state-approved to receive them. Today, a traveler's choices in China are infinite. Where to sleep, where to eat—every major city has hundreds of options. We've given you a few choices to consider for the major entry points of Beijing, Shanghai, and Hong Kong just to get your travels started. For restaurants we've specified a few famous places by name as well as general districts known for their dining options. We recommend you get an up-to-date travel guide, such as *Lonely Planet China,* to help plan the details of your journey.

Hotel Essentials

All large Chinese cities have a wide range of hotel options, from basic Chinese hotels with few amenities to international chains with high standards and prices to match. China uses a five-star rating for its hotels, but some places boast more stars than they have actually earned. Don't trust the rating; take a look around and ask to see the room before you commit. You should negotiate the price on every hotel room. The published rate is only the starting point; discounts of 10–50 percent or more can be easily had with a little bargaining. The

exception to this rule is during the major holidays when the increased demand for hotel rooms will make the high prices nonnegotiable.

Typical Chinese hotel rooms will consist of two twin beds. Rooms with beds big enough to share, such as a double or a king, are much less common. Extra twin beds can be brought into the room for a small fee.

Chinese youth hostels offer dirt-cheap dormitory beds, and unlike the reputation of hostels around the world, many of the Chinese hostels have a great atmosphere and offer extra amenities like bike rentals or access to a shared kitchen. Some hostels boast traditional Chinese courtyards and rooms furnished with Chinese antiques; to find the

© BARBARA STROTHER

Not only are Chinese youth hostels cheap, they can be quite charming. This one, the Xiangzimen Hostel, is in Xi'an.

good ones, look at the photos and guest ratings of one of the worldwide hostel-booking websites.

For check-in you'll need your passport, which will be used to fill in a form that is passed on to the Public Security Bureau (PSB) so they can keep track of visitors' movements. (In fact, if you stay with someone you know rather than a hotel, your friend is legally required to register your visit with their local PSB.) You'll also need to pay a deposit; many places now take credit cards, but hostels and smaller Chinese hotels may require a cash deposit.

BEIJING
Accommodations

Beijing is huge, about the same size as Belgium, so location is quite important in your choice of accommodation. Most prefer to be near the Forbidden City or the Chaoyang Central Business District, but other options put you near the airport or train station for a quick getaway. The most convenient accommodations are within walking distance of a subway station.

For high luxury with a price to match, the **St. Regis** (21 Jianguomenwai Ave., tel. 10/6460-6688, fax 10/6460-3299, www.starwoodhotels.com/stregis, $390 double) is considered by many to be Beijing's best hotel. For a uniquely

© BARBARA STROTHER

The Sleepy Inn Downtown Lakeside hostel in Beijing offers pleasant little spots to kick back.

Chinese experience, try **Haoyuan Guesthouse** (53 Shijia Hutong, tel. 10/6512-5557, www.haoyuanhotel.com, 930元/$136 double), a Qing Dynasty hotel located in a traditional *hutong* with a pleasant tree-lined courtyard.

The **Holiday Inn Lido** (6 Jiangtai Rd., tel. 10/6437-6688, www.beijinglido.holidayinn.com, $125 double) ranks high for its vast amenities but low for its location near the airport, which is far from the central city's attractions. For a pleasant hostel with a great location and helpful staff, try **Sleepy Inn Downtown Lakeside** (103 Deshengmen Nei Dajie, tel. 10/6406-9954, www.sleepyinn.com.cn, $44 private double, $9 dorm bed).

© BARBARA STROTHER

Donghuamen Night Market, Beijing

Dining

You'll find plenty of great eateries anywhere you go in Beijing, but the most pop-ular dining areas include the late night hot-pot restaurants along **Ghost Street,** the party-central **Sanlitun Bar Street** in Chaoyang, and the pubs that line the scenic banks of the **Houhai Lake Entertainment District.** Of course you have to sample Beijing Duck at the world's most famous chain, **Quan Ju De Roast Duck Restaurant;** the legendary location at 32 Qianmen Avenue (tel. 10/6710-1379) is where Fidel Castro, Yasser Arafat, and George W. Bush, Sr., have dined. For a taste of the exotic, the **Donghuamen Night Market** (around the corner from Wangfujing pedestrian street) offers strangely delicious—and some just plain strange—treats, including deep-fried scorpions and snake-on-a-stick.

SHANGHAI
Accommodations

Most tourists to Shanghai will want accommodation in Puxi, the main part of the city to the west of the river. This is where you'll find the famous Bund, Nanjing Road Pedestrian Street, Yuyuan Gardens and bazaar, and a whole lot more. Pudong, the newer part of the city to the east of the river, is the home of the financial district, making it a good option for those wishing to look into corporate opportunities. No matter where you choose, rooms can fill up fast in Shanghai; book early.

Pudong offers a chance to sleep in the tallest hotels in the world at the **Grand Hyatt** on the 54th to 87th floors of the Jin Mao building (88 Shiji Dadao/ Century Blvd., tel. 21/5049-1234, www.shanghai.grand.hyatt.com, $300 double) and the **Park Hyatt** on the 79th to 93rd floors of the new Shanghai World Financial Center (100 Shiji Dadao/Century Blvd., tel 21/6888-1234, www.shanghai.park.hyatt.com, $470 double). Conveniently located in the Shanghai Center on West Nanjing Road in Puxi, the **Portman Ritz-Carlton** (1376 Nanjing Xi Rd., tel. 21/6279-8888, www.ritzcarlton.com, $300 double) is considered to be the best business hotel in the city, with prices to match.

The historic, art deco **Shanghai Metropole Hotel** (180 Jiangxi Zhong Rd., tel. 21/6321-3030, www.metropolehotelsh.com, $72 double) is conveniently located within walking distance to both the Bund and Nanjing Road without the steep prices typical of the area; upgrade to a balcony suite for a spacious rooftop patio with a view. A few blocks north you'll find the popular **Mingtown Hiker Youth Hostel** (450 Jiangxi Zhong Rd., tel. 21/6329-7889,

TIME FOR TEA?

When it's time to give your feet a break from your fact-finding wanderings, China's teahouses are pleasant places in which to relax. Some offer traditional teas in a very sophisticated ambience, while others specialize in colorful and fruity *boba* teas (with or without the black tapioca pearls) and novelties such as swings instead of seats. It is typical at traditional teahouses first to order your preferred cup of tea, and then snacks like watermelon seeds or dried kumquats are often provided free of charge. Some places even offer a large snack buffet with enough variety to make a light meal. For those who prefer coffee, Starbucks has taken China by storm over the last few years; ironically there was even one inside the Forbidden City for a couple of years until patriotic complaints drove it out.

© BARBARA STROTHER

Picturesque flower teas "bloom" in the glass.

$9 dorm beds, $32–45 double). In addition to cheap dorm beds, this place also has a well-kept secret: a couple of charming boutique VIP rooms complete with king beds, sitting areas, and stylish little bathrooms for less than you'd pay for a basic hotel room elsewhere.

Dining

Shanghaiers love to go out, whether to catch a quick bite with friends or to party the night away at posh clubs. Cheap food can be found at little Chinese restaurants along side streets, but Shanghai is well known for being top-notch epicurean, both in Chinese cuisine and a vast array of global gastronomy.

Located on the 54th floor of the Grand Hyatt in the Jin Mao building, **Grand Café** (88 Shiji Dadao/Century Blvd., 54th floor, tel. 21/5049-1234, reservations required) offers incredible views of the city through its glass walls and an excellent international buffet. There are several other upscale restaurants here as well.

The best place to get Shanghai's characteristic *xiaolongbao* dumplings is **Nanxiang Steamed Bun Restaurant** (85 Yuyuan Lu, tel. 21/6355-4206), located across the pond from the Huaxingting teahouse in the Yuyuan bazaar. There's always a line, but it's worth the wait.

Xintiandi is a trendy pedestrian area on the eastern end of Huai Hai Street, with a collection of high-end restaurants and clubs in revamped old buildings. In the French Concession, **Maoming Nan Lu** (South Maoming St.) has long

© BARBARA STROTHER

Tired of Chinese food? Try Shanghai's American-style Blue Frog restaurants.

been known for its hip clubs popular with partying expats. Try **Blue Frog** (207–06 South Maoming St., tel. 21/6445-6634) for great American-style bar food in a stylish environment.

HONG KONG
Accommodations
Most visitors to Hong Kong will want to be located near the activity of northern Hong Kong Island (Central, Wan Chai, or Causeway Bay) or southern Kowloon in its bustling tip, Tsim Sha Tsui. Unfortunately these are also the most expensive areas for lodging, but the budget-minded can save money by staying farther from the center and taking advantage of Hong Kong's excellent transportation infrastructure.

Dubbed Hong Kong's poshest, **Peninsula Hong Kong** (Salisbury Rd., tel. 852/2920-2888, www.peninsula.com, US$450 double) is an architectural presence on the Tsim Sha Tsui harbor with unrivaled colonial elegance. **The Cosmo Hotel** (375 Queen's Road East, tel. 852/3552-8388, www.cosmo hotel.com.hk) in Wan Chai, an affordable boutique hotel, also offers 2-bedroom suites complete with kitchenette and living room perfect for traveling families.

Though we highly recommend youth hostels in China, we don't advocate them in Hong Kong, where they tend to be dirty, seedy, and tiny with few amenities for the price. If you simply must have dirt-cheap accommodations

© BARBARA STROTHER

the posh Peninsula Hong Kong

WELCOME TO CHINA

Kowloon's hostels: cheap and convenient but never deluxe!

that are right in the heart of it all, there are several hostels located at the famous **Chungking Mansions** (Nathan Rd., Kowloon). Check it out before you
commit to stay, and don't say we didn't warn you.

Dining

Hong Kongers love to eat out even more than Shanghaiers, especially since
homes in Hong Kong are so small (it's hard to cook in a kitchen the size of
a walk-in closet). Most residents like to eat very late; you can avoid the long
wait for a table if you dine a little early.

Your choice of amazing eating experiences in Hong Kong is practically
limitless. Stop by famous **Yung Kee** (32–40 Wellington St., Central, tel.
852/2566-1624) for delicious Cantonese dim sum served in the afternoon, or
for a plethora of local dishes at lunch or dinner. For a little romance, dine on
Victoria Peak at **Café Deco** (118 Peak Rd., tel. 852/2849-5111) overlooking
the city's lights far below, or its sister restaurant **Top Deck** (Shum Wan Pier
Dr., Aberdeen, tel. 852/2552-3331) on the top of Aberdeen's famous Jumbo
Kingdom floating restaurant boat. The restaurants at the **Fringe Club** (2 Lower
Albert Rd., tel. 852/2521-7251) mix gourmet food with fine art. Down the
block is **Lan Kwai Fong,** a bar/party street that's especially popular with the
expat community.

DAILY LIFE

© BARBARA STROTHER

MAKING THE MOVE

So you've done your research. You've learned about Chinese culture and the lay of the land, and you've discovered the work you want to do or the program you plan to study. You may have even picked up a little Chinese and fancy yourself ready for the lingual challenge. Now what? What are the next steps to get you settled on the other side of the world?

If you're lucky, you'll have an employer that will be managing your move, making all the arrangements to transport you and your household overseas. On the other end of the scale, you may have to handle every last detail completely on your own. Either way, it will still be up to you to decide exactly what to take and what to leave behind. When we first moved to China, we brought a lot of the wrong things and not enough of the right things. The first time a good friend came to visit, we were quick to request that he bring us thick socks and a stockpile of deodorant, and convinced him when he left to take home the unused sewing machine. You can do your friends a favor if you pack a little more wisely than we did.

© BARBARA STROTHER

Getting ready for the big move can be a busy and complicated time. If you have children, the younger ones may not understand what all the commotion is about; the older ones will understand all too well. When you add all the detailed paperwork and processes to manage, as well as saying goodbye to family and friends and perhaps a family pet, making the move can be quite a stressful time. Just make sure you don't get so caught up in the details that you miss out on the joy and thrill of this incredible adventure you are embarking on.

Visas and Residence Permits

The first step in making your move to China is to get a visa. Welcome to the web of Chinese red tape—and oh, what a web they weave. Unless you are only trying to get a tourist visa, leave plenty of time for obtaining all the documents you'll need. Two months is a safe bet, though the process can be expedited if necessary. The Chinese embassy typically takes around a week to process the application before it can be returned to you. Keep in mind, however, that most visas are only good for entry within three months of their issue date, so don't get your visa too far in advance.

OVERVIEW

Chinese visas are classified based on your purpose for being in China, such as tourism, education, or employment. To stay long-term in China, you'll have to be connected to an organization (the company you work for or the school you attend), which pretty much rules out the possibility of retiring there or just hanging out for longer than a tourist visa will allow. And if you're thinking of starting your own business in China or working in the country on a self-employed basis, you're going to have a very difficult time getting the entry visa you'll need, since all work visas must have a corporate sponsor.

If any of these difficult situations apply to you, our best advice is to hire one of the visa services in Hong Kong. Though expensive, they can sometimes work miracles (though if you have a strong conscience, you may not want to ask just how they were able to obtain that visa for you).

Visa applications are no longer accepted by mail; you'll need to walk it in to the nearest Chinese consulate or embassy, or hire a visa agent do it for you. All visas are classified as single entry, double entry, or multiple entry, and each has a different application fee that varies by country of citizenship. If you are in China on a single-entry visa but would like to leave the country temporarily (including visits to Hong Kong or Macau), you can have your

VISA TYPES

Visa Type	Name	Issued for	Length of stay	Residence permit needed?
L	*Luxing*, "travel"	Tourism and family visits	Typically up to 30 days, though longer requests may be granted	No
F	*Fangwen*, "visit"	Short-term study, lecturing, business visit, cultural exchange, job training, etc., of less than six months	Typically up to 30 days, though longer requests may be granted	No
X	*liuXue*, "study abroad"	Long-term studies or job training of more than six months	Residence certificate typically valid for one year, renewable annually	Yes
J-2	*Jizhe*, "reporter"	Foreign correspondents on a short trip for a reporting task	Variable	No
J-1	*Jizhe*, "reporter"	Resident foreign correspondents	Residence certificate typically valid for one year, renewable annually	Yes
Z	*renZhi*, "job/post"	Those coming to China for employment and their family members	Residence certificate typically valid for one year, renewable annually	Yes
D	*Dingju*, "reside"	Those expecting to permanently reside in China	Residence certificate valid for 10 years	Yes

visa entry type switched at your local Public Security Bureau (PSB). The PSB will also help you if you need an extension on your visa or residence permit; contact them at least a week before the visa expiration date to avoid the daily 500元 ($75) fine.

TOURIST AND SHORT-TERM-STAY VISAS

The simplest visa to get is a single- or double-entry L visa for tourists, which will allow you to stay in the country for 30 days, or longer if requested. Multiple-entry L visas are typically valid for one year, though each stay in the country cannot surpass 30 days without an approved extension (a maximum of two 30-day extensions can be requested while in China). Hong Kong and Macau have their own guidelines for tourist visas and allow many nationalities to stay up to 90 days without any visa at all (check the *Hong Kong and Macau* chapter for more information). To obtain an F visa for short-term study or a business visit up to six months in duration, you'll need to submit an invitation letter from the host organization. If you'll be returning regularly for business purposes and have documents to prove it, you can get a multiple-entry F visa good for up to two years. Check the Chinese embassy website (see *Contacts* in *Resources*) for more information on what kind of documents will suffice.

RESIDENCY VISAS

Residency visas (D, J-1, X, Z) are only good for getting you into the country; you'll then need a residency permit to stay in the country. Each type of residency visa requires different paperwork. To get a Z visa (issued to those coming to China for employment), you'll need to submit a Work Permit or a Foreign Expert's License, obtained by the company in China you will be working for, and a letter of invitation from your employer, as well as the marriage certificate and birth certificates for an accompanying spouse and children, respectively. A long-term-study X visa requires an enrollment letter and educational application form from the Chinese school. Journalist visas (J-1 or J-2) require both a letter from an employer and a letter from the Foreign Affairs Office. To get a D visa and subsequent green card for indefinite permanent work and residence in China, you'll have to first get an approval certificate from a local PSB in China. Unless you have close relatives who are Chinese citizens, D visas are difficult to get and are typically only rewarded to those who have resided in China for a minimum of five years without leaving the country for more than three months per year.

RESIDENCE PERMITS

It is not the visa but the residence permit that gives you the legal right to live in China. Once you arrive in China, you'll have 30 days to secure your residence permit. Your initial visa will expire within a few months, but your residence permit will function like a multiple-entry visa, allowing you to leave the country and return without an additional visa as long as the permit is valid. Three types of residence permits can give you the legal right to live in China. Permanent residence permits, a.k.a. the new "green cards," accompany the D visas and are renewable every 10 years. Temporary residence permits are for those staying more than six months but less than one year, such as visiting scholars or those doing job training. The Foreigner Residence Permit, typically good for one year and renewable annually, is standard issue for the majority

VISA SPECIFICS

Visa Type	Documents Needed for Application (Subject to Change)
L (Tourist)	Application with photo; passport
F (Short-term business; study less than 6 mos.)	Application with photo; passport; company invitation letter *extra requirements for 2-year multiple-entry visa; see China embassy website for details.
X (Study)	Application with photo; passport; Form JW201 or JW202; enrollment letter from school
J-1 (Journalist)	Application with photo; passport; company letter; Foreign Affairs Office letter
J-2 (Short-term journalist)	Application with photo; passport; company letter; Foreign Affairs Office letter
Z (Employment)	Application with photo; passport; work permit or foreign expert license; letter from employer; marriage certificate; children's birth certificates
D (Resident)	Application with photo; passport; Residence Approval certificate issued by the PSB

of foreigners working in China, though some qualify for a permit that is good for two years or more. With a valid residence permit you are allowed to leave the country and return, even if your initial entry visa has expired.

Physical Exam Certificate

Technically you are required to have a physical examination certificate for residence permits. We spent a lot of money getting all the health tests completed but were never asked to submit the paperwork. If, like us, you'll be entering on a tourist visa and then switching to a residency visa after you arrive, you may save a bit of money if you wait to see if they will actually require the physical, and then get it done in China. Some provinces require that the physical exam be done at a local Chinese health facility and won't accept your documents

Number of Entries Available	Cost for U.S. Citizens	Cost for Non-U.S. Citizens
Single entry:	$130	$30
Double entry, 6 mos.:	$130	$45
Multiple entry, 6 mos.:	$130	$60
Multiple entry, 1 year:	$130	$90
Single entry:	$130	$30
Double entry, 6 mos.:	$130	$45
Multiple entry, 6 mos.:	$130	$60
Multiple entry, 1 year:	$130	$90
Multiple entry, 2 years:	$130	$90
Single entry:	$130	$30
Multiple entry, 12 mos.:	$130	NA
Single entry (Residence permit automatically allows multiple entries):	$130	$30
Single entry, 1- to 10-day stay:	$130	$30
Double entry, 1- to 10-day stay each entry, 90-day validity:	$130	$45
Single entry (Residence permit automatically allowsmultiple entries):	$130	$30
Single entry (Residence permit automatically allows multiple entries):	$130	$30

from your home country. The best bet is to simply wait until you're told when, and how, to get the physical to avoid wasting money and time.

CHANGING VISA TYPES

It is illegal to be employed in China on an L or F visa (in other words, tourists and students cannot work in China). If discovered, illegal employees are fined, fired, and often deported. If you get a job offer while you're in China as a student or tourist, or if you come as a tourist and decide to stay for schooling, you can switch visa types at the PSB in most provinces. There are some locales, however, that require you to leave the country to obtain the new visa; most people accomplish this with a quick trip to Hong Kong. Either way, don't start work or classes until you have the correct visa in hand.

Along the same lines, it is illegal to engage in any news-reporting activities, such as journalistic interviews, if you are in China on a tourist visa. China likes to keep a close watch over the media, and you can be detained or deported for journalistic activities without having a J visa.

FAMILY MEMBERS

Accompanying spouse and children are given the same type of visa and residence permit as the one who will be employed or studying in China, though each family member will have to fill out an individual application and pay the application fees. If the stork should find you in China, you'll need to bring your new baby's birth certificate to the local PSB for registration.

China does not recognize gay or lesbian unions, nor do they extend any familial benefits to unmarried heterosexual couples. Significant others will have to apply for their own visa and residency with their own sponsorship.

If you have an employment visa and residency based on a family member's employment, you may find your own employment while in China. However, your new employer will then have to register your employment and file the necessary paperwork to make it legal.

ONCE YOU'VE ARRIVED

After you've moved into your new digs, you'll need to register with your local Public Security Bureau within 10 days. Bring your passport and all other documents showing your residence status. Your residence permit will be tied to your physical address, so should you decide to move, you will need to register the move with your current local PSB before the relocation date, and then register with your new PSB office after you've arrived at your new location. Failure to register with your friendly neighborhood PSB can get you deported.

You should also register with your embassy or consulate, either online, by fax, or in person when you arrive. If a natural disaster strikes or political unrest breaks out, they can and will do all in their power to help you—but only if they know you're there.

Foreigners and the Law

One final word of warning: The Chinese government does not appreciate foreigners breaking its laws, and they do not consider ignorance a justifiable excuse. We were interrogated like serious criminals, forced to sign a confession, and required to pay a hefty fine when it was discovered that our kids' residence permits had lapsed. Staying past your visa expiration or working without the appropriate visa will be punished. China even has laws forbidding entry to those "suffering from mental disorder, leprosy, AIDS, venereal diseases, contagious tuberculosis, or other infectious diseases"; if found out, visitors with any of these conditions will be kicked out. Our only question with these laws is, what if it was living in China that made you crazy to begin with?

Moving with Children

When we first announced we were taking our twin two-year-olds to the Middle Kingdom, our friends and family were concerned. To some, the idea of moving children to China sounds downright frightening. And we have to admit, there were times that it was frustrating and even frightening to have our little guys with us, though for the most part we were pleasantly amazed at what a great place China is to raise kids.

If you are preparing for a move to China with children, we think you're in for a real treat. The Chinese love kids, and little ones are given quite a bit more freedom just to be kids than they are in the West. School-age kids have great experiences attending top-notch international schools and making friends from around the world. Of course you'll have different trials living overseas than you would at home, and each age group presents its own challenges and rewards.

© BARBARA STROTHER

Finding ways for kids to keep the same hobbies they had at home will help their transition.

PREPARING KIDS FOR THE MOVE

Making a move overseas is stressful for every member of a family. The littlest ones have the hardest time understanding what is to come. Try to read books and watch shows about moving and about China (we had the video *Big Bird Goes to China* just about memorized before we left). Pack as much as possible from home that they are attached to, such as favorite blankets, toys, or movies, to keep things in their life somewhat familiar.

School-age kids and teenagers can get ready for the move in some of the same ways: by learning about

China and packing the personal items that mean the most to them. Giving older kids the opportunity to be involved in the decision-making, such as what house or apartment to choose, which room will be theirs and how to decorate it, and which school they will attend, helps as well. The choice to move to China may be out of their control, but empowering them to make other decisions will help them feel like their whole life is not out of their hands. Be sure to get the email and mailing addresses of their friends, and budget for extra phone calls to old buddies and grandparents during the adjustment period.

One good exercise to do during the move is to take stock of the things in your kids' lives that define who they are, including personal items, relationships, routines, events, hobbies, sports, etc. Be proactive in helping them find these things in China, or finding good replacements, which will make the adjustment much quicker.

MOVING WITH BABIES

With the abundance of inexpensive domestic help available in China, it can be easier to raise a baby abroad than at home. Most expats in China have an *ayi* (literally "auntie," a term used for any female providing domestic support). *Ayis* can handle everything from cooking, laundry, and cleaning to taking care of pets and, most importantly, child care. Some expat families with two working parents find it such a benefit to have the help of inexpensive *ayis* that they hire one for each child in the family. Even if you only use an *ayi* a few days a week for help with laundry and cleaning, you'll be able to spend more time with your kids and less time on domestic chores.

One of the worst things about living in China with a baby is the lack of equipment. Restaurant high chairs and public diaper-changing stations are rare. Public transportation doesn't allow for car seats; bumpy public sidewalks and a lack of elevators are not conducive to strollers. Child safety is not high on the priority list of many Chinese manufacturers or architects. At least department stores and supermarkets now carry a decent selection of baby items, though you'll pay much more for the quality imported items. Unlike the States, good used items are very hard to find.

MOVING WITH PRESCHOOLERS

Life with preschoolers in China is often much easier than in the West. Cheap toys are sold everywhere; kiddie rides are around every corner. Potty training can be easier in a nation where bathrooms are not requisite for taking care of your business (if you're male). On the other hand, emergency runs to public

FOREIGN BABIES ABROAD

The Chinese *adore* children – especially those that are very young, very cute, and very Caucasian. If you've ever wondered what it's like to be famous, just take a blond baby to a small Chinese town. They'll stare and point and follow you; they'll stalk your family with cameras like paparazzi. They'll try to touch your kids and pick them up and even take away their toys just to hear the cute little foreign kids cry. Many expat parents get in a routine of shielding their kids in public, ready to protect them from any grabby hands. If you've got extroverted children who love attention, they'll be in heaven, but if your little ones are afraid of strangers, they may find themselves in Chinese hell.

The Chinese truly believe that it takes a village to raise a child. This can have its perks, such as times when you and your mate can enjoy the rare uninterrupted dinner conversation because your kids are off playing with the restaurant staff. But in some ways the role of parental authority can be frustratingly weak in China. If a stranger wants to offer your child a candy or a snack (or, speaking from experience, a drink from their beer), they most likely won't ask you if it's OK first. If they feel you are not treating your child correctly, they won't hesitate to get involved, such as grabbing an icy drink out of the hands of a thirsty toddler (according to Chinese custom, cold drinks can bring harm to a small child).

This lack of deference to your authority as the parent may clash with your own cultural beliefs about parenting. Though at times frustrating, the pleasure of seeing your kids experience a foreign culture firsthand far outweighs the nuisance of the cultural differences.

bathrooms in China can be terrifying to adults, let alone kids who are already not so sure about this whole toilet thing to begin with.

Bring a few of their favorite things from home, and beyond that, they may just have to grow up a little faster than they normally would. Our boys had to learn quickly to sit in seats without the help of their booster chairs and sleep in big beds without a railing. Chopsticks can be a challenge to someone who's hardly learned to use a fork, but luckily Chinese soup spoons are available at every restaurant.

MOVING WITH ELEMENTARY-AGE KIDS

The elementary age is a great time to move to a foreign country. At this age kids are not yet so settled into their friendships as to create a catastrophe by leaving them, and still of an age to pick up a second language with amazing quickness. As long as you are moving to a major city, they'll have plenty of great school choices. Plus they'll retain much more of the memories of their time in China than the youngest ones will.

THIRD CULTURE KIDS IN CHINA

**PROFILES OF
AMERICAN SISTERS
AMELIA AND JOSIE**

In the 1960s, sociologist Ruth Hill Useem coined the term *third culture kids*, or TCKs, to refer to children who spend part of their impressionable years living abroad. These kids combine the influences of their birth culture with the new culture to create their own third culture. TCKs in China face their own unique challenges and rewards. Here are the stories of two American sisters, Amelia and Josie, who are growing up in China.

The Life of a Foreign Middle-schooler in China

My name is Amelia. I am in sixth grade and I live in Wuhan, China. I moved to China when I was in third grade. That year my family lived in a smaller town called Huang Shi. There weren't any other foreign kids there, and I spoke next to no Chinese at the time. That was a really hard year for me, but I think it helped me build a better relationship with my sister and my parents.

The classes in American schools are a lot bigger than my classes have been at the international school. This means that the teachers can pay more attention to each student individually here. I also know all the kids in the secondary school really well.

I think that living in a Wuhan-size city is best, even though I sometimes wish there were more foreign kids to be friends with here. In a smaller city there would be only a very small foreign community. It would prompt you to see Chinese people more, but there would be hardly anything to remind you of home. In a city with a bigger foreign community, there would be so many people that you wouldn't be very close with them. No matter how big

© JEFF CULP

Amelia and Josie

your city is you will find there are good things about every size.

Next year we are moving to Tianjin, which is near Beijing. They have more foreign products and a bigger school, but I will miss all the people I know. There is a boy there named Wei Hao. He is two years old and he has a liver transplant. We are trying to adopt him, but he can't leave his doctors so we are moving to Tianjin to be with him.

My suggestion to kids coming to China is to consider getting Facebook or emailing regularly. Some kind of way to speak to or to see friends or family back in the United States is very helpful as well. I suggest keeping a journal too. As a TCK, stress and emotions build up a lot. A journal is a good way to let your thoughts and feelings out.

Tales of a 10-year-old TCK

My name is Josie. I moved to China at age six and am now almost 10, so I have been here almost four years. I am now a fifth grade student at Wuhan Yangtze International School.

The Wuhan school is very different from American public schools. First of all, every class is one grade higher in math than in the United States. Also the school is a lot smaller! My class is the biggest class, and it has 15 people. I enjoy having fewer people in my class because it isn't as crowded.

I think Wuhan is a good city because I have grown to love this big industrial city that is so humid and polluted. This feels so much like my home because of how welcoming people are. There is always a friend or teacher to talk to because no one has anything better to do. It is bet-

ter than very small towns because there is just the right number of foreigners.

We are planning to move to Tianjin because there is a two-year-old boy there named Wei Hao who we are trying to adopt. This move is going to be very hard. Tianjin International School is a lot bigger and more developed than WYIS. I think that nothing can replace Wuhan, but this move is what is right, and I am willing to do it for Wei Hao.

I have had many challenges and rewards being in China. One challenge is that it is hard being away from all my friends and family. One reward is that I am learning Chinese as a child, so it is easier for me to learn it. Another reward is all my international friends. I have friends from Japan, Australia, Korea, Poland, and many more! One very special reward is how close I am with all the teachers. The teachers are like family to me.

It is a good experience for kids to live in a foreign country. Most Chinese people in small towns have never seen foreigners before, so they are amazed that you are there. Also it is wonderful seeing how happy everyone is to come to your house to practice English. There are so many TCKs just like you out there who have had the same experience as you. When you meet other TCKs there is a wonderful feeling of relief suddenly all through you, and you feel like, *Finally! Someone who came for the same reason as me.* Moving to China is also a good way to build a strong family. Families will grow very close because sometimes there is no one else there for you except your family. Moving to China is a true blessing.

As far as packing for this age, there are just a few things that are hard to find in China. If you'd like to have your own educational materials (whether for homeschooling or for supplements to regular school), materials for this age are difficult to get in many subjects, though the classics in English (adult classics made for kids, not kids' pop classics like Harry Potter) can always be picked up at large bookstores. Additionally, boys' clothing is best brought with you, unless your 9-year-old son *likes* to wear jeans with embroidered teddy bears.

MOVING WITH PRE-TEENS AND TEENS

Though perhaps the most difficult to move, this age can have even more amazing experiences in China than their younger siblings. School trips may take them to exotic locations; sports competitions may let them experience new Asian cities. The new friends they meet will be people they visit for years to come, jet-setting to Singapore or Australia to connect with old high school buddies. And learning Chinese language and culture will help them tremendously in the global business world of their future careers.

Being exposed to the multiculturalism of international schools can be both a blessing and a curse, however. Although you may be an American family that believes that children shouldn't ever drink alcohol, your kids will be exposed to new ways of thinking as they interact with friends from other countries who've grown up with wine or beer on the nightly dinner table. China does not enforce a minimum drinking age, meaning kids can get alcohol easily. The upside is that you won't have to worry about drinking and driving because it will most likely be a taxi or personal driver who's taking them around town. Drugs do exist in China, though nowhere near as plentifully as in the United States (drug dealers face execution in China). And the violence that has been plaguing U.S. schools will be a faint memory in this land of gun control.

Your teens won't miss American movies because they'll be able to pick up an unlimited supply of cheap pirated DVDs from the nearest sidewalk vendor. But being out of the country will also leave them a little out of the pop-culture loop, making it hard to return home without feeling like an outsider. Repatriation is especially tricky for teens and should be proactively treated with care.

Moving with Pets

If you are considering bringing Fluffy with you to the other side of the world, there are a few things you'll need to know first. Only those with residency visas are allowed to bring a pet to China. Some cities (especially Beijing) have strict requirements about how many dogs you can have as well as what parts of the city you can live in with a large dog, so be sure to research the latest regulations thoroughly if either of these conditions applies to your situation.

When you and your pet arrive at the airport, customs officials will require a health certificate and vaccination certificate from an FDA-certified vet verifying that Fluffy is fit and his shots are current. Then you'll have to pay a minor fee at the Quarantine Station, though the quarantine usually takes place at your own residence. Most likely an official will stop by your house to evaluate your pet's health within a month or two, including a stool check. If Fluffy passes, you can pick up your verification of vaccination, which you'll need to get him registered. All dogs (whether coming from overseas or purchased in China) are supposed to be registered and vaccinated for rabies annually; some larger cities require multiple photos of your dog, permission from your neighbors, and a fee up to 2,000元 ($300) to complete the registration process. When it's time to move back home, you'll need to bring your pet and the vaccination certificate back to the Vaccination Office, where you'll get a Certificate of Health. The airport veterinarian will check this paper before letting your pet leave the country.

Each airline has different requirements and fees for transporting pets, so do your research before you make your final decision. You may pay more to fly your pet to China than you would a child. Book early because planes often have a limited number of spots for animals. If all these steps sound too complicated, you can hire a service like PetRelocation.com to manage the entire process for you.

LIFE IN CHINA WITH A PET

What will life in China be like for you and your pet? Some things will be easier, especially if you have household help that can clean the litter box and walk the dog while you're traveling. On the other hand, few foreigners in China can afford a villa with a private yard, so your pet may have to adjust to apartment-dwelling. Pet supplies are sold at the big supermarkets, though you won't find much variety. If your pooch insists on moist canned food or if your cat refuses to use a box without the right kind of litter, you're going to have problems in China. As for veterinarians, local vets are cheap enough; those in big cities may

Caged grasshoppers and crickets are popular (and noisy) Chinese pets.

even speak English and use U.S. medications. Some foreign veterinary firms are moving into the market for those who prefer Western veterinary practice (with prices that match), though they may not be in your part of town. Keep a first-aid kit for your pet in case you can't get to your vet quickly in an emergency.

GETTING A PET IN CHINA

If you have to leave your pet behind, you can get a new one in China. Finding a pet in China won't be too hard—in fact, they'll come to you. Entrances to subways or areas around parks are common places for people to sell caged mice, hamsters, and baby bunnies for just a few bucks. So-called flower and bird markets have a variety of pets to choose from. Beyond the typical cat or dog you can go native with colorful birds or lucky crickets, both of which come in ornate Chinese cages and are kept for the music they make. Unfortunately Chinese pets for sale can often be unhealthy, diseased, or just too young to be away from their mothers. It's difficult to keep these animals alive for long. We personally cycled through 13 different pets during a 16-month stay in China (albeit nearly half were caged crickets); not counting the bird that got away, only the cat was still alive when we left.

Recent years have seen the growing popularity of expensive purebred dogs. It is not uncommon to see elegant Afghans, perky pugs, and more exotic species being walked down China's sidewalks. You'll still want to check out the living conditions of the pet before you buy it, if possible. Even purebreds purchased in China tend to be a little sickly.

What to Take

Deciding what to take will depend on how long you will be in China and what sort of a shipping budget you are working with. To get you started in your selection process, there are three broad categories that will help you decide what to pack: availability, an initial supply of necessities, and personal items. For everything else, try to leave it behind. Most expats find their Chinese homes much smaller than their Western homes, with very limited storage. Unless you are relocating with a long-term position in a corporation that provides a significant shipping budget, it's just not worth the cost and effort to bring much.

AVAILABILITY

China is a shopper's paradise: cheap clothes, handbags, watches, and scarves; gorgeous Chinese antiques and trendy Ikea-style furniture; elegant Asian art and funky Chairman Mao tchotchkes. There's enough retail therapy to keep you happily out of your shrink's office for years. But even with great deals and amazing finds, there will be some items you'll want that, no matter how hard you search, you just won't locate. Or you'll find it but it will be of such inferior quality or high price that you'd be better off just bringing it with you from home. Here are a few items in this category.

Leisure Items
- Reading material in English, in particular non–best sellers
- Board games
- Musical instruments (common instruments like guitars can be purchased very cheaply in China, but you get what you pay for)
- Bike helmets and specialized sports equipment (such as camping or rock-climbing gear)

Cooking and Baking Items
- Barbecue utensils
- Oven thermometer (if you are lucky enough to get an oven, it probably won't have dials marked in Fahrenheit.)
- Baking pans, pie plates, muffin tins, baking powder (the Chinese don't bake)
- Quality potato peeler, can opener, etc.

Food Items
- Maple syrup, salad dressing, yellow mustard, pancake mix, Western-style pickles, barbecue sauce, any Mexican food, coffee beans (instant coffee is

CUSTOM-MADE IN CHINA: CHINESE TAILORS

It can be difficult for foreigners to find clothing that fits in China. Because the Chinese are so much smaller, average-size Westerners struggle through the XXXL racks to fit a frame that would only be considered a medium back home. Only petite shoppers get to enjoy all those Chinese markets full of cheap clothing. For the rest of us, don't despair; help can be found at your local Chinese tailor.

Chinese tailors work inexpensively and quickly, turning out simple items in just a few hours. A friend and I once had a pair of pants and a couple of scarves custom-made while we enjoyed a long lunch – and paid less than $15 for it all. You can even get a suit custom-made in less than 24 hours, though for complex items like a suit or a qi pao (traditional Chinese dress), quality tailors may take two to three weeks to get the details right.

Chinese tailors are amazingly versatile in their skill. They can work from a photograph or duplicate a favorite piece of clothing you already own. Give them the dimensions of a friend or relative back home, and they'll create a one-of-a-kind custom-fit gift for someone who has never even set foot in the country.

Most tailors carry a small selection of fabrics, though you can buy your fabric elsewhere if you don't see what you like. Many cities have indoor markets with multiple tailors' shops congregated together. Silk shops in touristy areas or upscale department stores will also offer tailoring services, but you will pay quite a bit more for their quality work than for the little mom-and-pop tailor shop in your local neighborhood.

A tailor's quoted price will usually include the fabric and the labor, but make sure you clarify before they begin the work. At upscale shops that cater to the rich and foreign, a high quality suit or qi pao can cost several hundreds of dollars; tiny shops that serve the local

readily available), mayonnaise that isn't sweet, Thanksgiving foods (stuffing, cranberry sauce)
- Your favorite spices

Bathroom Items
- Deodorant, dental floss, tampons (major shampoo brands are readily available, including dandruff shampoo)
- Makeup—it is available at department stores but is often of the "whitening" variety

Clothing Items
- Clothing in large and tall sizes; bras above size 34C
- Large-size shoes (above 8 for women, above 10 for men)
- Men's swim trunks, if you don't like Speedo-style; women's swimsuits, especially bikinis, if you don't like the matronly modest look.

community can turn out a short *qi pao* for as little as $10 and a thin suit for around $50.

Both tailors and the ubiquitous street-side menders (look for hand-run sewing machines on the side-walks near older residential areas) will mend torn clothing, repair broken zippers, and adjust a hem to your height starting at just one or two kuai ($0.15–0.30) for simple tasks.

choosing fabric for a custom-made jacket

© BARBARA STROTHER

Household and Children's Items

- Construction paper, index cards, quality markers/sharpies (most other common office supplies are readily available)
- Items for the minor holidays such as Easter-egg dye (Christmas decor will be easy to find)
- Smoke detectors, carbon monoxide detector
- Quality toys (cheap toys are everywhere, but name-brand toys like LEGO are only at department stores and can carry a high price tag)
- Books and educational materials for older kids in English (there's plenty for preschoolers)
- Insect repellent (nonaerosol), quality sunblock, hand sanitizer
- Dryer sheets (assuming you'll have a clothes dryer, but you may not)
- Over-the-counter medicine for flu, colds, allergies, sinus problems, antacids, etc. (especially children's varieties), and a stockpile of vitamins
- Plug adaptors and electrical converters

PERSONAL ITEMS

The few personal items that you'll need to bring are mostly documents, such as birth certificates, immunization records, diplomas, marriage certificates, extra résumés, your will, banking and financial information, driver's license, health insurance documentation, and so on. There are also personal items you'll want for their sentimental value; you never know when—or how hard—homesickness will hit you. One of the best ways to get yourself through is to have a stash of items that make you feel those good "home" feelings again, things that celebrate who you are and where you come from, such as:

- Photos of your family, house, pets, and hometown—these are also great to share with new Chinese friends to show what your life was like "back home"
- Your favorite music, if it's not mainstream
- Your kids' most favorite toys and DVDs
- Supplies to do your hobbies or to enjoy your favorite way to relax

ONE-MONTH'S SUPPLY

There are a few things you will need to use immediately before you've had time to find where you can buy them. Items that you may find embarrassing to shop for (i.e. feminine hygiene products, condoms) are better brought with you in the beginning to help minimize the stress of the transition. If you are moving with a small child, think through what you will need for the first month and be sure to bring enough diapers, wipes, rash ointment, formula, and anything else you normally keep in the diaper bag. While many popular brands of hygiene items, such as shampoos and soaps, are readily available, you may want to bring a small supply of your favorite brands until you can determine where to buy them in China.

A WORD ON ELECTRONICS AND ELECTRICITY

Electronics are plentiful in China. It is easy to pick up digital cameras, iPods, computer components, the latest cell phones, and more. But contrary to what most foreigners expect, the prices are often considerably more expensive than in the United States, even for items manufactured in China (though still cheaper than in other places like Europe or Australia). According to Chinese law, all foreign-branded items that are made for export but consequently sold in China must include an import tax. Additionally, you'll have to deal with a lack of instructions in English, low product support for repairs, and voltage/outlet problems when you leave China. As a general rule, if you're only going to use the item in China, buying it there ensures the proper electrical components. But if you will be using the item long-term, even after you've left China, then you're better off buying it before your move.

The voltage in China is 220. Most buildings have outlets that will fit several configurations of plugs; adapters are easy to pick up at local markets if you have a plug that does not fit. Transformers are available for converting the voltage on small appliances, though it is not always easy to find the one you need (which is why we eventually sent back our sewing machine unused). If it's possible to buy your appliance there, it is often better to do so, rather than having to deal with finding and using a transformer.

Shipping Options

If you are only going to be in China on a short-term basis, you may be able to fit what you need to bring within the confines of your airline luggage allotment. If not, assess the extra weight and do a comparison between your airline's cost for excess baggage weight and the cost of mailing the extra items to your address in China.

If, however, you are moving to China on a long-term commitment, you may be looking at moving your entire household. We strongly recommend that you keep it as light as possible, planning on buying new stuff in China (which is cheap) rather than paying to have everything shipped over (which is expensive and a big hassle). You'll pay steep customs fees on some things, such as furniture and other "luxury" items. On the other hand, going light will give you reason to do more shopping while you are there. Hunting for antique furniture bargains is a favorite pastime for many expats.

There are some tricks to getting your stuff to China without having to pay expensive shipping. For example, we invited a good friend to travel with us during our move and used his extra luggage space for more of our stuff. If you know friends or family will come to visit you when you are overseas, you can leave boxes or suitcases packed and ready for them to bring along as part of their luggage if they are willing to do so. This trick also works in reverse; it's a great way to get some stuff home and save on shipping when you leave the country.

SHIPPING AND RELOCATION COMPANIES

If you need to ship much more than the airlines, or the local post office, can take, there are many relocation and shipping companies that can handle the job. Typically they will pack all of your belongings, get them ready for the high seas, and see them off at the port, then deliver them to your new home and unpack them. Household shipment from Middle America to the Middle Kingdom will put you out around $6,000 for a two-bedroom apartment up to $9,000 for a four-bedroom home, varying greatly based on the size of your shipment, extra services, and your specific destination.

You can save some money if you pack the boxes yourself, though often this job is best left to the professionals. You'll want to contact several companies that specialize in international relocation to get quotes. You have your choice of using Western-based companies that will subcontract the work when your shipment arrives in China, or a China-based company that will subcontract the initial packing and loading work. While some people prefer the comfort of working with someone who is from their own country, others prefer to trust the Chinese professionals who really know the complex customs laws and processes. There are also a few major companies, such as Crown Relocations, that have offices and staff in both locations.

You should plan on three months for your oceangoing shipping process from start to finish. Airfreight can be used for those items that you will want immediately. Standard airfreight will arrive in 7 to 14 days; express shipments will get the most crucial items to you in two to five days. You'll pay dearly for these options, especially express, so use them wisely.

DOCUMENTATION

Make sure you are fastidious about all the documents you must fill out with your shipment; otherwise you may be fined steep fees and/or your belongings may be impounded for several months while the problems are sorted out. Your international moving company will provide you with a whole folder full of forms and will let you know what other documents you will need that are specific to your situation.

Getting your stuff into the country is only half the battle; you'll need to get it all back out again (unless your move is permanent, of course). You'll need to hang on to all those original customs forms. The process for exporting your household goods out of China is about as complicated as importing them into China, and you'll have to prove you brought this stuff with you or you'll owe duty. Other paperwork to hold on to includes receipts for antique furniture purchased in China and verification that the antique is less than 150 years old (and therefore legal to export), as well as all receipts for significant purchases made while living in China.

HOUSING CONSIDERATIONS

Since most employers provide housing for foreigners working in China, chances are you won't be tackling the house-hunting process on your own. However, those who stay longer eventually desire a change from their initial arrangement: Experienced foreign teachers move out of school housing, second-term international students prefer to be off campus, and corporate expats may opt to buy a house.

Searching for the right place to rent or buy in China can be an exasperating experience. Among inflated real estate prices, doubts about the trustworthiness of your landlord or agent, and the difficulties of finding a place that has all that you're looking for, trying to find a place to call home can leave you stressed out. The best way to relieve some of that stress is to become as educated as possible about the process. This chapter can serve as a general guideline and a good starting place, but you'll have to get to know the market in your specific city as well.

We recommend that you don't try to find a permanent place to live right

© BARBARA STROTHER

off the bat. If you can, plan to stay in a temporary residence to get to know your new city before you sign a long-term lease or purchase a property. Students and teachers at Chinese schools should stay on campus at first; those with corporate budgets can reside at a serviced apartment until they find a place of their own. Inexpensive short-term furnished apartment rentals are also available, though it might take a little time to find one since most landlords prefer long-term leases.

Housing Options

Housing options in China primarily include apartments, dorms, and villas (houses), plus an occasional town house or traditional Chinese home. The majority of city-dwellers in China live in standard apartments, though some foreigners prefer a serviced apartment, which comes with all the bells and whistles of a luxury hotel.

STANDARD APARTMENTS

Standard apartments are the most common housing arrangements for both locals and foreigners alike. "Standard" is in contrast to "serviced," which are apartments run similar to hotel rooms complete with services like housekeeping and room service. Standard apartments vary greatly in quality, size, and cost.

Unlike the American system of apartment rental where one company owns the whole complex, apartments in China are purchased individually after they

© BARBARA STROTHER

Amenities at this upscale complex in Pudong, Shanghai, include a bird's-eye view of soccer and rugby matches.

HOUSING TERMS IN CHINA

- **Attached villa:** town house or duplex
- **DIY:** do-it-yourself home remodeling
- **Decorated:** finished (has flooring, doors, cabinetry, fixtures); may be furnished as well
- **Detached villa:** house
- **Furnished:** comes with furniture, appliances, electronics, and decor
- **Gardens:** green space and landscaping
- **Private garden:** yard
- **Secondhand home:** one that has been lived in previously
- **Serviced apartment:** an apartment run like a hotel
- **Undecorated:** unfinished (no flooring, doors, appliances, cabinetry, fixtures, etc.)
- **Unfurnished:** no furniture or appliances but everything else will be complete (flooring, doors, etc.)

are built. Though you may deal directly with the apartment's management company in paying your rent and other landlord-type issues, they are typically only performing this as a service to the individual who actually owns the apartment you are renting. There are, of course, companies who buy up blocks of apartments to rent them out, but it is rare for one company to own all the apartments within a complex. It is also possible for foreigners to buy their own apartments.

The average rents for apartments vary considerably from one city to the next. Hong Kong, Macau, Shanghai, and Beijing have some of the highest rents in the world; on the other hand, you can rent a nice apartment in smaller cities for as little as $100 to $200 per month. If you're in the market to buy, apartments are much cheaper than villas, starting as low as $30,000 in minor cities up to well over $1 million for a swanky place in Beijing.

The Range of Standards

Apartment choices cover a wide spectrum of amenities and prices. At the extremely cheap end, older and simpler Chinese apartments are rarely inhabited by foreigners unless they are in a tough financial situation. With these apartments you may have a squat hole in your bathroom instead of a toilet, and the entire tiny bathroom will serve as the shower stall. You may be washing your laundry by hand and hanging it on poles sticking out your window to

HOW BIG IS THAT APARTMENT?

Measurements for apartment sizes in China are given in square meters. The conversion between square meters and square feet is 1 square meter equals 10.76 square feet:

Square Meters	Square Feet
40	430
80	861
100	1,076
120	1,291
160	1,722
200	2,152
300	3,228
400	4,304

© BARBARA STROTHER

Apartments in Hong Kong can be quite tiny.

dry. The floors will be cheap linoleum or shiny fake wood that's warped and nicked. You may not have any heating or air-conditioning. All the pipes will be exposed in the kitchen, and you'll have no appliances except a portable cooking top. There's hardly any storage, and the rooms are so tiny that they remind you of the walk-in closets back home, which will be a faint memory since Chinese apartments don't have any closets at all.

Modern luxury apartments, on the other end of the spectrum, may have large garden tubs, Italian marble and real hardwood floors, central heat and air-conditioning, and broadband DSL access wired into the walls. Those that are designed with foreigners in mind will have a clothes washer *and* dryer, a built-in oven, a dishwasher, and lots of kitchen cupboards and storage closets, but you'll pay for these high-end amenities. Wall-to-wall carpeting is rare except in the nicest places with large numbers of foreign residents. The nicer the apartment complex, the more amenities will be located at the complex, such as convenience marts, beauty salons, health club facilities, swimming pools, tennis courts, restaurants, pubs, and coffee shops.

The bulk of the standard apartments available in China will fall somewhere in between these two extremes, with prices to reflect this. For the most part, you won't know exactly what a place will be like until you see it, but you can guess by its price tag at which end of the spectrum it may lie. Generally, when the prices are quoted in yuan, and the complexes don't choose cheesy English names, you can be sure that you are now on the local economy (as opposed to the "all foreigners are wealthy" economy). This will, of course, vary considerably based on which city you live in. A property advertised for $200 per month is likely to be decent in Xi'an but a dump in Beijing. And the Chinese toilets? In major cities, pretty much all apartments will come with Western toilets, though in places farther removed from Western influence, like Kunming, you may be surprised to find a squat pot installed into the marble floors of a beautiful new apartment. The apartments we've listed in the prime living locations of this book all have some level of international standards, though we don't guarantee that you'll get the dishwasher or the garden tub.

Floor-Level Matters

Chinese apartments are categorized as tall (i.e. skyscrapers) and mid-height towers. Buildings over seven stories are required to have elevators, which is why you'll see many places no higher than this in an effort to spare the extra expense. It's a great way to stay in shape if you live on a top floor, but it's not exactly convenient. Apart from the obvious benefit of great views, there are several reasons to pay attention to the floor level of apartments. The higher the apartment, the more likely it is to be posh. Higher floor levels garner higher prices, and every place listed in Chinese housing classifieds disclose the apartment's floor level in relation to how tall the building is.

Many apartments have luxurious two-story penthouses on the top floors.

© BARBARA STROTHER

Modern apartment buildings in China are built with luxury penthouses on the top floor. Often these penthouses are two stories tall and include rooftop garden areas. Driving around a Chinese city, look up and you'll see these penthouses, with huge walls of windows spanning both floors. Unfortunately these apartments are harder to come by as rentals because most owners choose to live in them rather than rent them out.

GET YOUR FENG SHUI ON

Feng shui, which literally means "wind and water," is a mystical belief that architecture, layout, and decoration, when done right, can direct the mysterious qi power into your life for blessing and prosperity. Feng shui uses the *luo pan*, a geomancy compass, to follow the guidelines of the *bagua* octagon, which has the yin and yang in the center symbolizing balance, surrounded by different compass points that correspond to natural elements and important life issues. The northern compass point, for instance, corresponds to the water element and relates to your front door, your career, your ancestors, and your ears (yep, you guessed it – feng shui is also used in traditional Chinese medicine). Whether you believe in feng shui or not, a basic understanding of it should give you a greater appreciation of the many idiosyncrasies of Chinese architecture.

According to feng shui principles, bathrooms and kitchens should be isolated so as not to disrupt the peace and quiet of the living spaces. Windows are placed not just to let in light but also to ensure the free flow of qi into and out of your home. The wealth corner must be decorated with items that symbolize prosperity; the love corner should have pairs of objects. A mirror in the dining room promotes abundance, but a mirror opposite the front door bounces the positive qi right back out of your house.

Perhaps the main idea of feng shui for your home is that the design will evoke simplicity, clean lines, and a lack of clutter. The bottom line is that feng shui results in homes with pleasant layouts, but whether it generates more qi or not, well, we'll leave that one up to you.

© BARBARA STROTHER

feng shui compass

On the other end of the scale, apartments on the first couple of floors are noisier, more vulnerable to burglary, and prone to have less privacy. Since gates and guards protect most housing in China, security isn't typically a major problem. Privacy can be a more important concern when an occasional curious landscaper or janitorial worker has no qualms about stopping their work to watch you through your windows. If you have small children or pets, you may be willing to deal with these potential issues in exchange for the convenient access to the green space outside where kids and pets can play.

Directional Matters

Most Westerners don't pay too much attention to which way an apartment faces, but direction plays an important role in Chinese real estate. For one, feng shui dictates certain blessings, curses, and luck that are closely associated with directions. If you're not a feng shui enthusiast, you may not find this very important to you; it plays a stronger role in purchasing than renting since it will affect the resale value of the home. As a Westerner, you'll probably be more concerned about the second reason direction is important: It can determine which TV signals you'll receive. If you're a sports or news addict, you may want to check first before you commit to a place where you'll never be able to get the big game on TV.

SERVICED APARTMENTS

Serviced apartments are rental apartments most often found on the premises of 4- and 5-star hotels, though there are a few chains that run serviced apartments outside of a hotel. These are designed for short-term rental from just a few weeks up to a couple of years. Although some are not much more than glorified hotel rooms, most were designed with the same types of layouts you would expect in a simple apartment: a small kitchen, a dining area, a living room, and one or two bedrooms with a matching number of bathrooms. A few may also have a balcony, but forget about having a yard or green space. Of course you wouldn't get a yard with a standard apartment either, but standard apartments often have parklike green areas where you can walk your dog, let your kids play, or practice your tai chi in the morning. Serviced apartments rarely have such spaces.

Serviced apartments are quite a bit more expensive than standard apartments due to the amenities they offer. Residents can take advantage of the hotel's fitness center, sauna, spa, swimming pool, room service, breakfast buffet, restaurants, concierge services, daily housekeeping, and the like. These places are typically staffed by English speakers who can take care of your requests and needs, which can be quite handy when you are new to the country and don't yet speak any Chinese. The flip side to this benefit is that residents tend to stay isolated from the local community, taking longer to learn basic conversational Mandarin and rarely making Chinese friends.

Serviced apartments are of course only available to rent, not buy. As a general guideline, you'll typically pay twice as much for a serviced apartment than for a standard apartment, but this can differ significantly based on location and what amenities the serviced apartment offers.

DETACHED VILLAS AND ATTACHED TOWN HOUSES

What most Westerners would call a "house" is called a "villa" in China. Whether detached with its own yard (called a "garden" in China), or attached as a duplex or in a row of town houses with small yards or shared green space, villas are typically the most expensive and most luxurious option in Chinese housing. Villas are always built in walled complexes with guarded gates and an English-speaking management company that serves the community around the clock. The villa market is still somewhat new to China, having come in on the wave of China's new economic wealth in order to cater to the growing wealthy class and to the increasing number of foreigners living in China.

AYIS

Quite a few expats hire locals to work as ayis. Ayi literally means "auntie," and a typical ayi plays the roles of nanny and maid and, like an auntie, eventually feels like a member of the family. They'll clean, do laundry, cook, and wash windows. They'll do your grocery shopping and help arrange any maintenance needed in your home. The nicer homes in China are built with ayi quarters, and the ayi typically stays the night during the week and goes back to her home on the weekends. Make sure you give her time off according to the Chinese holidays, and make sure you pay bonuses according to what's normal for your community (just ask your neighbors). To find an ayi, check with your real estate agency, or ask your expat friends' ayis for recommendations. Depending on the city, an ayi's pay ranges $150–300 per month for a full-time ayi, and a little more than half that for a half-time ayi. You'll feel guilty getting so much service for such a small amount of money, but the relationship won't always be easy. There's the language barrier and the strange food (river snakes, anyone?); she might not discipline the children according to your standards; and you might find her cleaning methods strange, such as when you catch her mopping the windows and rugs.

© BARBARA STROTHER

This Shanghai villa complex resembles a North American suburb.

Some villas are absolutely huge, even up to three, four, or five stories tall. They come in a large variety of styles: Mediterranean, mid-American, elaborate classical European, or minimalist Japanese Zen. Most places offer three to five bedrooms, a private garage, Western appliances, and gorgeous landscaping that you don't have to lift a finger to maintain. In addition, most villa complexes also have the added perks of swimming pools, playgrounds, a gym and sport facilities, gift and imported-foods shops, a pub, and a restaurant or two. Some have on-campus preschools (called "kindergartens") or classes for kids such as ballet and swimming, making them the best option for families with children.

As with serviced apartments, living in a villa complex tends to keep expats more isolated from the local Chinese community and less likely to learn the language. On the other hand, you'll be able to make friends with neighbors who come from all around the world.

Whether buying or renting, villas will take a big bite out of your wallet, which is why they are typically used by executives and diplomats who receive high expatriate compensation packages. Some start as low as $2,000, but others rent as high as $15,000 or more per month.

OTHER HOUSING OPTIONS
On-Campus Housing

A great number of foreigners living in China live on a school campus. English teachers are given apartments on the grounds of the school or college

© BARBARA STROTHER

Xiamen University dormitories

where they teach, and most foreign university students live in the international student dorms.

If you'll be a university student in China, you can expect to have a tiny dorm room, sometimes shared and sometimes private. In most international student dorms you'll have your own little bathroom, though the traditional style is a communal bathroom shared with the other students on your floor. At the best campuses, your room will have heat, air-conditioning, a desk, storage cabinets, and a television in a comfortable but simple environment, with a cafeteria and laundry room on the premises or close by.

As a teacher (regardless of what age group you'll teach), you should be given a small apartment on or near campus, which you'll probably have to yourself or share with another teacher if it's a two-bedroom. Your room arrangements are subject to negotiation; if it's important to you to have your own space, you can try to bargain for a better deal before the contract is signed. The housing will be provided free of charge, but you'll have to pay for some or all of the utilities. The apartment will be fully furnished and should come with a small washer and dryer (be sure to ask first!) as well as a microwave, cooking top, small refrigerator, and bottled water dispenser.

Roommates and Homestays

Another housing option to consider is to rent a room in someone else's apartment or to arrange a homestay. Both of these are great options for those who are serious about learning Chinese. Some real estate and classified ad websites such as www.locanto.cn have advertisements in English for people who are looking for roommates, both foreigners and English-speaking Chinese. Alternately, you can search the English magazines and websites dedicated to your specific city.

You'll also occasionally find a classified ad from a Chinese family or individual who wants to have a live-in native English speaker. Sometimes they will provide a free room in exchange for the language practice they'll get, especially for families that want their children to learn English well. Homestays are not as common in China, mostly due to the fact that such fraternizing with foreigners was forbidden before the recent opening-up policies. If you are interested in this option and can't find anything available online before you get there, consider posting your own classified ad. Given the Chinese fascination with learning English, there are bound to be plenty who would love to host a foreigner but have just never considered it an option before. One word of warning, though: Be sure you clear it with the local PSB (Public Security Bureau) before you move in. Chinese nationals who are housing foreign guests, even for a night, are required by law to report it to the PSB, and not all PSBs are clued in to the freedoms that foreigners now have.

Unusual Chinese Homes

Beyond the standard apartment and villa options, some Chinese cities offer more unique housing options. Cities like Qingdao, Xiamen, and Macau have

© BARBARA STROTHER

cat on a cold tile roof

old European villas, some of which are in extreme disrepair. In Inner Mongolia's countryside, people still live in yurts (felt tents), and close to Xi'an there's an area where homes have been built into hewn caves, complete with electricity but few other utilities. For those who are big on adventure, and in most cases with a big wallet as well, one of these unique options may appeal to you. Just don't expect it to be easy to find one or easy to live in. Beijing, however, has its *siheyuan*, old brick houses built around courtyards down mazes of narrow roads, which have become popular among foreigners in recent years. Though far from cheap, remodeled and updated units are a unique, traditional, and memorable housing option.

Renting a Home

If your employer won't be providing your housing in China, then you'll have the daunting task of finding an apartment or villa to call home. You'll have to sort through a wealth of options in location, size, amenities, and price, which may be easier with the help of a good real estate agent.

USING REAL ESTATE AGENCIES

Real estate agents in North America predominantly help clients buy homes, but real estate agents in China assist with both buying and renting. Each agency has its own properties available, and you'll know you've found one when you walk past a shop window covered with photos of apartments and villas. A few agencies in cities with large expat communities cater specifically to foreigners; the best way to find them is through online searches and through their advertisements in the local expat magazines.

The typical fee you'll pay for their services will be equivalent to one or two months' rent for the property you eventually decide on. They will take you around to see the properties you are interested in, find answers to all your questions about the place, and help negotiate terms with the landlord. The real estate industry is not as regulated in China as it is in the States, however, so you will need to make sure that you are comfortable with the trustworthiness of the agent you'll be working with. Some may take advantage of your lack of familiarity with the way things work to pad their own pockets a bit. You won't be on an exclusivity contract, so feel free to try other agents as well. The fees you pay are a commission on the property you choose, so you won't have to pay an agent that is unsuccessful in finding a home for you.

FINDING A PLACE ON YOUR OWN

You can also forgo the expense of using an agent and just do the legwork yourself. Expat magazines and websites often have classifieds with places available to rent. If you're already there, you can start asking around for leads as well; many people know someone who has a place to rent, especially since some of China's newly wealthy feel more comfortable putting their money into real estate investments than putting it into the stock market or the bank. If you see a complex that appeals to you, stop in and see what's available. Either the apartment management company will be able to show you apartments that are available to rent, or they'll direct you to posted rental ads with owner's contact numbers so you can set up a viewing appointment yourself.

By far the best way to get information is through the Chinese property-listing websites. Of course if you can't read Chinese well, you'll need to enlist the help of a Chinese friend to decode it for you. These online listings will tell you whether or not the home is being offered by the individual or by a company, and will give you the contact information for the landlord. Companies may be more trustworthy than an individual landlord when it comes to maintenance and other issues, although they will have much less flexibility to customize the rental agreement to your specific needs. Be aware, however, that when a potential landlord discovers that you are foreign, often the price immediately starts to rise. Price negotiations might be best handled by a Chinese agent before the landlord finds out you're not a local.

RENTAL TERMS

Most Chinese landlords are looking for a one- or two-year minimum lease agreement, though there are a few who are willing to do short-term rentals. Before you sign your new lease, be sure you are financially prepared to do so. Apart from the fees you'll pay your agent (if you used one), you'll also have to give your new landlord a security deposit. Some demand a six-month deposit, but you can probably negotiate just a one- or two-month deposit. Take your rent and multiply it by five to estimate the amount of cash you should have accessible to get into a new place. Monthly rental amounts are also negotiable, and in some places, the initial rental offering will be quite a bit higher than the landlord is actually willing or expecting to take. Usually you can get a decent discount if you do not require a *fa piao* (an official receipt that is submitted to your company for expenses and/or submitted to the government through the tax process).

How you pay your rent is also somewhat negotiable. Some landlords prefer

to be paid in 2- or 3-month incre-
ments rather than monthly. Some
will stop by to pick up your rent
payment in cash when it's due; others will prefer that you make a deposit into their bank account by a
certain date. The specific payment
details will have to be worked out
between the two of you, as well as
any other negotiable items concerning the apartment.

Furnished or Unfurnished?

Most apartments and villas for rent
come completely furnished, including electronics. On the other hand,
those rentals that are advertised as
unfurnished may not even have

© BARBARA STROTHER

Getting an unfurnished place allows you
to shop for furnishings to your taste.

basic appliances such as a stove or a fridge. If you would prefer to use your
own furnishings, or if you're interested in a presently unfurnished location
but need it to be furnished, it's all negotiable. Even if you'd prefer a different
type of furnishing than what is there, you can try to get them to swap it out
for you. Keep in mind, however, that if you're asking your landlord to remove
what's there, they'll have to do extra work as well as find a new place for the
items, so expect it to cost you a little in the bargaining. Some landlords with
unfurnished homes will let you pick out the furnishings within a certain budget, a great way to get the style you want without committing yourself to extra
possessions you'll have to get rid of when you leave the country.

Utilities and Services

Many rental agreements require you to pay for your utilities directly. Your
landlord will probably have all of your utilities turned on before you move
in. Monthly utility bills will arrive in the mail or at your door, and can be
paid at utility company offices, post offices, banks, by deducting the amount
from a Chinese debit card, or in some cases, inserting an I.P. card (the same
I.P. card that is used for making phone calls) directly into the electric meter.
The apartment complex provides trash receptacles, which are included in the
responsibilities and expenses of the property maintenance company. Typically

renters pay the apartment management fees as well, which are a set rate per square meter of the home.

Common utility expenses per month are: electricity 200元 ($30), gas 80元 ($12), telephone 30元 ($4.50), water 60元 ($8.85), cable television 30元 ($4.50), ADSL Internet 130元 ($19), and bottled water 38元 ($5.65) for two 4-gallon bottles, delivered. These figures will fluctuate by region, season, and size of your home, especially in the north, where you'll use more gas or electricity to heat your home. Electricity is 220 volts AC, 50Hz. While two-pin and three-pin sockets are standard, don't be surprised if your apartment has four or five different types of outlets.

Some landlords, especially in serviced apartments and high-end apartments, will provide a summary bill for utilities and request that you pay the landlord directly. This seems convenient, but you'd be wise to request a peek at the original bills so you don't get overcharged. In older apartment buildings, some of the utilities might be shared, in which case you'll be asked to pay a share each month, unless responsibility to pay the entire monthly bill rotates between the households.

MOVING IN

Before you start unpacking your boxes, you should give your new home a thorough inspection. Chinese housing sometimes may be subject to shoddy construction, so test all the taps, flip each light switch, flush the toilets, and make sure every door and window can be opened, closed, and locked. To protect your valuables, consider changing the locks soon after you move in. You should also register with the PSB and your embassy or consulate (see the *Once You've Arrived* section of the *Making the Move* chapter for more information).

Owning a Home

Many foreigners are surprised to discover that they now have the option of purchasing a home—whether an apartment or a villa—in Communist China. In fact, those that are investment-savvy claim that it's the only wise financial choice, given the rising economy and subsequent rise in home values. On the other hand, buying a home in China can be a bureaucratic nightmare that is not for the faint of heart.

For practical purposes, buying an apartment or buying a villa is the same process. In Chinese cities, building a home is not done by individuals but by real estate developers who sell each unit in a complex individually. Though rural Chinese do build their own homes, if foreigners wanted to try to build

DAILY LIFE

© BARBARA STROTHER

Hong Kong real estate property ads

their own home, they'd face an incredible amount of resistance and would probably be told it's not possible (though in China "not possible" is an easy answer that you will get all the time, whether it's true or not).

We recommend that you do not consider buying a home until you have spent a fair amount of time in this country, long enough to learn its ways and a fair amount of its language, and long enough to make sure you'll still love it here when the honeymoon stage has worn off and you're facing serious culture shock. That said, if you're convinced that buying a home is the right option for you right now, here are a few things you'll need to know.

THE RISKS

There are a number of risks involved with buying a home in China, including legal complexities, the chance of getting scammed (this country has more than its fair share of those who know how to manipulate the system to their benefit), the financial issues of the country's banking laws, and the possibility your property's value will drop in another real estate bust.

When you buy a home in China, you are technically only buying the building structure, not the land itself. All residential land is actually on a 70-year lease from the government, after which time they have the option to reclaim the land and recompense you according to what they think is fair. Homeowners do not have the same kind of rights in China as they do in the West, and it is not uncommon for local residents to get bought out of their homes and forced to move. The Chinese government just doesn't care all that much about your attachment to your home. They care quite a bit more about making way for "progress," and if your property happens to be in their way, you have no guarantees.

The chance that your home will be taken from you is slim, but the chance is great that you'll suffer from poor quality issues. No matter how beautiful the home looks when you purchase it, the quality of the place may immediately start to deteriorate. Chinese construction tends to take shortcuts when possible, and items manufactured for domestic purchase are often of extremely inferior quality. Stuff breaks, and repairs can be shoddy and jerry-rigged. A handyman you can trust to always do things right using the right materials and tools is a real treasure to find. The most you can do is be prepared to accept this as part of home ownership—or learn the skills of plumbing, carpentry, electrical work, and masonry, as well as the business of importing goods and materials.

NEW VS. SECONDHAND

The home-buying market in China is divided into two sections: homes that are newly built and those that have been previously lived in, referred to as "secondhand" in China. The buying experience can be quite different for each. In many cities, the competition for getting a brand-new home is so fierce that even before the houses or apartments are built there are long waiting lists of people waiting to buy. Some places have a lottery system where you pay to put your name in, and if you get lucky, you get to buy. Some places even charge you just to tell you the listed sale price on their homes. Buying a secondhand home is much less competitive, though if you see a place you like, you shouldn't take too long before you act.

With a newly built apartment or villa, you'll be getting what the Chinese call "undecorated." This doesn't mean it won't have art on the walls. In fact, with an undecorated place, you might not even get any walls! All you are guaranteed is an empty shell, though some will come a bit more finished. It will be up to you to "decorate" the home, which typically takes 2–3 months. You'll have to purchase (and have installed) all appliances, all cabinetry, all bathroom fixtures and light fixtures, and all flooring. You may have to oversee the building of walls where you want them and other construction details. You'll spend a lot of time at appliance stores and do-it-yourself outlets such as B&O and Ikea. Secondhand homes, on the other hand, will be finished and sometimes even fully furnished, although probably not to your liking.

Traditional Chinese kitchens can still be found in country homes.

HOW TO FIND A PLACE

The way to find a place to buy in China is not too different from the way to find a place to rent. Basically, you can choose between using a real estate agent or looking on your own, though the legal process becomes quite a bit more complicated with buying than renting, as do the risks. A third way to find a home to buy is to attend a home-selling convention, which some cities hold every quarter. At these events quite a number of properties are bought and sold. Some housing complexes schedule minibus tours from the convention grounds to their property to show off the homes for sale; others use photographs and detailed information. These events are in no way focused on foreigners, however, so you typically won't find a lick of English.

FINANCING AND MORTGAGE ISSUES

If you are purchasing a brand-new apartment or villa, the developer will probably have an exclusive financing agreement with a Chinese mortgage company that you'll be required to use. More competitive financing terms might have been found elsewhere, but at least you'll have the convenience of your developer handling the administrative details, which should fast-track the process quite a bit.

If you decide to arrange your own financing, you can use a foreign bank such as Citibank, Standard Chartered, or HSBC. Chinese banks that grant mortgages to foreigners include Bank of China, Industrial and Commercial Bank of China, and the Bank of Communications. Some of these banks only offer loans in renminbi, while the international banks offer loans in renminbi or dollars. For the renminbi loans, interest rates are based on a benchmark rate published by the People's Bank of China; dollar loans are based on the U.S. prime rate. Thirty-year mortgages are available, but more favorable conditions are offered for shorter terms. Few of these banks will finance the entire price of the home; most require a down payment of 20 to 50 percent.

OTHER RED TAPE

Real estate law changes every year, especially when it comes to foreigners. Before you get your heart set on buying a home, do a little research to be fully aware of the current local and national laws concerning foreigners buying properties. And because so many real estate deals end up in the courts, you should hire an attorney who has a proven track record helping expats purchase homes in China. You'll need permits for land use, construction, sales, and housing quality, and any error in the paperwork can invalidate your home purchase. Not every apartment or villa on the market can legally be sold to foreigners, and there are tax issues specific to expats. You'd hate to miss out on one of the tax breaks that are for foreigners only. Hiring an experienced lawyer should help you negotiate favorable conditions and minimize your chances of getting burned.

WHEN IT'S TIME TO LEAVE

When the time comes to pack up your bags and head back to your homeland (or on to new adventures), you can sell your home by listing it with a Chinese real estate agency. Keep in mind that regulations designed to drive out speculators sometimes require you to own your home for at least two years prior to selling it, or else you'll pay a stiff penalty.

After selling your Chinese home, you'll be stuck with a wad of renminbi that can be converted into hard currency after you jump through some administrative hoops. First, you'll have to apply to your local foreign exchange bureau, who'll then send the request to the State Administration of Foreign Exchange (SAFE). You'll need to submit a number of documents to SAFE, including receipts of foreign currency that you brought into China, original home-purchase documents, sale documents, and proof that your property taxes have been paid. Once SAFE is satisfied, they'll give approval to your bank to convert your loot into greenbacks.

Renting Your Home

If you want to hold on to your Chinese property but don't plan to live there, you can entrust the rental process to a real estate agent or to your complex's management company. Just be sure to pick an agency that has experience working with foreigners, especially if you plan to enjoy the rent proceeds from abroad.

LANGUAGE AND EDUCATION

China has always been a rich place for education. In ancient times, government officials were selected based on their intellectual prowess, and today placement exams are major life events that determine future prospects for high school and college students. On international standardized tests, Chinese students routinely outscore their Western counterparts in math and science. Today there are more Chinese people studying English than there are people in the rest of the world whose first language is English. Around 150,000 foreigners are currently studying in Chinese universities, and that number is expected to double over the next decade. Foreign children living in China now have multiple international schools to choose from in every major city. Living in a new country and learning a new language is tough, but we think students of all ages will find China's educational opportunities quite rewarding.

© BARBARA STROTHER

Learning Chinese

One of your biggest concerns about moving to China may be how you will communicate. Chinese is one of the most difficult languages in the world to learn—but that doesn't mean it's impossible. The written characters seem incomprehensible at first, but after some study you'll easily recognize many of them based on their pictographic roots. How can you forget that 三 means three? Thankfully, Chinese grammar is very simple. It follows the same subject-verb-object pattern as English, and there are no fancy verb conjugations, irregular verbs, or difficult past and future tenses. With enough study and practice, anyone can successfully learn to speak, read, and even write Chinese.

Most Chinese will not expect you to know Mandarin, so they'll be surprised and delighted if you can communicate beyond simple greetings. Putting forth the effort to use their language sends a powerful message of respect and goodwill. And because language and culture are intricately tied together, the more Mandarin you know, the more you'll understand the culture.

If you mastered three years of college-level Chinese classes, most people would consider you fluent for practical purposes. The benefit of studying in college is that you'll learn all four language abilities: speaking, listening, reading, and writing. Textbook smarts and street smarts, however, are two different things. Whatever classroom instruction you receive should be supplemented with real-life conversations with native Chinese speakers. This will help you with your pronunciation, and you'll pick up some idioms and the latest slang words. Most Westerners who are fluent in Chinese got that way only after studying Chinese in China diligently for at least two years.

HOW MUCH CHINESE DO YOU NEED?

How much Chinese you need to know depends on where you'll be in China, what you'll be doing, and how long you'll be there. If you are in Beijing, Shanghai, or Hong Kong, there are so many English speakers that it's possible to get by without learning much Chinese at all, especially if English is the language of your workplace. We know a few expats who've had the luxury of living and working in an expat enclave in China for over 10 years and have never learned to communicate beyond a simple thank you or excuse me. We also know quite a few foreigners who were extremely motivated and achieved conversational fluency after only two years in China.

If you're just going to be in China for a short-term assignment, you should strive to learn at least "survival Chinese," just enough to shop, eat out, travel, and make a little bit of small talk. After survival Chinese, you might strive to

DAILY LIFE

HOW ABOUT A CHINESE NAME?

Having a Chinese name will frequently come in handy for filling out documents and meeting locals who struggle with English. Chinese names most often consist of three syllables. The family name comes first, followed by one or two characters that make up the given name. For the family name, foreigners typically choose a Chinese family name that starts with the same sound as their English last name. Given names in Chinese can be just about any two words, but you should

either pick a cool name that describes you or one that sounds like your English name. One of the easiest ways to find a Chinese name is to look for the way your name has already been translated in Chinese – if you share your name with someone famous, most likely there's already a Chinese translation.

Stu chose "Situ"(司徒) after watching the movie *Stuart Little*. Situ also happens to be a respected family name in China, similar to the surname "Kennedy" in the States, making this a great choice for doing business in China. Barbara discovered "Ba Ba La" (巴巴拉) after buying a pair of Barbara Brand shoes in China. Because it is not a Chinese name, it sounds foreign and a little strange to the Chinese, but this made it easy for Barbara to recognize her Chinese name when she was a novice at Mandarin.

In addition to considering the meaning of the name and how closely it sounds like your English name, you may also want to weigh in how complicated the characters are to write and memorize. Before finalizing your selection, run it by a few Chinese people to make sure the name isn't too cheesy or a homophone for something offensive.

© BARBARA STROTHER

Get a bilingual chop made (while you wait).

be fluent in "phrasebook Chinese," meaning you've learned most of the words and phrases in a typical traveler's pocket phrasebook.

If you're making a long-term career move, however, you need an aggressive study plan that will move you toward proficiency as quickly as possible. Among other benefits, expats who speak Chinese make thousands of dollars more than those with the same skills and no language ability.

WRITTEN CHINESE
Characters

The written Chinese language is universally understood by those who speak Mandarin, Cantonese, or any of the other Chinese dialects. Many of the

DAILY LIFE

characters are also used in Korea, Japan, and Vietnam. There are about 3,500 simple Chinese characters, which can be combined to form at least 10,000 additional complex characters. For instance, placing the simple character for "sun" (日) with the character for "moon" (月) results in a complex word (明) that means "bright."

When separate words are combined to form a complex character, the individual parts are called radicals. Radicals hint at the meaning of the word, the pronunciation of the word, or both. Modern dictionaries list about 200 radicals, which are arranged according to the number of strokes. The character for "person" (人) has two strokes that resemble two legs, while the character for "big" (大) adds a third horizontal stroke, making it look like the person is now stretching out their arms to show how big the fish that got away was. Incidentally, the strokes always start at the top left and work their way down to the bottom right. In the example above the radicals are side by side, but they can also be on top of each other. Plenty of words combine more than two radicals, such as 众, which means "crowd"—this is easy to see because the word is made up of three radicals that individually mean "person." In Chinese, just as in English, three's a crowd.

Nowadays Chinese writing usually starts from the top left of the page and moves horizontally to the right, just as in English. But sometimes the characters are written in a more traditional order, vertically from the top to the bottom, or even horizontally from the right to the left.

© BARBARA STROTHER

practicing calligraphy

Simplified Characters

Back in the 1950s and 1960s, the government mandated that many written characters be simplified to have fewer brushstrokes in order to promote literacy. Previously a complex character such as 愛, meaning "love," required 14 brushstrokes to write. The simplified character, 爱, requires just 10 brushstrokes. Critics claimed that simplification would dumb down the language. For instance, when the word for "love" was simplified, the 心 radical, meaning "heart," was eliminated, but how can you have love with no heart?

Simplification was adopted in the mainland and eventually in Singapore, but those in Hong Kong, Taiwan, and Macau still use traditional characters. The foreign community is perhaps the greatest beneficiary of simplification because written Chinese is now much less difficult to learn.

Pinyin

Unlike English words, you can't sound out the pronunciation of Chinese words just by looking at them, so the pinyin system (literally meaning "phonetic spelling") was developed to help foreigners learn how to pronounce Chinese words. When we ignorant foreigners see 你好 we have no idea how to say it, but if we see the pinyin, *nǐ hǎo,* then we can give it the old college try. A pocket phrasebook with English, Chinese, and pinyin is an invaluable tool to help you start communicating like an old pro. You'll see pinyin next to the Chinese characters on street signs and product labels, and sometimes the pinyin spells out some pretty funny English words, such as *maxipuke,* the pinyin name of a popular brand of playing cards.

For a person who just wants to learn to speak Chinese without learning to read and write, pinyin will serve them well. We don't recommend this approach, however, because knowing how to read and write the characters is a crucial step not only toward language literacy but also toward cultural literacy. Being able to recognize characters on maps, street signs, menus, and ingredients labels makes life in China significantly easier. Besides, learning the characters can be a lot of fun, like solving a puzzle or deciphering a secret code.

Writing with Computers

Computers can now easily handle Chinese characters with adjustment of the display and input options. To find out how to adjust the settings within Windows, check Microsoft's website for tutorials. A language bar will allow you to switch easily between Chinese input and English input. In the Chinese input mode, you type in the pinyin pronunciation of the word, then you'll be given the most common character that matches the sound. Hit the backspace to see an additional list of characters to choose from.

Some websites will translate large blocks of text or whole web pages between Chinese and English, such as Alta Vista's Babelfish site (http://babelfish.altavista.com). These tools are only a starting point, however, since the translations are often very far from accurate. For a variety of other language tools, including a searchable dictionary of more than 40,000 words, check out www.mandarin-tools.com. Those with PDAs might also consider the PlecoDict application, a handy handwriting recognition tool and dictionary when you're on the go.

THE FIVE TONES

In Chinese, a single sound can have different meanings depending on the tone. Check out the different meanings for the sound "ba."

Pinyin	Character	Meaning
bā	八	eight
bá	拔	to pull out
bǎ	把	to hold something
bà	爸	pa, dad
ba	吧	an auxiliary word that functions like an exclamation point

SPOKEN CHINESE

When a Chinese word is written in pinyin, the diacritic marks above the vowels tell the speaker which of the five tones to use when pronouncing the word. The first tone is called the flat tone, signified by a flat line above the vowel, and it sounds high-pitched, a little like a man trying to imitate a female voice. The second tone is called rising because the pitch rises at the end of the syllable, such as when a person says "yes?" in response to a knock on the door. The third tone falls then rises, like when a person hears an unbelievable bit of gossip and responds "what?" The fourth tone is the falling tone, which sounds like you are impatient or angry. The fifth tone is considered neutral and can best be described as a relaxed pronunciation. It may seem a bit confusing, but don't fret—with time, practice, and exposure to native speakers, it will eventually come naturally to you.

The Chinese language has a huge number of words that have exactly the same sound, which is the source of an incredible amount of frustration for those of us trying to learn the language. For instance, the word for "kiss" is pronounced *wěn* and written 吻. The word for "mosquito" is pronounced *wèn* and written 蚊. In this example the words have different diacritic marks, but in a normal conversation you may struggle to figure out which tone was used.

Some words have exactly the same sound and tone but different meanings. In this case the context of the conversation determines the meaning. For example, the sound *wěn* can also mean "to cut one's throat." So if your sweetheart offers you a *wen,* we hope you can figure out by the context of the conversation (or at least by knowing the current status of your relationship) whether you're being offered a kiss, a mosquito, or to have your throat cut.

WHICH CHINESE?

When most people say Chinese, they mean Mandarin, a label that signifies this is the language spoken by the mandarins, the scholar-bureaucrats who

LANGUAGE COMPARISON

Area	Official Language	Primary Spoken Language	Written Language
Mainland	Mandarin	Mandarin	Simplified
Hong Kong and Macau	Mandarin	Cantonese	Traditional
Taiwan	Mandarin	Mandarin	Traditional
Singapore	Mandarin	Mandarin	Simplified

ruled imperial China for 2,000 years. But the Chinese call Mandarin *putonghua,* which literally means "the general language." In mainland China most people speak Mandarin because it's the official language and is used in public schools, though every region has its own local dialect as well.

There are eight major dialect groups within China: Cantonese (spoken in Hong Kong, Guangdong, Guangxi, and Hainan), Wu (spoken in Shanghai, Zhejiang, Anhui, and Jiangsu), Xiang (spoken in Hunan), Minbei (spoken in Fujian), Minnan (spoken in Hainan and Taiwan), Jinyu (spoken in Shanxi, Shaanxi, and Henan), Hakka (spoken by the Hakka nomadic group who settled in southern China), and Gan (spoken in Jiangxi and Hubei). A large number of the overseas Chinese migrated from southern China, so Cantonese and Hakka are commonly spoken in Chinatowns around the world.

WHERE TO LEARN
Outside of China

If possible, you should start learning Chinese in your home city before moving to China. More and more Western universities now offer 2–3 years of Chinese classes, or you can sign up at one of the language schools that can now be found in virtually every major Western city. Berlitz, for instance, has language schools in over 50 U.S. cities. Websites such as ChinesePod.com also offer online language lessons and other helpful learning resources.

Within China

The best way to achieve fluency is to enroll in a university program in China. At least one university in each large city has a Mandarin language program for international students. You'll also find privately run language schools that cater to foreigners. You can enroll in a group class or sign up for individual one-on-one instruction. Some crash courses are as short as 10 days, but most classes meet two or three times a week for a month. If you don't know any Chinese at all, after completing an intensive beginner's course you'll know about 250 words. This isn't too bad considering you need to know about 800 words for basic daily life, but you're nowhere near the 3,000 needed to read a newspaper. Language schools come in all shapes and sizes, so you should be able to find one that meets your needs. Foreigners who enroll in a school tend to learn at a much more rapid pace than those who just study on their own. The formal class setting provides structure, and people tend to be motivated to work hard at something after they've invested money in it.

Language Partners

An alternative to language school is to find a language partner. It can be more convenient, and there's usually no expense involved. Most language partners expect you to help them with their English half the time, and then they'll help you with Chinese for the rest of the time. Be careful, though, because a lot of the so-called language partners have ulterior motives such as having you help them get a visa, a job, or even a lover. Since there are many more Chinese than foreigners who want to partner up, you can afford to be choosy. If you're not learning from your partner, move on until you find someone you click with.

HSK

The Hanyu Shuiping Kaoshi (HSK) test is a Chinese-language proficiency test. Just like Chinese students who take the TOEFL test before studying in the United States, foreign students take the HSK to be placed at the appropriate level within a Chinese university. Foreign workers use their HSK scores to prove their Chinese-language ability to prospective employers. There is a preliminary level followed by three official levels scored on a scale of 1 to 11. Elementary is 1–3, intermediate is 4–8, and advanced is 9–11. A minimum score of 4 to 6 is required to be admitted to study in a Chinese university program taught in Mandarin, depending on the program (lower for sciences, higher for liberal arts). You can take the test in China or at a number of overseas locations.

General Education in China

The Chinese school system is structured very much like the U.S. system, with elementary, junior high, and high schools. Beyond that, there are universities and technical schools, most of which allow foreign students to enroll. The official school calendar is established by the central government each year and typically begins around September 1, ending around July 15 for summer break. The other major break is for Chinese New Year/Spring Festival, which typically runs for a few weeks sometime between January 15 and March 1.

COLLEGES AND UNIVERSITIES

China's higher education system includes universities, which function similar to Western universities, and technical colleges that provide vocational training in skills such as manufacturing, cosmetology, cooking, and technology. Students' test scores determine their options. There is no community college or junior college system, but a growing number of small private schools are filling in the gap. Unlike the universities, the private schools often don't require minimum test scores.

More than 50 Chinese universities accept foreign students. Beijing is the top destination for most, with Qinghua and Beida Universities at the top of the list. Shanghai is the second most popular study city, and Fudan and Jiaotong are the preferred schools. Other popular choices include Zhejiang University in Hanghzou, China's largest university and one of the top five academically, as well as Xiamen University, which has the added benefit of being near the beach.

Students come from all over the world and study just about every subject, including the arts, agriculture, economics, and both Western and Chinese medicine, but Mandarin remains the most popular. You needn't know any Mandarin to enroll in language classes; you can start out in a beginning class. Most foreign students who plan to study other subjects often start out with a year or two of Mandarin first. Some programs are taught completely in English or with a mixture of the two languages.

In 2008 the number of foreign students in China surpassed 195,000, which represents an annual increase of 20 percent year-on-year. The Chinese government has earmarked over $70 million for scholarships specifically for foreigners and has recently allowed a few of the top colleges like Zhejiang University to grant their own scholarships as well. China's education is so inexpensive that scholarships aren't even necessary.

The Chinese university system is almost identical to the U.S. system, with bachelors, masters, and doctorate degrees awarded. As in the United States, the academic calendar consists of a fall and spring semester, and most schools also have intensive summer programs. Admission is typically limited to the fall semester, which generally starts around September 1, so you'll need to apply in the spring at the latest. Be aware that at this point in time, a degree from a Chinese university may not be recognized by a Western employer, and credits from a Chinese university might not transfer to a Western university.

The tuition for one year of undergraduate study at Zhejiang University is around $3,000–4,500; masters and doctoral study ranges $3,400–6,800. A two-person room at the International Student Dorm rents for around $1,500 for the year. You'll shell out another $1,000 for cafeteria meals. In comparison, a year of medical school at a less famous university will only put you out

$3,000–4,000 a year, and that includes dorm and meals. Realistically, you'll need a few thousand more for traveling and for the psychological benefits of having a Western meal once in a while, not to mention all the karaoke and discos your classmates will drag you to.

Foreign Universities

While living in China it is possible to take courses from a number of foreign universities that have alliances with Chinese universities. The alliances could be as simple as just exchanging a couple of students or professors each year, or as complex as a joint-venture agreement with permanent facilities. The China Europe International Business School in Shanghai, which offers the highest-ranked MBA in Asia, was formed through such a partnership. Johns Hopkins University has a permanent site in Nanjing offering an MA in International Studies, and the University of Nottingham has built a large campus in Ningbo where both undergraduate and graduate programs are taught in a variety of disciplines.

ELEMENTARY AND SECONDARY SCHOOLS

Because both parents typically work in China, Chinese children typically start their schooling in a preschool (called "kindergarten" in China) as early as age 2, although every child is required to be enrolled in elementary school between the ages of 6 and 12. Junior high follows and lasts three years. The kindergarten, elementary, and junior high schools are assigned based on where the child lives, but at the end of junior high, a rigorous standardized test determines which high school the child will attend. If children do well on the test, they will surely be invited to a "good" high school where they'll be prepped for college. Have a bad test day and they might be relegated to trade school and perhaps a life of mundane work and low wages. After high school, students take another exam that determines which university they'll be admitted to, if any. Those who perform poorly on the exam can't attend university and will be off to trade school and/or the factory floor.

With the exception of a few fees for books, uniforms, and the like, public education through high school is free for locals, though foreigners will have to pay a nominal fee to enroll their children.

International Schools

Unlike some foreign posts where homeschooling is the only option for expatriate children, there are top-notch international schools in every major expat destination in China, typically covering preschool to 12th grade. The

STUDYING ABROAD IN CHINA

AN INTERVIEW WITH GEORGE XU AND LIN SUN, INTERNATIONAL STUDENT ADVISERS

With more than 3,500 international students in any given year at the prestigious Zhejiang University in Hangzhou, George Xu and Lin Sun have their hands full. As advisers to the Mandarin language programs, George and Lin are responsible for a diverse group of global students. Together they have a good bit of wisdom to share on being an international student in China.

Tell us about your students. Why do most of them come to China to study?
Lin: Many want to get a job related to China, or they want to have greater job opportunities by knowing another language. Traditionally American students have come for their own interest, but now they also come for job opportunities.

What is the ideal international student like?
George: Patient and active. International students have an opportunity to lead a very full life, full of trips and activities. We organize events for the students like singing contests, and there is a trend among local organizations to invite foreigners to events and trips in order to add international flavor. The students who can speak Chinese well are particularly popular.

What are the biggest challenges for foreign students?
Lin: Making friends with Chinese students, learning the real culture of China. It's a mistake to spend all your time in the international dorm and only make friends with other internationals.
George: If you really want to understand China and use this Chinese experience for your future jobs and personal life, you need to make Chinese friends. For English-speaking students this isn't difficult, because you are surrounded by people eager to learn English from native speakers.

Students should also try to understand the real China instead of only going to the pubs and bars and coffeehouses. China means more than this. The average Chinese doesn't like to go to the pubs.

What advice would you give to students new to China?
George: Try to be understanding of the differences between China and your home country. Some students are warm-hearted and truly interested in China on the one hand, but very impatient and unaware of the cultural differences on the other hand, which is always surprising and disappointing. International awareness is not that easy.

Another key issue in my mind is to be cautious not to go from one misconception to another. American movies and TV often show China as a very backward place where everyone practices kung fu and starts their sentences with "Confucius says . . . " You'll see that's not true, but on the other side don't go back to the United States thinking that every night is spent at bars and clubs. Don't engage by lingering in the bar too long or too late. Being surrounded by such people will give students the wrong impressions about China. Get a more comprehensive experience.

For those who want to study Chinese, what should they look for in a language program?
Lin: Because it's not usual for a Chinese university to place so much effort

George Xu and Lin Sun

on a Chinese language program, the big universities that already have lots of international students have the best programs. The private schools are less stable and can't offer as many opportunities for the students. For example, at Zhejiang University our students have more opportunities to attend social activities because in Hangzhou organizations come to our university first to invite foreigners.

Small universities might take good care of foreign students, but making international friends is a key part of being abroad, and in our college there are students from all over the world. Some students here even learn Korean or Spanish from other students, as well as learning about other cultures from around the world. Spanish has become popular, because we have students from Mexico, Spain, and Bolivia.

Why would you recommend Zhejiang University?

George: Zhejiang University is a great choice because academics should be the first consideration. There are, of course, other prestigious universities in China, but Hangzhou is a city that is particularly suitable for expat life. It's not too big and not too small; not as crowded as places like Beijing, not as much hustle and bustle as Shanghai. Hangzhou is easy to get around, and the cost of living here is relatively low.

What about scholarships?

George: In the past, scholarships always came from the government, but the university has recently been authorized to give scholarships directly. Only the prestigious colleges get this privilege. We offer 30 international student scholarships per year, which cover tuition as well as all accommodation and some living expenses.

What are the qualifications for the scholarships?

George: Universities are encouraged to pick students coming from good universities around the world. Our university especially encourages doctoral students, and we are eager to enroll those successful and talented students from educationally developed countries like the United States.

English-language schools tend to follow either an American or British curriculum, with the latter often offering the International Baccalaureate college-prep program. The student population at the international schools is incredibly diverse; when our children attended an international school in Shanghai they had classmates from more than a dozen different countries. Unfortunately, current mainland Chinese government regulations only allow those with a foreign passport to attend the international schools, so your children probably won't have too many local Chinese classmates, though students from Hong Kong and Taiwan are permitted.

There are plenty of advantages to putting your children in an international school. For one, your kid's classmates will come from families of diplomats and business leaders that have a strong commitment to the value of education. Teachers often have higher qualifications than what is typical in the public schools in the United States. It's not uncommon for an elementary school teacher at an international school in China to have a doctoral degree, and quite a few of the teachers are seasoned veterans who've decided to finish out their careers on the international scene. Another advantage is that the schools regularly put on community events that will give your family the opportunity to get plugged into the expat community. The main disadvantages of international schools are the high price, which can easily cost $25,000 or more per student per year in the prominent cities (although cheaper locales will be closer to the $12,000–20,000 range), and the lack of integration with the local Chinese community.

Local Schools

You can also enroll your children in a public or private Chinese school, which will cost considerably less than the international schools. Your children will probably excel in math and science and will quickly learn Mandarin. Be aware, however, that if your child can't speak Chinese, the adjustment process could be quite stressful for your littlest ones. There are quite a few private English preschools available, however, that are run by either foreigners or Chinese. Since most Chinese schools start teaching English very early on, your older child may have classmates who can converse in English. Other than the English teachers, not many other teachers or staff members will speak English.

Private schools in China follow the same division of ages and grades as the public schools. Many of these private schools are semi–boarding schools, where the kids stay on campus for the business week but return home to their parents on the weekends. This is true for all ages, even some preschools, though boarding is not required.

While the cost of attending a Chinese school will be nowhere near what

© BARBARA STROTHER

A poster about puberty hangs on the wall of a Chinese school in Shanghai.

you'll pay at the international schools, you'll still have to pay fees for books, meals, and administration. These fees will be nominal for public schools but are much higher at private schools, where you may pay as much as half of what you would pay at an international school in the same city.

It is quite rare for expats to send their kids to public school in China as most fear that their child would receive an inferior education. In a private Chinese school you are much more likely to find top-notch teachers and more Western educational values (such as creativity and a rich learning environment) than in public schools, which often focus on rote memorization and have dismally blank concrete walls. Hong Kong's schools are the exception, however; see the chapter on Hong Kong for more information. There are also a handful of mainland public schools, primarily located within special economic and development zones, that enjoy a good reputation among the local expat community. If you are interested in considering public school, you'll want to tour the facilities during a school day to see firsthand if this will work for your family.

Homeschooling

Homeschooling has grown in popularity around the world, which gives families the freedom to travel extensively and spend more time interacting with the foreign culture. Some apartment and housing complexes with high ratios of foreign occupants have informal homeschool co-op groups. If you're looking for other homeschoolers to connect with, check the local expat magazines and websites for your city or ask around at the foreigners' church services. Though Chinese bookstores offer a variety of educational materials in English for the preschool to early elementary ages, you'll need to import your own materials for older grades.

HEALTH

In many ways the Chinese have a much healthier lifestyle than Americans. At a time of day when most Americans are hitting their snooze button, many Chinese are hitting their local park for tai chi exercises and ballroom dance practice, followed by their daily commute by bicycle. Chinese meals can be high-vegetable, low-meat, low-sugar affairs that keep the cholesterol and the weight down. And traditional medicine shops do a brisk business in dried snake, seahorse, and ginseng root, believed to work wonders for one's vitality and longevity.

Adopting a traditional Chinese lifestyle may add a few years to your life, but there are plenty of influences that will take away from it as well. Diseases tend to float around rural China with fluidity. Food-borne illness can make those with sensitive stomachs run for the squat pot a little too frequently. And if contaminated food doesn't do you in, the traffic might. Nevertheless, when you need it, you'll find adequate health care available, from international medical facilities, Western doctors, and imported drugs in major cities

© BARBARA STROTHER

to inexpensive local clinics where your antibiotic prescription may come with a few vials of murky green traditional medicine. And if any health situation proves too serious, medical-evacuation choppers offer transportation to the nearest place that can help.

Hospitals and Clinics

The greatest horror stories you'll ever hear about China are about what happens behind hospital doors. Nowadays most of the stories about recycled needles and contaminated medical environments are simply urban legend, though substandard and even harmful health care does still exist in more remote places. The best way to keep from becoming one of these horror stories is to do your research. Look around the facility, ask lots of questions of the staff, and seek out reviews of other foreigners who have firsthand experience.

The health facilities in China's prime cities can be divided based on their management, whether foreign-run (including joint-venture facilities) or domestic-run (including both private and public facilities). The public system is further divided into district-based clinics and city-based hospitals, many of which have VIP wards for foreigners and wealthy locals.

If you find yourself in need of specialist care, many medical facilities (both foreign and domestic) have specialists on staff that they will bring in as needed. China also has numerous small hospitals that specialize in one area of medicine, which you will be referred to if your situation demands it.

FOREIGN-RUN HOSPITALS AND CLINICS

Hospitals run by foreigners are the most expensive option for health care in China, but they are also the most trustworthy. You'll pay dearly for their services, so you'll want good insurance first. A procedure at an international facility can regularly cost more than 10 times what the same procedure would cost at a public hospital. Fortunately the international health institutions are more likely to accept your insurance (check first!), so you won't have to pay out of pocket and wait for reimbursement. Some of these facilities also require membership before you can take advantage of their facilities.

Hospitals and clinics that are wholly foreign-owned are typically staffed by expatriate doctors; joint-venture facilities are often managed by a foreign company but staffed by foreign-trained Chinese personnel. There shouldn't be much difference in medical treatment between the two, but philosophy of practice can differ greatly, such as how much information to give a patient or to what degree a patient is allowed to make choices in their treatment. Staff

TCM 101: A PRIMER

You pick up a pack of normal-looking pills at the local pharmacy labeled "stomach care tablets." But hidden in the fine print, the active ingredients include starfish, ginger, oyster shell, and a few obscure roots and rhizomes. Welcome to traditional Chinese medicine, a.k.a. TCM.

In the States, TCM has a reputation of being strictly an alternative therapy, but in China it is an integral part of the modern health care system. You'll likely have ample opportunity to try a little of this 3,000-year-old folk medicine while there. Here's a little basic information to get you started.

THEORIES

- **Five Elements:** All of your body's organs are associated with a specific element, such as wood for the liver, fire for the heart, earth for the spleen, metal for the lungs, and water for the ears. Medicinal herbs are also similarly categorized. If an herb causes dry skin, it would be called a "fire" herb. To control the "fire" ingredient you'd add a "water" ingredient; to help a "wood" problem in your body, you'd take a "water" herb.

- **Meridian System:** In TCM, the meridian system is made up of lines that show the connections between organs and other areas of the body. If an acupuncturist puts a tiny needle into one point on your body, it is believed to benefit the other parts of the body that lie along the same meridian.

- **Yin-Yang:** a belief that all things should be balanced, represented by the popular black-and-white symbol. To have optimal health you must reach your balance point, and certain foods are believed to do this. While Asian ginseng helps your yang, American ginseng helps your yin. Dried duck gizzards, on the other hand, will balance out the yin and yang of any recipe.

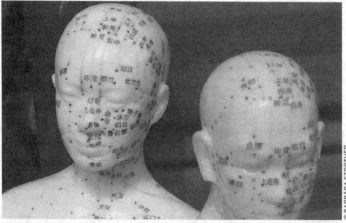

meridian pressure point models

© BARBARA STROTHER

DAILY LIFE

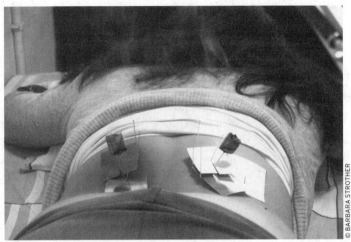

© BARBARA STROTHER

acupuncture and moxibustion

DIAGNOSTICS

TCM practitioners are trained in observing subtle changes in the body, and may examine your tongue, ears, and face, the tenderness of your abdomen, how you smell, or how your voice sounds. Then they'll classify your symptoms into external or internal, yin or yang, cold or hot, and psychological or physical, and prescribe a treatment plan accordingly.

TREATMENTS

- **Acupuncture:** the practice of sticking tiny needles into various points of your body to stimulate healing. Some swear by it; others just swear when getting it.

- **Herbs and Food Therapy:** a mixture of natural ingredients to fit your specific needs. Classical mixtures come in all forms: pills, syrups, plasters and liniments, tablets, liquid extracts, and tea infusions, as well as foods to add to your dinner menu to get your qi back in balance, such as bird's nest soup for beautiful skin and strong spleen, and apricot kernels for the lungs. Seahorses alone are beneficial for the kidneys, circulation, swelling, frequent urination, wheezing, and impotence – the Viagra of the sea.

- **Moxibustion:** Herbal leaves are burned on or near a point along the body's meridian system to stimulate acupuncture points.

- **Qi Gong, Tai Chi, Chinese Martial Arts:** The Chinese martial arts serve as exercise but more importantly focus on balancing your qi – your internal energy or life-force – performing physical movements that bring a certain sense of spiritual balance.

at foreign-run hospitals and clinics will be fluent in English; there may also be a variety of other languages represented. You'll find several foreign-run hospitals and clinics in China's biggest cities, though smaller key cities may have just one or none at all.

DOMESTIC-RUN HOSPITALS AND CLINICS

Any foreigner can take advantage of the public hospitals and clinics in China, paying the same amount as the locals do to get the same treatment. These facilities do not take appointments; just show up and join the waiting crowd. You'll pay the basic fee when you arrive at the registration desk, then pay again before each test or treatment you require. An increasing number of hospitals in larger cities are now accepting credit cards for payment. You'll have to contact your insurance company later for reimbursement if you need it, though medical procedures are so much cheaper in China that you might not even want to bother. A recent trip to a clinic for a sprained ankle (including doctor visit, pain medicine, and an x-ray that we were able to keep) cost less than $20 total.

Chinese medical care often includes the choice of Western or traditional Chinese medicine. If you prefer Chinese medicine alone, most towns have hospitals that are solely dedicated to it, though just about any Chinese doctor at any medical facility in China can (and will) prescribe a traditional option in addition to his Western recommendations.

Be aware of the cultural differences in medical practices between China and the West. Chinese doctors sometimes refuse to supply copies of medical records, lab results, or X-rays. Some have been known to strongly discourage patients from seeking a second opinion, and refuse to listen to requests from patients concerning their own treatment. While domestic-run health care can be a bargain, you might pay for it in lack of service-oriented professionals.

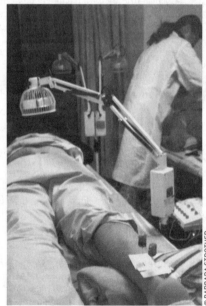

traditional Chinese medicine clinic

© BARBARA STROTHER

Rural hospitals can be as backward as the backwoods they're located in. Foreign residents in smaller cities tend feel more comfortable traveling to the closest larger cities for treatment, while others prefer to head directly to Hong Kong's trustworthy medical facilities for all their health needs. You'll have to judge your situation for yourself to determine what options you are most comfortable with.

City-Level Hospitals

City-level public hospitals are thought to offer better overall medical service than the smaller district-level clinics. They keep advanced and specialized medical equipment and prescription medications on hand. Some also offer VIP wards (called *gaogan bingfang*), where you can pay extra to be treated in a comfortable private room, potentially with English-speaking staff that will be more attentive to your needs. In fact, Global Doctor and other foreign medical firms run clinics inside some of these VIP wards. Though the docs are still often Chinese and have a Chinese way of doing medicine, they will be thoroughly Western-trained. You'll get sound medical care, but you may not get the autonomy we enjoy in the United States, such as the ability to make your own decisions about childbirth methods.

District-Level Clinics

District-level clinics offer the convenience of being close to your neighborhood and having much shorter wait times than larger hospitals. A typical visit to a district-level facility, such as a checkup or treatment for a minor ailment, should take less than 30 minutes, whereas visiting a city-level hospital for the same reason could take three or four times longer. Fees are lower at your local clinic, though so will be the amount of English spoken. Some expats make the mistake of dismissing this option before checking it out, but you never know when you'll find a nearby doctor you like who speaks English and is thoroughly trained. If your ailment is more complicated than a simple cold or rash, however, you should go directly to a city-level hospital with more advanced technology.

OTHER TYPES OF CLINICS

By the looks of some Chinese smiles, you might think that there are no dentists in China. On the contrary, whether or not the locals choose to take advantage of them, China has many fine dental and orthodontic services, often charging a small fraction of the cost of their American counterparts. Many large hospitals include dentists and orthodontists, as well as other specialists such as ophthalmologists. Major cities offer eye-care centers with Western-trained professionals; some cater specifically to English speakers. And if you want to give traditional Chinese medicine a try, some hospitals and clinics focus on TCM as their specialty.

CHOOSING A MEDICAL FACILITY

We recommend checking out all the options in your area before you actually need them. You'll want to confirm that gloves are always changed between patients and needles always come from sealed packages, and make sure you don't see anything with blood on it left sitting around. You'll also want to know how the hospital is managed, such as what types of payment and insurance are accepted, if you can specify which doctor you would like to see, and how long the typical wait time is. Find out what they charge for visits and for a few common medical procedures. The U.S. Embassy's website (www. usembassychina.org.cn/uscitizen/medical.html) lists recommended medical providers by city and includes some listings for dental, orthodontic, and ophthalmologic clinics.

If you'll be working for a Chinese employer who is providing health benefits, check to see if they require that you use a specific facility. If you'd prefer to not use their choice, be sure you are aware of the financial consequences of using a different facility. When we worked at a Chinese school, we were able to take advantage of the school's on-site clinic for most of our medical needs, such as common colds and immunizations for our kids. When we had problems

a medical facility in Guangzhou

© BARBARA STROTHER

beyond their scope, they would refer us to the district clinic or tell us which city hospital could best help us. At our nearby district clinic, our helpful doctor spoke English, the wait time was short, and the fees were minimal. The city-level hospital, however, proved both time-consuming and difficult to find answers to our questions, though the facility was quite clean and modern.

When you've decided which health facility to rely on primarily, be sure to keep their business card in your wallet. In an emergency, you'll want it to show to a taxi driver to get you to your hospital. Don't bother waiting for an ambulance to take you there; ambulances in China do not come with sophisticated medical equipment, and the drivers often have little or no medical training.

Insurance

Currently China has no adequate system of private health insurance, so you'll want to make sure you are insured prior to your move to China. Many U.S. policies do not cover services received outside the United States. If your insurance does cover Chinese medical expenses, you will typically have to pay up front and file for reimbursement later, though foreign-run hospitals may take your insurance.

You'll want to make sure that your insurance policy covers emergency medical evacuation since it can cost up to $100,000 should you need it. Check your policy for psychiatric treatment as well; stress and depression are common among expats as they learn to adjust to a new environment without their close friends and family nearby.

You may consider choosing a provider that includes the services of SOS International, or purchase a personal SOS membership yourself. As the world's largest medical assistance and evacuation company, SOS maintains relationships with over 150 hospitals across China that they have approved for treatment of foreigners, as well as the Chinese military and commercial airlines to arrange for medical evacuation when needed. Their convenient 24-hour hotline operators can answer medical questions and recommend where to get quality medical assistance in any corner of the nation, including their own clinics in Beijing, Tianjin, Nanjing, and Shenzhen (see *Resources*).

If you are thinking of saving money by not carrying any medical insurance, here's the situation. If, during the time you are in China, you will only suffer very minor ailments, such as colds or the occasional rash or stomach flu, and you don't mind going to the cheap local Chinese clinics, you could save a ton of cash. On the other hand, if you find yourself with a serious medical situation (such as injuries resulting from one of the frequent traffic accidents), you'll have to pay up front for all the expensive tests and treatments. If you can't pay, you may have a very difficult time getting the medical attention you need. And if it's serious enough to warrant a medical evacuation to better facilities in Hong Kong or the United States, let's just say we hope you have a very, very wealthy uncle who loves you dearly.

Pharmacies and Prescriptions

You shouldn't have to walk far to find a pharmacy in China. In most cities you'll find one every block or two, marked by a green cross. You can also pick up medications at hospitals and foreign health clinics, both of which charge more but have stronger safeguards against the possibility of getting counterfeit medications. The foreign clinics will carry the imported medications you are used to, but you'll pay much more for them than you would back home. On the other hand, many common Chinese medications (even prescription drugs) sell for just a few dollars.

AT THE PHARMACY

Finding a pharmacy may be easy, but finding English in that pharmacy will not be. You'll be lucky to find one that keeps a bilingual medical dictionary, or that has any staff who can speak a lick of English, let alone medical terms. Fortunately many of the Chinese medications will have the drug's generic name in English on the box, although all directions and precautions will be

preparing natural prescriptions at a traditional-medicine pharmacy

© BARBARA STROTHER

in Chinese. When you do find the drug you need, be sure to keep the box to show it to the pharmacy the next time you need it.

The process of getting prescriptions filled in China is similar to what you would expect in the United States, except it is solely paper-based. You'll need your doctor in China to give you a prescription paper, which you will then take to the pharmacy (no computerized records of prescriptions are available, and don't expect to have your doctor call in a prescription for you). Chinese pharmacies will not recognize a prescription brought from your home country; you'll have to take that prescription to a local doctor to obtain a new Chinese prescription.

Pharmacists can help diagnose basic medical symptoms and prescribe over-the-counter medications. Unless you already speak Chinese, the trick will be in how to communicate your symptoms, and how to know for sure that the pharmacist has understood you correctly. A pharmacist's advice is best sought for ailments that are visual, such as rashes. Better yet, bring a fluently bilingual friend with you to translate.

OVER-THE-COUNTER DRUGS

Chinese pharmacies carry some over-the-counter medicines that are similar to what you'll find in the States, though nowhere near the variety. Your local convenience store and supermarket may also carry a very small amount of over-the-counter medications. It pays to stock up before your move on items like daytime and nighttime cold/flu pills, allergy pills, and all kinds of children's medications, all of which are not easy to find in China. If you are partial to certain brands, you should bring them from home as well.

It used to be that many drugs requiring prescriptions in the United States were available over-the-counter in China, a convenient and cheap way to avoid having to go to a doctor when you're running low on a regular medication (we do not, however, advise self-diagnosis of medical ailments). With recent changes to the law, many of these drugs now require a prescription, although you can sometimes find a pharmacy that will sell them to you if you agree to sign a waiver releasing the pharmacy from any responsibility for your risk. These rules are much more lax in smaller cities. In fact, some people find it convenient to pick up a few handy packs of general antibiotics when traveling since small-city pharmacists rarely ask to see prescriptions, an easy way to solve simple problems like bladder infections that get so much more complicated if you have to communicate the issue across language barriers with Chinese doctors.

STASI'S CHINA CHALLENGE

AN INTERVIEW WITH STASI AMATANGELO

Stasi Amatangelo has had complicated health issues for as long as she can remember. Her medical history reads like a medical dictionary: rheumatoid arthritis, fibromyalgia, ulcerative acid reflux, Crohn's disease, colitis, and a long list of allergies that include fish, protein, citrus, and dairy with a little mold, nickel, and hypersensitivity to medicine thrown in.

Stasi first traveled to China as a college student and came home knowing that she wanted to return. So when she was offered a position teaching English at a top high school in Wuhan, China, she had to think long and hard about the potential health risks.

Tell us about your decision to move to China.

My two greatest fears in coming to China were that I would not be able to find the medications that I needed and that I would not get proper health care in case of an emergency.

As for the first fear, it turned out to be true. The medications that I take daily are not used in China; I had to purchase a year's supply of the medications and bring them with me. The second fear has also come true. When I was most recently sick with what they guessed was a parasite, the doctors were unable to treat me. Returning to the States was not possible because of how weak I was, and it was only after my mother brought me medications from the United States that I started to get better.

Despite the health issues, I loved my first year and decided to return for a second. I really enjoy the people, what I do, and the culture.

What health issues have you had to deal with in China?

I've had flare-ups of some of my preexisting illnesses as well as strep throat, pneumonia, and chicken pox. I also had a skin-eating bacteria on my right arm, but the doctors never gave it a name. Most recently I was ill for two months, but the doctors were never able to diagnose me.

Traveling in China with these illnesses and allergies is a challenge. Finding adequate medical care and medications is next to impossible. Choosing to live in Wuhan was a choice to live without dependable health care for a time. Living in a city like Shanghai, Beijing, or Hong Kong would be so different; with the Western influence and population in those cities, things like health care are much more efficient.

Trying to find food to eat in China is also a task in itself. Many times I am faced with offending my hosts by not eating the food prepared. It is a difficult balance of respecting the culture and being wise as to what I can eat.

What have been your experiences with Chinese hospitals?

To be honest, I have not had good experiences with the Chinese health care system. The instruments and facilities are not always properly sanitized and precautions (such as proper covering for taking X-rays) are not always used. You are unable to make an appointment, so waiting in a four-hour line is unavoidable, and then you are treated as a "number" in a line and not as a patient.

What about traditional Chinese medicine?

As far as traditional Chinese medication goes, I have been more lucky.

I have had many headaches since being in China and have found that their medicine teas and acupuncture do work. I don't use them in place of my Western medication, but I have found that the tea and acupuncture have helped my headaches and tension when used along with the normal medication I am already taking.

What advice would you give about health care in China?

Trust your body. I have learned to understand my body much more clearly since being here. I have realized that if I need something, I have to insist that it gets done. Chinese often times do things one way and one way only, but that might not be the way that you need, so you have to stand your ground and not move until you get what you know your body needs. It helps to have a good translator willing to fight for you at the hospital. Oftentimes Chinese friends will just agree with the doctor because that is what they are taught, but sometimes the doctors are wrong. I generally call my doctor in America and ask for his advice first, then proceed to the Chinese hospitals and tell them what tests, procedures, or medication prescriptions I want them to do.

What are the best things about living in China as a foreigner?

The best things about living in China are being able to try new foods, learn about traditional customs, celebrating different holidays, and traveling. I have traveled more in my time here in China than I have ever and might ever again. I have enjoyed building relationships with my neighbors, coworkers, and students. They are treasures I will never forget.

As a nation, China grabs onto a lot of Western influences and catches on quickly to new trends. China is breaking out, and it's been wild watching it grow and develop right before my eyes. The memories I have made living in China, even the crazy medical memories, are all a part of who I am now. I feel like I have grown so much from it all.

Stasi Amatangelo

COURTESY OF STASI AMATANGELO

DAILY LIFE

AVAILABILITY OF PRESCRIPTION DRUGS

If there is a prescription you know you will need while in China, you should verify its availability before you go. If you have a membership with one of the medical services for foreigners such as SOS, Worldlink, or Global Doctors, check with them before you go. Some medications are not yet available in the mainland, but just about anything can be picked up in Hong Kong. Some common prescription drugs, such as birth control pills, are available over-the-counter in China, though you may have a hard time locating them in smaller or more remote cities. It is best to assume that you won't be

Maybe these critters contain your cure!

© BARBARA STROTHER

able to get the medication you need and plan accordingly. If you decide to bring a stock of your needed drug with you, be sure to keep the original prescription handy in case you are stopped by customs.

HERBAL MEDICINE

If you are interested in trying traditional Chinese herbal medicine, look for a pharmacy that specializes in it. You'll know them by their jars of brined snakes and ginseng on display.

Diseases and Preventative Measures

China has plenty of diseases floating around, though most can be avoided by using vaccinations and a healthy dose of wisdom.

VACCINATIONS
General

As with any travel, you should make sure your diphtheria, polio, and tetanus immunizations are current before you leave. Vaccination requirements and recommendations specific to China should be obtained from your doctor or the Centers for Disease Control (www.cdc.gov, 877-FYI-TRIP, 877-394-8747) for up-to-date information. As a general rule, immunizations for hepatitis A and B are recommended. Hepatitis A, caught through contaminated water or food and poor sanitation, is quite widespread, and China is considered high risk for hepatitis B, spread through contaminated blood, needles, and syringes.

Tuberculosis (TB), spread through respiratory droplets, is a prevalent problem throughout China. The vaccination is only recommended for children younger than five and adults at very high risk since it prevents serious complications of the disease but may not protect you from getting TB in the first place.

Rural or Subtropical Areas

Typhoid is not an issue in China's modern cities, but if you plan to travel off the beaten path, poor sanitation and contaminated food and water may put you at risk. The vaccine is only needed if you'll be spending considerable time in rural areas.

Japanese encephalitis is a threat in rural areas and is also carried by mosquitoes. Although very rare, the disease can be quite deadly, especially to children; on the other hand, the immunization is quite expensive. We were fortunate to get the vaccine free for our children at the Chinese school where we taught; you may also want to wait until you arrive and try a Chinese hospital for a cheaper vaccine. (Don't try this with the most important vaccines, however, since you risk not being able to find a hospital that carries them.)

Malaria, spread by mosquitoes, is only a threat to those bound for Hainan Island or southern Yunnan Province. If traveling or staying in these areas, you'll want to protect yourself from mosquito bites.

SARS

The Severe Acute Respiratory Syndrome (SARS) outbreak of 2003 was a scary time for people around the globe, but none so much as the residents of China. SARS originated in China and rapidly spread around the world via airline travelers, infecting over 8,000 people and killing over 800 in 33 countries. The threat has passed, and China has long been declared SARS-free. After being sufficiently shamed over the initial outbreak, the Chinese government has put a rapid detection system in place to deter a similar outbreak happening in the future. Currently a SARS vaccine is in the testing stages and should be widely available in the case of a future recurrence.

AVIAN FLU

Avian flu, a.k.a. bird flu, is a deadly disease that is passed from infected fowl to humans mainly through contact with body fluids, such as when butchering an infected chicken or coming into contact with bird feces at a live animal market. From 2003 to 2006 about 200 people contracted the disease, and more than half of them died from it. Most cases of bird flu have occurred in Vietnam and southern China. Medical science experts are concerned that if the virus mutates into a form that is easily transferred between people, there could be a pandemic that would leave hundreds of thousands dead in its wake around the globe.

At the time of writing, both China and the United States are in an advanced stage of testing effective vaccines, though no vaccine is currently available to the public. A drug called Tamiflu is believed effective in treating it, and this has led many governments to stockpile the drug in case of a pandemic. Ironically, Tamiflu is created from ingredients that come from China and are used in traditional medicine, such as star anise.

The best way to protect yourself from bird flu at this point is to simply avoid contact with live birds, including any water or surfaces that could become contaminated by infected birds. Eating poultry, as long as it is well cooked, poses no threat.

AIDS

The first reported case of AIDS in China was in 1985. In 25 years, that one case has grown to an estimated 700,000 HIV/AIDS patients, according to China's government statistics (meaning the number may actually be much higher due to unreported cases). AIDS now ranks as the third-deadliest infectious disease in China. Many of the initial cases were a result of contamination through poorly managed blood donations.

The best precaution against AIDS (as well as hepatitis B and C) is to avoid the activities associated with these diseases, such as unprotected sex and drug use. Be aware that the quality of Chinese condoms can be dangerously lower than American standards. You should also safeguard yourself from contaminated blood by refusing any needle or syringe that was not opened from a sterilized package in your presence, and perhaps even bringing your own needles and syringes if you'll be spending time in rural areas without modern medical care. If you are already HIV-positive, the Chinese government doesn't even want you to bother coming. Chinese law prohibits anyone "suffering from mental disorder, leprosy, AIDS, venereal diseases, or other infectious diseases" from entering the country. While you may be able to slip in on a tourist visa, you'll be required to get an HIV test if you'll be in China longer than six months. This policy may soon change, however, as government talks are currently underway to repeal the ban on individuals with HIV/AIDS.

Environmental Factors

MOSQUITOES

They are annoying. They buzz around your ears in the dark, and their bites make you itch like mad. And in the rural backwaters of China, mosquitoes can also give you potentially fatal diseases like malaria and Japanese encephalitis. Even in the city, mosquitoes can get into your house, hotel room, or college dorm, coming in through the drains even if you keep your windows securely closed. Luckily there are several ways to keep the little buzzers at bay.

For walks in the woods or along waterways, keep a travel-size can of bug spray with DEET handy. Inside your home or hotel room, China's plug-in repellents with replaceable pads work wonders. One cool bug-repelling device that sells for less than $2 is a battery-operated bug zapper that resembles a plastic tennis racket-except the metal strings have an electric charge. It kills flies and mosquitoes in mid-air with a satisfying pop as their small bodies go up in a tiny flame. While good at killing bugs, this racket is not, we discovered, a good way to play a trick on a friend by daring him to touch the electric wires, unless you like to see grown men cry.

FOOD AND WATER

Overseas travel invariably includes some sort of trouble for the tummy, and China is no exception. Caution must be taken to wash all fruits and vegetables. Lettuce and leafy vegetables that hide stubborn dirt can be placed in a quart of water with a couple of drops of bleach; rinse with drinking water before consuming. Overall it's good to follow the standard advice of, "Wash it, boil it, peel it, or forget it."

Tap water is not recommended for drinking in China, and in fact, most Chinese don't drink the water. The problem with tap water isn't so much bacteria as it is chemical and mineral contaminants, such as lead. You shouldn't have a problem using the tap water to wash vegetables or brush your teeth. For drinking water, bottled water is available everywhere. Hotels provide each room with bottled water and a daily thermos of boiled water. Apartments come furnished with water dispensers, and new bottles will be brought to your door with a quick phone call to the management company. Ordering water at restaurants will typically get you either a bottle of mineral water (for a charge) or a glass of water that has come directly from a bottled water dispenser or has been boiled (for free). To request a free glass of cold water that's safe to drink, order "leng de bai kai shui."

Traveler's diarrhea does happen in China, but not nearly as often as you would expect. The truth is, in this country so focused on starches (rice, noodles, or dumplings at every meal) more foreigners experience the opposite problem—constipation. In fact, one of our colleagues used to risk drinking tap water in small quantities in the hopes that its contaminants would help her stay more regular. (Of course, we don't recommend this.)

DAILY LIFE

DIRTY FOODS

When we returned home from China, it wasn't the immense beauty or the ancient culture that I missed most – it was the food. Not just any food; the dirty food. Food of dubious origin sold from the back of a bike by illegal street vendors; food from grungy little two-table "restaurants" down dark alleys. *Dan chao fan* (egg fried rice) never tastes as good as when it's made in a wok that's due for its annual washing.

A trip to China would not be complete without savoring some of the delicious and dirt-cheap sidewalk foods, such as grilled lamb kebabs, tea-boiled eggs, spicy squid on a stick, and roasted sweet potatoes from mobile drum-barrel ovens. Nonetheless, caution should be taken. Look for food that is cooked over a flaming fire or sizzling griddle while you watch, not precooked. Stay away from meat that has been sitting out in the sun or exposed to flies. Be sure that any foods kept in water, such as pineapple on a stick, has not been soaking in tap water; if in doubt, buy bottled water and give the fruit a thorough rinse before you indulge. And if you are concerned about the cleanliness of your chopsticks or bowl, use hot tea to do a quick rinse.

© BARBARA STROTHER

street snacks

The name may not sound appetizing, but these bottled drinks will keep you well hydrated.

THE ELEMENTS

China is a land of extremes, and those extremes can take their toll on your health. Heatstroke and sunburn are common in areas as diverse as the tropical south, arid northwest, and the intense sun of the high Himalayas. On the other extreme, hypothermia and frostbite are possible in the frigid northern winters and the high elevations of China's dramatic peaks. Altitude sickness is a serious problem in Tibet that can be fatal if precautions are not taken. Use wisdom to protect your health in all of China's natural extremes; use sunblock, hats, and drink plenty of liquids to protect from the sun; wear adequate warm clothing and gloves to protect from the cold; and rest when your body is telling you to slow down.

POLLUTION

China claims the infamous distinction of having 20 of the 30 most polluted cities in the world. Efforts to improve the situation, like locating factories beyond the city limits, are unfortunately offset by increased car ownership, trading vehicle emissions for factory emissions. Beijing and northern industrial cities struggle most with pollution, though no city is immune; even the smallest mountain villages can produce a fair amount of dirty air since coal is still used for heating and cooking. Some days the pollution indices, reported daily or weekly by the media in most major cities, exceed the World Health Organization's recommended maximum level by three or four times or more.

If you already have heart or respiratory problems, you may have a very

© BARBARA STROTHER

doing their best to keep the parks clean

difficult time adjusting to the air in China's cities. To contradict the effects of the air pollution, use a humidifier and an air purifier, try to keep your home as dust-free as possible (not an easy task!), and keep plenty of green plants around to pump fresh oxygen into your air. If you long for a deep breath of the good stuff, drop by one of the oxygen rooms offered at some hospitals, hotels, and serviced apartments (though Beijing doctors recommend that you don't leave your home at all when the city's pollution index is soaring).

SMOKING

Factories and vehicles aren't the only ones polluting the air in China; smokers are playing their part as well. This is a nation with a serious nicotine addiction problem. One third of all cigarettes smoked per day worldwide are smoked in China, and 3,000 Chinese die every day from smoking-related diseases. As the top producer and consumer of cigarettes, China is blowing a lot of secondhand smoke. Fortunately the government is starting to do something about it. Many cities are starting to follow Shanghai's lead to ban smoking in public places, such as schools, supermarkets, teahouses, restaurants, cinemas, public transportation, and, long overdue, hospitals (where, incidentally, 60 percent of doctors smoke). Unfortunately, though the laws are on the books, little is done to enforce them. On the other hand, if you're a smoker, you'll still find plenty of freedom in China-not to mention cigarettes so cheap and plentiful that it makes nonsmokers wonder if they should start the habit just to take advantage of the bargain.

SPITTING

Regardless of the numerous "No Spitting" signs, fines for lawbreakers, and even antispitting squads, almost everyone spits in China. Male, female, young, old-you'll hear them hocking up loogies all around you. It's not only disgusting (especially when you lean up against something and come away with a green glob of goo on you), it's also the means for spreading tuberculosis and SARS. On its par is the frequent "farmer's blow"-holding one nostril closed to blow the contents of the other nostril onto the ground below. There's not much you can do about the spitting and the blowing, of course, except to be careful where you walk, sit, swing your arms, and rest your bags. And don't forget to wash your hands frequently.

Safety

ACCIDENTS
Traffic

They say in China the most dangerous thing you can do is walk across the road. With over 200 fatalities and 800 injuries due to traffic every day in the country, crossing the street (or riding in a taxi, or hopping on a bus, or pedaling your bike down the road) is not to be treated lightly. Pedestrians never have the right-of-way in China. To be safe, use the growing number of pedestrian overpasses and underground crossings to get to the other side of a busy street; their entrances are sometimes hidden inside a nearby shopping mall. It takes some time to learn to cross a street like the Chinese do; the best way to maneuver it is to wait for a group, putting the locals between you and the oncoming traffic.

Household

In addition to traffic dangers, expats face a greater chance of household accidents in Chinese houses and apartments. Sometimes gas appliances are not sufficiently ventilated, resulting in a buildup of lethal carbon monoxide, and there have been U.S. citizens who have died in their Chinese homes because of this. Pack a carbon monoxide detector with you before you come, and make sure you have good ventilation when your appliances are installed.

It goes without saying that no matter where you live, in your home country or abroad, you should always keep smoke detectors and fire extinguishers in good working order throughout your house. Create a fire-escape plan for the whole family and do a few trial runs until everyone is comfortable with the routine. Pick a meeting place outside the scope of potential danger. In

© BARBARA STROTHER

If you haven't got a fire truck, apparently a bike will do.

China the emergency number to reach the fire department is 119; ambulance/medical emergency is 120 (though taxis are faster).

NATURAL DISASTERS AND OTHER CATASTROPHES

Trains collide, airplanes crash, earthquakes destroy, political unrest breaks out, and wars start. We sincerely hope that none of these catastrophes will touch you during your time in China, and chances are they won't. Nevertheless, you should be prepared for the worst. The best thing you can do to help yourself and your family on the chance there is such a major event is to register with your embassy or consulate (see the *Once You've Arrived* section of the *Making the Move* chapter for more information). If they don't know you're there, they can't warn you of rising political unrest, or advise you of the right time to get out of the country. If they know you live in the area hit by a natural disaster, they'll be eager to make sure you are OK.

CRIME

Foreigners are seldom the victims of violent crime in China. The country as a whole has a low crime rate. Most expats feel safer in China than in their hometown; just knowing that individual gun possession is unheard-of in China makes a huge difference. Usually the most crime you'll need to worry about in China is pickpockets, con artists, and other scammers. The riffraff of China don't want to hurt you; they only want to share your wealth (with or without your consent). Take the usual precautions to guard your money and your belongings, and be wise when it comes to doing business on the streets. If you do find yourself the victim of a crime, dial 110 to get the local police (a.k.a. PSB, the Public Security Bureau), or just chalk it up to experience. Major cities staff the 110 call center with English speakers.

If, on the other hand, you are the law-breaker, watch out! Playing with the Chinese law is a very foolish thing. Don't assume that because you are a Westerner, the worst they will do is deport you. They have the right to sentence you to the same punishment a Chinese offender would receive. There are currently hundreds of foreigners serving prison terms in China, many for economic crimes like tax evasion and fraudulent business deals, as well as selling pirated DVDs and other counterfeit goods. But serious crimes, including drug trafficking, can be punished by the death penalty, and foreigners have been executed in China for such activity. In a country where even white-collar crimes like government corruption are punishable by public execution, you just don't want to get on their bad side.

Crimes Against Women

As a female traveler, I've had my bottom pinched by Russians and my lips kissed by an Argentine I had just met. I've been propositioned in Costa Rica and frisked by a passing Turk. I've had a family in Iran insist I sleep in their train berth to protect me from the single men in my assigned compartment. But in all my time in China, I have never been inappropriately treated by a male. While caution should always be exercised, most American women feel much more comfortable walking alone after dark in China than they would anywhere in the States.

The majority of crimes against women in China happen within the context of relationships. China has been on the slow end of believing that date-rape is truly rape, and instead tend to consider it simply a private matter between the couple. Domestic violence is a serious problem in China, especially in rural areas, but this won't affect you directly.

CHILD SAFETY

If you're off to China with kids in tow, there are a few safety concerns you should be aware of. To start with, many of the most basic safety restraints that we would never live without in the West aren't even available in China. Seat belts are ubiquitously absent in the backseats of taxis. Infant car seats can be purchased, but they will be quite impractical unless you have your own car or a regular hired car-and-driver at your disposal. Bike helmets and protective sports pads are also difficult to find because the Chinese rarely use them.

© BARBARA STROTHER

There's no shortage of fun activities for kids in China's public parks.

One of the best things about living in China with kids is the abundance of children's activities. Tiny cars, mini merry-go-rounds, inflated bouncing rooms, obstacle courses—all these and much more can be found easily as your family explores a city. But before you give in to the desperate pleas of your little guys, take a second to look things over. Equipment is simply not maintained in China; you never know when something will break. Call me overprotective, but I would never let young children ride a roller coaster at any Chinese-run amusement park. Besides, just because someone calls it an activity for kids does not mean that you can trust it to be safe for them. When we agreed to let our boys try a park's archery range, we didn't realize the arrowheads were genuinely razor sharp. The Chinese aren't known for taking safety precautions. You'll find plenty of pedal boats and bumper boats on ponds and lakes, but you won't find any life jackets.

Child abduction is not a common problem in China. Though your kids will almost certainly not be taken from you, you might very well misplace them. The swarms of pushing crowds in busy areas can easily separate you from your children. Stay close, keep emergency contact info on your child at all times (hidden in a shoe or sewn into a coat or backpack), and be sure your older ones know exactly what to do if they can't find you. Or better yet, get everyone in the family their own cell phone and make sure even the littlest ones know how to use it in an emergency. We always discuss a recognizance plan with our kids before subway rides on the off chance that we get separated while trying to enter or exit the train. Luckily China is a place where people adore children, especially foreign ones. Most kids who go missing are eventually found having a grand old time with a group of delighted Chinese adults.

Tourism can pose additional threats to kids. We once spent two days cursing ourselves as foolish parents as we hiked up and down Yellow Mountain with our three-year-olds in icy weather—nobody told us we'd be on the edge of slippery sheer cliffs most of the time. And I can still feel the fear when I remember taking them on a sightseeing ski-lift ride in Nanjing where one wiggle could have slipped them through the bars and sent them dropping to the treetops far below us. In both cases we didn't realize the potential life-threatening danger to our children until we were past the point of no return. It won't take too many harrowing experiences like these before you'll get a good feel for what is appropriate for your kids.

Travelers with Disabilities

If you are a person with a disability and are considering a move to China, you will want to think long and hard about that decision. China has only recently started to entertain the idea of building with consideration of people with disabilities. Though there is a much stronger push now to provide wheelchair-accessible facilities, they are currently few and far between. Photos in train brochures show beautiful attendants pushing smiling elderly men in wheelchairs along the station platform, but you won't find enough space to maneuver a wheelchair on most trains, nor accessible bathrooms. Stairs are everywhere in China; elevators are rare.

When you do find the rare accessible facility, it will often have a less-than-politically-correct translation, such as the wheelchair ramp recently noticed marked "pathway for deformed man." The Chinese also have a cultural tendency to unabashedly stare and point and ask strangers questions that make Westerners uncomfortable. It takes a very strong and even stubborn person to face the physical and emotional difficulties of living in China with disabilities. As long as you're determined and have correct expectations, you can make it work, and it's likely that in the end you won't regret the decision to go.

EMPLOYMENT

Thirty years ago, the first wave of expatriate workers in China were English teachers employed by universities. Today, teachers still make up a significant part of the expat workforce, but the opportunities for foreigners to work in China have widened considerably thanks to the economic boom. Foreign-owned and Chinese companies alike are hiring expats with skills in transnational management, global marketing, engineering, and more. And these days, teaching doesn't just mean being an English teacher. Chinese schools often welcome English-speaking instructors in a variety of disciplines, and teachers for international schools are in high demand due to the many expat families flocking to China. Whether you work for a local or international firm, are an executive or a teacher or something entirely different, you should expect your time in China to be a boon to your career. Working in China will give you the kind of cross-cultural experience that today's globally minded employers highly value.

© BARBARA STROTHER

The Job Hunt

Expatriates working in China will have vastly different experiences depending on whether they work for an international or a Chinese employer. Generally speaking, the international companies, schools, NGOs, embassies, and the like treat their employees according to labor customs in the home country, while many Chinese employers follow local human-resources standards, which might mean lower pay and less-generous benefits. In recent years the Chinese have been rolling out the red carpet to keep their foreign workers happy, but the Chinese red carpet just isn't as plush as that of most international firms.

WORKING FOR AN INTERNATIONAL EMPLOYER

Positions at China branches of multinational corporations (MNCs) are becoming increasingly competitive. With China' s growing prominence as both a manufacturing and supply base as well as a burgeoning consumer market, many MNCs are focused on China as the linchpin of their global strategy in the short and long term. Ambitious employees recognize the importance of being part of the China scene as a promising way to climb the corporate ladder.

For those who are successful in gaining a position at an MNC in China, expat compensation packages can be quite generous because you might qualify for more than one type of pay. First, the base pay is given according to the normal wages in the home country. Cost-of-living allowances might also be offered (even if you're able to get by on less). And you might even get the "hardship" pay, especially if your destination will be outside the key expat cities of Hong Kong, Shanghai, and Beijing. Expats who work for international firms are sometimes paid as much as 125 percent of the typical salary in the home country. And let's not forget the legendary benefits package that you might get that includes luxury housing, travel, a few more days (in some cases, weeks) of vacation, a private car and driver, and private-school tuition for the kiddies. Many expat compensation packages are no longer as generous as they were in the good ol' days, but working for an international employer is still an excellent way to go.

WORKING FOR A CHINESE EMPLOYER

Chinese employers rarely even come close to offering the same lucrative packages that international businesses offer, but they'll still pay you more than they'll pay their own countrymen. You might expect to earn 1.5-2 times the amount a local would earn in your position, especially for those in the teaching field. Chinese employers may provide additional benefits that their foreign

DAILY LIFE

DAILY LIFE

© BARBARA STROTHER

One of the perks of Chinese corporate culture: game rooms to foster good employee relations.

competitors don't; for example, Chinese schools typically offer free housing, cafeteria meals, travel bonuses, Internet access, use of the school health clinic, and potentially other services like an on-campus barber or foreign-exchange services. It can take extra time and patience, however, to learn to function in the Chinese business culture. Differences in cultural work concepts can prove frustrating, such as ideas about formal power distance (i.e., to what degree can a lower employee approach a higher one) and the sharing of information (i.e., you may not be told the dates of your upcoming vacation until just a day or two before it starts). But in the end, working for a Chinese employer typically leads to having a greater command of Mandarin and more Chinese friends.

THE HIRING PROCESS

Like any job search in today's Internet society, you'll probably apply for jobs in China via email, hopefully followed by phone interviews. If you are applying for a position with a major corporation, you'll have a series of in-person interviews and probably undergo a few weeks of training before being sent abroad. Because this gets expensive for the company, they often prefer to hire from within, unless the position requires a high skill level that you happen to fulfill. Management- and executive-level recruiting will probably be handled by a third-party human-resources firm, not the actual employer.

Landing a job with a Chinese firm will be done via email and phone. It's not likely the company will fly the candidate to China for the interview; they prefer to fill these positions with people who already live in China. But for high-level or highly skilled positions, an international human-resources firm in the United States might do the hiring.

Discrimination in Hiring

Human-resources managers in the United States work extremely hard to keep their companies out of costly discrimination lawsuits, but since Chinese society is not as litigious, Chinese employers are more open to discuss topics that are taboo in the United States. A job posting from a Chinese company might specify the ideal age and even list some of the personal characteristics they prefer. Don't be surprised if you find a job posting like, "Tall beautiful single women wanted as account managers." In fact, most Chinese employers require that you submit a photo with your application.

If an employer asks your age, they are probably interested in a person with a certain level of life experience. If the employment ad notes a married person with children is desired, that indicates that the employer is looking to hire someone who will stay in the position for a long time. If you are a young person who is newly married, you might be discriminated against because the employer fears you'll miss lots of workdays when the babies come.

Such discriminatory hiring practices are more likely to occur with a Chinese firm than with an international firm. Hiring practices at an international company would typically follow the same laws and customs of the home country.

BUSINESS AND MEDIA
Where to Look

The best way to find a job in China is to use your personal contacts. If you aren't blessed with such *guanxi,* then the Internet is typically the second-best option, unless you have the skills and experience to work with an executive recruiting service. Multinational companies advertise heavily on job sites like www.monster.com, while Chinese companies tend to use www.zhaopin.com. You can post your resume at Chinajobs.com and wait for the employers to come to you. If you're already in China, you can also check out the classifieds in your city's English magazines or attend one of Chinajob.com's annual job fairs. Obtaining a position from within China is less likely to include a nice employment package (such as free housing or paid travel home) since you may be labeled a "local hire."

What Employers Want

To a business, the ideal expatriate worker has the right mix of hard skills, soft skills, and language skills. Hard skills in demand include technical skills (including both IT and manufacturing processes), financial skills, international marketing skills, and legal skills, especially lawyers familiar with international trade laws. Having the right hard skills and credentials may land you an interview, but the soft skills like flexibility, maturity, people skills, and cross-cultural competency are what will help you secure a job offer. Not everyone can cope with the stress of living and working in a cross-cultural setting, so lots of expats end up going home before their contracted time is up. The expat "failure rate" for China has been reported to be as high as 70 percent. Human-resources personnel know the average Joe won't cut it in China, so expect to be scrutinized heavily before being offered the job. Employers want someone who can project a positive image for the company, and they certainly want to avoid the expense of sending an employee home early.

Having the right mix of hard skills and soft skills will qualify you for an excellent job in China, and promotions and pay raises will come quicker and easier than you'd expect back home. But if you want to start out ahead, the best thing you can do is learn Chinese. The best-paying jobs require a conversant level of Mandarin. Positions that require Mandarin fluency listed on websites such as www.monster.com tend to pay as much as $30,000 more than the same job without the language requirement. Even if you aren't fluent, any Chinese language ability will be beneficial in this job market.

TEACHING
Where to Look
English-teaching jobs or university teaching jobs tend to be filled via email and telephone contacts with the school directly or through a placement agency. A quick Internet search will result in numerous sites listing English-teaching jobs. Try www.ejobfair.com for thousands of positions at Chinese educational institutions across every region of China, including even remote and minority areas.

Some placement agencies match teachers with Chinese schools, provide predeparture training, and only charge a modest fee for the service. On the other end of the spectrum, some organizations, particularly those with a religious affiliation, provide the same placement service but require that their teachers raise a significant amount of funds prior to placement in a Chinese school. These funds will pay your living and travel expenses as well as health insurance, training, and ongoing support from the organization. To find a position without the help of an agency, the job fairs for foreigners held annually in Beijing and Shenzhen are a good place to meet face-to-face with potential employers if you are already in China.

DAILY LIFE

© BARBARA STROTHER

The door is wide open for foreign teachers in China.

International school teaching positions tend to be filled at the major job fairs each year hosted around the globe by the three main recruitment agencies: COIS, Search Associates, and ISS (check their websites, listed in the *Resources* section of this book, for the upcoming fair dates and places). Candidates need a government-issued public school teaching certificate and should plan to attend the fair to participate in on-site interviews. If you can't make it to one of the fairs, the best way to search for international school positions on the Internet is through a paid subscription to www.tieonline.com.

What Schools Want

English-teaching jobs typically require that you are a native English speaker and have a college degree-any subject will do; it doesn't necessarily have to be in TESOL (Teaching English to Speakers of Other Languages) or English, though the best schools may require it. American English is preferred, but the King's English will suffice. To land a position teaching English at a top university, you'll probably need a TESOL certificate. Having a master's degree isn't necessary to get a teaching job, but it will earn you considerably more in monthly salary. English teachers have primarily worked in the colleges, but quite a few high schools, middle schools, and even elementary schools are now employing foreigners as teachers. More and more Chinese schools are also hiring foreigners to teach subjects other than English. There are also a fair number of jobs at the new private schools teaching both English and other subjects. Just be careful, though, because an unproven new school might not provide you with stable employment or make good on their financial promises.

To teach subjects besides English at the universities, you'll need at least a master's degree, and more and more they want PhDs for full-fledged professorial work. Most of this work is still compensated according to local standards, which is still enough to live on in China, but nowhere near what a college professor would earn in the States. If, however, you are a highly regarded scholar who can bring prestige to the school's reputation, you'll be compensated according to international standards.

Teaching at an international school in China is an excellent option for those who already have their teaching credentials. The schools are run according to the standards in the home country, so if you have the appropriate college degree and teaching certificate (regardless of the state or nation that issued the certification), you're qualified to teach at an international school. Husband and wife teaching teams are popular, in part because the schools can save on the money they spend for teachers' housing.

English-Teaching Contracts

An English-teaching contract is a short document that specifies the teacher's workload and the compensation and benefits provided by the school. The contract will probably be signed by the school principal and faxed to you while you are still in your home country. Although the contract is a legally binding document, promises often go unfulfilled. Ask the school to put you in contact with people who have previously taught there so you can find out what you're getting into before you take the plunge. As long as the contract is satisfactory to you and the school has good references, you should be fine. On the other hand, the Internet is filled with stories of teachers who were victims of a bait-and-switch scam, where their salaries were lowered, or they were housed in tiny dormitories, or their airfare wasn't reimbursed, and so on. Using a proven placement agency can help you avoid getting scammed if you don't mind paying the extra money for their services.

A typical contract will specify the number of teaching hours; 15 is the benchmark for full-time teaching. If you have a higher salary, you might be expected to go up to 20 hours or more, which is a heavy load considering the time spent in meetings, grading, lesson planning, and participating in extracurricular events like English Corners or clubs.

The contract will also specify the teacher's monthly salary, which is typically paid for the 10 months that you'll be teaching and the 11th month when you'll be traveling or returning home. A good contract will also specify that the pay is "after tax," meaning that the school will pay your income tax separately rather than deducting it from your salary. On a one-year contract, schools pay for round-trip airfare; for less than a year, they may pay half or less. Since some teachers have been known to leave before the contract is fulfilled, the schools prefer to reimburse you for half of your ticket when you start, and then pay you the other half when you finish teaching. Your contract should also specify free private or shared lodging, health care, cafeteria meals, and travel bonuses.

Perhaps most importantly, your school should provide you with the necessary paperwork to get a Z work visa. If they tell you, "just come over on a tourist visa, and we'll work it out when you get here," you take the risk that the school may be unregistered and you'll be an illegal worker. On the other hand, since your Z visa will be tied to your specific employment, coming on a tourist visa buys you and your employer a little time make sure the arrangement will be a good fit for both of you. To stay legal, however, you should have the Z visa in hand before you actually start your regular teaching schedule.

MOONLIGHTING

Picking up some moonlighting work is a good way to make extra pocket cash. There are an unlimited number of opportunities to cash in on the foreign way you talk, look, or write. Don't be surprised if you are stopped on the street and offered work as a movie extra, model, translator, narrator, or tutor. Our kids were once paid to play with pool toys; the resulting photos were used on product packaging that would eventually make its way to Target stores in the States. A couple of Russian girls we know of were paid $1,000 per day to do high-fashion runway modeling in Shanghai, even though they had no previous modeling experience (their height and long blond hair helped). Although Caucasians tend to be the more sought-after subjects for the camera, even Asian foreigners can get acting gigs when studios need someone who is a native English speaker. Some employers request that their workers not moonlight, though many expats find ways around this, justifying it by their need for the extra dough. Keep an eye on the classifieds in the local English magazines and websites for your city for opportunities. If you're a student, check the billboards at the international student dorms or let your adviser know you're interested since organizations often contact them for leads.

Starting a Business

Some brave souls seek their fortunes as foreign entrepreneurs in China. In such a booming economy, starting a business in China can be a rewarding experience. If you want to be self-employed in China, you'll have to find a way to get your initial visa without having an employer issue an invitation. The best way around this obstacle is to get a "starter" job, or even register for a semester of classes as an exchange student, either of which will give you your entry visa. Then, once you are there, you can work on the legalities of getting your visa type switched when you need to.

With the Western expat community in China growing exponentially, some of the best small-business opportunities focus on serving this niche market, such as specialized import stores, relocation services, or international restaurants offering the foods foreigners miss most in atmospheres that feel like home. Professional services are another business opportunity since expats in China often don't know where to go for legal advice, document notarization, or to have a will drawn up.

Another wide-open business opportunity is serving the Chinese population who are interested in your language and cultural expertise. Your native English-language ability might be your most marketable skill in China. We once ran a microbusiness recruiting English teachers to come to China to

© BARBARA STROTHER

In this tiny factory started by a foreigner, women with handicaps make quilts to become self-supporting.

HIRING LOCALS

Quite a few expats hire locals for services including domestic help, drivers, *kuai di* (couriers), language tutors, and the occasional construction worker to help with repairs or remodeling around the house. All of this employment is customarily handled off the record, without the formalities of work permits, taxes, and the like. And the workers pre- fer it this way since many of China's laborers are unregistered workers from the countryside who don't possess official work permits for employment in the big city. Don't worry about what may seem like very low wages – expats tend to pay more than market wages, and unregistered workers are earning much more than they could back home.

DAILY LIFE

work in Shanghai high schools. With a little bit of business savvy, opportunities in tutoring, translating, or acting/modeling could certainly be developed into viable businesses.

THE PROCESS OF STARTING A BUSINESS

Once you've decided to take the entrepreneurial road, your next steps will be quite complex. As with any business start-up anywhere in the world, you first need research the viability of your plan. Talk to other expat entrepreneurs in your city and learn from them the ins and outs of running a small business.

We advise you to start your new business with a trusted local partner because Chinese laws place many restrictions on foreign ownership. You'll need to register with the Ministry of Commerce, the State Administration of Industry and Commerce, and the various tax authorities at the national, municipal, and local government levels, along with proof of sufficient start-up capital, before you get the green light. Depending on the industry, the start-up capital the government requires to see in your bank account can be extremely high, regardless of the actual initial investment your new company will require.

Along the way you'll be faced with the decision to be an upstanding, honest, law-abiding citizen, or take the ethical low road, such as operating under the table on a cash basis. As an "emerging" economy, that's just how much of Chinese business gets done. Playing by the rules, while difficult, is necessary for a legitimate business to start out on the road to long-term success. To play by the rules, however, you first need to know what the rules are, and they are way beyond the scope of this book. If you are seriously considering starting a business that includes employing others besides yourself, we recommend you contact one of the numerous corporate consulting firms that specialize in this kind of work.

AN ENTREPRENEUR'S LIFE

AN INTERVIEW WITH MARK SECCHIA

Although most business expats in China are working for "the man," some have found success going it alone and forging their way as small-business entrepreneurs. When Mark Secchia was required to do an internship for his MBA at China Europe International Business School in Shanghai, he decided to use the opportunity to start his own business instead. With fund-raising and business plan in hand, he and a few colleagues founded Sherpas, a service that delivers meals from Shanghai's gourmet restaurants to their customers' front doors.

Mark knows what it's like to take on the difficult task of starting up an entrepreneurial venture in China. Weathering the China challenges, Sherpas now has more than 200 employees and delivers meals from nearly 200 restaurants throughout Shanghai, Suzhou, and Hangzhou.

What first brought you to China?

I first visited in 1989 back when Americans couldn't even use Chinese money – we had to use special tourist money. The place was exciting, cheap, dusty, crazy, loud, and confusing. But I moved to China because of love. Not because of my (eventual) love for the country, but because my girlfriend moved here to teach English, and I followed. It was only supposed to be a one-year trip, but over 10 years later, we are married and still here.

What gave you the idea for Sherpas?

My wife and I would both get home at about 8 P.M. on weekdays. We didn't really like to cook, so we ordered a lot of deliveries. At that time, it was only Chinese food and pizza that were available for delivery. So we started calling other restaurants, and most of them said the same thing: They don't do delivery, even though lots of people ask for it. So I saw the supply and the demand and figured there was a market for it.

What have been the biggest challenges of running a small business?

In 1999, opening a company was a lot more difficult than it is now. Just trying to understand where to register the office and how to handle the administrative details was a nightmare. Now there are dozens of companies that can do it for you for a few thousand dollars. Back then there were only a few, and their fees were much, much higher. So to avoid the high fees, we actually stood in the lines and got the permit approvals ourselves. It was a long, very confusing process. Once we got up and running, the actual food-delivery part of our business was the hardest part to solve. Getting the order correct, not shaking it up, not tipping it over, not letting it get cold – they were all very difficult to do. Our couriers were not used to understanding the importance of food presentation and how important it was for the food to maintain its temperature. It sounds trivial, but it almost killed us in the beginning.

Can you give us some idea of the financial aspects of starting a business in China?

It took us 18 months to get cash-flow positive. I started losing my hair and gaining weight around month number 12. It is a big responsibility knowing that our staff was living on their salaries month-to-month, and we needed to get cash to them every month. The staff was fiercely loyal to me and the company, and if I could not pay them for it, it would be the biggest failure of my life. It actually took about four years before I could start to pay back my investors. In my business plan, I thought it would take two years. Luckily, for the growth of my business, my suppliers finance our growth. This is because we take the food from the restaurant and pay them back in about 45 days. So as we worked at about a 20 percent growth rate, it did not affect our cash flow. The last few years we have averaged over 50 percent growth.

What other jobs have you had in China?
In order, I used to be an English teacher, a project manager for Amway, sales manager for *That's Shanghai* magazine, and the general manager of *City Weekend* magazine. Mixed in were a few entrepreneurial failures that my ego prevents me from listing.

How have your impressions of China changed over time?
I now think of it as controlled chaos. Things tend to work out fine – you just have to let go of the desire to understand the "why" of everything.

What do you miss about life back in the States?
I sorely miss college basketball and, of course, my family.

What do you think are the most difficult challenges as an expat in China today?
The drinking and partying. We arrived in our early 20s, and there wasn't much else to do on the weekends except congregate and head to the bar. This is a dangerous routine that has impacted the health of many of those around me. Have fun – just go slowly.

COURTESY OF MARK AND LAURIE SECCHIA

If someone wanted to follow in your footsteps, what words of advice would you give?
It is easy to get the feeling that this economy is like a bullet train whizzing by and you just can't find a way to slow the train down enough for you to hop on. Just look for an opportunity. They are everywhere. Ignore the hurdles. Realize that when operating in China, forgiveness is easier to obtain than permission. Just get out there, and chase your dream.

Mark and Laurie Secchia

DAILY LIFE

Chinese Business Practices

CROSS-CULTURAL MANAGEMENT

If you're moving to China to take a management position, congratulations on your promotion. If this career move involves managing Chinese employees, however, there are cultural workplace dynamics specific to the culture that you should be aware of. One of the primary predictors of management success in China is the ability to treat your employees like family. The Chinese expect their supervisors to play the role of an uncle or aunt, someone who shows concern for their personal lives and even helps them through nonwork difficulties when necessary. Many industries are experiencing very high turnover rates,

© BARBARA STROTHER

the ubiquitous business cat, believed to bring fortune to your business

and attrition has become one of the greatest struggles of multinational corporations in China; promoting a sense of family among your staff is one of the best ways to combat this trend. Chinese employees will be loyal to a manager who shows concern for each individual employee.

GUANXI

As someone who will be working in China, you will need to be very aware of how *guanxi* will affect your business relationships. First of all, *guanxi* can be hard to break into. Even if you have the best possible product, price, and service, you may not get the sale if your competitor already has an established relationship with your potential client. Or your competitor may have better *guanxi* to offer, especially if they have a relative in a strategic government office or have a large budget to use on "gifts" for clients. Business in China is best done when it is *not* all business. Patience, and much effort put toward relationship-building, is in order. Getting to know your client (What is his family like? What are her hobbies?) and treating them to dinners, gifts, and special privileges are important for building business in China.

SAVING FACE

As you interact with the Chinese in business, never forget the concept of saving face. If you suggest a better way to do a task, a Chinese businessperson may refuse to accept your ideas, regardless of how good they may be. To some, accepting your ideas would be to admit that they are either intellectually inferior to you or that they haven't been doing their job well enough to begin with. You may feel that they won't heed your suggestions simply because they aren't their own original ideas-and you'd be right. If you find yourself working with someone who is like this, and your ideas are important to you, you may need to get creative in how you suggest them so that it won't cause them to lose face. Make them think it was their idea to begin with.

WINING AND DINING

In the West, business deals are mostly made on the merits of the contractual relationship. In the East, you won't even get around to contractual concerns until you've finished a number of rounds of wining and dining. Even if the business deal makes sense to you and your Chinese counterpart, you'll still have to participate in a number of banquets in addition to the obligatory business meetings. And don't forget the *guanxi* of banquets-for every banquet they host for you, you're expected to host one for them. Some Chinese businessmen won't trust you until you've gotten drunk with them, smoked their cigarettes, and had at least one John Denver karaoke marathon with them, which may or may not end with an offer of a female companion for the night. It's their

© BARBARA STROTHER

business lunch, expat style

way of building a relationship, and a strong personal relationship leads to a strong business relationship. If you prefer not to participate in something for health, religious, or other reasons, just explain that to your host. They'll understand, but you'll still have to put forth a lot of effort to build the relationship in other ways.

Contract Law

Contracts are legally binding in China. When a contract is breached, the offended party can seek financial damages and an order from the courts that would force the other party to make good on its original promises. To some Chinese a contract might be seen as more of a suggestion than a binding agreement. The biggest difference in contracts between the United States and China is in how contract disputes are resolved. If arbitration fails, then the courts must resolve the dispute. American judges resolve contract disputes based on the principle of "good faith." If your company signed a contract to purchase 1,000 widgets, then you are obligated by good faith to honor your promise and purchase the widgets. Chinese judges might rely more on reason than the principle of good faith. If your company suddenly has no reasonable need for the widgets, then you might not be expected to purchase them, even though you previously promised to do so. Most business transactions work out just fine, but if you do find yourself in a breach-of-contract situation, be prepared for the worst.

If, on the other hand, you are the one reneging on a business contract, you need to take careful steps to bring about a peaceful resolution. There are a number of American businesspeople currently serving prison time in China for business deals gone bad, and you don't want to join them. Since China's admission to the World Trade Organization, corporate criminals are facing stricter penalties, especially in internationally sensitive areas such as intellectual property violations.

FINANCE

Historically the Chinese economy has been a cash-based system. In the past, few people had personal bank accounts, and no one had a checkbook or credit card. The only sources of credit were loans from relatives, friends, village elders, and loan sharks. But today, like everything else in China, the financial system is changing. People are taking their life savings out of ginger jars and depositing them into bank savings accounts or investing in stocks or real estate. Thanks to the rise of e-commerce, credit cards are starting to gain popularity, and banks are now issuing more mortgages, student loans, and even personal loans to the credit-worthy.

All this progress comes with certain challenges. The exchange rate is continually inching lower, meaning your dollars won't go as far as they used to. And that old infuriation that's second only to death—the income tax—is now a harsh reality in China. We've made every effort to fill this chapter with useful practical information that's up to date, but keep in mind that the rules of

© BARBARA STROTHER

finance are constantly changing, and the interpretation and enforcement of the rules still vary from place to place. Use this chapter as a guide, but hire professional help if your finances are complex.

Cost of Living

The living standard for all Chinese people has risen dramatically in recent years, but unfortunately so has the cost of living. China's three most cosmopolitan cities, Shanghai, Beijing, and Hong Kong, now rank as some of the most expensive places to live in the world, although these statistics are based on a comparable Western lifestyle. Buying a car and a house with a yard in Chicago is much, much cheaper than doing the same in Beijing; but the difference is you don't *need* to buy a car or a house with a yard in Beijing, and you can get by nicely with much less. Compared to the United States and especially to Europe, living in China can still be a bargain. In the second-tier cities, such as Tianjin, Hangzhou, or Qingdao, your cost of living will be about 25 percent lower than in Beijing or Shanghai, and in inland cities such as Chengdu and Xi'an you can live on less than half of what you'd need in the first-tier cities.

Besides location, the other major cost of living factors to consider are

© BARBARA STROTHER

With a growing upscale market, China is not always a bargain.

© BARBARA STROTHER

A menu board shows prices for Western food.

housing and lifestyle. Housing in China can cost as much or more than what you'd pay in the West, and much more if you want something comparable in size and quality to what you'd get back home. The good news is that most employers provide housing, so there's a chance you won't have to pay a dime for the biggest expenditure that keeps China's cities on those most-expensive lists. If you do have to pay for your own housing, do plenty of research into housing costs in your city to make sure you can afford it before accepting the position. If you're willing to live like the locals and don't mind riding a bus or bike instead of taking cabs, eating noodles instead of steak, and taking trains instead of airplanes, the Middle Kingdom can be an incredible bargain.

HOW MUCH MONEY DO I NEED?

In the early days, employers provided housing (often including utilities), health care, and transportation for their expat workers, so you just had to figure out how much money you needed for food, clothing, souvenirs, travel, entertainment, and other daily necessities. Employers today still consider China a hardship post, but not as "hard" as before, so the benefits packages have been scaled back in recent years. This is especially true for those who go to China for one purpose, such as studying or teaching, then hire on with a business. (These types are often labeled "local hires," and since the employer knows you're already somewhat acclimated to the culture and lifestyle, you won't receive the same benefits package as an expat recruited from abroad.)

Prior to accepting your new job, do some research into the prevailing wages for your position and the cost of living in your assigned city. There are plenty of opportunities to work in China, so you needn't settle for a low-paying job or one with subpar benefits. China won't always be a bargain, so choose a position with a decent salary, and you should have an excellent lifestyle and even be able to save a few bucks for your future.

Minimum

In deciding how much money you need to live on, we suggest no less than 3,500 元 (around $520) per month for a single person who doesn't have to pay for housing. In first-tier cities this amount will only provide a bare-bones existence, but in cheaper cities it can buy you a middle-class lifestyle. Even though this income is the same as that of locals in teaching or administrative positions, an expat's expenses will be higher than those of a local, especially when you consider the cost of imported foods, international phone calls, Western restaurants, and the tendency to depend on taxis rather than navigating the complex local public transportation

OUR FAVORITE RIP-OFFS

In China, as anywhere in the world, you do well to trust the kindness of strangers. But, as everyone who's ever worked in the hospitality industry knows, tourists often have a fat wad of cash that makes them easy targets for rip-off artists. Listed below are some of our favorite rip-offs; sadly, many of them were learned firsthand. Unfortunately you'll discover your own creative scams as you travel in China. If the rip-off is for a lot of money, you might consider contacting the police; otherwise just grin, bear it, and learn from the situation.

- **The False Bottom:** The top 20 percent of your tea canister is tea, the bottom 80 percent is newspapers. The beauty of this scam is that it might take months before it's discovered.

- **Rotten Food:** Food vendors, like the guys with the ice-cream stalls, don't throw out the rotten food, presumably so they can get a refund from their supplier, but when an unsuspecting out-of-towner walks up, why not just sell it to him?

- **Not My Kung Pao:** If a waiter screws up an order, the locals will reject the food, putting the waiter in a bad situation with the restaurant boss. If foreigners are dining in the same restaurant, they might just serve it to you, and even though you didn't order it, you'll be charged for it. Always compare your restaurant bill with the dishes that actually arrived at your table.

- **Meter's Broken:** Your taxi driver claims the meter is broken and quotes a flat price for the journey that is probably way higher than you should be paying.

- **Each Passenger Pays:** If you fall for the "meter's broken" line, and agree to a flat fee for the taxi ride, when you get to your destination, the cabbie demands that each passenger pay the agreed-on amount.

- **Kickback Cabbie:** You tell your cab driver, "Take me to Ba Da Ling Great Wall." He drops you off at a big gate with Ba Da Ling written above it. You pay the $5 to get in, but then realize you aren't at the Great Wall, you're at some lame little museum. Before you realize you've been ripped off, your cabbie has pocketed his kickback, and lies to you, "I didn't know, I've never been here before."

DAILY LIFE

system. Foreigners who like to avail themselves of China's hip club scene will spend considerably more on drinks alone. For 3,500元 per month, you'll be able to afford some budget travel and a few Western meals once in a great while, but you'll have to go without many things that your expat peers will be enjoying. It's not much fun surviving on instant noodles and street food while your expat comrades are enjoying a Montana burger, fajitas, and cold Heineken at the local Blue Frog. Living on the cheap might also hinder you from hanging out with Chinese peers because the Chinese who run in expat circles are typically well-educated professionals, and their own incomes will be well above 3,500元.

© BARBARA STROTHER

- **Post-Qing Dynasty Antiques:** In the dark alleys of Beijing, people will whisper to you, "Hey mister, buy Ming Dynasty vase?" The thin film of dirt covering the vase makes it look authentic enough, but when you show it to a real expert, he'll tell you what you've purchased is a "post-Qing Dynasty" vase. Since the Qing was the last dynasty, any vase made today would meet that description.

- **Tea Ceremony:** This one's a Beijing specialty. A friendly college student (often a cute flirty girl) offers to show you the city sights, and your tour ends up at a "tea ceremony" shop where you'll be encouraged to purchase some exorbitantly priced tea and presented with the bill for the expensive "ceremony."

- **One-day Watch:** All over town, you can buy the souvenir watch with Mao waving to the masses or a shiny fake Rolex. They're called one-day watches because that's how long they will work.

- **Fake Waiter:** A friendly man helps the waitress take your order at a restaurant. She thinks he's with you, and you think he's the restaurant manager. He'll present you with the bill at the end of the meal, and after you pay him, he disappears. Then the waitress appears, demanding payment.

- **Karaoke Kickback:** Some cute, flirty college girls take you to a karaoke bar. The place is a dive, so you don't worry that the menu doesn't have prices. After a few songs and a lot of drinks, the girls vanish and a tough guy shows up with your extremely high bill.

© BARBARA STROTHER

If you like to do a lot of shopping, you'll want a budget that will accommodate your passion.

Average and Luxury

For a comfortable lifestyle in a first-tier city, we'd recommend 5,000–12,000 元 ($740–1,770) per month, which will give you the freedom to regularly purchase imported foods and beverages, eat out at Western restaurants, visit the sights in your city, shop at the malls, and travel to the far corners of China. Outside the most expensive big cities, this range will be enough for a comfortable life even if you have to pay for your own housing. But in Shanghai, Beijing, or Hong Kong, housing will add considerably to this amount unless you can make some sacrifices.

If you plan to do a considerable amount of traveling, shopping, and eating out, and especially if you want high quality or spacious housing, you'll need a salary comparable to or greater than an American salary. Modern conveniences in the Middle Kingdom generally carry modern price tags.

For a luxury lifestyle, the sky's the limit in China. If you require a villa-style house and will be sending a couple of kids to an international school, housing and schooling alone will cost you well over $100,000 a year outside of the first-tier cities, even more in Shanghai and Beijing, and considerably more in Hong Kong. Of course, most expat families share these expenses with their employers.

MONTHLY EXPENSES
Housing and Utilities

If your employer doesn't provide your housing, then you should expect to pay

DAILY LIFE

no less than $600–1,000 per month to rent a modest two-bedroom flat in Beijing or Shanghai, and even more in Hong Kong. You can save money if you're prepared to make a lot of sacrifices or share a place with roommates. In other cities, rents will be at least 25 percent less. On the housing high end, a Western-style suburban house in a gated community can rent for $10,000–15,000 per month or more.

Common utility expenses are: electricity 200元 ($30), gas 80元 ($12), telephone 30元 ($4.50), water 60元 ($8.85), cable television 30元 ($4.50), ADSL Internet 130元 ($19) and bottled water 38元 ($5.65) for two 4-gallon bottles, delivered. Of course these figures fluctuate, especially in the north where you'll use more gas or electricity to heat your home.

Food and Other Necessities

Food can be very inexpensive in China. If you don't mind a steady diet of rice and vegetables, a single person can live on $100 per month. For our family of four, a typical weekly shopping outing at Carrefour for groceries and household necessities runs around 500元 (about $75). That figure could be much lower for someone who could do without the Western foods we like, such as American breakfast cereal, cold cuts, imported canned goods (tuna, corn, etc.), imported dairy products (butter, cheese), and imported chocolate (the local variety just doesn't do the trick for us). It could also be much higher for those who like to shop the organic food aisles and for gourmet treats at the specialty supermarkets or stock up on imported wines.

Medical Expenses

Medical expenses vary widely. Large local employers (especially schools) typically have a clinic with a nurse and perhaps even a physician who will see you for free or for a nominal fee. The district hospitals and clinics are also quite cheap. A recent visit for a sprained ankle cost less than $20 for registration, doctor visit, Western pain medicine, traditional Chinese medicine, and X-rays (which we were allowed to keep). On the other hand, the Western health care system frequented by the diplomatic and business community is often priced according to Western standards.

Schooling and Household Help

If you put your children in a Chinese school, you'll have to pay fees to cover books, meals, board (if needed), uniforms, and administrative costs. The costs vary widely among the schools but are nowhere near the high cost of the international schools, which cost $15,000–30,000 per child per year, with schools in second-tier cities on the cheaper end. The cost to attend a private Chinese school is usually about one-third to half of what you'd pay at an international school in the same city.

For help around the house, you can hire an *ayi* for about 2,000元 ($300) per month for full-time (40 hours per week) assistance with cleaning, laundry, cooking, and taking care of kids and pets. *Ayi* fees are cheaper in smaller cities and get more expensive in upscale housing complexes with lots of foreigners (if you find a good one, pay her well or your neighbors might steal her away). In places like Hong Kong it's customary to also provide live-in housing, assuming you have the room. Unlike in the mainland, many domestic helpers in Hong Kong are Filipino and are therefore fluent in English.

Entertainment and Travel

The cost of entertainment and travel also varies widely in China. Traveling from Shanghai to Beijing by plane costs around $170 one-way for a full-fare reservation, while the same trip by train, hard-sleeper class, is only $45. To travel really cheap you can take a long-distance bus, half as expensive as the train but twice as grueling. Hotels can get quite pricey, but fortunately a growing number of trendy and quaint hostels offer beds for as little as $10 or less per night. Likewise, entertainment can be just as satisfying on the cheap if your idea of fun is watching DVDs (which you can get for a buck or two) or eating out with friends at inexpensive Chinese restaurants (where you can feed a whole group for less than $20). But if your entertainment includes symphony concerts, designer fashion shows, or partying until dawn with a continuous stream of mixed drinks in hand, you'll need to have a nicely padded wallet. Many expats sink a large chunk of their salary into their bar habit; an imported beer or nice glass of wine can easily cost $10 at a nice club.

Shopping

Between the bargains and the bargaining, one of the most fun aspects of living in China is the shopping, especially in the local markets. For those with high tastes and a high cash flow to match, China's shopping districts are filling up with international designer stores like Tiffany, Gucci, and Coach that are the real deal but offer no deals. The price tags at high-end stores often list prices as high as or higher than what you would find at the same store back home. At the markets, however, it will take trial and error to discover just how low the negotiations can go. Plenty of times you'll boast to a friend

BIG-BOX RETAILERS IN CHINA

Store	Ownership	Specialty
Auchan	French	Similar to Carrefour but with a larger wine selection.
B&Q	British	Home improvement.
Carrefour	French	The biggest and best megastore, selling clothes, bikes, hardware, electronics, household goods, and a huge grocery section that includes imported foods. The ground floor usually consists of specialty retailers.
Ekchor Lotus	Thai	A slightly less-impressive version of Carrefour.
E-Mart	South Korean	Hypermarket with quite a few Korean products.
Isetan	Japanese	High-end department store selling apparel, food, household goods, and various other products.
Metro	German	A bulk warehouse-style store requiring a membership.
Trust Mart	Taiwanese	Huge hypermart, but no imported food section.
Wal-Mart	American	Carries few imported items and mostly caters to local shoppers.

DAILY LIFE

about how little you paid for something, only to discover your friend got it for half as much.

Megamarts like Carrefour, Wal-Mart, Trust Mart, and Metro can be found all over the big cities and even in some of the smaller ones. As in the United States, these stores are chock-full of the types of goods consumers demand in their everyday lives. There are also plenty of smaller mom-and-pop shops that tend to offer better service without the maddening rush-hour crowds of the megamarts.

Your city will probably have some specialty markets where similar goods are sold by multiple vendors under the same roof, such as shoe markets, electronics markets, antique markets, and of course the fresh food markets (which most people call a wet market, but we fondly use the term "hepatitis market"). These markets are open during the day, but the really fun markets are the "night markets" where city streets or sidewalks are closed off to make way for vendors of silks, pirated DVDs, name-brand knockoffs, and fake antiques.

YOU PAID HOW MUCH FOR THAT?

In China you can expect most things to cost less than in the United States. Here's a list of common items that you might purchase and their prices (in 2009):

Item	Cost in China
Bus fare	$0.15
Pint of local beer from the store	$0.45
Apples, 2 lbs.	$1
DVD	$1
Pack of cigarettes	$1
Haircut at a barber shop	$1.50
Big Mac sandwich	$2
10-minute taxi ride	$3
T-shirt	$3
Doctor's visit without insurance	$6-15
Pampers diapers, 20-pack	$7.50
Haircut and style at a salon	$8
Hostel dorm bed	$8
Low-end bicycle	$30
Mid-range restaurant meal for 4	$30
Mid-range hotel room	$50
1,000-mile train ride	$100
New compact car	$5,000
Luxury car	$50,000

© BARBARA STROTHER

Temple Street Night Market, Hong Kong

© BARBARA STROTHER

night market bargaining in Hangzhou, communicated by calculator

BARGAINING

Bargaining is expected in markets and small shops, but not in large department stores or supermarkets. The best way to discover if there is room to bargain is to ask, *Keyi pianyi yidian ma?* (Can you go a little cheaper?), a hard phrase to memorize but one that will save you lots of dough. They'll reply with either *bu keyi* (nope) or *keyi* (sure), in which case you can proceed to bargain. The rule of thumb is to cut a seller's price in half and eventually settle on a price around two-thirds the original quote, though at markets that cater to foreigners the "real" sell price may be as little as 10–25 percent of the original amount quoted. A good way to discover a fair price is to check out the item in two or three different shops, keeping in mind that in China you often won't get the true price until you've started to walk away.

In the beginning you'll be overcharged quite a bit, but don't worry about it. If the price sounds good to you, go for it. Have fun and be happy that you are helping the local economy. As your Chinese-language skills improve, they'll see that you aren't a fat-cat tourist but someone who is really in the know. They'll give you better prices just for speaking the language.

Some belligerent foreigners who don't understand the bargaining game criticize the quality of the goods or insult the seller with their words or body language. Try to remain polite—negotiating is a fact of life in Chinese commerce, and it is all part of the ritual. Making a seller lose face will not help your efforts. You'll know you've arrived as a bargainer when after fierce and seemingly antagonistic negotiation you enjoy a good laugh with the seller and they offer you a freebie and a cup of tea. Now you are starting to fit in.

Banking

Despite how modern China has become, cash is still king in the Chinese economy. Consider your check-writing days over, and except for megamarts and high-end hotels and restaurants, most businesses won't accept your credit cards either. You'll have to get used to carrying around wads of cash with you. Whether or not you should open an account at a Chinese bank depends on how you are paid, and how you plan to manage your cash-flow needs. The risk that your home will be burglarized is pretty minimal, but since it's fairly simple to open a local bank account, why take chances? Unless you have reason to believe the authorities will seize foreign assets again like they did back in 1949, your money is safe in a Chinese bank.

OPENING AN ACCOUNT WITH A CHINESE BANK
Renminbi Accounts
To open an account with a Chinese bank, just show up with your cash, your passport, and any other Chinese identification you might have, including your residence card and foreign expert card. Fill out the forms, make your deposit, and you're ready. You'll be given an ATM card, but don't expect to be issued a checkbook. Your initial deposit should be in cash to simplify matters. Once your account is established, you can deposit checks from foreign banks, but it can take up to four weeks for them to clear.

Multicurrency Accounts
Opening a renminbi account is pretty straightforward, but if you want to open a "multicurrency account," you'll have a little more paperwork, possibly a higher minimum to avoid monthly fees, and possibly higher fees per month. With these accounts you'll have the flexibility of getting

Agricultural Bank of China

© BARBARA STROTHER

MANDARIN MOOLAH

You probably know what bucks, greenbacks, and smackers are, but how about *kuai, qian,* and *jiao*? This list should help you figure it all out.

Equivalent pinyin term	Characters	What's it mean?	in 元	U.S. equivalent
Renmimbi	人民币	Literally, "the people's money"	1	U.S. dollar
Yuan	元	Informal for renminbi	1	dollar
Kuai	块	Slang for renminbi	1	buck
Jiao	角	Literally means "horn"	1/10	dime
Mao	毛	Slang for *jiao,* literally "feather"	1/10	dime
Fen	分	Literally "point"	1/100	penny
Qian	钱	Money		

other currencies when you need them (dollars, euros, yen, etc.), such as for an extended trip out of the country, as long as you give the bank advance notice and pay a small fee. You can also switch between currency types if you want to try to make a profit from the fluctuation in currency rates.

With multicurrency accounts, your deposits, checking, and savings can be in U.S. dollars, Hong Kong dollars, British pounds, euros, Japanese yen, Canadian dollars, Australian dollars, Swiss francs, Singapore dollars, or good old Chinese renminbi. HSBC, for example, offers multicurrency accounts that integrate up to nine different currencies in one single account. Interest rates on multicurrency accounts also vary according to the type of international currency, with typically higher rates for Australian, British, and U.S. currencies and lower rates for Singaporean and Japanese currencies.

INTERNATIONAL BANKING

China's financial sector has opened up, and the authorities now allow certain foreign banks to operate in the country. Today you can physically conduct all of your banking at a branch office of an international bank such as the Standard Chartered Bank or HSBC, both headquartered in London, or the New York–based Citibank. These banks aspire to be just like your neighborhood bank back home and offer just about every financial service you might need, including multicurrency accounts, renminbi accounts, foreign exchange, credit cards, ATMs, loans, and even mortgages for purchasing real estate in China.

DAILY LIFE

FOREIGN CURRENCY

At the time of writing the yuan–dollar exchange rate is just under 6.8:1. The State Administration of Foreign Exchange in Beijing has established some very tight foreign exchange policies. For instance, there are a limited number of foreign currencies that are convertible into Chinese yuan, and reconversion from yuan back to the foreign currency can be difficult. It used to require the original exchange memo or proof of income earned in China, but nowadays you can simply walk into a bank with your passport and stack of renminbi to exchange. Theoretically there is a

the world of *high* finance in China, pun intended

© BARBARA STROTHER

cap on how much you can exchange in a day (currently around $500), but actual experience differs. You may get refused without explanation, or you may have no problems exchanging renminbi into several thousand U.S. dollars. You won't, however, be able to circumnavigate the system by trying to do a second exchange at another bank, because the transaction is submitted in real time to the State Administration of Foreign Exchange, which monitors transactions. For those that want to exchange a large sum, some have found it helpful to recruit a (trusted) Chinese friend to handle the transaction.

ATMS

ATMs are very common in China and relatively easy to use. Almost all of them have English instructions, though many don't have English on the receipts. You'll typically be charged $3–8 per transaction to access money from an international account, depending on whether the Chinese bank has a partnership with your bank. If your ATM card is from an account at a Chinese bank, you'll only be charged a nominal fee of around 2元 ($0.30).

Most ATMs have limits of 1,000–3,000元 ($150–450) per transaction, but some will allow you two or more transactions in a row (with transaction fees every time). To avoid incurring high fees from a foreign bank account, you may prefer to get a larger share of your pay in cash. We typically kept a few thousand renminbi stashed in a homemade book safe in our house, and hoped our *ayi* would not suddenly get the urge to read our English books.

FOREIGN CREDIT CARDS

Don't cut up your credit cards just because you are moving to China. Take at least one with you, and forget all the cool advertisements about MasterCard and American Express, because if any card will be accepted, it's going to be a Visa. Although credit cards will be of little use to you in the everyday street economy of China, they can be quite useful for online shopping, booking airline tickets, and paying at hotels and some restaurants. Unfortunately you'll lose a lot in conversion rates.

CHINESE CREDIT CARDS

It is possible, but not easy, for an expat to get a Chinese credit card, especially a dual-currency one. Local debit cards are much easier to come by. Some organizations, such as Ctrip, one of the best websites for making discounted flight and hotel reservations, will only accept local cards. The easiest way to get a Chinese credit card is through your employer; talk to your finance department to see if they can help you get a card from the bank that holds their business. If you're trying on your own, you'll need to provide proof of income (stamped with your company's official chop), proof of residing in China for over a year (i.e. a residence permit), and it will help quite a bit if you also have proof of property ownership (i.e. a mortgage). If these requirements don't fit your situation, try adding an employer recommendation letter, or better yet, get a good Chinese friend to sign a guarantee document. Now, that would be a good friend indeed.

CHECKS

Most banks will not accept foreign checks unless you leave them some collateral, such as your bank card. Because almost no one accepts checks as a form of payment, you can generally count your check-writing days as over when you reach the Middle Kingdom. Some expats receive financial support from their home country in the form of checks. With a check you won't be able to walk away with cash from the teller window; the Chinese bank will only deposit the funds into your account once they've received the funds from your home bank, which can take as long as 3–4 weeks. The funds can either be deposited into your account as renminbi or as dollars if you have a multicurrency account. Checks are treated like cash deposits when it comes to exchange rates, and there should be no fee associated with depositing them. In the end, however, it might be simpler to keep your U.S. bank account open and have checks sent there, then access the funds through an ATM in China.

TRAVELER'S CHECKS

Traveler's checks are not that useful for expats because they are only redeemable at high-end hotels and certain banks. Considering the fees you pay when you get them, the lousy exchange rate you're likely to get, and the inconvenience of finding a place that will cash them, they don't seem like such a great idea. But if you worry about misplacing your money, burglary, or an *ayi* with sticky fingers, you might prefer traveler's checks. We've used them while leading travel groups when it didn't seem wise to carry $20,000 in cash. For die-hard fans, you can get traveler's checks in U.S. dollar denominations at certain branches of major Chinese banks.

ELECTRONIC FUND TRANSFERS

You can wire money to China from a U.S. bank (or any bank, for that matter). You'll just need to give the U.S. bank the cash and the account number, bank code, and address of the bank in China, and pay the fees. This process should be relatively easy and quick, but sometimes it can take as much as a month for the full transaction to be completed. You might have better results using Bank of China, which has branch locations in New York City and Los Angeles, or an international bank, like HSBC, that has locations in the United States and in China. Western Union can also wire money for a lower fee, but since the money doesn't go into a bank account but waits for pickup by the individual, this process is less trustworthy (though usually faster).

Wire transfers at a bank typically cost around $40–50. A cheaper option, if it fits your circumstances, is to deposit the funds into your U.S.-based bank account and access the funds in China via an ATM. Just leave a few deposit slips with your parents or someone else you trust, and they can easily add funds to your account when you need it.

Getting Paid

The way you are paid as an expat working in China depends on the type of employer you work for. You might receive all of your pay in China; all of your pay could be deposited into your bank account back in your home country; or you might receive a portion of your pay in China while the rest is deposited into your account back home.

Keep in mind that U.S. dollars do not circulate in China's markets, so they

ZHONGGUO RENMIN YINHANG

中国人民银行

拾圆

© DOMINI DRAGOONE

10-yuan notes

DAILY LIFE

won't do you much good unless you are leaving the country soon. Chinese authorities want the renminbi to remain the unit of exchange, and they don't want money leaving the country. They want you to spend your dough in the country rather than export it. So go ahead, shop a little—it's good for the economy!

IN CHINA

If you get paid in cash, your employer can choose to exchange a percentage of your renminbi pay into U.S. dollars for you. They will inform you what the maximum amount is that you can exchange into dollars. Just make your request well in advance of payday to give your company enough time to go to the bank. Our old employer preferred to pay 70 percent of our pay in cash renminbi, while the rest was in U.S. dollars. We could always exchange the dollars for renminbi if we needed them, but sometimes it was convenient to have dollars on hand, especially for traveling abroad or reimbursing a visitor who brought us items we had requested from home.

If you work for a Chinese company or university, you'll probably receive all of your pay in China, and you might be paid in cash renminbi. Every two weeks you'll have to show up at your employer's cashier window where you can sign for a brick of money. With all large transactions it is customary for the recipient to count the money before signing for it. Remember to be discreet, because your brick of cash may be many times thicker than your Chinese counterparts around you.

If your experience is like ours, you'll sometimes be pleasantly surprised that your pay is a little more than you had expected. It's probably not an error—Chinese employers often surprise their employees with small bonuses, especially around the time of the local holidays.

IN THE HOME COUNTRY

Most international businesses will give you the option of depositing a portion of your pay in your home-country bank account. This is especially beneficial if your pay is considerably higher than your monthly spending. A young couple we know saved so much money over a three-year stint working in China that they were able to pay cash for a small house when they returned to the States. Check with your human-resources department to find out what pay options are available to you. If you *are* the human-resources department, you can learn the official regulations from the Local Labor and Human Resources Agency, the government agency in charge of such matters. Keep in mind, however, that the official party line is not always an accurate representation of how business is done in China, so you might be better off getting advice from a management consulting firm such as BCG, PricewaterhouseCoopers, or China Consulting Association.

WHAT IF I DON'T GET PAID?

Some expats who work for unprofitable Chinese companies or cash-strapped schools have been met at the cashier's window with dull stares and apologies of *mei you, mei you* (don't have, don't have). If payday is on a Friday, you probably won't be able to complain to management until they return on Monday. How you resolve the situation depends on you. If you consider your work in China to be humanitarian work, then a delayed paycheck is little more than an inconvenient nuisance compared to the greater good that you are accomplishing. But if you're not into forced humanitarianism, let your employer know that missing a payday is unacceptable. If you let them delay your pay once, you can count on it happening again. You'll have to confront your boss, and no matter how tactful you are, such a confrontation will most likely result in a loss of face for your boss. As a result, your relationship might never be rosy again. Choose your battles wisely.

You can also try your luck in China's relatively young court system, but don't get your hopes too high, especially because your boss will probably have more *guanxi* in the local community than you. Some expats whose pay has been withheld have gone on strike, refusing to work until paid. If the problem persists, you may want to look for other employment or return home early if there are no other options.

Taxes

As an expat in China you will likely be required to pay taxes both in China and in your home country. Ask your employer to help you sort out your tax liability *before* accepting the assignment. Your "Z" work visa will be based on the employment contract, so make sure your benefits package is structured for the best tax efficiency before the contract is presented to Chinese immigration.

China has tax treaties with the United States (and plenty of other countries) that are ostensibly set up to prevent individuals from being double-taxed, but the treaties are also designed to help each country catch the cheats. As you can imagine, penalties for tax evasion are far more severe in China than in the United States. In the United States you'll get a slap on the wrist and a fine, but in the Middle Kingdom you'll earn a free vacation at the "behind bars" resort. And since the tax bureau is now connected to the immigration bureau, if you're going to be busted, it's likely to happen at the airport just when you were planning to leave. Wave good-bye to your loved ones—it might be a while before you see them again.

Whether you'll be required to pay the Chinese Individual Income Tax (IIT) depends mostly on how long you have lived in China. If your stay is less than 183 days (90 days if you're from a country that doesn't have a tax treaty with China), you'll be exempt. If you're in China between 183 days and one year, you'll pay IIT on services performed inside China even if the company you work for is not Chinese. For those who've exceeded a year but have stayed less than five years, IIT is additionally required for all paid work performed outside of China that was done for Chinese establishments. Stay for more than five years and you'll be required to pay IIT on all worldwide income, regardless of who paid you or in what country you were paid (though you will also qualify for a foreign tax credit).

CHINESE INCOME TAXES

Back in the glory days of communism, nobody in China paid income taxes. The government was content to earn its money from the income generated by the state-owned companies. Now that capitalism has a foothold in red China, the standard of living has vastly improved, but alas, now everyone must pay the despised Individual Income Tax (IIT). Most fringe benefits are not subject to the IIT, including travel and relocation allowances, housing (unless you are paid a cash stipend), health care, language school, meal and laundry allowances, home leave, motor vehicle expenses, and the educational allowance for

DEATH AND TAXES

If you've been
in China for . . .

90 days	You are now a "tax resident" and must pay Chinese income tax (unless you are a citizen from a country with an income tax treaty, such as the United States).
183 days	You are now a "tax resident" and must pay income tax on all of your income earned in China (even if you are a citizen of a country with an income tax treaty).
5 years	Your total worldwide income is subject to Chinese income taxes.

dependent children. Official invoices for all these benefits must be submitted to tax authorities within a month of incurring the expenses.

The IIT in the mainland is a progressive tax just like in the United States. The first 4,000元 ($600) of your monthly salary isn't taxed, but for wages up to 20,000元 ($3,000) you are taxed 20 percent (after a 375元/$55 standard deduction); for wages 20,001–40,000元 ($3,000–6,000) the tax rate is 25 percent (after a 1,375元/$200 deduction), and so on. The highest tax bracket is income over 100,000元 with a marginal tax rate of 45 percent and a deduction of 15,375元 ($2,275). When you consider that 100,000元 is only about $15,000, 45 percent seems quite high; China's IIT rates are among the highest in Asia.

Workers in Hong Kong pay a 16 percent flat income tax on annual income. Similar to the U.S. system, the gross annual income figure is adjusted downward based on personal, child, charity, mortgage interest, adult education, retirement savings plan, and other deductions. To avoid double taxation, those who split their work between Hong Kong and the mainland should consult the guide on the Hong Kong Internal Revenue Department's website.

Unlike the United States, where income taxes are paid once a year, in China they are assessed each month. Employers typically handle the tax burden for their employees. They'll withhold the tax from your salary and pay the State Administration of Taxes on your behalf. Annual tax returns should be filed by the end of March.

Since tax laws are constantly changing and tax avoiders face harsh penalties, we suggest you consult a tax expert if your situation is complex. Companies such as Deloitte Touche Tohmatsu offer all sorts of legal and financial consulting, including tax advice, but as always it's best to start with your company's human-resources department.

U.S. INCOME TAXES

U.S. citizens who live and work in China still find themselves under the thumb of the IRS. Some U.S. expats who work for non-U.S.-based companies (such as teaching at a Chinese school) choose not to report any income because they know their employer will not report any income to the IRS. If the income is too low to warrant any U.S. taxes anyway (a salary under roughly 5,000元 per month as of 2009), you're not required to file a return.

There are several ways to reduce U.S. taxes on your Chinese income. The most popular option is to claim the Foreign Earned Income Deduction. You can treat around $90,000 of your foreign income as not taxable, and you can also add the foreign housing exclusion of items like rent and educating dependent children. A second option is to declare a foreign tax credit, subtracting the taxes paid to China from the taxes you owe the United States. So if you owe Uncle Sam $5,000 this year, but already paid Uncle Mao $1,000, you just have to pay Sam $4,000. A third option is to deduct your Chinese taxes from your income level so that you pay U.S. taxes on a smaller amount. You cannot combine these options, so pick the one that works best for your situation. Or better yet, consult an international tax expert and let them pick the option that works best for you.

Investing in Chinese Stocks

So, you've heard of all the capitalists striking it rich in this great bastion of socialism, and you want a piece of the action too, eh? It is true that millionaires have sprung up like bamboo after the rain, but most of these nouveaux riches got that way through entrepreneurial exploits based on their *guanxi* with powerful Party officials. As a so-called "emerging" market, there are still plenty of opportunities for investors to earn a reasonable return, but speculators should beware. As with anything Chinese, or Asian for that matter, investing is a complex matter with many subtleties unappreciated by the typical Westerner.

HONG KONG STOCK MARKET

Hong Kong has long had its own stock exchange, and the free flow of investment cash was an important part of the prosperous little region's success. The Hong Kong stock market primarily consists of stocks of companies based in and around Hong Kong. Mainland China–based companies whose shares are traded in Hong Kong are known as H-shares. "Red chip" stocks are from those mainland China companies that are largely controlled (30 percent or more) by mainlanders, especially the Beijing government. H-shares and red chips are valued in Hong Kong dollars and enjoy a much rosier reputation than stocks traded on the Shanghai or Shenzhen exchanges, but compared to Hong Kong–based companies, H-shares and red chips are thought of as inferior investments. There are no citizenship restrictions on purchasing shares of stock for companies listed on the Hong Kong exchange.

© BARBARA STROTHER

Hong Kong, banking and finance headquarters of Asia

SHANGHAI AND SHENZHEN STOCK MARKETS

In Shanghai and Shenzhen individual company stocks are either classified as A-shares or B-shares. Most of the A-share companies are controlled by the Chinese government. They are valued in yuan and can only be purchased by Chinese citizens or "qualified foreign institutional investors," meaning large financial services companies with at least $10 billion in assets, such as Merrill Lynch. B-share companies have their stock valued in U.S. dollars (on the Shanghai Stock Exchange) or Hong Kong dollars (on the Shenzhen Stock Exchange) and can be purchased by locals or foreigners. Whether deserved or not, the B-share companies have a poor reputation and are thought of as struggling companies whose best chance at making money is by having some deluded foreigner purchase their stock. In other words, you can't buy A-shares, and you shouldn't buy most B-shares, so you'll just have to figure out another way to strike it rich in China.

Of course not all of the B-share companies are dogs, so if you really want a piece of the action, you can open a trading account with a Chinese broker just like in the United States. Since most stock trading happens electronically now, you might consider opening an account with one of China's electronic brokerages like CITIC Securities.

INTERNATIONAL STOCK MARKETS

The best way to directly invest in China's economy is by purchasing Chinese company stocks that trade on international stock markets. Numerous Chinese companies are listed on the New York Stock Exchange, such as China Eastern Airlines (CEA) or China Unicom (CHU). A handful of others trade on the NASDAQ exchange, and hundreds are available over the counter. The bottom line is that numerous Chinese stocks can be purchased using a typical U.S. broker as easily as you would purchase a U.S.-based company's stock. In this scenario your dough is subject to U.S. investment laws, so it is presumably safer.

MUTUAL FUNDS

Besides the obvious "buy low, sell high" advice, you might consider the old "diversify your investments" advice, in which case you should put your money in a mutual fund whose investments are primarily in Asia generally or China specifically. Some of the larger U.S.-based financial services companies offer mutual funds consisting of Chinese-only securities, and there are also a few mutual funds that hold securities from all over Asia. Fidelity's China Region mutual fund, for instance, holds stocks from Taiwan, Hong Kong, and the mainland in many major industrial sectors. In such a mutual fund, the return on your investment should mirror the overall Chinese economy's performance, so you're unlikely to lose your shirt, but you also won't strike it rich.

DAILY LIFE

COMMUNICATIONS

For hundreds of years, expatriates in the Middle Kingdom resolved themselves to a life of isolation, but now it has never been easier to stay in touch. Though some forms of communication have not yet reached Western standards, others have surpassed those in the United States in both technology and efficiency. When you pick up a telephone, it'll work (even though you might not fully understand what the caller is saying). When you mail a package, it'll get there—maybe not as quickly as you'd like, but it'll get there. Mobile phones work better in China than they do in North America; texting became a mainstream part of Chinese popular culture long before American youths started exercising their thumbs. Instant messaging is a regular part of life and business in China. Books, magazines, and newspapers in Chinese and English are plentiful, as are television channels. Nowadays most cities have at least one or two dedicated English-language channels plus planned English programming at various times of the day.

Although access to media communications may be favorable, the content

© BARBARA STROTHER

may at times be less so. Media is one industry that is still completely controlled by the government. All books, magazines, newspapers, television broadcasts, films, and music come under the scrutiny of Big Brother's eye. Taboo subjects are banned, and the law dictates that all media must function in the role of upholding the Communist Party and avoiding all politically or morally subversive material. Interpretation of what counts as subversive is at times in direct confrontation with the Western ideals of freedom of the press and the right to information. Though censorship is alive and well in China, there are often ways around it. It won't take long before you'll discover the tricks to getting around the Great Firewall of China.

Telephone Service

Just like in the United States, ordinary telephone service is everywhere, and it works quite well. You can expect phone lines to be installed already in your home, and your landlord will probably have already turned the service on for you. Just don't expect the wall jacks to be conveniently located. If for some reason your landlord hasn't already turned on the phone service, or you are the rare expat who purchases a brand-new home that hasn't been wired, you'll have to stop by the local branch of China Telecom to arrange installation. Bring a Chinese friend with you to help you interpret and navigate the process.

LANDLINE SERVICE

It costs about 25元 ($3) per month for telephone service. In most cities you won't be charged for the local calls you make; instead you'll receive a flat-rate phone bill each month. A few cities have measured-rate service where you are charged for local calls. In Xiamen, for example, China Telecom will give you around $10 in credit each month. If you gab a lot and reach the limit, they'll turn off your service until you pay your bill. In high-end housing, including villas and serviced apartments, you'll probably never see a phone bill; it will be built into the cost of your monthly rent.

In general, you can expect telecommunications expenses in China to be less than half what you'd expect to pay in the States. Long-distance domestic calling rates average about 0.7元 ($0.10) per minute. Direct-dial international calls from China should be around 8元 ($1.20) per minute, though most foreigners nowadays prefer to use a VoIP service like Skype for their international calls. Your home phone bills can be paid at your bank; give the teller your phone number to find out what you owe for the previous month.

LET'S PLAY CARDS!

This handy guide will help you make sense of the different telecom cards for sale at the ubiquitous street kiosks.

I.C. card	The original cards actually had tiny "integrated circuits" built in, but nowadays it's just a simple magnetic strip that you swipe at the pay phone or just dial a string of codes like the IP card. The rates are higher than the IP card, but you don't have to dial as many codes, and supposedly the quality is better.
I.P. card	The fancy abbreviation is for "Internet Protocol," which refers to the fact that the voice signal is converted to digital packets and sent across the Internet. The quality might be lower, but so is the price. You also have to dial a lot of codes before calling. You can use the IP card for direct-dialed domestic or international calls from pay phones and regular telephones.
Mobile phone card	All mobile phone service is prepaid, so you'll have to buy one of these to add airtime to your account.
SIM Card	Small electronic chip that gives your mobile phone its own unique ID.

CALLING CARDS

If you worry about gigantic phone bills giving you sticker shock at the end of the month, you should consider purchasing prepaid phone cards. These cards are readily available at newsstands, convenience stores, and kiosks. The rates are discounted though somewhat ambiguous, but at 50–200元 ($7–30) per card it is easy to control how much you spend. The I.C. and I.P. cards are the most common calling cards.

A typical 100元 ($15) China Telecom I.C. card is good for about 200 minutes of local calling, about 120 minutes of long-distance calling within China, or about 12 minutes of calls back to the United States or other countries. Although everyone has a mobile phone in China, the I.C. pay phone cards are still useful because of the "dead zones" where there is no mobile signal (like subway stations). An I.C. card might

Telecom, ancient style

© BARBARA STROTHER

also come in handy if your mobile phone's battery goes dead. These cards are inserted directly into the pay phone, so you won't have to type in a bunch of numbers or try to follow instructions in Mandarin.

The most economical prepaid card is the I.P. card, which can be used from a pay phone or landline, such as in a hotel room or university dorm room. A typical 100元 ($15) I.P. card is good for about 330 minutes of local calling, about 250 minutes of long-distance calling within China, or about 50 minutes of international calling. The hassle of the I.P. card is that you'll have to dial a long string of numbers (as many as 35 digits!) to connect your call, and often there are no English instructions to guide you through it.

VOIP

The cheapest way to make international calls is to use VoIP (voice over Internet Protocol) service. To make free Internet calls, you and the person you're calling will have to download the software, and then you can make voice calls as long as you are both online. You can also use the service to call traditional phone numbers, but you'll have to pay a small fee for this service (but it's still way cheaper than direct-dial long distance). Leading companies include Europe-based Skype (and their Chinese partner Tom Online) for PC users and iChat for Macs. Skype now offers a service that routes your calls to you from a local number in the country of your choice. Now Grandma can dial a local number from her kitchen phone, and you can answer it on your laptop sitting in a teahouse in China.

HOTLINES

In every city there are informational hotlines that are accessible from landlines or mobile phones. These hotlines can connect you to emergency services, directory assistance, or weather information, to name a few. In larger cities most will be available in English. The national number for police is 110; ambulance

USEFUL COMMUNICATIONS NUMBERS

110	Police
119	Fire
120 or 999	Ambulance, medical emergency
114	Local directory assistance
115	International assistance
117	Time
121	Weather

is 120; fire is 119; and information operators are 114. There may also be a medical emergency hotline number that will connect you to Western medical personnel—of course if you are not already a paying customer, you can't expect too much help. There are also translation-service hotlines that will help you communicate with the locals for a subscription fee. All these hotline numbers are listed in the Yellow Pages; if you're lucky, your city will have an English-language version.

Mobile Phones

There's a saying that "even the beggars have mobile phones in China." In 2008 there were over 600 million mobile phone subscribers in China, and that number grows by 20 percent every year. This is due in part to their extreme affordability. Since Chinese cities are so densely populated, they need fewer cell towers to provide user coverage, resulting in cost savings they can pass on to their customers. Mobile phone service is both high quality and low cost, so you shouldn't have any problems. Make sure you pick from the top three companies (China Mobile, China Telecom, and China Unicom), and choose a phone with style, because in China, the ubiquitous mobile phone makes a strong statement about your personality and social status. And get your thumbs warmed up—your Chinese friends will prefer to communicate with text messages.

Even ancient warriors have mobile phones in China.

© BARBARA STROTHER

BUYING A MOBILE PHONE

Signing up for mobile phone service is pretty simple. Unlike in the United States, you won't have to sign a service contract. But you also won't be given a free phone. You'll have to purchase the phone, which will cost 270–4,000 元 ($40–590) depending on the features and style you want. If your city has an electronics market, start there—they'll have the best selection and the coolest new phones. Every major shopping center and all the megastores like Carrefour and Wal-Mart also have mobile phone counters, as do the mom-and-pop shops.

There's also some phone recycling among expats. Before you arrive, ask your host if they know of anyone who is leaving who wouldn't mind off-loading their phone. If you really want to go on the cheap, ask one of your young hip Chinese friends (assuming you have one) to find you a secondhand phone. Since these hipsters demand the latest styles, you can easily pick up last year's model for next to nothing.

SIM CARDS AND AIRTIME

When you buy a new phone you'll also need to purchase a SIM (subscriber identity model) card from one of the Chinese telecommunications companies such as China Mobile or China Unicom. This 0.5-square-inch computer chip slides into the back of your phone and uniquely identifies your phone's number to the mobile network. The card will cost you around 100元 ($15) and should include 30–50元 of airtime. Ask the vendor to show you their available numbers so you can try to pick one that's easy to remember. Of course all the lucky numbers (with lots of 8's) will already be taken; avoid any numbers with unlucky 4's.

After purchasing the phone and the SIM card, you still need to buy the airtime from the telecom company that issued your SIM card. After you've paid for the airtime card, just scratch off the silvery stuff to reveal the numbers, type them into your phone, and you're ready to start flapping your gums again. You'll have to pay extra to get the ability to make international calls on your phone (make the request when you first purchase your SIM), or simply use a prepaid I.P. calling card on your mobile phone to save money.

When you use the phone while traveling, you don't have to worry about expensive roaming charges because most mobile phone service is considered "nationwide coverage" even though they don't label it as such. Airtime is typically good for three months, then you lose it if you don't use it.

USING A U.S. MOBILE PHONE

Technically any GSM phone will work in China as long as it's set up for international access through your home carrier. Many mobile phone companies have reciprocal agreements, so even if you are "roaming" in China and make a few calls on your GSM phone, you won't be billed directly by the Chinese company. The calls will show up on your home-country carrier account, and you'll be charged an arm and a leg. To avoid the roaming charges, you can swap the SIM for a Chinese one when you arrive, but only if your phone is unlocked. Be sure to verify if it is unlocked or not before you go.

If you don't already have a GSM phone or if you don't want to mess with swapping the SIM, just plan on getting a new phone in China. Even for visits as short as a few weeks, buying a cheap China-based phone will come in quite handy.

Internet Access

In China, Internet access is more advanced than in the United States, where the Internet was invented. In fact, there are now more Internet users in China than in any other country in the world. Most Chinese computer users have leapfrogged dial-up and gone straight to broadband. The typical Chinese computer connects to the World Wide Web using a broadband DSL connection and often a pirated version of Microsoft software ($1 from the same guy down the street who sells DVDs from the back of his bicycle).

© BARBARA STROTHER

Wi-Fi hotspots are popping up everywhere.

THE GREAT FIREWALL OF CHINA

When the Communists first rose to power 50 years ago, the free press was replaced with a Soviet-style propaganda machine. The government has loosened a bit since the glory days of the revolution, but all media and communications are still subject to censorship today.

Television, movies, and print media typically paint a rosy picture of life in modern China. The media industry is one of the few remaining areas of Chinese commerce where foreign companies are not allowed to have majority ownership. Moreover, it is written right into their laws that all media must uphold the Communist government and protect the people from subversive influences.

The boom in Internet use in China has made censorship quite a bit more challenging for the government. The "Great Firewall of China" has been put in place, and many websites are blocked, especially those related to Tibetan independence, democracy, religious expression, or pornography. Wikipedia, blog-hosting sites, the BBC, and other foreign news media sites are often inaccessible in China, especially in the wake of a politically sensitive event. Even companies like Yahoo and Skype have been pressured into sharing information about their users with the government. Yes, even your Skype phone calls might be tapped while in China.

Censorship exists in China, but to what extent Big Brother is watching you, nobody knows for sure. Nevertheless, it's far better to be safe than sorry: try to avoid talking or emailing about taboo subjects. It's safest to keep your thoughts to yourself or save these topics for face-to-face chats.

contributed by James Bezjian

BROADBAND

Every major city has multiple broadband Internet service providers. Ask your pals which company they'd recommend, but generally speaking there's little difference regarding service and price. Of course you could play it simple and just go to the nearest China Telecom office and sign up for service. ADSL service starts at around 120元 ($18) per month for unlimited access and varies depending on the speed. Nowadays most housing already has DSL set up before you move in. If you have to install it yourself, it will cost around 300元 ($45), which includes the modem.

INTERNET ON THE ROAD

Most Chinese hotel rooms have extra phone jacks that you can use for dial-up Internet access; some even offer Wi-Fi. If you'd rather travel light and leave the laptop at home, you can surf the Web and check your email on the computers at your hotel's business center—most hotels, four-star and up, have business centers and charge from around $2 up to $15 per hour, depending on the class of the hotel.

You can also visit one of the local Internet cafés. Every city has Internet cafés, but you'll be amused that few of the customers actually go to surf the Web, preferring instead to play PC games. The typical Internet café is dimly lit, grimy, and full of heavy smoke; and most are hard to find unless a local takes you. The charge is usually around $0.50–2 per hour, and you'll need to bring your passport to sign in. There are also "upscale" Internet cafés with comfy settings, fancy drinks, and clean workstations, though these are very rare. A growing number of teahouses, coffee shops, and restaurants offer Wi-Fi; most require a food or drink purchase to get "free" access.

Accessing the Internet through mobile phones has become increasingly popular in China in recent years. If you have a GSM phone, you'll need to apply for GPRS service from your mobile service provider before you'll gain access to the Web. With licenses for 3G networks recently issued to China Mobile, China Unicom, and China Telecom, cell phone users can now surf the Web at near-broadband speeds, make video phone calls, play video games, and shop on the go.

INSTANT MESSAGING

Online chatting via instant messaging services is a vital part of the Chinese business and social scene. Take a quick walk through just about any office

STAYING IN TOUCH WORLDWIDE

Whether you live in China or anywhere else in the world, you can make it easier to stay in touch with your friends and family back home by subscribing to certain worldwide communications systems. Everyone knows that you can check your email in any Internet café on the planet as long as you have a Web-based email account such as Hotmail or Gmail. What you might not know is that a lot of these companies also offer Internet-based phone numbers and fax numbers. They'll assign you a U.S.-based telephone number so you can easily receive faxes and voice messages through your email account.

You can also set up a permanent P.O. box in the United States and request to have your snail mail and packages forwarded to your China address either as they arrive or periodically. The post office will charge you fees for boxing your mail and forwarding it to you. This system makes it easier for your loved ones to send you stuff, and when you move around, you won't have to mail out those annoying change of address notices. If you receive a lot of packages from private shippers like UPS, then you might consider getting a permanent P.O. box with a private company such as Access USA. It charges a small setup fee, a monthly fee, and then a per-kilogram fee for express delivery of your mail and online purchases.

in China and you'll see professionals in cubicles typing away on MSN (a.k.a. Windows Live Messenger). Though MSN is required for work communication, the younger generation prefers QQ, a colorful instant messaging service primarily used by young Chinese to meet new people and chat with friends. You'll need to be adept at using these for the sake of successful business and social networking the Chinese way.

Postal Service

Your expat buddies may advise you not to use the Chinese mail system, complaining that China Post is a stereotypical government bureaucracy that will lose your letters, pilfer your postcards, and break your boxes. They may convince you to use FedEx, UPS, or DHL. However, we've mailed letters and boxes from post offices all across China for the last 15 years with no major problems (not including slow delivery), and our advice is the opposite of what you'd expect. You may want to think twice about using FedEx and UPS because they are still relatively new on the scene and still struggle with the complexities of China's bureaucracy, especially with customs issues. If you are in a hurry, use DHL, or China Post's new Express Mail Service, which is available in the larger post offices.

© BARBARA STROTHER

the traditional way to deliver packages in China

SENDING AND RECEIVING MAIL

Letters and postcards can be mailed within China for just a couple of yuan or less, depending on the destination. Airmail letters or postcards to the United States currently cost around $2. Package rates within China are just above 100 元 ($15) per kilogram, and packages sent internationally via surface mail cost a little more than 200元 ($30) per kilogram. International packages can also be airmailed, but the rates will be at least quadruple the surface mail rates. Options like delivery confirmation and certified mail are not available in the Chinese postal system.

Sending or receiving packages can be a sensitive matter. To mail a package you'll always have to show your passport and fill out some paperwork. To receive a package at the post office it's the same story, except for those lucky occasions when they decide just to drop off the box at your place, which is more likely if you use your work address instead of your home address.

When shipping a package, you'll be required to purchase an official postal box, so bring your items with you unpackaged (along with your own packing material if they're breakable). The postal workers will look through your stuff for contraband before they smother the box with packing tape.

If you are shipping something abroad, write the address in English, and your package should arrive just fine. Airmail takes about 5–10 days to reach the United States from China. Surface mail can take as long as two months. If people are sending you mail from abroad, they can write your Chinese address in English/pinyin and it will most likely reach you, but it's best to include Chinese on the parcel. A bilingual business card attached to the package will help significantly, as will a mobile phone number where they can reach you if they can't find you.

Media

NEWSPAPERS

Major English-language daily newspapers include the *China Daily* and Hong Kong's *South China Morning Post*. Most Chinese cities also now have their own daily English newspapers, like the *Shanghai Daily*. Chinese papers are considerably smaller than American ones and sell for just 2–5元 ($0.30–0.75).

If you are a sports fan, you'll be able to keep up with American basketball, but you might as well forget American football and baseball. Instead, you might find yourself developing a strange new interest in cricket and rugby. To stay abreast of world affairs you'll have to use the Internet. In fact, to stay

© BARBARA STROTHER

Fashion magazines are very popular in Chinese cities.

abreast of Chinese affairs you'll also want to use the Internet; due to government censorship these English papers will often give you a sense that all is rosy in China even when you know it's not.

MAGAZINES

All print media is extremely affordable in China. Walk in any direction for five minutes and you'll soon find a newsstand loaded with newspapers and magazines. Even if you aren't fluent in Mandarin, you might still enjoy a local magazine once in a while. Most of the magazine will be in Chinese, but often one or two articles will be in English, and surprisingly, most titles and picture captions are bilingual. (I guess they know we just want to look at the pictures anyway.) A growing number of U.S. magazines are now available in Chinese versions, including the top fashion and home decorating publications. English magazines published outside of China are much harder to find, but local English magazines that cover the events and highlights of a city are common.

BOOKS

Books and literature have always been highly esteemed in Chinese culture. Today, you'll find numerous bookstores in every Chinese city. Small bookshops pop up in the quirkiest places, and as in the United States, you'll find bookstores near universities. The big cities have massive multistory bookstores that are worth a visit. Usually one whole floor is dedicated to foreign-language books. You'll find a decent number of the English classics, and a few of the most recent nonfiction best-sellers, but not much in the way of popular novels. Because of the increasing number of Chinese who are taking college courses in English, you'll also find a generous selection of textbooks and scholarly books in English. There are also special foreign-language bookstores in the major cities that have high-quality English books with high-quality prices.

© BARBARA STROTHER

an inviting bookshop at Fudan University in Shanghai

TELEVISION

Television is dominated by the numerous CCTV (Chinese Central TV) channels. The programming consists of quirky game shows, soap operas set in ancient times or sappy Chinese opera, news programs (all good news, of course!), and propaganda shows that highlight exciting new advancements such as a new pedestrian bridge or a calligraphy contest at an elementary school.

You can get cable television that will get you a few English-language channels and even HBO movies. The desktop decoder box costs around 1,000 元 ($150), but you might get one free from your landlord or from your local cable TV company. Monthly fees for cable TV are only around 30元 ($4.50), which might already be built into the cost of your rent.

Satellite TV is now common in China, especially in the high-rise buildings where the management company has purchased a license for the entire building. You can also pay to have personal satellite service if you have a place to install the dish facing the proper direction, such as a rooftop or a balcony. Getting a private dish allows you the freedom to choose a package of channels that fit your interest. Most satellite services, however, only provide illegally pirated access to networks from the Philippines or Thailand. If the channels they offer are really good ones, chances are the service is not legit.

Speaking of pirated entertainment, it is also quite popular in China to watch U.S. television programs over the Internet. Some Chinese sites upload the latest episodes, complete with Chinese subtitles, within 24 hours of the program's original airtime in the States. In this way, millions of Chinese can keep up to date on *Desperate Housewives, Grey's Anatomy,* and *Prison Break.*

RADIO

Like television, most Chinese radio programming is targeted to Chinese listeners. Some of the stations play a mix of Western music and Chinese pop music, especially sappy love songs adored by junior high girls. Numerous stations take their cues from Chinese opera and broadcast humorous stories and high-pitched traditional singing. Quite a few expats prefer to build up their music CD collection (just $1 for pirated music CDs from the street vendors; or just a few bucks in music stores, where coincidentally the music is probably also pirated).

You can also catch English broadcasts like Voice of America or BBC News in the larger cities. The language might be simplified since the broadcast might be intended for locals who are studying English. Needless to say, living in China might cause you to fall somewhat out of touch with world affairs, but on the other hand, just think of how much you'll be learning about China.

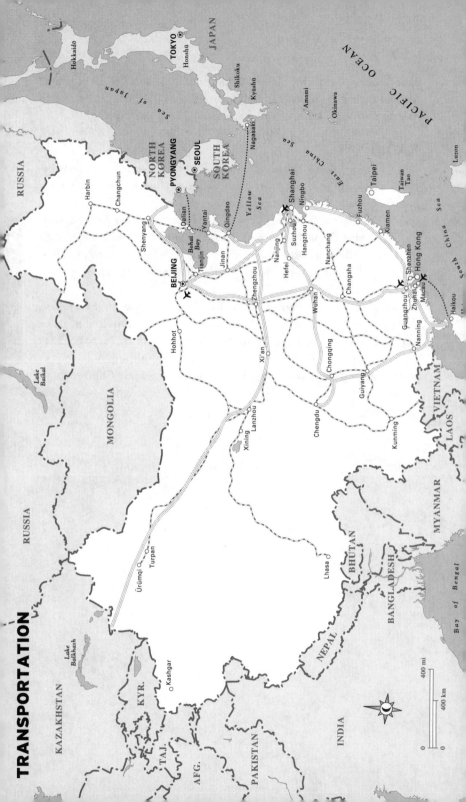

TRAVEL AND TRANSPORTATION

The Chinese transportation network is as vast and diversified as the colorful nation it crosses, from the world's fastest commercial train in Shanghai—the Maglev—to plodding donkey carts on the outskirts of Beijing. On any given day airplanes connect more than 160 cities, trains can deliver you to all but the most remote regions, and buses will take you even further to little villages barely touched by the modern world. And as the Chinese government continues to invest 15 percent of its GDP in transportation and logistics annually, the system is always expanding and improving. On the other hand, some of the quaintest traditional methods for getting around, such as rickshaws, pedicabs, and motorcycle taxis, are being outlawed in larger cities to keep up with modern times.

Much of your time in the Middle Kingdom will be spent in the middle of the masses on the move. A given day could include a complex chain of transport options. Our commute to church included a bike ride to a city bus to the subway. To get to our favorite shopping district, we took a taxi to a river

© BARBARA STROTHER

ferry to the local bus. And did we mention cheap? You'll pay a tiny fraction of the cost in Western countries to be whisked around in cabs, trains, buses, and boats.

By all means, get out there and experience the wealth of travel options in China—it will make your stay rich with unique experiences. Hop in a rickshaw, sleep on a train, fly to remote regions, and store up memories, photos, and tales to tell for years to come.

By Air

Although it is possible to arrive in China via ship in the east, train in the north, or four-wheel drive in the west, more than likely your introduction to China will be via one of China's international airports. Direct flights from a half-dozen U.S. cities take around 12 to 16 hours. Most international arrivals to the mainland come through Beijing, Shanghai, or Guangzhou, but more than 20 smaller cities have opened up to international flights from major Asian cities. These numbers have grown dramatically over the past few years since a goal was set to open over 50 cities to receive direct flights from the United States by the year 2025.

Within China, around two dozen domestic airline carriers can shuttle you among the country's airports with reasonably efficient service. The longest distances can be pricey, especially if discount fares are sold out. For example, a full-fare one-way ticket between Guangzhou and Urumqi costs 2,840元

© BARBARA STROTHER

hazy sunrise at the Beijing Capital Airport

(about $420) and Shanghai to Lhasa around 2,760元 (about $400) one-way, doubled for round-trip. Shorter flights, such as Beijing to Dalian or Guangzhou to Guilin, will run you around $200 round-trip, or even less than half that amount for discounted fares on the cheapest airlines. Prices typically decrease as the departure date nears; often you'll find deep discounts on flights that leave in two weeks and even cheaper if it's just a day or two away. In fact, if you use a Chinese travel agency to provide a fare quote, some will ask you to call back when your travel date is just two weeks out.

To book a flight, you'll find local travel agents and airline booking offices plentiful on China's city streets. Alternately, most hotels have a reservations desk staffed by English speakers who can make your travel arrangements for a small service fee. You can also book flights online (see *Resources* for Web addresses). Prices are often given in one-way fares; double it for round-trip, and estimate an additional 25 percent to upgrade to business class or 60 percent to upgrade to first class. Kids under 12 get a 50 percent discount; babies under 2 pay just 10 percent of full fare.

While Chinese domestic airlines now boast safety and service comparable to Western airlines, take note that traveling by plane isn't always the best way to get around the country. For shorter distances, or traveling any distance with children, we enthusiastically recommend taking the train.

By Train

The trains in China are a budget traveler's dream. Vast, reliable, and cheap, the train network can now get you to every corner of this giant nation complete with picturesque views of countryside and villages. Attendants regularly wheel snack carts down the aisles offering potato chips, fresh-fruit cups, instant noodles, watermelon seeds, meal boxes, warm beer, and hot water for tea; longer rides also have a dining car where Chinese chefs will whip you up a number of Chinese dishes. Not all train journeys offer the same level of cleanliness and comfort, however, so it is important to understand the Chinese system of ticket classes and train numbers.

In a socialist effort to rid itself of class distinction, Chinese train tickets opt for monikers that don't make a statement on the worth of the individual. There are no first- or second-class citizens here; only those that opt to purchase one of the following tickets: hard seat, soft seat, hard sleeper, and soft sleeper. The terms "hard" and "soft" do not literally describe the softness of your resting place—nowadays, all seats and bunks are padded.

TYPES OF TRAIN TICKETS
Hard Seat

If you value comfort and cleanliness, you'll want to avoid the hard-seat section on all but the shortest train routes. Although dirt-cheap (about $6 for a four-hour ride from Nanjing to Shanghai; about $2 Shanghai to Suzhou, less than an hour), hard-seat cars are often packed tight with travelers sitting shoulder to shoulder on upright benches that are *supposed* to fit just three. On longer rides the floor fills up with discarded shells of nuts and tea-boiled eggs, watermelon rinds, litter, green spatters of spittle, and an occasional wetness from a toddler clothed in the traditional open-bottomed pants. And don't even think about using the hole-in-the-floor, handrail-on-the-wall, squat pot "toilets" after the first few minutes into your hard-seat journey. When the train jolts, the watery mess will splash from the floor up your pant leg. Hard-seat class is recommended for only three occasions—if you want to travel dirt cheap on a super-short trip, if you want to rub shoulders (literally) with the locals and experience the hardship of "real China," or if you have your heart set on a trip and all the other tickets are sold out. Have fun—just don't say we didn't warn you.

Soft Seat

Soft seat is a great improvement over hard seat. A ticket in this class will get you an assigned seat (no overbooking allowed) on a carpeted train car featuring lacy curtains, tablecloths, seat covers, air-conditioning, and clean

Train travel is a relaxing way to see the country.

© BARBARA STROTHER

bathrooms with choice of Western toilet or Eastern squat pot. Slightly more expensive than hard seat (in comparison, Shanghai to Nanjing runs $10 to $16 depending on the speed, around double the cost of hard seat but still cheap), this class offers a pleasant environment for you and your friends to sip tea and play cards while watching terraced hills and rice paddies pass by. Unfortunately soft-seat cars are only available on a few of the shorter trains between major destinations.

Hard Sleeper

For overnight journeys, hard sleeper is our favorite way to travel. Six bunks in an open compartment face a corridor with fold-down window seats. Pricing is based on the bunk's position. The highest bunk is the cheapest, offering little headroom but a good option for tall travelers who can stretch their feet out into the corridor without bothering anyone walking by. The bottom bunk is the most expensive due to its conveniences: under-bed storage, easy use of the mini-table and hot water thermos, and a convenient place to sit during daylight hours. Unfortunately everyone else will also find your bottom bunk a nice place to sit, and you may long for the American ethos of personal space. Alternatively, many foreigners find the middle bunk the best option. With a middle bunk you can choose when to join your bunk-mates in a game of *xiangqi* (Chinese chess) and when to hide away comfortably on your bunk with your iPod and a good book. Sample fare: Beijing in the north to Guangzhou in the south, 22 hours, $64).

Soft Sleeper

If you cherish your privacy, a soft sleeper ticket will buy your way into a two- or four-bunk compartment with locking door and the ability to control the lights, speakers, and vent. The newer trains also boast individual TV screens and outlets for laptop use. The luxury is reflected in the price, though, and for some destinations soft sleeper is as expensive as flying, but keep in mind you are also saving the expense of a hotel night when you sleep on the train. The most common soft-sleeper route is the Shanghai–Beijing express train, 12 hours, $72.

BUYING TRAIN TICKETS

Most major cities have a ticket window at the train station specifically for English speakers. Or, for a service fee, use a local travel agent or hotel ticket-reservation desk. Biannual train booklets with intricately detailed timetables and ticket pricing can be purchased near the ticket windows at the station. No English versions are available yet, and the guide is complex, but if you can work your way through it, you can come up with all kinds of exciting travel plans. For a quick reference, enter your destination at www.chinahighlights .com/chinatrains for information on the trains that cover your desired route.

Train tickets usually can't be purchased by individuals more than three or four days ahead of your travel date. The exception is during key holiday seasons, when the tickets go on sale a few weeks ahead of time. These tickets are very hard to come by, however, since millions of Chinese will be crisscrossing the nation during the Chinese holidays to visit family and do touring of their own. The best way around these complications is to trust the purchase to a Chinese travel agent who can work their connections to obtain your tickets in advance. As for return tickets, most can't be purchased until you reach your destination station (a stressful reality for anyone who has to get back to work in time), but as China's train system becomes computerized, some round-trip tickets can now be purchased at major train stations.

Kids get a discount on train tickets based on their height. The littlest ones can share your bunk, saving money and giving parents peace of mind that their tiny tots won't fall out of the bunk with the occasional jolts of the train. Compared to the discontent of being strapped into a plane seat, the freedom kids have on the train to walk around and climb on the bunks far outweighs the lack of good rest a parent may get being squeezed between their little snoozer and the edge of the skinny bunk.

TYPES OF TRAINS

All trains in China have an alphanumeric label based on their age and speed. Train numbers starting with a D are the newest and fastest express trains in the fleet, followed by Z trains, each boasting its own "luxury" perks. Comfortable compartments (by Chinese standards) may offer amenities such as personal TV screens, individual reading lights, wireless Internet access, a place to plug in your laptop, a menu with both Western and Chinese options, and even breakfast delivered in bed in the morning. Heck, they even give you complimentary noodles if it's your birthday (birthday song not included). The majority of the D trains have only soft sleepers, but the prices are not that much higher than the cost of hard sleepers on older trains traveling the same route.

The T trains used to be the fastest and most luxurious class of express train before the Z and D trains were released in 2004 and 2008, respectively. These T trains feature all classes of seats and sleepers and crisscross the country in every direction. The next step down, K trains, are a little slower and cheaper still. Trains labeled with an N, or those without any letters at all, are slower and older, dirty, and dirt cheap. You'll encounter these trains most often if you like to head off the beaten path because they don't usually run between major tourist cities (and if they do, they'll stop at every Podunk town between them).

As a general guideline for overnight routes, T trains add a couple of hours to the Z train schedules, and D trains subtract an hour or two; K, N, and numeric trains add at least four to five hours or more with a decreased price and a decreased comfort level.

Two bits of advice for train travel: First, don't lose your ticket on the train because you will have to show it to exit the station at your destination. And second, travel light. You'll have to lug your bags down several flights of stairs to board the train. Escalators going up are common enough in China, but down escalators are much rarer, even in train station areas where you'd think they would find it rather helpful to provide them. Besides, the baggage space is small—you may have to share your skinny bunk with your chubby Samsonite if it doesn't fit in your luggage area.

SUBWAY

While you'll probably use the long-distance train system on breaks and holidays, daily you'll probably find yourself on a different sort of train—the subway. Residents of Hong Kong, Shanghai, Beijing, and Guangzhou (and to a lesser extent, Tianjin, Nanjing, and a handful of other cities with expanding

© BARBARA STROTHER

Hong Kong's metro system is fast and efficient.

subway systems in the works) will want to be intimately acquainted with the subway system in their city. Often faster than taxis and always cheaper, the subway is the most efficient mode of transport around China's crowded cities. Most cities prorate the fares based on distance, though some have a flat use fee. Typical fares run between 2元 and 8元 ($0.30–1.20); tickets are purchased at booths or machines displaying subway maps that show the fare for each stop. Multiuse passes are an even easier way to ride, especially in Hong Kong where the so-called Octopus card can be used for more than just the subway, including vending machines, parking, and stores like 7-Eleven.

You'll find the Chinese subways to be quite English-friendly. Arrival announcements in most cities are made in English as well as Chinese, and route maps give the names of stations in pinyin as well as characters. The biggest drawback of the subway is the pushing and jostling that goes on as the masses force their way onto overcrowded trains at rush hours. As with any crowded subway system around the world, watch your bags and pockets for wandering hands.

By Bus

LONG-DISTANCE BUS

Long-distance travel by bus can be rather slow and uncomfortable. There are few times when self-arranged long-distance travel is best by bus. For instance, short distances such as Shanghai to Hangzhou can take the same amount of time by train or bus, but if you are located closer to the bus station than the train station, it may save time and money. Because the demand is less (except during major holidays), tickets are cheaper and easier to come by than other modes of transportation. Besides, China's long-distance buses can get you to even the tiniest of mountain hamlets, which is their greatest appeal—offering unparalleled first-hand experience of the China your grandparents saw in picture books when they were children.

The buses plying the most popular routes will be relatively clean, comfortable, and air-conditioned, with some showing movies during the ride. If your destination is small or remote, however, you may get stuck on an overpacked, under-padded ratty old bus with farmers taking bags of live ducks to the market.

Sleeper buses offer reclining seats or two-tier bunks, the cheapest way to spend the night and reach your destination at the same time. Check out the bus before you commit, though, because some of the sleeper buses are quite dirty.

All long-distance buses will stop for meals and bathroom breaks at places that will give you great stories to tell of your bravery and adventurous spirit.

Our advice: bring your own snacks, and drink as little liquid as possible on these trips, especially if you are female.

Tickets

Except for major holidays, you can just show up at the bus station and buy a ticket on the day you want to travel—just get there early enough to accommodate for the possibility of long lines and communication woes. Try to get as much information as possible on your options. They may sell you a ticket on the next departing bus without bothering to mention that if you waited another half hour, you could upgrade your seat on the jalopy to an air-conditioned luxury bus for a fraction more. Tickets can be purchased at marked windows or directly from the attendant on the bus.

CITY BUSES

For those who don't live close to a subway line, the public bus system can take you just about anywhere in the city—that is, if you can find the route you need. Bus-stop signs list the routes, but without a lick of English or even pinyin, it can take quite a bit of effort to figure it out. City maps, however, list bus numbers along each street. If your English map doesn't show bus numbers, pick up a Chinese map at the nearest bookstore, train station, or tourist site and compare the two to find the route you need. Typically you won't have to wait more than 5 or 10 minutes for the next bus to come.

Public buses are dirt cheap, typically just 1元 ($0.15), unless you choose an air-conditioned bus (labeled with a K or a snowflake) for the exorbitant rate of 2–3元 ($0.30–0.45). When traveling in the summertime with toddlers we found these air-conditioned buses a great place for our kids to catch a quick nap while we enjoyed a cheap city tour sans heat wave. If there is no coin-drop when you get on, you'll pay the conductor. Just take

Double decker trams and buses are a fun way to navigate Hong Kong.

© BARBARA STROTHER

a seat and she'll come to you. Some common routes feature double-decker buses, some with an open roof on the second level. Most buses stop running around 11 P.M.

When you do get settled into the Chinese neighborhood you'll call home, experiment with the local buses. You can always grab a cheap and easy taxi back home if you end up stranded in an unknown part of town. Riding buses through the neighborhoods is how we found some of our favorite restaurants, tailors, and markets. You never know what you'll discover. Be aware, though, that rush hour can be unpleasantly jammed full of shoving, elbowing locals who may be a little too interested in what's in your wallet.

By Boat

In China you may find yourself more often afloat than you would back home. Boats are a part of the spice that gives China its unique flavor, such as dragon boats on idyllic lakes, morning commutes by Hong Kong ferry, and gondolas still plying the ancient canals of river towns.

Not so long ago, traveling long distances by ship in China could open up a whole world of high-seas adventures. Sadly, as roads, railways, and air routes become more efficient, many of the old passenger ship routes are being discontinued. A few good routes still exist, though, protected by the poor accessibility via land to these destinations. Dalian's peninsular location provides numerous options for traveling by boat, as well as the many islands and inlets of the South China Sea around Hong Kong, Macau, and Hainan Island.

RIVERBOATS

Riverboats, although sometimes excruciatingly slow, offer an unparalleled view into life along China's waterways as they meander China's inland rivers and canals. Luxury cruise lines glide along the Three Gorges from Chongqing to Wuhan on one of the most famous river cruise routes in the world. The Three Gorges cruise cabins are comparable to 3- to 5-star hotel rooms but with a much higher price. Other less-glamorous river routes, such as Nanjing to Shanghai along the Yangtze or Hangzhou to Suzhou along the old Grand Canal, offer slow passage in less-than-luxurious rooms with an up-close look at life along—and on—the river. For any Yangtze River trip, keep in mind that the closer you get to the sea, the wider the mighty Yangtze becomes—eventually too wide to see anything except a dull expanse of muddy brown water in all directions.

DAILY LIFE

© BARBARA STROTHER

The Hong Kong harbor is always busy with boats, ships, and ferries.

CITY FERRIES

There are a handful of cities in China that use ferries in their everyday commuting. Hong Kong, with its hundreds of islands, depends on its extensive ferryboat system to keep its island-hopping commuters on the move. On a much smaller scale, Shanghai's ferries can be the fastest—not to mention most scenic—way to cross between Puxi and Pudong if both your origin and destination lie close to the river. At less than $0.25 per trip, you get to avoid the bridge and tunnel traffic, and you can even bring your bike or motorcycle across the river if you'd like. Ferry routes are marked on most city maps.

By Car

They say the most dangerous thing you can do in China is walk across the street. Every day, traffic accidents claim the lives of 300 people in China, and more than 85 percent of these fatalities are due to negligent drivers. As the national economy continues to boom, car ownership is multiplying at a dizzying rate, filling the streets with more inexperienced drivers and new vehicles than the roads can hold. Despite the risks and the major traffic congestion, getting around on four wheels—whether by taxi or private car—is probably the way you'll most often get to where you need to go.

TAXI SERVICE

Compared to other major cities around the world, China's taxis are cheap and plentiful. Beijing has five times more taxis than New York City. While taking taxis daily would be cost-prohibitive in most countries, Chinese cabs cost just a few bucks per ride. Taxi fares start around 12元 ($1.75) for the first three to five kilometers and 2元 ($0.30) for each kilometer thereafter, varying by city and type of taxi. Tips are never expected for a typical ride, although daily rentals expect a little extra for their services and may want you to pick up the lunch tab as well. Except for rainy days and rush hours (and especially rainy rush hours), it should be relatively easy to find a cab. Just step up to your nearest street curb and start waving your hand. Any movement will do since cabbies intently watch foreigners for the slightest sign that their taxi services may be needed. If you tell the driver where you want to go and he turns you down, it may be that he is holding out for a higher fare, or it may be that regulations forbid him from taking the route needed to reach your destination. Some cities limit the number of cabs that can use busy tunnels or bridges on certain days and times.

One of the most difficult aspects of using cabs is the lack of English spoken

A TAXI OF ANOTHER COLOR

When you hear the term *taxi cab*, what do you picture? Something with four wheels, no doubt, perhaps a yellow car with a rectangular light on top. But in China you may be surprised to find what the local taxi service looks like. In Turpan, donkeys pull you through the city in wooden carts covered in colorful rugs. Along Suzhou's canals and Beijing's *hutongs*, three-wheeled bicycles called pedicabs offer a comfortable bench seat for two behind a thick-calved pedaler. In Nanjing's Confucian Temple area, rickshaws take you to your shopping destination powered the old fashioned way – the feet of the coolie. River towns built around waterways offer gondola taxis, and elsewhere motorcycles are enclosed in sheet-metal compartments resembling micro-minivans.

By all means, if your journey is a short one, use the local transport. They are a great way to celebrate the adventure of living in China. They may be slower, but they allow you more opportunity to take in the sounds and smells and back-alley sights of the world you are traveling in. You'll never think the same way about what it means to take a "taxi" again.

© BARBARA STROTHER

The nickname for these motorcycle taxis is *ben ben che*, "stupid stupid car."

by drivers. If you find one that can say more than "Hello," consider yourself lucky—and get his phone number to request his services regularly. Otherwise, the most foolproof way to communicate with a taxi driver is on paper. Grab a business card from your hotel or a business near your home for the return ride. Have a bilingual acquaintance jot down your destination in Chinese. Or point to your destination location on a map—but do *not* make the assumption that your driver will be able to use that map to find his way around.

Scams

DAILY LIFE

Most taxis have meters and do not try to rip you off. If, however, the meter isn't working in your cab, you have the right to refuse to pay. For the most part, metered taxis are honest, to the point of offering discounts if they took a wrong turn or missed the right street. Watch out, though, for unmetered taxis such as pedicabs or the little *mian bao che,* literally "loaf of bread car," which are funny little vans that often hang out at train stations waiting for groups toting excessive luggage. Fares for unmetered rides need to be agreed on and negotiated before you get into the vehicle because, as one expat put it, "The price of a ride depends on the length of your nose." Make sure that the amount is the total, not a per-person rate (a favorite trick played on unsuspecting tourists), and carry small bills to pay the exact fare. If you spend any length of time traveling around China, you will eventually be the victim of a conniving cabbie. Disagreements with drivers over fares can get quite ugly; you're better off just letting it go.

If you do feel that you are being taken advantage of by a taxi driver, be sure to write down his license number, posted in front of the passenger seat, as well as the phone number for the cab company (also posted within the cab). If your disagreement is with a rickshaw or pedicab driver, or some other private taxi service, look for a nearby police officer to help you negotiate the situation. Often seeing someone in your party go after a man in uniform will make your driver immediately give up his attempted scam. You can also call 110 to summon police help, which is staffed by bilingual operators in larger cities.

DRIVING

With the extensive and highly efficient public transportation available, driving your own car is really quite unnecessary. Driving is a tricky affair in China. A better way to get around by private car is to hire a driver. But if you have your heart set on getting behind the wheel, here is what you will need to know.

The first step to getting behind the wheel is deciding whether or not it is the right choice for you. Can you read enough Chinese to maneuver the streets safely? Where will you be driving? If your destinations lie mostly in the central city area, you'll spend most of your time searching for the elusive parking spot. How are your defensive driving skills? Chinese streets are filled with new, inexperienced drivers. Will you be in the country for a year or less? Then it won't be worth your time to muddle through the complex process of getting a permanent license, though you may consider applying for a temporary license (three months maximum). We recommend that you spend a fair amount of time observing the traffic situation in your Chinese city before you make your final decision.

Driver's Licenses and Traffic Laws

If you still have your heart set on getting behind the wheel, you'll have to get a local Chinese driver's license because international licenses aren't recognized in China.

Temporary driving permits for foreigners can be obtained from the Public Security Bureau for a maximum of three months. The permit is supposedly limited to small automatic cars, and you're supposed to attend mandatory lessons on Chinese driving rules. Having the temporary permit will allow you to rent a car in China.

To get the official driver's license, first take your U.S. or international driver's license to an official translator and stop by a hospital for a physical exam (local clinics don't count). Next up is a written test, which in major cities is available in English; if not, you will be allowed to bring a translator with you. Bring a few passport photos for the application, your residence permit and passport, your translated foreign license, and money to cover the fees. When the process is complete you can return in a week for your coveted card. You can avoid a lot of the hassle if you choose to just pay an organization like the Foreign Enterprise Service Corporation (FESCO, www.fescochina.com) to handle the whole process for you.

Once you've found your way legally into the driver's seat, you'll find the rules of the road a bit ambiguous. Traffic weaves all over the road ambivalent to marked lanes. Chinese drivers feel they can do just about

traffic signs

© TYLER CHRISTIAN

anything they want as long as they use their horns to blaringly announce their intentions, such as going the wrong way down a one-way street, running red lights, playing chicken in oncoming traffic to pass a slower vehicle, forcing left-hand turns directly into oncoming traffic, and driving in bike lanes and even on sidewalks. The idea seems to be that if you see—or hear—them, you're supposed to get out of their way. Speed limits are regularly posted, less regularly followed. Mobile phones are off-limits for drivers; seat belts are required in all seats (though these laws are not often enforced). Be aware that hidden traffic cameras are abundant in some areas, so even though you don't see any police, they are watching you, and they know how to find you. If you do find yourself the lucky recipient of a ticket, you'll be required to go to the traffic police station nearest the spot where you broke the law to pay the fines.

RENTING OR HIRING A CAR AND DRIVER

Unlike the thriving rental industry in Western nations, the car rental industry in China is in its infancy. A few of the prime U.S. rental agencies are opening locations throughout China, such as Avis and Hertz, where cars can be rented for local use starting around $100 daily. You'll need to have either a temporary Chinese driving permit or a regular Chinese driver's license in order to rent a car for self-drive.

The preferred way to rent a car in China includes hiring a driver as well, which is a great way to get around without having to personally hassle with the complicated traffic, tricky navigation, and nonexistent parking. Comfortable cars and vans can be reserved ahead of time through a travel agent or hotel desk or directly with a car rental agency; alternately, you can negotiate a flat day rate with any cabbie driving by. Many businesspeople opt for a long-term hire arrangement with a specific car and driver. In these arrangements you'll be chauffeured around for a specified number of hours per week for a flat fee, getting you and your spouse to work, bringing the kids home from school, or running around on errands and sightseeing activities. Extra hours require an extra per-hour rate, and the driver can use his off time to seek other fares. The best way to find someone is to ask for recommendations from others who have personal drivers, but you can also use an agency for a higher fee. Monthly rates for daily car-and-driver service from an agency start around $1,300.

You can also hire a driver for your own personal car. One option is to hire a taxi driver, which allows you to see them in action before you make the job offer. Alternately, agencies that place *ayis* can also help you find a driver, or your *ayi* might have a relative she would gladly recommend. The expected monthly pay for a personal driver is around 3,000元 ($450) in Shanghai, much less in cheaper cities.

BUYING OR LEASING A CAR

Since the bureaucratic challenge of bringing your own vehicle into China is rarely worth the money or effort, you may consider buying or leasing a car during your stay. You'll see plenty of sedans and minivans made by Hyundai, GM/Buick, and Volkswagen on the road, as well as lots of micro-cars made by Chinese companies like Chery. Even high-end cars are on the rise, with plenty of Cadillacs, Range Rovers, Hummers, and even Lamborghinis. After tariffs, these luxury vehicles can cost as much as three times more than in the States. New car dealerships are popping up around the country; bring your PRC license if you want to test-drive. If you'd prefer used over new, second-hand-car markets in major cities will have plenty to pick through, but the level of trustworthiness of the sellers is hard to gauge. As with many other major purchases, the easiest way to buy a used car is to pick one up from another expat who is on his or her way out of the country.

The costs associated with buying a new car include the price of the car, registration fee, emissions test, appraisal tax, road tax, user tax, license plate, and insurance. Sticker price for imported luxury cars such as BMW and Mercedes can be found in the $100,000 range; locally made cars are a little more affordable, such as the ever-popular Buick, starting around $26,000; the Chevrolet Aveo hatchback, in the $10,000 range; or a Chery QQ for just under $5,000. Since the government controls the number of license plates issued each month, competition for new plates can drive the prices much higher—around $4,000 or $5,000 in competitive markets but a mere couple of hundred yuan in more rural areas. License plates with lucky numbers, such as all 8's, fetch ridiculously high prices at auction. With monthly maintenance, tolls, and insurance, you can plan on spending at least an extra $3,000 annually.

Foreign residents who have worked in China for over a year can apply for auto loans to cover no more than 60 percent of the cost of the vehicle. You will also have to prepay the insurance for the whole term of the loan. The easiest way to get a car loan is through the car dealership, since banks require the title before a loan is issued. Some dealerships may be hesitant at first to pursue car loans for foreigners; be persistent and offer solid proof of security.

Instead of buying a car, consider leasing. Benefits include a lower down payment and no responsibility for repairs and maintenance. You will need to provide an upfront deposit in the range of $2,000–4,000, depending on the value of the car to be leased, as well as your ID card, passport, and local driver's license. Of course, the downside of leasing is that in the end, you don't have much to show for all those payments you made, and you'll have paid much more for the car than its original price.

DAILY LIFE

© BARBARA STROTHER

a classic motorcycle with sidecar in Shanghai

A WORD ABOUT MOTORCYCLES

Motorcycles and motor scooters can be quite cheap in China, starting around $250 for a scooter from your local Carrefour or other large retailer. No license is required for the scooters—just keep them on the bike lanes and sidewalks. As for motorcycles, you will need a Chinese driver's license. D licenses cover all motorcycles, including those with sidecars and motorized tricycles, while an E license covers just two-wheelers. In an effort to curb traffic problems, some cities have banned motorbikes outright from the central city and major roadways. Others have forbidden all bikes over a certain age. Additionally, the number of motorcycle license plates is fixed per city. If you buy a bike without a plate, you'll have to jump through quite a few hoops to get one. Because of the changing laws concerning motorcycles, be sure you check out the latest situation in your city before investing in one. The best way to get the latest scoop is to find a local riding club, which can often be found listed in the classified sections of English-language city magazines.

By Bicycle

Car ownership may be on the rise in China, but bicycles are still the number-one way to get around. Most roads in Chinese cities include an ample bike lane, making it much easier to navigate on two wheels than in the West, where city planners don't consider bikes a standard mode of transportation. You'll see whole families on one bike, or bicycles used as delivery trucks. A local appliance shop in our old neighborhood used traditional two-wheel bikes for deliveries, with a refrigerator strapped to each side of the bike and one stacked on top of the others. You might not carry your furniture around with you, but bike baskets make handy spots to throw purses, briefcases, groceries, or laptops. We once had a bike we affectionately termed our Chinese minivan: Two extra seats for our two toddlers and three baskets made it possible for just one of us to take the kids to do the weekly grocery shopping.

The rules of the road for biking are simple. Stay to the right except to pass. When you hear the sound of a car horn or another bicyclist's bell, get out of the way. If you want to pass a pedestrian or another biker in front of you, use your own bell to signal your intentions. And think twice about riding double with a person of the opposite sex, which can signify that you are dating.

Bikes are very cheap in China—often in both price and quality. The cheapest models start around $30. Luckily mobile bike repairmen sit around the sidewalks with carts full of spare tires and replacement parts ready to fix your flat or broken brakes for a few coins while you wait. (You'll find them next to street-side tailors doing the neighborhood mending with their ancient hand-operated sewing machines.)

One word of advice for buying a bike in China: Don't get one that looks fancy. Cool-looking bikes tend to disappear quickly no matter how well you lock them up, and a plain- or old-looking bike is the best protection against theft.

riding bikes on top of the ancient city wall in Xi'an

© BARBARA STROTHER

PRIME LIVING LOCATIONS

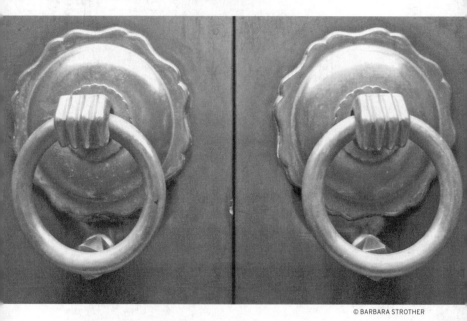

© BARBARA STROTHER

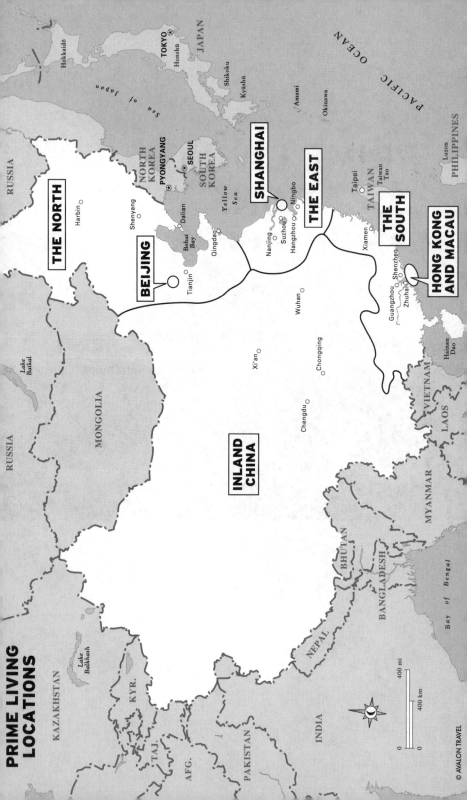

PRIME LIVING LOCATIONS

THE NORTH

BEIJING

SHANGHAI

THE EAST

THE SOUTH

HONG KONG AND MACAU

INLAND CHINA

RUSSIA

KAZAKHSTAN

MONGOLIA

RUSSIA

Lake Baikal

Lake Balkhash

KYR.

TAJ.

AFG.

PAKISTAN

INDIA

NEPAL

BHUTAN

BANGLADESH

MYANMAR

LAOS

VIETNAM

Bay of Bengal

Hainan Dao

Harbin

Shenyang

Dalian

Bohai Bay

Tianjin

Qingdao

Xi'an

Chengdu

Chongqing

Wuhan

Nanjing

Suzhou

Hangzhou

Ningbo

Xiamen

Guangzhou

Shenzhen

Zhuhai

Taipei

Taiwan Tao

TAIWAN

PHILIPPINES

Luzon

PACIFIC OCEAN

Okinawa

Amami

Kyushu

Shikoku

Honshu

Hokkaido

JAPAN

TOKYO

Sea of Japan

NORTH KOREA

PYONGYANG

SOUTH KOREA

SEOUL

Yellow Sea

400 mi

400 km

© AVALON TRAVEL

OVERVIEW

This *Prime Living Locations* section is designed with two types of people in mind. For those who have the opportunity to choose their destination in China, these chapters will help you make an informed decision. But most foreigners moving to China won't get to choose where to live; their employer will have already done that for them. For those of you who have been assigned to a specific location, the information on these pages will give you a solid introduction to what to expect in your new home away from home.

For the sake of this book we've divided the country into seven sections. China's major cities are covered in the *Beijing, Shanghai,* and *Hong Kong and Macau* chapters, while the *North, East, South,* and *Inland China* chapters cover the best places to live in each of these broad regions. Don't be surprised if you don't see your favorite vacation spot on these pages; quite a few places are great to visit but difficult to live in. We've chosen to cover the places that can offer the best quality of life for foreigners, based on factors like the size

© TYLER CHRISTIAN

of the city's expat community and the accessibility of Western amenities like imported groceries, high-quality housing, international schools, and Western health care.

Beijing

Proud capital and seat of power, Beijing wields an amazing amount of influence over this vast nation. All provinces live by Beijing; they set their clocks by Beijing time and speak Beijing's Mandarin dialect in their schools, businesses, and local government.

This city is the heart and soul of the nation, and the presence of central government is strongly felt here. In fact, politics is one of the main reasons why many foreigners come to Beijing, from diplomatic positions at one of the many embassies to journalists who keep the world informed of what this mighty giant is up to.

Compared to Hong Kong and Shanghai, Beijing is much more "Chinese" than its cosmopolitan cousins. Though its immense skyline is decorated with copious glassy skyscrapers, this city still feels old, due in part to the gloriously stubborn existence of *hutongs,* the labyrinthine neighborhoods dating back hundreds of years. It's also the center of the Chinese performing arts, celebrating the rich culture of this ancient nation's unique culture with its Chinese operas, acrobat shows, and traditional orchestras.

© BARBARA STROTHER

Tiananmen Square

WHERE TO LIVE IF . . .

Not sure which place is best for you? Here are a few priorities you may
want to consider.

If you . . .	Choose . . .
Want to learn Mandarin	A smaller city with few foreigners, which will force you to use the language, or areas that speak Mandarin without strong accents, such as the northeast. Avoid areas with prevalent dialects like Guangzhou and Hong Kong.
Want to get by without learning much Chinese	A big city with a large English-speaking population. Hong Kong is the best choice, followed by Shanghai, then Beijing.
Anticipate a future career move	One of the key business cities with a multitude of opportunities for foreigners. Shanghai and Hong Kong top the list.
Want to save money or live on a shoestring budget	A smaller city, an area with less foreign influence, or an inland location. Consider Ningbo, Xi'an, Xiamen, Zhuhai, or Chengdu.
Want to have an active nightlife and/or social life	Shanghai, Hong Kong, or Beijing. Avoid smaller cities.
Want to travel cheaply and easily to see a lot of China	A central city that makes for easy train departures in all directions, like Wuhan; Chengdu for easy access to minority regions and majestic scenery.
Want or need to frequently travel to other countries	A northern port town for flights to Japan and Korea; for inexpensive flights around Southeast Asia, try Guangzhou or Hong Kong.
Want to interact with minority cultures	A smaller city in a minority region, although some are restricted for foreigners. To stay in a major city with minority populations, try Xi'an for the Muslim minorities, Chengdu for Tibetans, or Kunming for a variety of local groups.
Despise hot, muggy summers	The northeast or high elevations. Avoid the Yangtze River cities (the muggiest locations in China), especially Wuhan and Chongqing.
Despise long, frigid winters	A southern city that boasts spring weather year-round such as Zhuhai, Macau, Xiamen, Shenzhen, or Guangzhou. Avoid the west and the north.
Need access to high-quality Western medical care	Hong Kong, which is by far the best, though Beijing and Shanghai also have plenty of Western medical services and hospitals.
Have health issues that would be exacerbated by air pollution	Xiamen, Dalian, Zhuhai, or one of the other cities that have made considerable progress limiting pollution. Avoid industrial cities, especially in the north and inland.
Need a lot of sunshine or get depressed with too many gray-sky days	Lhasa or Kunming for the most hours of sunshine in a year. Avoid Chongqing and Chengdu, which have the fewest hours of sunshine annually.

PRIME LIVING LOCATIONS

Unfortunately Beijing is often weighed down with thick gray smog. Harsh winters and occasional dust storms blowing in from Mongolian deserts add to the challenges of Beijing residents. But the city is in the midst of massive change, thanks in part to the vast enhancement efforts for the 2008 Olympics. Improvements to infrastructure and industry are quickly turning this city into a world-class destination.

Shanghai

With over 20 million residents and growing, Shanghai is not only the largest city in China, it's the largest in the world by population. In this flourishing commercial and financial center, East meets West in a striking blend of world cultures. Historic European buildings stand regally along its busy river, a reminder of its colonial past, while Asian temples and old-style Chinese neighborhoods hint at a more ancient culture. The real heart of Shanghai is in its fast-paced business and social scenes. This city is all about energy, and it is hard not to feel the excitement pulsing behind its futuristic skyscrapers when you first arrive. This place is also all about money, and Shanghaiers have a reputation for focusing their lives on the pursuit of conspicuous wealth. Businessmen in $1,000 suits jet about in shiny new Buicks, Bentleys, and

Shanghai's Pudong skyline at night

© BARBARA STROTHER

THE BIG THREE: ECONOMIC REGIONS

Within China there are three key city clusters that together are responsible for the majority of the nation's gross domestic product.

- **The Yangtze River Delta:** central eastern cities located on the Yangtze or near where the river meets the East China Sea, including Shanghai, Nanjing, Suzhou, Hangzhou, and Ningbo.
- **The Pearl River Delta:** southern cities located on or near where the Pearl River meets the South China Sea, including Guangzhou, Shenzhen, Zhuhai, Macau, and Hong Kong.
- **The Bohai Bay Economic Rim:** northern cities located on or near the Bohai Sea, including Beijing, Tianjin, Dalian, Yantai, and Qingdao.

Hummers to high-powered business meetings; the young and beautiful get all decked out in designer labels for yet another night out on the town.

Some compare Shanghai with New York, some with Paris—though don't go expecting either or you may be disappointed. As for expat amenities, Shanghai can't be beat among mainland cities. You'll be able to get just about anything you want here, though you may pay dearly for it. Your money will also buy you more decisions here than in other parts of the country, from what kind of world cuisine to eat for dinner to what architectural style of luxury villa to live in (Mediterranean stucco or Bavarian village? Japanese Zen or sleek ultra-modern?). Shanghai offers more opportunities to forget, for just a little while, that you are living in China—something that foreigners in smaller cities long for when the culture shock and the homesickness come on strong.

Hong Kong and Macau

The return of Hong Kong to mainland China in 1997 and of Macau in 1999 made these areas official Special Administrative Regions (SARs) of the People's Republic of China, although they retain their own laws, currency, and taxes. Though the British governed Hong Kong for 150 years and the Portuguese ruled Macau for 400 years, these spots have always maintained their Chinese character, along with a bit of European flair. Yet so many years of independence from the mainland have given both Hong Kong and Macau a unique flavor that you won't find anyplace else in the mainland.

Hong Kong is as cosmopolitan as China gets. Its urban islands boast a plethora of international restaurants, posh shopping malls, and five-star hotels amidst a dizzying array of skyscrapers and neon lights. It's the place mainland China expats run to when they need dependable health care, when they want to shop for something they can't find in the mainland, or when they need a break from the "real China." It's not all glass and glitz, however. A trek out to one of the outlying islands will put you on sandy beaches and pristine hiking trails for a much-needed infusion of the natural world.

Macau, on the other hand, is limited by its size in what it has to offer. Located opposite the Pearl River Estuary from Hong Kong, the peninsula and islands that make up Macau are tiny, home to half a million people packed into eleven square miles. Most are drawn to Macau for its historic old Portuguese charms or its sparkly new casinos—it's the only Chinese city where casino gambling is legal.

While both Hong Kong and Macau come with a lot of perks, they also come with a hefty price tag. Their real estate and cost of living are among the most expensive in the world. But if you've got a lot of money to spend, this is as good a place as any to spend it. Both Hong Kong and Macau consistently make it into the top 10 best places for expats to live in Asia.

The South

The best word to describe southern China, both literally and figuratively, is steamy, a land of summer typhoons and successful tycoons. Guangdong Province holds the economic powerhouse of the Pearl River Delta cities, including three top destination cities for expats: Guangzhou, Shenzhen, and Zhuhai. It's also home to Hainan Island, where the tropical sun and surf have garnered it the nickname the Hawaii of the Orient. Up the coastline in Fujian Province, Xiamen Island has captivated foreigners with its charm for centuries.

Guangzhou City, also known as Canton, has served as a major international port since the days Arab traders exchanged their Muslim religious influence for a bit of silk and tea during the Tang Dynasty. British merchants replaced the Arabs in the 19th century, and modern-day Guangzhou reflects these many years of foreign influence. The Cantonese have a reputation for strong entrepreneurial spirit, cosmopolitanism, and above all, a taste for very strange foods.

The city of Shenzhen is the gateway between Hong Kong and the mainland, and it's strictly business. As the PRC's first experiment with foreign investment, Shenzhen is a new and prospering boomtown, jockeying with Shanghai for the position of having the wealthiest residents. Directly across the Pearl River is the city of Zhuhai, the gateway to Macau and another booming Special Economic Zone. Along with their economic success, both Shenzhen and Zhuhai boast clean air and pleasant living environments with easy access to the perks of nearby Hong Kong and Macau.

Up the coast and beyond the mountains of Fujian Province, the city of Xiamen covers two islands and a bit of the mainland. Its seaside gardens and meandering lanes of old Mediterranean-style villas reflect Xiamen's history as a colonial port city, while its thriving new upscale commercial areas and pristine beaches provide pleasurable pastimes.

The East

East China consists of the two provinces surrounding Shanghai, Jiangsu and Zhejiang, which make up the Yangtze River Delta economic cluster. This is one of the wealthiest areas in China, where even the farmers live in towering four-story homes.

As the saying goes, "In heaven there is paradise. On earth there are Suzhou and Hangzhou." For centuries these two cities in eastern China have had a reputation for their physical beauty: Suzhou for its ancient gardens and Hangzhou for its famous West Lake. The effect of having such a relaxing natural environment has given Hangzhou residents a laid-back demeanor, unlike their workaholic Shanghai neighbors. Both Hangzhou and Suzhou have a thriving tourist industry, with highly developed amenities and businesses that cater to foreigners.

Farther north, Nanjing holds strong historic significance as the site of the Kuomintang headquarters and the Japanese massacre. This ancient city is once again starting to come into its own, adding amenities like a modern subway system and international luxury hotels. Some say Nanjing is like Shanghai

PRIME LIVING LOCATIONS

© BARBARA STROTHER

golden dragon in Hangzhou

before the development of Pudong—on the brink of great things but still a sleepy city.

Ningbo, on the coast south of Shanghai, is smaller and sleepier still, mostly known as an important trade port city as well as the jumping-off point to beautiful Putuoshan Island. Booming business in Ningbo's commercial hub has brought a growing community of foreigners within its borders.

In eastern China you can have the best of both expat worlds—the feel of a smaller town, including a somewhat cheaper cost of living, with easy access to Shanghai's boundless cosmopolitan amenities.

The North

The northern region surrounds Beijing and follows the coastline from Shandong Province, through the Bohai Bay Economic Rim, and up to the cold borders with North Korea and Russian Siberia. In the north, opportunities abound for getting out into nature, from digging your toes into the sand to digging your ski poles into fresh mountain snow. Hiking takes a spiritual twist with a climb up Mount Tai, a mandatory pilgrimage for devout Taoists. And the hilly landscape of Hebei, crisscrossed by the Great Wall and dotted with historic temples, is the play land of city-weary Beijing residents.

Bordering Beijing, Tianjin Municipality is one of the four cities that stand independent from a province, along with Shanghai, Beijing, and Chongqing. Tianjin's reputation is often linked with nearby Beijing, though there is plenty here for it to rest on its own laurels. Tianjin is one of the most prominent and influential industrial and port cities in China. Its history as a concessionary port is reflected today in its varied architecture.

Heading northeast from Tianjin, the region once grandly referred to as Manchuria is now known as "The Rust Belt," with its closed state-owned factories and unemployed workers. The Chinese government is determined to redevelop the area, however, and Liaoning's provincial capital, Shenyang, is the epitome of these efforts. This historic city has come into its own as a prime expat destination within the last few years. In contrast, Liaoning's other prominent city, the charming port of Dalian, has long been a flourishing seaside resort, having escaped the industrial decline and dismal reputation of its neighbors.

The north's most famous coastal city, Qingdao, is Shandong Province's pride and glory. This place savors a reputation for good beaches and even better seafood. Home to China's most famous beer and historic old Bavarian villas, Qingdao is full of surprising delights.

Inland China

Inland China, covering the bulk of the nation's geography, is home to colorful minority villages and the ancient Silk Road, the world's highest peaks and one of its lowest points, gorgeous natural scenery and the mighty Yangtze River that divides the Middle Kingdom into north and south. Though tourists come by the droves, the lack of resources for foreign residents has kept all but a small percentage from settling here. There are scores of inland cities with a tiny handful of expats teaching English or studying Chinese, but only three cities have a strong enough mix of international amenities to be considered prime destinations: Wuhan in Hubei Province, Chengdu in Sichuan Province, and Xi'an in Shaanxi Province (though Kunming and the Chongqing Municipality are up-and-coming contenders).

The cloudy city of Chengdu is known for its spicy Sichuan cuisine, its portly pandas, and its time-honored teahouses. It's a growing city that is quickly climbing its way up in international importance. In the past, visitors simply passed through colorful Chengdu on their way to Tibet and other exotic locales nearby, but nowadays foreigners are discovering that Chengdu is not such a bad place to set down some roots.

Wuhan and Chongqing, the front and back gates to the popular Three Gorges, are known as two of China's furnaces because of their blazing hot summers. Wuhan, nicknamed China's Chicago, is a sprawling commercial city and key transportation hub between the inland and the prosperous east, with a colorful history of foreign missionary activity and political uprisings.

The last of the prime inland locales is the most famous worldwide: Xi'an, home to the legendary terracotta warriors. Xi'an has an amazing history that dates back 5,000 years. It was China's pride and glory when it served as the well-traveled gate of the Silk Road. Xi'an still reflects those strong Turkic influences today, with its renowned mosque and Muslim quarter.

© BARBARA STROTHER

petting a kitten at a remote Buddhist temple

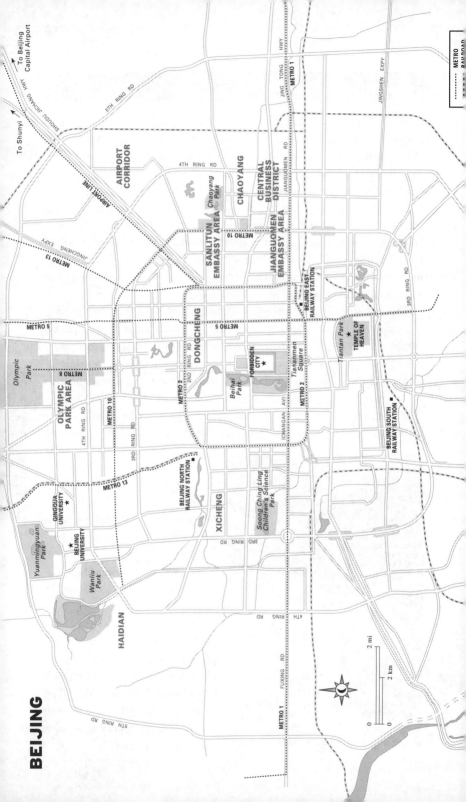

BEIJING 北京

For centuries Beijing has served as the political heart of the Middle Kingdom. Foreign invaders, Chinese emperors, and Communist hard-liners have all bitterly fought for control of this city, understanding that to rule China, you must begin in Beijing. From Kublai Khan with his Mongol hordes to the marauding Manchu invaders, Beijing has served as the base for dynastic rule and foreign invasion. It was here that Mao Zedong established the People's Republic of China in 1949 after defeating Chiang Kai-Shek's Nationalist army. Today, Beijing maintains its role as the center of China's political system. The cluster of foreign embassies is located in Beijing, and the city hosts a significant number of foreign journalists.

For years, Beijing's core focus has been government and heavy industries such as steel, machinery, and textiles. In recent years, however, Beijing has emerged as an important high-tech center. The city boasts the most educated workforce in China and contains hundreds of research institutes and universities,

© BARBARA STROTHER

© BARBARA STROTHER

souvenirs for sale at the Great Wall

including Beijing University and Qinghua University, the top two schools in mainland China. Foreign tech companies such as Motorola, Siemens, and Microsoft now have major operations in the city.

Beijing is home to about 17 million other residents, a number that's been growing by half a million annually in recent years due to the influx of migrant workers. Han Chinese make up 95 percent; the other 5 percent are China's numerous minority groups and foreigners.

Beijing has undergone a major upgrade in recent years due to its hosting of the Olympic Games in 2008. This citywide facelift has given Beijing a modern international flair, but at the same time much of the new construction has retained its ancient charms. The new National Stadium (a.k.a. the Birds Nest), National Aquatics Center (a.k.a. the Water Cube), Grand Theater (a.k.a. the Egg), and CCTV Tower (a.k.a. the Big Underpants) are putting Beijing on the global map of cutting-edge modern architecture, giving rival Shanghai some tough competition.

The city's expat scene is also on the rise with an increasing number of businesses that cater to foreigners, such as international restaurants, coffee shops (there are now more than 70 Starbucks in the city), and especially upscale Western-style housing. Foreigners living in Beijing have never had it so good. If the city could only gain control of its pollution woes, life in Beijing could be ideal.

© BARBARA STROTHER

bicycling near Tiananmen Square

PRIME LIVING LOCATIONS

THE CHARACTER OF BEIJING

Beijingers proudly consider themselves the "true Chinese" and have been known to look down their noses at their "uncivilized" brethren from other cities and provinces. Compared to their cousins in China's other first-tier cities, Beijingers see themselves as less materialistic, more loyal, and quite a bit more sophisticated. Beijing's hallmark cuisine, Beijing (Peking) Duck, is considered by many to be the best meal you can get in China, and to some even the best in all of Asia. Expatriates, and especially tourists, have found Beijing a wonderful place to discover historical China. With the Great Wall, the Forbidden City, the Temple of Heaven, and Tiananmen Square, how can you go wrong?

For all its culture and history, the character of Beijing is also heavily influenced by its political role as the nation's capital. It was here in Tiananmen Square where the Cultural Revolution was kicked off as thousands of young Red Guards frenetically waved Mao's little red books. Of course, the results of the Cultural Revolution were disastrous, and China's creative class has struggled to find safe middle ground somewhere between artistic freedom and Communist censorship. Today, Beijing has a burgeoning modern art scene, and contemporary galleries feature works that make shocking statements about life and politics in China in a newfound freedom of expression.

Despite its reputation as a culturally and historically rich place, some regard Beijing as a congested city that is choked by pollution, traffic, and the

© BARBARA STROTHER

preparing Peking Duck, considered by many to be the best meal in China

red tape of the city's army of bureaucrats. In Beijing it's more obvious than in other parts of the country that Big Brother is watching you. And like a typical tourist town, there's a bustling scam industry that preys on unknowing tourists. You'll have an awesome time in Beijing for sure, but don't kid yourself: It's not a question of *if* you'll get ripped off, but *when*.

The Lay of the Land

The Beijing Municipality is slightly smaller than the state of New Jersey. It is hilly in the north and flat in the core city and south. The Forbidden City and Tiananmen Square serve as the geographic center of the city, and other important government structures are aligned directly to the north and south. The city center is circled by a series of seven concentric ring roads (although the 2nd, 3rd, and 4th ring roads are the ones you'll regularly use). Wide north-south boulevards connect with similar east-west roads, creating a grid street pattern. As long as you stay on these main roads, you'll navigate the city like an old pro in no time. Wandering off these main arteries into Beijing's infamously crooked *hutong* alleys is a sure-fire way to get lost, but also a great way to mingle with traditional Beijing.

Surrounding the Forbidden City north of Changan Avenue are Xicheng and Dongcheng Districts. Both are characterized by their historic *hutong* neighborhoods and the courtyard homes of famous literary and political players of the past. Xicheng is also home to Beijing's urban lakes, including Beihai, imperial gardens turned into a large park, and Houhai, a popular entertainment district where trendy bars and upscale restaurants line the edge of the picturesque lake. South of Changan Avenue has a reputation as being some of Beijing's working-class neighborhoods where you're more likely to find the so-called "Chinese apartments," in other words, the real China.

Farther northwest of the city center you'll find the Haidian District, which is home to the Summer Palace, numerous universities, and the Beijing Zoo. Directly to the east of downtown is the Chaoyang District. Here you'll find Sanlitun and Jiangguomen, two neighborhoods with lots of embassies and large expat populations. Besides the embassies, Sanlitun is most famous for its restaurant and bar scene on Sanlitun Road, with dozens of old watering holes, new restaurants, and modern shops.

The Beijing Capital Airport is about a 30-minute drive to the northeast of downtown. There are numerous new expat enclaves that have been developed along this route, quite a few with upscale villa-style housing with architectural styles from around the globe.

Surprisingly the central business district (CBD) is not located in the center of town but to the east of Tiananmen Square between the 3rd and 4th ring roads. The area has undergone major redevelopment to make it an attractive place for office buildings, and plenty of high-end housing is available here to serve the businesspeople who work nearby.

© BARBARA STROTHER

taking a stroll near the Forbidden City

CLIMATE

You'll be pleased that Beijing's weather follows the four distinct seasons, but sadly three of the seasons tend to be inhospitable. Winter (December through March) can be harsh, with daytime temperatures around 30°F and extra air pollution from a few remaining coal-fired electric plants and heaters. Since joining the World Trade Organization and hosting the Olympics, the government has felt pressure to clean up the environment, but with all the industrial growth and the explosion of privately owned automobiles, it's anybody's guess whether Beijing will ever be a "green" city.

Beijing breakfast

© BARBARA STROTHER

In springtime (April and May) the weather is more bearable with temperatures around 50°F, but spring also brings wicked sandstorms blowing in from the nearby Gobi Desert. By the time summer arrives (June through August), the annoying sands will have been replaced by scorching sun, 90°F temperatures, and dripping humidity. So you are left with the brief fall season (September through November) to enjoy clear skies and comfortable 70°F weather.

LANGUAGE

The standard Mandarin language, also called *putonghua* (common speech), is based on the Beijing dialect. However, Beijingers famously add a nasal *er* sound to the end of many words. Even the greenest *laowai* should be able to pick out the Beijing accent after just a few days. If you're in China to learn Mandarin, being here will give you the opportunity to learn the language in its purest form, but unfortunately you'll also pick up the strong nasal accent.

CULTURE

Beijingers boast that their city represents the culture of all of China. Considering Beijing's ancient cultural heritage and its contemporary arts scene, this reputation as cultural center may be well deserved. Most Chinese cities have some ancient sites that the locals are proud of, but few can match those found

© BARBARA STROTHER

Bajiao Amusement Park in Beijing

in Beijing. At the geographic and spiritual center of town, you'll find Tiananmen Square and the Forbidden City, the home of the emperors. The Summer Palace is found to the northwest of the city center. And who can match the Great Wall, which is just an hour's drive north of town? You can also visit the ancient Ming Tombs along the way.

Beijing is famous for its world-renowned traditional opera, calligraphy, folk dancing, and acrobatics. Much of China's famous literature also came out of Beijing, including works by Lao She (*Rickshaw Boy*), Lu Xun (*The True Story of Ah Q*), and the feminist Zhang Jie (*Love Must Not Be Forgotten*).

The contemporary music scene in Beijing is also pretty vibrant. The city is a major stopover for DJs from around the world who play every night in packed clubs with all sorts of themes. For those with more highbrow tastes, the city boasts about a dozen concert halls and over 30 theaters, including the impressive new National Grand Theatre. There are also numerous sports sites hosting a variety of professional and international competitions, including those that were built for the 2008 Olympics. All in all you'll find plenty to do every day and night in Beijing, if you can only find the energy to keep up the pace.

Where to Live

Though you'll find foreigners dwelling in every random corner of the city, there are several key areas with significant expat populations. Historically, expatriates in Beijing have lived near the embassies just east of Tiananmen, especially in the Sanlitun and Jianguomen neighborhoods. Nowadays this eastern part of the city is still crawling with expats, but it extends to cover more territory in Chaoyang District, including the CBD. Students and scholars typically live on or near campus near the universities in the Haidian District to the northwest of Tiananmen. The northeastern Shunyi District and the airport corridor connecting the city to the new airport have

PRIME LIVING LOCATIONS

© BARBARA STROTHER

a pleasant Beijing bike ride beside Hou Hai Lake

recently experienced much suburban development, including a variety of villa neighborhoods to cater to the numerous expat families associated with Beijing's multinational firms.

EAST CHAOYANG DISTRICT

If you enjoy the excitement of life in the big city, then Chaoyang District may be just right for you. This densely populated area is abuzz with the workings of commerce as commuters, workers, businesspeople, and bureaucrats do their daily thing. The embassy districts of Sanlitun and Jianguomen are about three miles east of Tiananmen Square, and the CBD continues along Changan Avenue to the 4th ring road. Chaoyang District has attracted quite a few foreign firms and expatriates who work and live in the area. Consequently the area is host to quite a few foreign businesses that cater to the needs and tastes of this expat enclave. Almost all of Beijing's international schools are located either here in Chaoyang District or in Shunyi District.

Sanlitun is best known for its bar scene, but for entertainment options that don't involve heavy drinking, you can visit your fishy friends at the Blue Zoo aquarium, catch a game at the Workers' Stadium, or fly a kite at Ritan Park, built in the 16th century as a temple to the sun god. If all else fails, there's always some of the best shopping in the city, including the Sanlitun Yashou Market and the Silk Market for cheap knockoffs, the upscale Lufthansa Center and China World Trade Center complex (with the added fun of an ice rink in the basement), and the Friendship store, an old faithful Beijing institution. Chaoyang is also well connected to the transportation system, with several subway stops, the main train station, and a quick getaway to the airport from the district's northern areas.

There is a wide range of housing options available in Chaoyang, though most foreigners live in high-rise apartment towers. These towers function as mini-cities because they have so many amenities. In addition to the comfortable luxury apartments, people find the towers an attractive place to live because of the restaurants, imported-foods stores, salons, gyms, swimming pools, and indoor playgrounds for the little ones. Of course all of this doesn't come cheap.

On the low end, you can rent an 85-square-meter one-bedroom apartment for as little as $800 per month at a place like the Kang Bao Garden near the Workers' Stadium. A typical two-bedroom apartment has about 150 square meters and rents for around $2,000 per month. On the high end, you can rent a 4-5 bedroom apartment with over 300 square meters for as much as $6,500 per month at a place like the Beijing Golf Apartment by Chaoyang Park.

Serviced apartments are available throughout the district. They tend to rent for about double the price of a normal apartment. At the aptly named Embassy House, for instance, you can rent a two-bedroom serviced penthouse with just over 200 square meters starting around $5,500 per month. A larger place with over 300 square meters will run you $10,000 per month. Though most serviced apartments are located in hotels, others are in office buildings (which means you can no longer blame the traffic for making you late for work).

Because the area was developed before villas became popular in Chinese housing, your options for villas are limited; most who require a villa are forced to flee to the suburbs. The exception is the East Lake Villas near the Canadian embassy. Though the homes here are smaller than what you'd get in Shunyi, they offer a lot of charm with their "Suzhou Garden Style." A three-bedroom villa with 150 square meters costs $4,000-5,000 per month; the luxury model with five bedrooms and over 300 square meters costs up to $10,000 per month.

Rents are high in Chaoyang because most of these properties are built according to Western standards, and landlords know most expats here are paying for rent with their employers' money. You might be able to rent a modest apartment from a local for less than half the rates quoted above, though you may have extra responsibilities as well, such as setting up the utilities.

HOW ABOUT A *HUTONG?*

Hutongs, literally "alleyways," are the ancient crowded little courtyard neighborhoods only accessible by maddeningly crooked alleys too narrow for cars. Beijingers proudly boast that the *hutong* is a unique symbol of Beijing. Though sometimes dirty and decrepit, *hutongs* do have their charms, and for expats who want to experience the real China, renting an old courtyard house in a *hutong* may be just the thing.

Living in a *hutong* is all about communal living. Children play together in the narrow alleys and courtyards while adults gossip and sip tea. The tight quarters make everyone get to know each other, but it can also be a drag, especially if your *hutong* has communal bathrooms.

Most of the *hutong* homes rented by foreigners in Beijing are in Xicheng District near Houhai Lake or Dongcheng District near the Lama Temple. The Ju'er *hutong* has emerged as an expat ghetto; the foreign families in this *hutong* make up almost half of its residents.

Homes in *hutongs* are called courtyard houses because you'll get a nice private outdoor courtyard as part of your house. A growing number of these old homes are being renovated for the wealthier class to live in, some under the direction of world-renowned architects and designers. Of course such luxury comes at a price. A 100-square-meter home rents for about $4,000 while a designer 250-square-meter place can cost up to $10,000, though you can find simple places for as little as $1,200 per month. But for those expats with new urbanist leanings, the *hutong* might be just right.

© BARBARA STROTHER

a traditional Beijing home renovated to modern standards

SHUNYI DISTRICT

The Shunyi District is out on the 6th ring road northeast of the city center and directly north of the Chaoyang District. Because of Shunyi's proximity to the Beijing airport and the availability of undeveloped land, the area has emerged as a major industrial area in the last few years. Quite a few high-tech firms have chosen to locate here, including those in the aviation, automotive, optical, electronic, and biopharmaceutical sectors. Though the numerous farms in this suburb have earned the area the nickname of "granary of the capital," Shunyi and the adjacent Airport Corridor have become a hot spot for expat families with generous housing budgets.

So many villa complexes have been built here that some have begun to call Shunyi "Levittown" in a nod back to the 1950s planned suburbs. And the resemblance is striking: Inside the gates of the walled compounds, children ride their bikes on the sidewalks, kick soccer balls on manicured lawns, and dogs are walked every evening. It's enough to make you forget you're living in China.

There are quite a few recreation options in Shunyi. A few luxury golf courses do a brisk business with the expats. Those looking for a more adventuresome time will appreciate the skiing centers and the theme parks. Agrotourism and folk custom tourist venues are also popular here.

Shunyi is also the site of the 2008 Olympic swimming, diving, and equestrian events. New facilities for these were constructed along with numerous other major infrastructure projects. Shunyi is making a major transformation from sleepy farmland to cutting-edge high-tech zone, and if you can handle the construction dust, you might find it a pleasant place to live.

With its convenient international schools and a number of foreign-based shopping outlets, Shunyi has proven to be popular among expatriate families with children. The walled compounds create a sense of security but can also isolate you from the real China. Unlike the urban areas, Shunyi doesn't have too many hangout spots. And since Shunyi is a sprawling suburb, you'll need a car or taxi to take you where you need to go, which means you'll miss out on a lot of Chinese street life that you'd otherwise experience if you were biking or walking in the urban center.

The area near the airport where the southwestern tip of Shunyi District meets Chaoyang District is sometimes called the "Central Villa District" for its many auspiciously named complexes, like Dragon Villa, Merlin Champagne, and Yosemite. The complexes consist of upscale detached villas (some of the nicest in China), and some also have town houses and apartments. Each complex boasts its own amenities such as swimming pools, tennis courts, imported-foods stores, cafés, billiard rooms, playgrounds, and more. The Beijing Riviera even has its own skate park. All residents of the complex can enjoy all of the amenities equally regardless of whether they rent the smallest apartment or the most luxurious villa.

Housing prices in Shunyi are not a bargain. Two- or three-bedroom apartments rent for around $1,500 per month at the lower end, though there aren't as many available here since most compounds focus on villas with only a couple of low-rise apartment buildings on their premises. Serviced apartments start around $2,000 per month for a small place. Townhomes, which are basically duplexes with small yards, rent for around $2,000-5,000 per month for a two- to four-bedroom place. Villas, which are Shunyi's specialty, start out no lower than $3,000 and can be higher than $12,000 per month. A four-bedroom villa at Yosemite has about 400 square meters and rents for around $5,500 per month, which is typical for villas in this area.

HAIDIAN UNIVERSITY DISTRICT

The Haidian District, northwest of the city center, is the intellectual capital of Beijing. Haidian District is home to 80 universities, including Beijing University and Qinghua University, the top two schools in China. In addition to the universities, Haidian earned its brainy reputation as a result of the cluster of technology companies in the area. Back in the 1980s the Zhongguancun high-tech zone was established, encompassing most of the Haidian district. The zone designation created numerous incentives for high-tech businesses to locate in the area. Since then, thousands of companies now call Haidian home, including quite a few foreign firms like Cisco, HP, IBM, Intel, Lucent, Microsoft, P&G, and Canon. The area is a virtual who's who of high-tech business, and today Zhongguancun is known as China's Silicon Valley.

For fun in Haidian, most expats tend to hang out in the bohemian restaurant and bar scene that has developed just outside of the campuses. Young hipsters especially appreciate the trendy Wudaokou neighborhood near the Beijing Language and Culture University. Haidian also boasts some of the best outdoor parks in Beijing. If you're tired of Beijing's urban grind, maybe you could use a day trip to Fragrant Hills Park, the Purple Bamboo Forest, or the Botanical Garden. You might also enjoy visits to the zoo, the National Library, and the Beijing Exhibition Center, all located nearby.

Most of the foreigners who move to Beijing to teach or study end up living somewhere in Haidian, most likely on campus. Foreign students are offered dorms that are usually about as comfortable as dorm rooms in the United

States, and profs and teachers can expect to be put up in a well-equipped campus apartment. Those who work in the private sector typically choose to rent a nearby apartment if they don't have kids; expat families tend to commute from Shunyi or Chaoyang, where there are many more options for educating foreign kids.

Apartments in Haidian are a bargain compared to the other expat neighborhoods. You can rent a 60-square-meter studio apartment here for around $600 per month. A larger place, such as a three-bedroom 200-square-meter apartment at the Dong Sheng Yuan, will only run you around $1,200 per month.

Without much demand for them, serviced apartments are not common in Haidian, and there are very few villas here. Though new villa construction projects are planned for the suburban areas nearby, for the time being, expats that work in Haidian with budgets big enough for villas will most likely commute from Shunyi.

Daily Life

EXPAT SOCIAL SCENE

Expats come to Beijing for a variety of reasons. Most of the foreign diplomatic corps is plopped down here, as well as journalists that cover the country's economic and political news. Beijing's large cluster of universities attracts thousands of foreign students each year, and unlike the early days, the foreign students aren't coming just to study Mandarin, and foreign professors aren't here just to teach English. The new economic development zones have also successfully attracted numerous foreign firms to Beijing with their workers in tow, especially around Shunyi and Haidian.

Twenty years ago just about every foreigner from the West living in Beijing knew one other. Today a vast expatriate community has emerged and is making an impression on the Beijing social scene. The expatriate crowd is now served by a wide variety of Western-style housing, schools, shopping, restaurants, bars, nightclubs, and even the type of club where people meet because of some common interest (besides drinking).

Beijing has over 100 clubs run by expats. Quite a few of the clubs are established based on the home country of the members, including Canadian, Dutch, Italian, Polish, and even the Black Beijing club, whose members are African Americans. Some expats with intellectual leanings have formed a writers' club, a philosophy club, and a chess club. Quite a few of the clubs are alumni organizations, mostly associated with major U.S. universities. Rotary

FOREIGN BABES IN BEIJING

AN INTERVIEW WITH AUTHOR RACHEL DEWOSKIN

In 1994 Rachel DeWoskin moved to Beijing to take a position in a public-relations firm and ended up becoming an overnight sensation as a Chinese soap opera star. An estimated 600 million Chinese viewers watched as her character, Jiexi, seduced a married Chinese man and stole him away to the United States. She tells of her experiences both on and off screen in her hugely popular book, *Foreign Babes in Beijing: Behind the Scenes of a New China* (W. W. Norton & Co., 2005), which has been translated into multiple languages and is being made into a Paramount movie. Although she currently resides in New York City, she returns to China several times a year and plans to live there again someday.

Why did you decide to go to China?
I moved to Beijing because, after 17 years of American childhood and student-dom, I wanted to go somewhere no one else I knew was going. I wanted excitement and a jolt of culture shock, and I chose China because it was both unfamiliar and familiar. My father is a sinologist, and I spent my childhood summers riding overnight trains across internal China, peering up at giant Buddhas, climbing staircases to temples, and sleeping in the guesthouse beds of revolutionary heroes. As a kid, my first impressions were of food and words: banquets where my brothers and I ate sea slugs, "horse whip" soup, and turtle, and I learned to sing "Are You Sleeping" in Chinese. The words in Chinese are, "Two tigers, two tigers, run very fast, run very fast. / One has no eyes, one has no tail. / How weird! How weird!" Those lyrics are the first Chinese I ever learned.

Why did you stay in China as long as you did?
I loved it. The more I stayed, the less I knew, and the more I wanted to know. My impressions of China changed the way anything changes when it starts out strange and then becomes familiar. At first, Beijing seemed to me a set on which other people acted out lives I could never know anything about. And then later, it seemed like home.

What advice would you give to someone who wants to get into acting in China?
My role came by way of a fairly typical combination of randomness and *guanxi*. If you want work in TV, just be sure to read the script before you sign the contract.

and Toastmasters have branches, as well as the exclusive Capital Club, which only admits senior foreign biz types.

Weekend warriors will want to join one of the expat sports clubs—there are plenty to choose from, including rugby, soccer, ultimate Frisbee, hockey, climbing, and the new national sport of China, basketball. There are also a number of organized children's leagues, such as those at the Lido Country Club.

**What were the greatest rewards and frustrations of
your time in China?**
The greatest reward was the constant feeling of being alive, of having to
work at daily interactions and conversations. The greatest frustration?
The constant feeling of being alive, of having to work at daily interactions
and conversations.

**What do you think are the most difficult challenges
faced by expats in China?**
Being an expat in China is a mostly glorious and addictive business. Learning Chinese and speaking it with confidence is a challenge, but mainly,
expats in China consider the delight of full-time life there to be one of the
world's well-kept secrets.

What are the benefits of living in China as a foreigner today?
Access to endlessly interesting material, fabulous food, 1.3 billion potential
friends. If you have a chance to go, you should absolutely go. And stay as
long as you can.

© BARBARA STROTHER

PRIME LIVING LOCATIONS

RESOURCES

Beijing now has significant online and print media that target the English-
speaking crowd. English-language newspapers include the *People's Daily* and
the *Washington Post: China Version.* Politically minded types will appreciate the
Beijing Review, which is published weekly in Chinese, English, and four other
languages. For the lowdown on economic, industrial, and business news, check
out *Business Beijing* and *Beijing This Month,* both published monthly in English.

HORSE KILL CHICKEN: THE ART OF MASSAGE

One of the Chinese words for massage sound just like "horse kill chicken," *ma si ji.* At the Beijing Massage Hospital you can get an excellent, and cheap, "horse kill chicken." In fact, in every Chinese city you'll find massage salons, including some that specialize in blind masseurs. Most charge around $10 for an hour-long treat. Or even cheaper, barbershops and salons often throw in a free head, back, and arm massage as part of the haircut. Stay clear of the pink-light barbershops, however, where the ladies will offer more than the standard massage late at night.

Chinese spas are a cheap form of entertainment. Many stay open 24 hours, and some include Ping-Pong tables, billiards, a movie room, or an Internet café. If you're too relaxed to head home after a deep tissue massage and a good soak in the Chinese bath, you can stay and sleep for free. In fact, some Chinese looking to save money sleep at massage parlors and skip the hotel room altogether. Keep it in mind if you ever accidentally lock yourself out of your apartment without your wallet.

© BARBARA STROTHER

spa ad

That's Beijing and *City Weekend* are free weekly entertainment magazines on local happenings, restaurants, and bars; you can learn a lot about the city just by reading the classifieds. These magazines also have companion websites, which can provide invaluable information about Beijing even before you move there.

HEALTH CARE

The health care system in Beijing is considered the best the mainland has to offer. The care is affordable, and quite a few of the doctors can speak English and have been trained according to the high standards of Western hospitals. The top local hospitals include the Sino-Japanese Friendship Hospital and Beijing Union Medical Hospital, which was originally built in 1917 by American philanthropists, namely the Rockefeller Foundation. Each has separate VIP wards for foreigners. Both of these hospitals accept medical insurance from the United States. There's also the Beijing Massage Hospital. Even if you're not sick, you might want to invent some ailment just so you have an excuse to seek treatment here!

Beijing's only private hospital run by foreigners is the United Family Hospital in Chaoyang District. It is staffed by international physicians, dentists, and surgeons and has childbirth facilities, an intensive care unit, and an emergency room. If you only need a simple clinic instead of a hospital, you can find international-quality medical clinics at two hotels (Beijing International SOS Clinic at the Kunlun Hotel, and Hong Kong International Medical Clinic in the Swissotel) and one at a shopping center (International Medical Centre at the Lufthansa Center). If traditional Chinese medicine is your thing, you can try the Pingxintang TCM Clinic in Wangfujing, or the Yanhuang TCM Clinic in the Dongcheng district.

SCHOOLS

Beijing has more than a dozen choices in international schooling for foreign families. The bulk of the international schools in Beijing are located around the 3rd ring road where the Chaoyang and Shunyi Districts come together. These schools include the Australian International School Beijing and the Beijing BISS International School. The British School of Beijing in Sanlitun is the main international school operating in the embassy neighborhood, and the Beijing City International School is the most convenient option for those living in the CBD. Over the years some schools moved their campuses from

© KEVIN SEMDOMRIDGE

Students show off their kung-fu skills at an international school.

PRIME LIVING LOCATIONS

© BARBARA STROTHER

Xiushui Market

downtown out to newer "greener pasture" facilities in Shunyi, including the International School of Beijing (one of the city's largest) and the Western Academy of Beijing.

SHOPPING

For many years, visitors to Beijing have shopped for the city's four famous handicrafts: cloisonné, ivory, jade, and lacquerware. Today, it's a different story. This once-proud bastion of hardscrabble communism has emerged as a shining mecca of consumerism. You can now buy just about anything in Beijing. Formerly scarce items as mundane as a stick of deodorant or as fancy as a new Bentley are readily available-that is, if you know where to look, and if you've got the dough to pay.

Shopping Areas and Major Stores

Wangfujing Street is one of Beijing's busiest shopping areas. It runs north-south and is located two large blocks east of Tiananmen Square. Here you'll find the Beijing Department Store, the mammoth Xinhua Bookstore, the Foreign Language Bookstore, and a wide variety of shops selling everything you might need (and plenty of things you don't need). It is a pedestrian street, so you'll find it an excellent place for window shopping and people watching. There are also plenty of ethnic restaurants in this area selling food from faraway places like Xinjiang, and its snack street is legendary for its unusual delicacies, such as scorpion, grasshopper, and silk worms.

Wangfujing caters to internationals and internationally minded locals, while

Xidan is the trendy shopping area favored by locals. Xidan is two major blocks west of Tiananmen Square running north and south along Xidan Road. The main shopping mall is the higher-end Xidan Shopping Center, with lots of electronics, jewelry, and clothing stores. For real upscale shopping similar to what you'd find in high-end department stores back in the States, try the glamorous Lufthansa Center just north of the Sanlitun embassy neighborhood.

Beijing has numerous megamarts stocking food, clothing, housewares, and just about everything else you need for daily life. Wherever you end up living, you should be close to a Carrefour because there are now nearly a dozen in the city, not to mention Sam's Club, Wal-Mart, Metro, Ikea, and the like. Of course there are local grocery stores and general merchandise stores in every neighborhood, but the foreign megamarts are often your best bet for those hard-to-find items that expats can't live without like cheese, root beer, or Legos for the kiddies. The showroom of Villa Lifestyles can also hook you up with all the goodies you'll want to use for outdoor entertaining at your villa, such as high-end gas grills, hot tubs, and trampolines.

Markets

Ready to brag to your pals back home about the sweet prices you're paying for cool stuff? If so, then you'll need to hit the street markets. Leave your credit cards behind, bring plenty of cash, and dust off your bargaining skills.

In the embassy district on Jianguomen Road you'll find the Xiushui Silk Market, a popular place to go for cheap clothing, luggage, toys, and lots more. The labels might not be real, but the good deals are. Another favorite is the Hongqiao Pearl Market on the east side of the Temple of Heaven. You'll find lots more than pearls here, including mobile phones, watches, and the usual knockoff clothing. Another market worth checking out is the Sanlitun Yashou Market for clothing (and startling prices), designed with the foreigner in mind. All of these markets are several stories tall.

© BARBARA STROTHER
shopping for an Olympic jacket

Whichever markets you end up shopping at, understand that these markets operate on the fringes of the law. Don't expect much customer service after the sale, do expect counterfeit (and often substandard) merchandise, and don't be surprised if your favorite place to shop vanishes overnight, the latest victim of a government crackdown on intellectual property rights violators.

Getting Around

Beijing is relatively flat, which makes it an ideal place to own a bicycle. For short trips most Beijingers pedal to their destination. Avoid the temptation to buy a fancy bike like those in the movie *Beijing Bicycle,* because bike thieves are well-armed with bolt-cutters, and your bike won't last very long (just like in the movie). For crosstown trips, you'll appreciate Beijing's well-developed network of taxis, subway lines, and public buses. Pedicabs are a relaxing way to be chauffeured around the *hutong* neighborhoods and the central lakes.

BY TAXI OR PRIVATE CAR

The easiest way to get around Beijing is to simply hail a taxi. You can also hire a car and driver or hire a single taxi for the whole day. Traveling by car is often not the speediest way to get around, especially during rush hour. With the emerging middle class now hitting the road, Beijing's gridlock often resembles

Pedicabs replace taxis in Beijing's narrow *hutong*s.

© BARBARA STROTHER

Los Angeles's. When the traffic is heaviest it can take less time to ride a bicycle than to ride in a vehicle, even to somewhat distant destinations. Nonetheless, taxi rates are still pretty reasonable, starting at a 10元 ($1.50) minimum and charging 2元 ($0.30) per kilometer.

BY SUBWAY

Beijing's subway system will efficiently move you around town for just a couple of *kuai*. Line 1 runs from the west side of the city through Tiananmen Square and on to the east along Changan Avenue, connecting the key commercial centers of Xidan, Wangfujing, and the CBD. Line 2 is a circular route following the path of the 2nd ring road. Line 13 runs to the northern suburbs, including the university district, and loops back to Line 2. Line 5 runs north-south a few blocks east of Tiananmen and passes through two areas famous for temples, the Lama Temple and the Temple of Heaven. Line 13 follows the 3rd ring road on its northern and eastern path. Other lines run to the suburbs and the airport, and half a dozen new lines are scheduled to open over the next three years.

BY BUS

A complex network of bus routes can take you virtually anywhere in Beijing (or further into every corner of China if you can handle the ride). The busiest routes typically have clean air-conditioned buses, but there are still quite a few junkers on the road. To figure out a route, purchase one of the local maps or have a local friend help you. The days of live chickens and ducks on public buses seem to have come to an end, but you'll still have to deal with the sardine-packed passenger system at rush hour. If you like mosh pits, then you may enjoy riding the bus. You don't have to worry about your personal safety or getting groped, but you should definitely keep a hand on your wallet or purse.

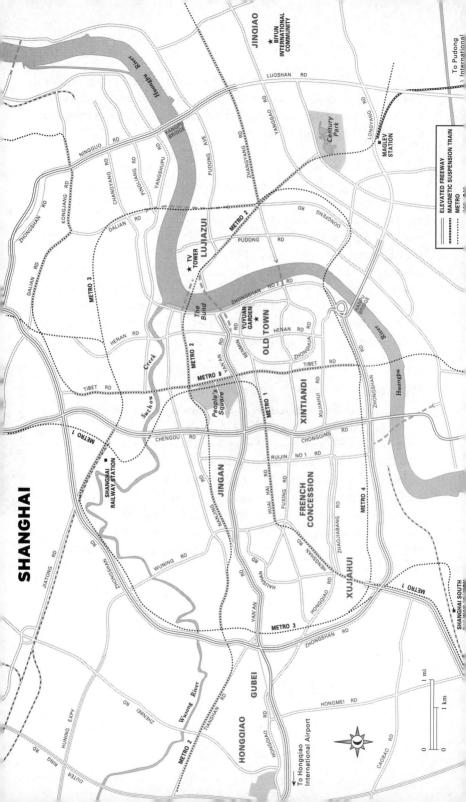

SHANGHAI 上海

Paris of the East; Pearl of the Orient. Whatever nickname you prefer, one thing's for sure: Shanghai is the China of the future. Whether ruled by cut-throat gangsters, foreign merchants, or communist rebels, Shanghai has always been on the cutting edge of what's new and what's hot in China. While the rest of China struggles to find the right blend of tradition and modernity, Shanghai continues marching onward as the nation's leader in business, economics, and pop culture.

Shanghai ranks at the top of just about every list that compares Chinese cities, including quality of life, average income, housing quality, low crime rates, best infrastructure, abundant recreation, numerous business opportunities, and on and on. This city has the world's busiest port. Its Maglev is the world's fastest commercial train. Its Financial Center is the world's tallest skyscraper. Its futuristic skyline is unparalleled by any other city in the world.

With a population greater than 20 million, Shanghai is the largest city in China, and by many counts, the largest in the world. The city's bustling

© BARBARA STROTHER

economy continues to attract large numbers of Chinese from other provinces (many of whom are unregistered migrants) and a giant foreign population. In an apparent bid to maintain its position as the most cosmopolitan city in China, the local government's goal is to increase the number of foreigners living in the city to up to 5 percent of its total population. Shanghai residents tend to be stylishly dressed, well spoken, and well mannered. From the view of other Chinese people, Shanghaiers have a reputation for being stylish yet

© BARBARA STROTHER

Some of the world's tallest skyscrapers are in Shanghai.

pretentious, talented but arrogant, industrious but workaholic, and perhaps a little too greedy.

Since Shanghai serves as China's financial and commercial center, we might also call the city the New York or London of the East. The powerful Shanghai gangsters of old have been replaced by equally influential bankers, financiers, and investors from across China and abroad. The Shanghai Stock Exchange is the busiest exchange in mainland China, and the city is host to more than 10,000 foreign firms. Including nearby Jiangsu and Zhejiang Provinces, the Yangtze River Delta accounts for a third of China's import and export activity.

Shanghai's economic growth is most evident in its building boom—there's a saying that half of the world's construction cranes are in this city alone. Nowhere in the world will you find a more impressive architectural collection of buildings than in the Pudong New Area, a showcase for the who's who of the world's best architects. Unfortunately the boom is not without its downsides, and housing costs are some of the highest in the mainland. If, however, your pay is based on an international standard, and your employer provides your housing, you may find yourself deciding, like so many expats who've come before you, that Shanghai might be a nice place to spend the rest of your working years.

HISTORY

Compared to the rest of the Middle Kingdom, Shanghai is a very young city. For centuries it was just a modest fishing village (Shanghai literally means "on the sea"). In the 16th century it became a proper city when a city wall was erected to keep out the Japanese pirates. The British took control of much of the area as a concession for winning the Opium War of 1842, followed by the French, Americans, Russians, Japanese, and others who established their own settlements. For the next 100 years, the foreign concessions covered most of the city and had their own municipal governments and even their own police forces. The International Settlement was north of the Huangpu River in what is now the Hongkou District, and the French Concession is southwest of downtown and still shows strong evidence of its colonial roots.

By the 1850s Shanghai had developed into a major international trade port, especially for the bustling opium and tea trades. The foreign powers had little interest in development of a harmonious society, and for the next 100 years, the city was characterized by lawlessness, gambling, prostitution, and opium addiction.

The party ended in 1949 when Communist forces took control of the city. Although Mao sent the foreigners packing, Shanghai has never shaken

PRIME LIVING LOCATIONS

PRIME LIVING LOCATIONS

its reputation as a place where money is more important than following the rules, and where no pursuit is nobler than having a good time. As a result of the economic reforms of the 1980s, the city began to reattract large numbers of foreign firms. In the resulting economic miracle, Shanghai has reclaimed the prosperity and glamour of its youth. The cost of progress, however, is pollution, congestion, destruction of historic neighborhoods, and the struggle to provide affordable housing for its legally registered residents as well as its 6 million migrant workers who have flocked to Shanghai to pursue their own dreams of riches and prosperity.

The Lay of the Land

The muddy waters of the Huangpu River divide Shanghai into two parts. The older part of town is known as Puxi, which literally means "west of the Pu River." On the other side of the river, you'll find Pudong ("east of the Pu River"), which in the past 20 years has undergone a miracle transformation from rice paddies to ultramodern development. Most historical sites of interest to tourists are in Puxi, while Pudong is the site of the city's financial district and an export processing zone that has attracted a large number of multinational firms.

On the Puxi side of the river is the Bund, a wide pedestrian river walk where tourists and lovers take in the breathtaking views of Pudong's skyline across

© BARBARA STROTHER

A giant scale model of Shanghai hints at the city's incredible size.

SHANGHAI BOOKS

- *In Search of Old Shanghai* (1982) by Ling Pan is considered the authoritative history of Shanghai. Sadly it is out of print but worth reading if you can find a secondhand copy.

- *Life and Death in Shanghai* (1988) details Nien Cheng's suffering during the Cultural Revolution of 1966-1976.

- *New Shanghai: The Rocky Rebirth of China's Legendary City* (2000) by Pamela Yatsko describes Shanghai's return to its position as the most dynamic city in Asia.

- *Shanghai Diary: A Young Girl's Journey from Hitler's Hate to War-torn China* (2004) is Ursula Bacon's story of moving from Europe to the Shanghai Jewish Ghetto as an 11-year-old girl.

- *The Shanghai Green Gang: Politics and Organized Crime, 1919-1937* (1996) is a scholarly book by Brian G. Martin detailing the exploits of Shanghai's most notorious gang, led by Pudong native Du Yuesheng, the godfather of sin city.

- *Shanghai Messenger* (2005) by Andrea Cheng is a fifth grade-level kid's book that tells the wonderful story of an American-Chinese girl who connects with her Chinese heritage while visiting Shanghai.

the river. The backdrop of the Bund is a collection of fabulous colonial-era buildings highlighted by the elegant Peace Hotel, a previous haunt for Shanghai's high-roller crime bosses, politicians, and foreign dignitaries. The Las Vegas–style neon lights of Nanjing Road, a busy pedestrian shopping street, will guide you from the Bund to People's Square and People's Park. This large city park was originally the site of the Shanghai horse racetrack, but today it houses three museums and a theater and also serves as the city's transportation hub and cultural center.

The major north–south roads in Puxi are named after China's provinces, and the east–west roads are named after the major cities. A few blocks south of People's Square is the site of the old walled Chinese city currently known as Old Town, or the Yuyuan neighborhood, named after its famous gardens and bazaar. A few long blocks to the west of Old Town and People's Square is the upscale French Concession, home of most of the foreign consulates. The Hongqiao-Gubei District is farther out to the west, and is home to a large enclave of expatriates near the Hongqiao airport.

Across the river in Pudong is the Lujiazui Financial District, home to the Shanghai Stock Exchange, numerous banks, and three of the world's most impressive skyscrapers, the Oriental Pearl Tower, the Jin Mao building, and the World Financial Center, currently the tallest in the world by roof height.

© BARBARA STROTHER

Shanghai summers bring frequent and sudden rains.

About a 10-minute cab ride to the southeast is the Jinqiao District, home to numerous foreign firms and the bustling Biyun International neighborhood, where foreigners practically outnumber locals. Shanghai's new Pudong airport is located about 50 kilometers from Lujiazui to the southeast.

CLIMATE

The best season in Shanghai is springtime (March–May) with its pleasant temperatures around 65°F and the city's famous flowering trees that create "petal storms" around town when the breeze blows. Summertime lasts from June through August. The days are long; the temperatures are hot (frequently above 90°F). Shanghai averages about six inches of rain each month in the summer, so things might cool down a bit during afternoon storms, but Mother Nature quickly takes her revenge with exhausting tropical humidity—don't even bother trying to hang up your laundry on these days; it simply won't dry.

It finally cools down in the fall season, which runs from September through November. Average fall temperatures are around 65°F. Shanghai winters last from December to February, and with daytime temperatures as low as 30°F, it can get a little cool, but it almost never snows. You won't have too many blue-sky days in the winter thanks to the combination of weather and pollution.

LANGUAGE

People who grew up in the city will speak the local Shanghai dialect, which some say sounds like Japanese. The Mandarin spoken here, the official language of schools, government, and business, has no difficult accent, unlike the heavily accented Mandarin spoken in Beijing and so many other regions of China. Fortunately for expats, there are enough locals who speak English that you can get by in Shanghai without learning much Mandarin, though we wouldn't recommend it.

CULTURE

Compared to most Chinese cities, Shanghai has relatively few historically significant cultural sites due to its short history. Shanghai's true cultural identity is best represented by the city's pop culture scene. Since the 1920s, when Hollywood brought its trade to China, Shanghai has served as the center of China's film industry, and the city regularly hosts major international film festivals. The city itself has starred in dozens of movies, including recent flicks *Mission Impossible III, Shanghai Triad,* and *Godzilla: Final Wars* (in which the Oriental Pearl Tower is destroyed). Despite the ubiquitous DVD bootleggers on every street corner, Shanghai's movie houses do a brisk business showing the latest films. The art deco Cathay Theater on Huaihai Road has been showing Hollywood flicks since the 1930s, when Americans were its main customers.

The "Paris of the East" nickname aptly describes Shanghai's role as fashion

PRIME LIVING LOCATIONS

SHANGHAI ON THE BIG SCREEN

- ***Mission Impossible III:*** The continuation of the spy theme, this time partly set in Shanghai.
- ***Shanghai Express:*** This 1930s movie is set during the civil war that overthrew the last emperor. Marlene Dietrich stars as Shanghai Lily, who rides a train to Shanghai. Shanghaiers were outraged with the film's portrayal of them as bandits, and they threatened to jail the director if he ever set foot in Shanghai.
- ***Shanghai Ghetto:*** A documentary of the sad tale of Jewish refugees who fled Nazi Europe in World War II and settled in Shanghai.
- ***Shanghai Kiss:*** An endearing love story interwoven around the tale of an Asian-American who has inherited his grandparents' home near the Shanghai Bund.
- ***Shanghai Surprise:*** This super-cheesy movie starring Sean Penn as a tie salesman and Madonna as a (*gasp!*) missionary got horrible reviews, but it is actually a fun, lighthearted movie that's enjoyable as long as your expectations aren't very high.
- ***Shanghai Triad:*** This movie shows a 1930s Shanghai ruled by gangsters.
- ***Temptress Moon:*** When the head of a wealthy Chinese family dies, his daughter tries to manage the household but gets entangled in opium and a love triangle. Set in Shanghai in the 1920s, the movie portrays the struggle between Westerners, gangsters, and the Japanese for control of the city.

A worker naps in front of an upscale Shanghai shop.

capital of China and its "eat, drink, and be merry" attitude. The city has authentic ethnic restaurants featuring the cuisine of at least 50 different countries, including Brazil, France, Ireland, Mexico, and Turkey (complete with belly dancers, of course), to name just a few. The French Concession, where most of the consulates are located, has always been the home of the international restaurants, clubs, and the like, but in recent years these places have cropped up in all corners of the city.

Where to Live

Where you live in Shanghai will most likely depend on where your job is located. Because the city sprawls out like the Los Angeles metro area, commutes from one side to the other take up to two hours, even more during rush hours.

Most of the diplomatic corps tend to live in apartments in the French Concession, where the 30-plus consulates are located, including American, Australian, British, and Canadian. Those working in finance will probably be located in Lujiazui, Pudong. Families tend to prefer Hongqiao and Jinqiao, where there's plenty of green space, large villas, and excellent international schools, while singles prefer downtown with its vibrant energy, numerous shopping venues, and exciting nightlife.

DOWNTOWN SHANGHAI

Within Puxi, the Bund marks the eastern edge of downtown, and the Suzhou Creek is considered the northern edge. The southern and western edges are somewhat arbitrary, but for clarity we'll exclude from downtown the Old Town neighborhood because few foreigners live there, and we'll cover the French Concession as a separate section. A couple of key areas for foreigners downtown include the Jing'an district, and on its far western side, Xujiahui.

Downtown Shanghai is characterized by small, densely built city blocks with plenty of tall skyscrapers and highly congested city streets—a Chinese version of Manhattan. Living downtown can be an exciting experience, with its appealing museums, concert halls, shopping, restaurants, and nightlife. It's relatively easy to get around on foot, by local bus, or by subway. The drawbacks of living downtown are the congestion and the pollution. There are no international schools in downtown Shanghai, so the few foreign children unfortunate enough to live here must endure daily commutes to their schools in the suburbs. One of the nearest international school is the Shanghai Community International School in Changning, due west of downtown.

Virtually all of the downtown housing is in apartments. The demand has been very high in recent years, driving up prices, but the real estate bust of the global financial crisis should apply downward pressure on prices. Rents for an average two-bedroom apartment downtown start around $1,000 per month. Apartments in the high-rises overlooking People's Square rent for around $2,500 for a two-bedroom place, and up to $10,000-plus for a 350-square-meter five-bedroom penthouse. Serviced apartments are available at the numerous upscale hotels, such as at the Portman Ritz-Carlton, which has long been an important hub of expat activity with its imported-foods store and entertainment facilities. At the Portman, also called the Shanghai Center, rents for serviced apartments with 1 to 4 bedrooms (100 square meters, up to 380 square meters for penthouses) range $2,400–11,000 per month.

© BARBARA STROTHER

Xintiandi

FRENCH CONCESSION

Back in pre-communist days, most foreigners lived and worked just north of downtown in an area known as the International Settlement, but the French built their own settlement to the west of the Chinese city, just southwest of the present-day People's Square. While the International Settlement has been replaced with newer construction, much of the French Concession still retains its original colonial charms. Today, the French Concession is characterized by its historic Western architecture, its upscale shopping, and its foreign consulates. You can walk around the tree-lined streets and take in the historical sites, including art deco buildings from the 1930s, Sun Yatsen's former residence, and the site of Mao's first congress of the Chinese Communist Party.

The area is a must-see for tourists, but it is also quite popular among expats because of the excellent shopping, the Hengshan Road church with its services for foreigners, and the numerous international restaurants, especially at Xintiandi. The restaurant selection in the French Concession includes Mexican, Brazilian, French, Italian, Turkish, Thai, and so on, some of which are housed in old historic homes. The popular bars and clubs here range from seedy to sophisticated, especially on the diverse bar streets of Maoming, Hengshan, and Xintiandi. There are no international schools in the French Concession except for one for preschoolers.

Housing in the French Concession mostly consists of apartments, but you can rent one of the older historic villas or remodeled lane houses. On the other hand, there are a few modern villas on offer in this area, such as the Thomson Garden, where 200-square-meter three-bedroom town houses rent around $6,000 per month. Rents for small 100-square-meter two-bedroom apartments in this area start out around $1,500 per month and top out as high as $10,000 or more for a large four-bedroom penthouse in one of the high-rises.

HONGQIAO AND THE WESTERN SUBURBS

The Hongqiao area is located in the western suburbs. The area is relatively flat but is not pedestrian friendly due to the long city blocks and wide boulevards. Hongqiao was originally developed in the 1970s as a foreign trade zone complete with an international airport that anchored Hongqiao's bustling logistics business. Hongqiao has played second fiddle to Pudong over the past 20 years, but a mishmash of foreign firms, in a variety of industries but especially in manufacturing and logistics, have still chosen to locate here. Around these core industries, a massive service sector has arisen that includes office buildings, hotels, and exhibition centers. There are plenty of excellent options for schooling in Hongqiao as the area is home to Shanghai's largest and most established international schools. The Gubei neighborhood in the center of Hongqiao is getting a reputation as Shanghai's "India Town" because there are so many expats from India in this area, though most of Hongqiao's foreign residents come from all over the globe. Minhang District is also an up-and-coming area for foreigners.

Hongqiao has every sort of housing, including villas, serviced apartments, and regular apartments, but the area is known for its numerous villa complexes. On the low end, you can rent a smaller three-bedroom town house with about 250 square meters for around $2,500 per month. On the high end, a five-bedroom 650-square-meter villa at Le Chateau rents for $15,000 per month. Numerous apartment rentals are available in Hongqiao, mostly in high-rise towers. Rents start out around $1,500 for a modern 120-square-meter two-bedroom and quickly climb as high as $7,500 for larger, fancier places, such as the 365-square-meter four-bedroom apartments at the lush Shanghai Racquet Club complex.

LUJIAZUI FINANCIAL DISTRICT

Lujiazui is China's Wall Street district. The Shanghai Stock Exchange is located here, as are the headquarters for many of China's largest banks. Lujiazui is located in Pudong directly across the river from the Bund. While the

© BARBARA STROTHER

the Pearl Tower in Lujiazui

Bund is China's strongest reminder of its colonial period, the Lujiazui skyline proudly symbolizes China's future. From the space-age Oriental Pearl Tower to the country's tallest building, the Shanghai World Financial Center, there's no greater display of architecture. As you wander around Lujiazui, you can still find an occasional traditional *shikoumen* home with its trademark stone entryway, but most have been razed to make way for the steel-and-glass skyscrapers.

On the ground in the shadow of the skyscrapers, Lujiazui's sidewalks are busy with crowds of tourists, shoppers, and the suits who work in the office towers. Although it's crowded, it's easy to get around on foot or by bike. Century Avenue starts at the Oriental Pearl Tower and runs southeast, where it ends at the giant steel sundial near the entrance of Century Park. With its massive pedestrian plazas, time-themed sculptures, and rows and rows of trees, some have suggested the avenue is the Chinese version of the Champs Élysées.

You can move around Lujiazui efficiently on the subway or the bus, and you can easily travel between Lujiazui and Puxi on the passenger ferries, subway, or via the psychedelic passenger tunnel. The roads can get quite congested, so taxis aren't always the best way to get around, especially during the rush hour gridlock or when it rains.

Besides high-finance companies, Lujiazui also houses a number of upscale hotels and a few massive shopping centers, including Babaiban, Shanghai Times Square, and the Superbrand Mall. The Pudong river walk here is Pudong's version of the Bund but more suited for jogging or cycling since it's much less crowded. For other fun outings, Lujiazui also hosts the new Shanghai Ocean Aquarium, the Lujiazui Golf Club, and the Science and Technology Museum. Besides a few small kindergartens, there are no international schools in Lujiazui, though there are several in nearby areas of Pudong.

There's no room for villa housing in urban Lujiazui, but there are plenty of high-rise apartment towers. Shanghai's formerly hot real estate market kept developers building upward and onward until the housing bubble burst, and in Lujiazui there seems to be more housing than jobs, which has kept the rents perhaps lower than they should have been. Yanlord Town, one of the area's most popular complexes, has two-bedroom flats with 100-plus square meters starting around $1,000 per month (but climbing closer to $7,000 for a large and luxurious 5-bedroom with close to 300 square meters). Modest two-bedroom apartments elsewhere can still be rented for just $600 per month. Of course serviced luxury apartments are also available. The swanky Ascott Hotel has fully serviced apartments that start around $2,300 for a small 85-square-foot one-bedroom, and up into the $12,000 range for a spacious 375-square-foot four-bedroom.

JINQIAO BIYUN INTERNATIONAL COMMUNITY

Jinqiao, a suburb in central Pudong, was established as an Export Processing Zone in the 1990s and has been rapidly developing ever since. A few farms still remain on the fringe, but they continue to give way to the rapid development of industrial sites and high-priced housing. The area is relatively flat and easily bikable, but as with most Chinese suburbs, distance to the central amenities makes residents dependent on cars, either their own or taxis.

The eastern end of Jinqiao is industrial and home to companies specializing in electronics, automotive, appliances, and biotech. Some of the larger foreign firms include General Motors, Kodak, Whirlpool, and Corning. Just to the south of Jinqiao is the Zhangjiang High-Tech Park, which has recently attracted a number of foreign firms that include Du Pont, Honeywell, and Roche.

The western half of Jinqiao consists mostly of housing, shopping, and schools. This area is known as the Biyun International District, and there is no greater concentration of Westerners in China than in Biyun. With two large international schools within walking distance, you're just as likely to see blond kids here as Chinese ones. Quite a few of the businesses cater to expats also. Carrefour is the retail center of Jinqiao, and next door you'll find a variety of international restaurants and shops. A great way to spend a Sunday afternoon is watching a local soccer match from the Blue Frog restaurant terrace while enjoying the best burger in China. Other amenities of interest to expats include two top-tier golf courses (Thomson and the Shanghai Links); the new Abundant Grace Protestant church and the Jesus Sacred Heart Catholic church, both with English-language services; and the China Europe International Business School, which has been ranked as having the number-one MBA program in Asia.

Housing in Jinqiao is among the best quality you'll find in China, and it has the prices to prove it. There are more than a dozen villa complexes here, starting around $3,000 per month for a three-bedroom 250-square-meter place at Luoshan Oasis and going as high as $14,000 per month for

a soccer field in the Biyun area of Pudong

© BARBARA STROTHER

PRIME LIVING LOCATIONS

a five-bedroom 600-square-meter place at the Regency Park. Thomson and Shanghai Links both have villas right on their golf courses. There are dozens of high-rise apartment complexes in and around Jinqiao with rents as low as $500 for a small 85-square-meter one-bedroom apartment and up to $6,000 per month for a four-bedroom 320-square-meter place at Green Court in the heart of the Biyun neighborhood. The smaller, cheaper places will be farther away from Biyun Road.

Daily Life

EXPAT SOCIAL SCENE

Shanghai's social scene is legendary. The city's reputation as a place where the in-crowd stays out late every night drinking, dancing, and flirting can be quite realistic. You'll find bars and nightclubs, even gay bars, throughout the city but especially around the French Concession. Maoming Road and the Xintiandi area are both hopping spots just south of Huaihai Road. The recently gentrified Xintiandi area has quite a few upscale restaurants, bars, and coffee shops that are popular with foreigners.

Since the opening up of the 1970s, the earliest expats in Shanghai were teachers and students at the various university campuses across the city. Today there are tens of thousands of international students attending Shanghai's universities, including the prestigious Fudan and Jiaotong Universities. Officials estimate the number of international students will exceed 50,000 by 2010.

True to its cosmopolitan reputation, Shanghai has well over 100 expatriate clubs, some based on nationality, including clubs run by Belgians, Brits, Canucks, Italians, and the list goes on and on. There are also quite a few alumni clubs, and all sorts of groups for the artistically minded, including writing, books, music, painting, and dance (salsa, anyone?). If sports are your thing, Shanghai's expats meet to participate in every imaginable sport, including cycling, fencing, golf, rugby, running, squash, Ultimate Frisbee, and dozens of others. There are a few charitable organizations that you can get involved with that support orphanages or perform other good works. Still other clubs are organized according to the needs of families, such as moms' groups that set up play dates for the little ones.

RESOURCES

For English-language newspapers, you can read the *Shanghai Daily* or pick up an English magazine like *City Weekend, 8 Days,* or *That's Shanghai,* which provide up-to-date info on local sights and events. *That's* is a must-read for all expats. The advertisements are a great way to find the local businesses that cater to the expat community, and its classified ads can help you find just about anything, including real estate, jobs, language partners, or even a sweetheart. Other English magazines are dedicated to local real estate or business, such as *Shanghai Business Review.* Many of these magazines have companion websites that can be useful, especially if you are trying to learn about the city from abroad.

HEALTH CARE
In recent years Shanghai's local hospitals have begun to win the trust of the expatriate community. Three hospitals, all in Puxi, have special foreigner clinics: the Huashan Hospital, Huadong Hospital, and the First People's Hospital near the Bund. The Ruidong Hospital in the Jinqiao area of Pudong also serves foreigners.

If you work for an international company, you'll probably be covered by the Parkway Health system (formerly World Link) or a similar provider that follows international standards. There are five Parkway health and dental clinics located in various areas of Puxi as well as one in Pudong. The Shanghai United Family Hospital, with two locations in Puxi, is another good option, as is the Shanghai East International Medical Center in Pudong.

SCHOOLS
The Hongqiao area is home to Shanghai's largest and most established international schools. The Shanghai American School (Puxi branch) has large elementary, middle, and high schools; technology labs; and impressive sports facilities that include an aquatic center. The Yew Chung Shanghai International School, which follows a British curriculum, has a campus in Hongqiao and a boarding school in Gubei. The Shanghai Community International School and the British International School each have three campuses to serve various areas of the city.

There are a number of international schools in and around Jinqiao. In the heart of Biyun, the Concordia International School is a top-notch college prep school with an American curriculum and a Christian emphasis. Next door is the Pinghe Bilingual School, a boarding school where most of the students come from the wealthiest families in China. A number of the students are foreigners (about 5 percent are Westerners) whose parents want their children to learn Chinese fluently. The Dulwich British School is just a few blocks away. A half-hour's drive to the east is the Shanghai American School

BLUE FROG IN RED CHINA

AN INTERVIEW WITH RESTAURATEUR BOB BOYCE

After a steady diet of rice and noodles, expatriates from the West tend to develop cravings for Western food. Sometimes a Big Mac with a red-bean milkshake and a taro pie just doesn't cut it. That's where Bob Boyce comes in. A longtime resident of China, this Montana native has built a successful restaurant business that is satisfying expat palates across the Middle Kingdom while also introducing locals to the "best of the West" cuisine.

Tell us about your business.

I run a company based in Shanghai that includes restaurants, bars, and catering. Blue Frog, which opened in 1999, was one of the first independent restaurants in Shanghai to serve classic Western food in a comfortable contemporary atmosphere with warm service, all at a reasonable price. It has since become a Shanghai institution, with seven venues throughout the city, a Macau location at the Venetian, and two venues in Beijing, with additional venues opening soon in Shanghai and Beijing. KABB in Xintiandi is a more sophisticated bar and grill serving luxe comfort food with a great, approachable wine list. It's also something of a "see and be seen" place here in Shanghai. We also have a catering arm that does a full range of events, from large corporate functions to small house parties.

Bob Boyce

How did you end up in the restaurant business in China?

My first job in China was with a relocation company, which stationed me in Guangzhou and Shanghai. Along the way I noticed that in these important international cities, typical Western food was scarce. I thought the expat community would embrace a casual restaurant with great quality, a consistent product, a reasonable price, and the friendly service you'd expect back in the States. At heart, all my restaurants are about being able to unwind in a relaxed setting with great food and drinks.

What are some of the most difficult challenges of running a business in China today?

There is an acute skilled-labor shortage. Finding staff with depth of experience is difficult, and it will continue to be difficult for many years to come. We have approached this challenge by instituting a training program to develop entry-level staff into managers, but obviously, this is a longer-term solution.

What first brought you to China, and what were your initial impressions?

I first came to Beijing in 1994 to study Chinese. Even back then, China seemed like a place with huge potential for adventure and opportunity. The

COURTESY OF BOB BOYCE

sheer volume of people was a sharp contrast to my home in Montana. The diversity within that volume was another initial impression – people may have all looked like Han Chinese, but once you went beyond the surface, there were so many differences. I saw people with everything, and people with nothing. I was amazed at the sharp contrasts. You could spend a dollar, have a great meal, and be full – or walk across the street, spend $200, and also have a great (but very different) meal. That is actually something that is still happening today.

How have those first impressions changed over time?
It's not that my first impressions have changed so much as that China has evolved. When I first arrived, there really was no middle class – just the very poor and the very rich. Now there is an increasingly affluent middle class, and more and more opportunities available, no matter their backgrounds. We have these *ayis* in our organization who can't read or write and come from extremely poor backgrounds, but they are now able to send their children to school. Their kids are fearless; they look me, a foreigner, in the eye and shake my hand, and they have the same chance of achieving their dreams as anyone else. That's a huge change.

What are the best things about living in China as a foreigner today?
The vibe of the place. Everything is on the go and in a constant state of change. Also, the people can be amazingly hospitable and welcoming. I've stayed here all these years because I love the energy of Shanghai, the people, making sense of everything. It's amazing, and I love the opportunities available. Frankly, I don't know why anyone would be anywhere else!

PRIME LIVING LOCATIONS

© BARBARA STROTHER

(Pudong branch) with its sprawling 23-acre seaside campus located adjacent to the Shanghai Links golf course.

SHOPPING

Nanjing Road, Shanghai's most famous shopping street, consists of Chinese and international department stores, specialty stores, and restaurants. It's a wide pedestrian street filled with thousands of Chinese shoppers and quite a few foreigners, especially tourists. Its futuristic neon lights and the modern architecture are straight out of *Blade Runner*. For clothing, the Silk King here on Nanjing Road is an obligatory if overpriced stop on the foreign dignitary circuit. While you search for the perfect fabric for your custom-made *qipao* (traditional dress), check out the dozens of pictures of heads of state who have shopped here before.

For upscale name-brand shopping, try Huaihai Road in the French Concession, Plaza 66 on West Nanjing Road, the Super Brand Mall next to the Oriental Pearl Tower in Lujiazui, or the Grand Gateway in Xujiahui. Along Huaihai Road you can start by hopping on one of the double-decker buses to check out the area before you empty your wallet at some of the priciest, trendiest shops this side of Paris. There are also close to 100 big-box retailers in Shanghai, including quite a few foreign-owned stores such as Carrefour, Wal-Mart, Metro, and B&Q. For items unique to villa living like trampolines, hot tubs, gas grills, or pool tables, try the showroom of Villa Lifestyles.

MARKETS

Shanghai's Xiangyang market was once one of the best-known markets in all of China. Originally it was a narrow alley where vendors sold thousands of pairs of Nike sneakers, Gucci heels, and North Face gear that made its way out of the back door of the factory or was just plain counterfeit. The market had expanded to a large outdoor square carrying more goods, especially pirated DVDs and fake Rolexes. The "Respect Intellectual Property Rights" sign at the entrance was always good for a few laughs because if you removed all the counterfeit goods from the market, you'd be left nothing but a few silk scarves. Sadly the government ordered the market closed in 2006. Many of the fake-goods vendors have ended up at the underground market adjacent to the Science and Technology Museum subway stop in Pudong.

For antique trinket shopping in Shanghai there are two markets in the city center and a cluster of furniture shops in the western suburbs. The Dongtai Road Market just south of Huaihai Park consists of a couple of narrow streets filled with shops overflowing with yesterday's treasures (and plenty of fakes that

gourd decorations for sale

look a lot like yesterday's treasures). The Fuyou Antiques Market is a jam-packed four-story building in Old Town a few blocks from of the Yuyuan bazaar. Save time to wander the numerous shops of the Yuyuan area in Old Town; you never know what you'll find here. The center of Yuyuan is great for the typical tourist purchases, but wander farther afield down stray alleys to find where the locals shop for cheap. All Shanghai expats head here when they're searching for odd random things (a Santa Claus outfit, funky wigs, Chinese lanterns, hand warmers, red envelopes, and random tools, to name a few from experience).

For gorgeous antique Chinese furniture, you should try the Hongqiao suburbs, where there's a cluster of a dozen or so large warehouses packed with antique furniture for sale. Most of the shops, like Hu and Hu (a favorite among expats) will refinish the piece according to the look you want. And compared to the flimsy furniture sold at the local furniture stores, or even at Ikea (near the Shanghai Stadium), the cost of antique furniture is really quite reasonable, but keep in mind you'll have to pay to ship it back home at the end of your stay in China.

Throughout Shanghai there are numerous other local markets that rarely make it into the English-language guidebooks. Most neighborhoods have vegetable markets, toy and electronics markets, and "flower and bird" markets that carry all kinds of pets and bonsai trees. Just ask your Chinese friends where they shop and you're likely to find some good markets nearby.

Getting Around

Except for the older parts of the city, Shanghai is not a very pedestrian-friendly place. The new areas and suburbs consist of large sprawling blocks that cause a lot of people to park their bikes and take taxis instead. If you really want to get around on the cheap, Shanghai has hundreds of buses that'll take you anywhere in the city—if you can figure out the routes, have a lot of time on

© BARBARA STROTHER

your hands, and don't mind the throngs of other riders. To cross from Puxi to Pudong and back, you can take the local passenger ferry, even bringing your bicycle or motorcycle with you. More often than not, though, you'll zip around town using some combination of taxi and subway.

BY SUBWAY

The Shanghai subway is the longest track in all of China, with more than 3 million riders on an average day. It's currently in the middle of an ambitious 40-year plan to build a spiderweb of around 20 subway lines to link every district of Shanghai, including the far suburbs, islands, and even out to Hangzhou. Connected to the subway system is the Maglev, the world's fastest commercial train, which takes about 20 minutes from the terminal to the airport. At 270 miles per hour, it puts quite a few roller coasters to shame.

As of this writing there are eight functional subway lines, though several new lines and extensions will soon be open for transit. The Number 1 subway line extends north past Shanghai Circus World, through the main railway terminal, south through People's Square, then jogs southwest to the south railway station and beyond. The Number 2 subway line starts in the far west and connects the Hongqiao airport with People's Square before dipping under the Huangpu River into Pudong's financial district and on to the Maglev terminal. The Number 3 line is an elevated light-rail train that connects the south railway station within a half loop around the western side of the city before turning north at the main railway station. Line 4 runs a loop around the central city. Line 6 is the only line that runs exclusively in Pudong, and it follows a more-or-less northeast to southwest trajectory. Lines 5 and 9 serve the southwestern suburbs.

HONG KONG AND MACAU

There's a certain excitement and exhilaration to Hong Kong and Macau, two areas located just east and west, respectively, of the Pearl River Delta off the southern coast of the mainland. These two have always been, and continue to be, popular spots for foreigners to live, work, and play—and for good reason. Time spent living in one of these locales will be a once-in-a-lifetime experience.

Hong Kong and Macau share many geographic, historical, and political similarities. Both comprise a peninsula and islands. Both were settled and governed by foreigners and have retained their international flavor through the years that the mainland was "communized" and closed to outsiders. Both are now technically part of the People's Republic of China but are classified as Special Administration Regions (SARs). Being a SAR guarantees a large measure of autonomy to maintain their capitalist economy and local rule, an arrangement made under Deng Xiaoping's principle of "one country, two systems."

Expats headed to either of these locations will have a very different experience

© BARBARA STROTHER

PRIME LIVING LOCATIONS

from those headed to the mainland. You won't feel the heavy hand of the central government here. Hong Kong and Macau are much closer to Western nations in their culture and outlook. In fact, Macanese and Hong Kongers who live in mainland China are given many of the same privileges as foreigners, including attending church services and international schools that require a foreign passport.

Despite their similarities, each of these spots has its unique flair. Hong Kong's fame comes from its role as a fast-paced center for international business, finance, and some of the world's best shopping. Macau, on the other hand, enjoys a laid-back reputation founded on its colonial charm and its casinos. Macau is much less sophisticated than its sibling across the water and slightly cheaper as well—though if you're looking for a bargain, you're better off in the mainland.

Hong Kong 香港

Hong Kong is a city unlike any other in the world. It's a place where ancient meets modern, secular meets sacred, and East meets West. Buddhist and Christian faithful stop by their local temple or cathedral as they go about their day, while Chinese and Western business types make their fortunes in glimmering skyscrapers nearby. Neon lights guide you to some of the hippest nightlife in Asia, while in the New Territories and surrounding waters, farmers

© BARBARA STROTHER

It is not uncommon in Hong Kong to stop by a temple or church as you go about your day.

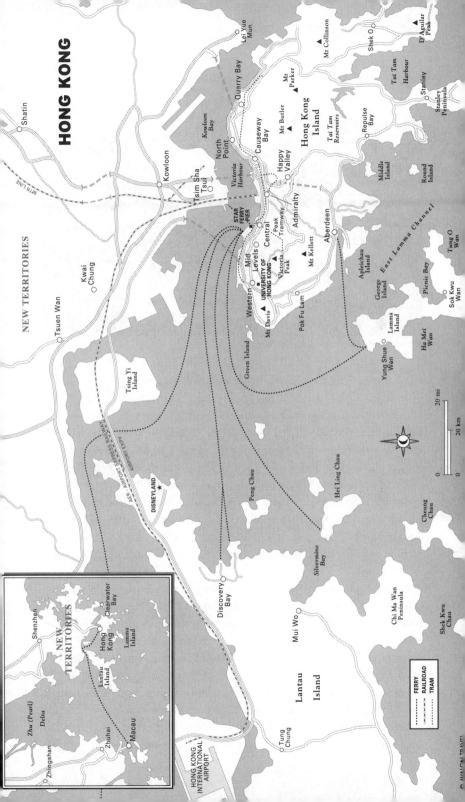

ancient and new in North Hong Kong

© BARBARA STROTHER

and fishermen ply their ancient trade with skills passed down over a dozen generations. Colonial architecture, street names, and vehicles traveling on the left side of the road show the influence of the British, yet over 6 million Chinese residents remind you that you are in the Orient. Whether it's picturesque temples with incense sticks burning or the Hang Sang Stock Exchange with multimillion-dollar deals cooking, Hong Kong is an exciting place.

Hong Kong hasn't always been this way. When the British took control in 1841 as a concession granted by the Treaty of Nanking, the Hong Kong islands were little more than muddy islands deforested by firewood pickers. Today, the islands are green and lush, the result of the vigorous British reforestation of Hong Kong, including the introduction of hundreds of new species of foliage.

Many people have an image of Hong Kong as a single island covered with concrete and skyscrapers. In reality, only about a fifth of Hong Kong's islands (and the Kowloon Peninsula) are urbanized. The remaining area includes plenty of farmland, mountain parks, and beaches. The deep waters surrounding Hong Kong and its location near the South China Sea and the mouth of the Pearl River have made it a naturally strategic hub of ocean shipping for hundreds of years. Its name literally means "fragrant harbor," a reference to the sandalwood incense production that could be smelled by sailors at sea.

Over the past 150 years Hong Kong's laissez-faire economic system has been a magnet for international investment. Hong Kong is a literal textbook example of free market capitalism at its best. Its combination of low taxes, limited regulations, and an industrious labor force have turned this once-sleepy archipelago into one of the world's foremost economic powerhouses.

The Hong Kong story does have a dark side. Hong Kong's idyllic tropical-island location also means it suffers from regular typhoons. The population density also puts Hong Kong residents at risk of diseases such as SARS and the bird flu. The laissez-faire government situation, although it has benefited business, has also proven fertile ground for organized crime. The notorious gangs, known as triads, are major players in black markets around the world. Their specialty? You name it—extortion, smuggling, drugs, pornography, counterfeiting, and piracy (both the waterborne type and the distribution of copied intellectual property, especially DVDs and software).

Hong Kong has never been rich in natural resources, and its economy has always been built on trade. The engines driving Hong Kong's economy today are in finance, banking, insurance, telecommunications, tourism, entertainment, and shipping. The sweatshops of old have been moved across the border into Shenzhen, and today giant cranes hoisting hundreds of containers into oceangoing ships have replaced the sweaty coolies and the picturesque junks in the harbor.

Close to 7 million people call the city of Hong Kong home, including nearly a half million expatriates, many of whom are of Chinese descent—having left during darker times, they are returning now that Hong Kong's standard of living is virtually the same as elsewhere in the world. Americans and Canadians now outnumber the once-predominant Brits. There are also large communities of Thais, Indians, Pakistanis, Japanese, and a plethora of Filipinos, many working as domestic helpers.

In 1997 the British turned control of Hong Kong over to the People's Republic of China. PLA troops quietly crossed the bridges in trucks and assumed the defense posts previously held by the British military. Unlike in the mainland, the PLA here does not make itself very visible. The Hong Kong Police Force, on the other hand, maintains the peace. Though ownership of Hong Kong reverted from the British back to Beijing, the Hong Kong SAR still has its own local government that manages most governmental affairs, retaining its own currency and laws.

THE LAY OF THE LAND

The Hong Kong SAR consists of Hong Kong Island, Lantau Island, the Kowloon Peninsula, the New Territories, and more than 200 smaller islands. Hong Kong Island is the original British territory and remains the center of

PRIME LIVING LOCATIONS

© BARBARA STROTHER

Hiking paths on Lantau Island are a serene break from the bustle of the city.

government and business activity for the region. The Kowloon urban area is on the tip of the peninsula across Victoria Harbour from downtown Hong Kong. The remainder of the peninsula is known as the New Territories, which make up more than 90 percent of the SAR. There are quite a few small towns, farms, fisheries, beaches, and mountain parks in the New Territories. Lantau Island, to the west of Hong Kong Island, is a beautiful mountainous area. More than half of Lantau is set aside as parkland, and a network of hiking trails crisscrosses the mountain linking its Buddhist and Trappist sites. The northern shore of Lantau is the site of the new international airport, and its farmland is rapidly giving way to development. The impressive Tsing Ma Bridge connects Lantau to Kowloon. Several smaller islands are home to residential communities, all of which utilize ferries to connect to the rest of Hong Kong.

Climate

Hong Kong's climate is subtropical and similar to that of Hawaii, which shares the same latitude. The fall season, September and October, is the most pleasant. The days are warm enough for fun days at the beach, and the ocean breezes make for cool relaxing evenings. You'll never see snow in winter, though you might encounter some ice if you hike the mountain peaks on the chilliest of days. The misty months of March and April bring warmer temperatures, around 70°F. The hottest months are May through August, with temperatures above 90°F and frequent rains pushing the humidity close to 100 percent.

Language

In Hong Kong quite a bit of English is spoken, so it's entirely possible to get by with English alone. If you want to learn Chinese, you'd probably be better off living somewhere in the mainland, where you'll be forced to use it to communicate. Those that plan to make Hong Kong their home will be better off studying Cantonese because it's spoken throughout the region, but Mandarin is also becoming more common since the SAR reverted back to the PRC. Street signs are written in both traditional Chinese characters and in English.

Culture

Much of the local culture in Hong Kong centers around food. Hong Kongers love to eat out, and you'll find lines to get into many restaurants until late in the evening. With its unique blend of eastern and western cuisines as well as the grand diversity of international cuisines found here, eating in Hong Kong is a pastime that has a never-ending source of pleasure.

Hong Kong's pop culture wields a powerful influence in China, the rest of Asia, and even in the West. Hong Kong's fashionable Cantopop musicians are worshipped throughout the mainland, and its movie stars like Jackie Chan and Bruce Lee (even though he was born in San Francisco) are well-loved around the globe.

Other popular leisure activities in Hong Kong include horse races at the Happy Valley and Sha Tin courses, world-class arts performances and concerts, traditional Cantonese opera, shopping, playing mahjong, and spending time outdoors on Hong Kong's green mountains and sandy beaches.

WHERE TO LIVE

You'll find expatriates living in just about every corner of Hong Kong. When deciding where to live you'll have five major regions to choose from in the Hong Kong SAR: the north side of Hong Kong Island, the south side of Hong Kong Island, Kowloon, Lantau and Lamma Islands, or the New Territories.

In cost-of-living studies, Hong Kong is often among the top 10 most expensive cities, more expensive than New York and Los Angeles but slightly less than London. Housing will be your most expensive budget item. In fact, nearly 50 percent of Hong Kong residents live in public housing projects because they are unable to purchase homes amidst the notoriously high housing costs here.

North Hong Kong Island

With its bustling city streets and massive skyscrapers all lit up with neon

Chinese characters, the northern side of Hong Kong Island is the Hong Kong you've seen in photographs and movies. You can find expats living in every neighborhood in northern Hong Kong. Central is the financial and commercial hub of Hong Kong, and since so many expats work in finance, the area of Central, Western, and the Mid-levels has always been the premier location for expatriate living. Other key areas here include Admiralty, Causeway Bay, Happy Valley, Wan Chai, Kennedy Town, and North Point. North Hong Kong Island is also home to the University of Hong Kong, drawing international students to the area.

Living in the North Hong Kong districts can be exorbitant and crowded, especially around Central, but there are a number of amenities that might make living here worth it. Public transportation, especially the Mass Transit Railway (MTR), makes getting around easy. It's also home to one of the coolest ways of getting around: Every day thousands of people use the Mid-levels outdoor escalator (the longest in the world) to traverse its steep hills. Some escalators only run one direction and are switched from downhill in the morning to uphill in the afternoon and evening to accommodate the commuters. The restaurants, nightlife, and shopping are also legendary here, including the Lan Kwai Fong party zone and nearby Fringe Club arts center. The zoo is in this area, and there are a number of parks, including the Victoria Peak Garden at the top of the peak tramway. There are also plenty of churches, shopping centers, food markets, and hospitals.

Housing in North Hong Kong is some of the most expensive in all of Asia,

© BARBARA STROTHER

the view from the Peak: North Hong Kong Island in the foreground and Kowloon in the distance

a neighborhood park in North Hong Kong

and at times perhaps in the entire world. The prime living location is the Mid-levels, where a tiny one-bedroom 500-square-foot apartment rents for about HK$15,000 (US$1,900), and typical two-bedroom 800-square-foot apartments start around HK$20,000 (US$2,500). A serviced apartment in northern Hong Kong only costs a few thousand more unless it's at one of the swankier hotels.

Just up the mountain at Victoria Peak you'll find the expensive homes of the rich and famous, where rents can easily reach HK$300,000 (US$40,000) per month. (If you have to ask, you can't afford it.) You'll also find expat-friendly housing in other areas of North Hong Kong, such as Happy Valley, North Point, and Causeway Bay, where the rents are more or less what you'd pay in Central. Lower rents can be found farther from Central, such as in Kennedy Town to the west, but you might be the only foreigner in your neighborhood. Rents in Kennedy Town start around HK$10,000 (US$1,300). Check the local classifieds for even better bargains if you can get by with a tiny living space.

South Hong Kong Island

The southern half of Hong Kong Island is less developed than the urban north and is primarily known for its sandy beaches. While expatriate singles and couples often prefer the hustle and bustle of northern Hong Kong, expatriate families tend to prefer the quieter natural environment of the south. The south side boasts a long coastline with numerous beaches, bays, and inlets, but it also has the usual smattering of temples, parks, and shops. The giant Ocean Park with its pair of celebrity pandas also draws plenty of visitors. There are quite a few quaint villages along the coast, but the main towns are Pok Fu Lam, Cyberport, Aberdeen, Repulse Bay, and Stanley. As for public transportation, buses serve this area well (although because of the terrain, they are not very speedy). Plans are underway to bring the subway here, but currently there are no trains that serve southern Hong Kong.

© BARBARA STROTHER

PRIME LIVING LOCATIONS

© BARBARA STROTHER

South Hong Kong Island is perfect for beach lovers.

The Pok Fu Lam area on the western coast of Hong Kong Island, with its slow pace and the tranquil confluence of mountains, beaches, and parks, is a fave of expat families. Many of the expats here work at the University of Hong Kong or at one of the many IT firms nearby, especially at the Cyberport. The Queen Mary Hospital is also in Pok Fu Lam, one of the most established hospitals in Hong Kong. International schools include the Kellet School and the West Island School, both British, as well as the Kennedy School. Most of the housing in Pok Fu Lam is in high-rise buildings. The rent for an 850-square-foot two-bedroom apartment will start around HK$25,000 (US$3,300).

Aberdeen, Repulse Bay, and Stanley are other southern towns favored by expatriates. A number of country clubs are here, including the American Club, the Hong Kong Country Club, and the Royal Hong Kong Golf Club. For mariners, there's the Aberdeen Marina Club and the Aberdeen Boat Club. The top schools in the area include Aberdeen's Canadian International School and British South Island School as well as the Hong Kong International School (HKIS) with campuses in Repulse Bay and Tai Tam. Incidentally, HKIS is considered one of the premier schools in Asia. Housing costs on the south side, although by no means a bargain, can be more affordable than in other parts of Hong Kong, and you have a variety of housing options to choose from, including high-rise apartments, low-rise apartments, luxury villas, and even boats (there's a whole community of people, including a few expats, living on boats in the harbor at Aberdeen). Small one-bedroom apartments in Aberdeen

open-air pubs on the waterfront in Stanley

© BARBARA STROTHER

PRIME LIVING LOCATIONS

can be rented for HK$10,000 (US$1,300); larger three-bedroom places go for around twice that. Gorgeous sprawling villas with amazing views along the hills of southern Hong Kong rent for around HK$250,000 (US$32,250) per month, and you'll find a few simpler and smaller town houses and villas that rent for less than half that amount.

Kowloon and the New Territories

The Kowloon Peninsula is directly north of Hong Kong Island across Victoria Harbour. The British took possession of Kowloon as a concession of the Tianjin Treaty of 1858. Today Kowloon is a densely populated urban area. The Tsim Sha Tsui region at the tip of the peninsula is the heart and soul of Kowloon. The Hong Kong Polytechnic University is here as well as a number of museums, a coliseum, public parks, and more than a few of the world's largest corporations. Tsim Sha Tsui has numerous restaurants and nightclubs, not to mention shopping

neon lights in Kowloon

© BARBARA STROTHER

opportunities galore at public markets, megamalls, and everything in between. The northern part of Kowloon is less steel and concrete and somewhat more traditionally Chinese. Kowloon is a favorite for Americans, as evidenced by its American schools: Concordia International School and the American International School.

Housing costs in Kowloon, while high, are not as steep as on Hong Kong Island. The cheapest studio apartments in the heart of Tsim Sha Tsui rent for around HK$10,000 (US$1,300) per month, while a two-bedroom place in Tsim Sha Tsui can be rented for HK$22,000–32,000 (US$2,800–4,100). Elsewhere in

Tai Po Temple, New Territories

© BARBARA STROTHER

Kowloon expect to pay HK$12,000–18,000 (US$1,500–2,400) for a two-bedroom apartment with around 700 square feet.

The New Territories were "new" back in 1898 when the British first leased them from the Chinese. Today the New Territories are mostly rural with a few small towns. Most expats who choose to live in the New Territories choose to do so because they either want to be immersed in Chinese culture so they can learn the Cantonese language, value the country setting, or are just desperate to avoid Hong Kong's high rents. The International Christian School, one of Hong Kong's top institutions, is located here in Sha Tin, drawing expat families to the town. A number of foreigners have also chosen to live in Clearwater Bay and Sai Kung. Both areas have plenty of green space, fresh air, nice beaches, and excellent opportunities for outdoor recreation. Housing rates in the New Territories are the most affordable in the SAR. A 1,300-square-foot three-bedroom apartment can be rented for just over HK$20,000 (US$2,600). You'll find a few smaller villas in the central New Territories for as little as HK$35,000 (US$4,500) per month, though the large and luxurious ones with excellent locations near the coast will rent for three times that amount.

Lantau and Lamma Islands
With beautiful natural settings, Lantau Island and Lamma Island have

© BARBARA STROTHER

© BARBARA STROTHER

a view of Discovery Bay on Lantau Island

excellent beaches and mountainous hiking trails. Modern development has grown in Lantau in recent years. The new international airport is here, as is the new Hong Kong Disneyland, situated on Lantau's northeastern point. The luxury homes and international school in Lantau's Discovery Bay have attracted a significant expat community. Travel between Lantau Island and Hong Kong is easy using the MTR's Gold Line or ferries, and both taxis and buses ply the island's roads. Lamma Island, on the other hand, can only be reached by ferry, and there are no cars on the island. But rents are cheaper on Lamma, and there is a sizable expat community that enjoys the secluded and laid-back life here.

You can find some of the newest and cheapest housing in Lantau. Housing costs range from as low as HK$7,500 (US$1,000) per month for a small 300-square-foot one-bedroom apartment up to HK$50,000 (US$6,500) for a three-bedroom town house with a private yard. Detached luxury villas at Discovery Bay rent for US$15,000 or more and have over 2,000 square feet and a private pool. On Lamma Island you'll find 1- or 2-bedroom apartments in the HK$4,000–6,000 range (US$500–775), many with balconies and mountain or sea views. Unlike housing just about everywhere else in Hong Kong, Lamma prohibits buildings over three stories tall, so you won't have any high-rise apartment towers here.

DAILY LIFE
Visa Requirements

North Americans and most Europeans are allowed to visit Hong Kong for up to three months without a visa. If you will be working in Hong Kong, however, you should arrive with the correct visa in hand, as it can be quite difficult to change your visa type from tourist to business once you are there.

Anyone who resides in Hong Kong for more than 180 days is required to apply for a Hong Kong identity card at the Registration of Persons Office. To work in Hong Kong you'll need to secure an employment visa from the Chinese embassy or consulate in your home country, or by applying directly to the Hong Kong Immigration Department. If you find you really love this place, after legally residing in Hong Kong for seven years you are eligible for permanent residency. Dependents are not allowed to work on their spouse's visa and must apply for their own, but they still need to be sponsored by an employer first.

Finance
MONEY

Hong Kong has its own currency, called the Hong Kong dollar, which is broken into 100 cents. Because the Hong Kong dollar has been pegged to the U.S. dollar, the exchange rate doesn't fluctuate much (US$1 = HK$7.75). There are numerous ATM machines in Hong Kong, making it convenient for you to withdraw Hong Kong dollars, even from your bank account back home. Unlike the mainland, there are no limitations on how much currency you can bring in or out of Hong Kong. Cash transactions in PRC renminbi are becoming more common, and Hong Kong banks now offer yuan accounts.

MOVING IN

When it's time to move in, you'll need to have the utilities connected. To hook up your utilities, you'll first need to pay deposits of around US$100 for all utilities, including water (and sewage), electricity, natural gas, telephone, cable TV, and broadband (if you choose). Utility bills will be mailed to you, and most can be paid through automatic bank draft, at an ATM machine, using a payment processing service on the Internet, by mail, or in person. Typical monthly expenses for an average-sized Hong Kong home are HK$50 (US$6.50) for water (although it will be billed every four months), as much as HK$1,500 (US$200) for electricity if you run your air-conditioning frequently, HK$300 (US$40) for natural gas, HK$100 (US$13) for telephone, and HK$250-500 (US$32-64) for broadband and cable television. You should also consider changing your locks and getting a steel safety door installed when you move in. Though Hong Kong is not a violent place, burglary can be an issue here.

You can also use major credit cards here, but some shopkeepers will tack on a service fee of 5–10 percent. Quite a few locals use the Octopus smart card for purchases. Originally designed for use on the public transportation system, some restaurants and shops now accept payment with the Octopus card.

TAXES
There are no sales taxes or capital gains taxes in Hong Kong. You will, however, have to pay a 16 percent personal tax on your earned income. Personal income tax does not apply to income from investments, rentals, interest on your bank account, and the like. Although the tax rates are comparatively low, at the end of your first year in Hong Kong the Inland Revenue Department will mail you a bill for the tax on your first year's earnings, and a bill estimating the tax on your second year's anticipated earnings. You'll have to pay both bills within a couple months of each other, so be prepared financially. Your tax bill can be reduced with deductions similar to those in the U.S. system (mortgage interest, health care, senior care, and education are all tax-deductible). Taxes can be paid monthly if you want to avoid the lump sum at the end of the year; most people choose to pay every six months. Unless you have one of the generous expat employment compensation packages where your employer pays your taxes for you, you'll have to pay taxes yourself.

RETIREMENT
Just about everyone working in Hong Kong participates in the Mandatory Provident Fund (MPF) established by the government. In the MFP program, employers and employees both contribute funds (about 5 percent of the employee's salary) into a savings account designated for retirement. Numerous local banks participate in the MFP programs. You can collect the money when you retire or leave Hong Kong. If you already have a retirement plan through your company, such as a 401(k), you can avoid participating in the MFP.

Expat Social Scene
The expat community in Hong Kong has formed social clubs for just about every interest, such as cricket, squash, and softball, and there are quite a few clubs for outdoor recreation, including hiking, windsurfing, boating, diving, and the like. Hong Kong's numerous churches and the international schools also provide opportunities for expats to connect to the foreign community.

For nightlife, Lan Kwai Fong is one of the most happening areas. Located in Central, this area's abundant restaurants and bars attract large numbers of expats every night. Just to the south is the Soho area, another popular hangout spot with its diverse international restaurants and numerous watering holes.

Other popular nightspots where you can get your groove on include Tsim Sha Tsui and Wan Chai.

Resources

Hong Kong has a number of high-quality English-language newspapers and magazines. The two local newspapers are the *South China Morning Post* and the *Hong Kong Standard,* but you can also get the *Asian Wall Street Journal,* the *International Herald Tribune,* and even *USA Today.* Hong Kong is also the base for the *Far East Economic Review* and the *Financial Times. BC*

Lan Kwai Fong is the most lively expat party zone in Hong Kong.

© BARBARA STROTHER

Magazine is a general-interest magazine that covers current events and restaurant and club reviews. It also has a rich classifieds section where you can find everything from used cars to pets and roommates. For the politically minded, there's the *Hong Kong Voice of Democracy.* Most of these publications have handy websites as well.

Health Care

Before traveling to Hong Kong, make sure your immunizations are up-to-date. With its tropical climate and crowded subways, you should do your best to avoid catching a nasty case of typhoid, tuberculosis, or hepatitis A or B. Hong Kong's doctors and dentists are trained according to Western standards, so you shouldn't worry about the quality of care you'll receive, but unfortunately you'll pay Western prices for the care. You'll want to make sure you have ample medical insurance if you live in Hong Kong.

The emergency telephone number is 999. There are also medical hotlines (2882-4866 and 2300-6555) that can help you with just about anything related to health care, including directions, fees, and so on. There are excellent hospitals located throughout Hong Kong; three of the best medical facilities include Queen Mary Hospital in Pok Fu Lam, Queen Elizabeth Hospital in Kowloon, and Prince of Wales Hospital in the New Territories.

Schools

In mainland China, expat families put their children in the international

Many of Hong Kong's schools are run by churches.

© BARBARA STROTHER

schools, but in Hong Kong the local schools offer a more viable option. The Hong Kong school system is modeled after the British system, with the first six years at primary school followed by three years at a junior secondary school and finally 2–4 years at a senior secondary school. The style of education is characterized by rigid discipline (including uniforms), learning through a lot of rote memorization, and challenging exams. About half of the public schools teach in English, and the rest use Cantonese or a mixture of English, Cantonese, and Mandarin. Most Hong Kong schools are run by Christian organizations and are either subsidized by the government or funded through private tuition.

Additionally, there are close to 50 different international schools with curricula from the United States, Britain, Canada, Australia, and other non-English-speaking places. The list is a virtual United Nations, with names such as American International School, Australian International School, Canadian International School, French International School, Japanese International School, Norwegian International School, and so on. You'll find them located all over the SAR.

Shopping

Hong Kong has a reputation for its materialism and consumerism, and its status as a shopper's paradise is well deserved. You'll find shops large and small throughout the SAR, but especially in Kowloon and northern Hong Kong. In fact, you won't even have to go looking for them; much of the Hong Kong

© BARBARA STROTHER

Get a little relationship advice while you're window shopping.

subway system forces you to walk through malls to reach your subway train whether you want to shop or not. Some of the most famous upscale shopping centers include the nine-story Times Square in Causeway Bay; Pacific Place in Central; and Harbour City, one of the largest malls in Asia, in Kowloon near the cruise-ship terminal.

Your grocery bill in Hong Kong will be high if you plan to keep a Western diet. A pound of beef can cost as much as $20 or more for the good stuff imported from Australia. Local food, however, is affordable, especially vegetables and the abundant seafood that's so fresh it'll still be swimming when you buy it. You'll probably do a lot of your grocery shopping in convenience stores and small groceries like Park-n-Shop and Wellcome; most of Hong Kong doesn't have the space required for the big megastores.

Kowloon has several street markets where you can buy knockoff clothing and pirated goods, such as Ladies Market (with goods for guys and gals), Goldfish Market, Flower Market, Fa Yuen Street Market, and the famous Temple Street Night Market, where you can also grab a bite to eat at an outdoor restaurant. Across the harbor back in Hong Kong's Central neighborhood, you'll find the "Lanes," Li Yuen Streets West and East, where there are numerous street vendors. The Stanley Market in Stanley is another popular bargaining spot.

GETTING AROUND

A vast public transportation system of taxis, subways, buses, streetcars, and ferries makes it easy to get around Hong Kong.

By Taxi

Taxi fares start around HK$15 (US$2) for the first two kilometers. The color of the taxi indicates its assigned zone. In urban areas the cars are red; in the New Territories they are green; and in Lantau Island taxi cabs are painted blue. A red disk visible in the passenger side of the windshield lets you know the taxi is available.

By Subway

The Mass Transit Railway (MTR) is a modern system of subway lines connecting the major parts of the SAR. Depending on distance, typical fares cost between HK$5 (US$0.65) and HK$30 (US$3.85). Seniors, children, and college students qualify for the "concessionary" fare, which is about half the full fare. Fares can be lower if you purchase a discounted tourist pass, or if you use the Octopus smart card that uses radio signals to pay the fare so you never even have to take it out of your wallet or purse to use it.

Several lines designated by colors traverse Hong Kong in multiple directions. The stations match the color of the line, making it easy to determine if you've found the right train when changing lines. The teal line connects the Hong Kong station in Central with the new international airport; a one-way airport fare is HK$100 (US$13). If you're headed to the mainland, the old Kowloon Canton East Railway (now merged with the MTR) will take you straight to Shenzhen, stopping at several New Territories towns along the way.

By Bus

A complex network of buses and minibuses connects all points far and near in the Hong Kong SAR. Some of the buses are double-decker, and some of the top decks are open-air, a pleasant way to see the city in good weather. A letter in the route name indicates something special about the route. For instance, the letter *M* used as a suffix indicates that the route connects with the MTR. Bus fares range from as low as HK$2 (US$0.25) up to HK$45 (US$5.80); fares on air-conditioned buses are slightly higher. The bus routes are posted at all bus stops and are not difficult to learn to use, unlike the complex list of characters for buses in the mainland. Most buses take either cash or the Octopus card.

By Streetcar

There are streetcar routes all along the north side of Hong Kong Island. Board the streetcar in the back and head up to the second deck for sightseeing. For HK$2 (US$0.25), there's perhaps no better way to see the sights in such a traditional Hong Kong way. The famous Victoria tram is a funicular train that ascends to Victoria Peak, where you can take in an awesome bird's-eye view of Victoria Harbour and the Kowloon skyline.

By Ferry

Numerous ferries cross Victoria Harbour and connect to the outlying islands. The famous green-and-white Star ferries charge only a few Hong Kong dollars for a quick 10-minute harbor crossing. Ferries and turbojets also connect to faraway places such as Macau and Zhuhai.

By Car

If you feel the need to have your own car, you can purchase one for about the same cost as you'd pay in the United States, but you'll pay the exorbitant "first registration" tax and numerous fees that can literally double the amount that you pay for the car. The steep fees are intended to discourage car ownership in an effort to keep traffic and pollution minimized. Only about 10 percent of those living in Hong Kong own their own cars.

Macau 澳门

The former Portuguese colony of Macau is the Las Vegas of the Orient. It is the only place in China where gambling is legal, and whether it's cards, dice, slots, ponies, F-1, or greyhounds, the Macanese know how to gamble and have a good time. Like Hong Kong, Macau is also a Special Administrative Region (SAR) retaining its own currency and local rule. But unlike Hong Kong, Macau is quite small. Its land mass is only 2 percent the size of Hong Kong's, and its population is only around 500,000.

Over 400 years ago, merchants from Portugal established a trading post at Macau. It was the first European colony in all of Asia. Catholic missionaries and military men accompanied the merchants, and the area was developed like any other European city, complete with imposing forts and baroque cathedrals that still exist today.

While Macau is a bit cheaper than Hong Kong, it is still considered one of the most expensive places to live in Asia. If you're deciding between the two,

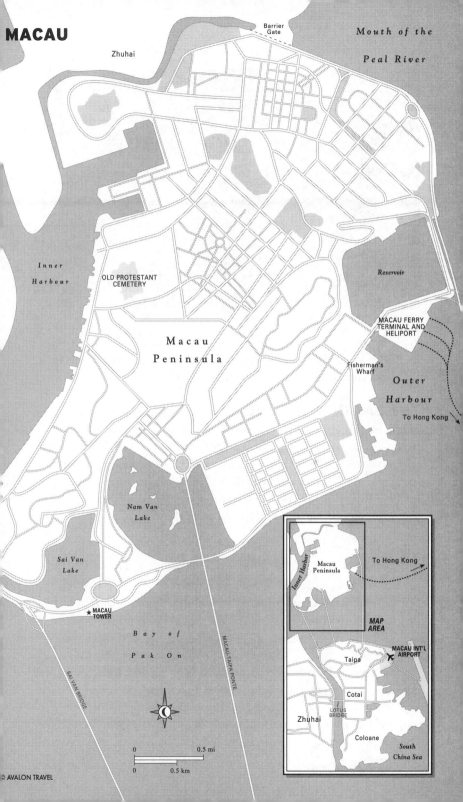

© BARBARA STROTHER

inside the Venetian Hotel & Casino in Macau

it's good to know that salaries in Macau are typically on par with pay in Hong Kong, but your money will go much farther here.

THE LAY OF THE LAND

Macau consists of a peninsula connected to mainland China and the two islands of Taipa and Coloâne, which are technically now one island due to a land reclamation project that links them. The Chinese city of Zhuhai is across the border to the north, and Hong Kong is 70 kilometers to the east across the Pearl River Delta. Ferries to Hong Kong take about an hour, or you can take a helicopter if you're in a hurry (and money's no object).

Climate

Macau shares the same subtropical climate as Hong Kong. Summers, starting in April, are hot and humid with occasional typhoons in July and August. September through December is the most pleasant time of the year: warm, dry, and always sunny.

Language

Though street and place names are primarily in Portuguese, Cantonese is the common language of the day, though you will occasionally hear conversations in Portuguese. In areas frequented only by locals, you might struggle if you only know English, but because Macau is an international tourism destination, English is spoken widely in and around the tourist areas.

WHERE TO LIVE

In recent years the Macau real estate market has skyrocketed, making it one of the most expensive places to live, trailing just behind Hong Kong. Real estate prices are typically advertised in dollar amounts, though those dollars are Hong Kong dollars, not U.S. dollars. And unlike in the mainland, size is given in square feet, not square meters. The property market is brutally competitive in Macau, so be sure you're really ready to act when you go looking for a new home. You may find places sold right out from under your feet if you so much as take a week to think about it.

Most of the population is concentrated within the Macau peninsula, so most of the housing is located there, but newer housing has recently been built in Taipa and Coloâne, some of it designed for Western tastes. New luxury developments are going into the Cotai Strip, the reclaimed land connecting Coloâne and Taipa that is becoming Macau's version of the Las Vegas strip. There are very few villas in all of Macau, so no matter which part you choose to locate in, you will more than likely live in an apartment.

Another option for where to live is in Zhuhai, just across the border. Some of the benefits of living in Zhuhai include cheaper and better-quality housing, cheaper general cost of living, better choice of international schools, and for language-learning purposes, simplified characters and more Mandarin spoken than in Macau. The major drawback is the daily commute through the border crossing, which can be quite slow at typical rush hour times due to the number of locals that live in one place but work in the other. See the Zhuhai section of the chapter on the South for more information.

© BARBARA STROTHER

a neighborhood with typical Macanese flair

Macau Peninsula

Though the Macau Peninsula covers just a quarter of the SAR's total land mass, it's home to the majority of the population. The peninsula is where all the activity of the city takes place. Most major facilities and tourist venues are here, and its compact design makes it easy to walk or take a short taxi or bus ride anywhere you want to go. It's also the most expensive of the three. At the Lake View Mansion on the Nam Van Lake, you can rent a sprawling 3,500-square-foot luxury apartment with four bedrooms and gorgeous views for as much as HK$35,000 (US$4,500). Expect to pay $800–1,200 for most 2- or 3-bedroom apartments here with features like clubhouses and resort-like tropical pools. On the lower end of the scale, a small local studio apartment can be rented for HK$4,000 (US$515) if you don't need any extra amenities.

Taipa

Taipa is the middle ground between the crowded yet alluring Macau Peninsula and the quiet countryside of Coloâne. If you'll be working on the Cotai Strip, living in Taipa will be an easy commute. It's also home to the International School of Macau. The Kingsville, one of Macau's most luxurious apartment complexes, is located here, complete with a swimming pool, a gym, and an easy walk to area restaurants and shops. Apartments with three or four bedrooms rent for HK$12,000–28,000 (US$1,500–3,600). Ocean Garden is another popular spot; a 1,200-square-foot two-bedroom apartment with views of the hill and the sea will put you out just HK$6,000 (US$775) per month. For the budget-minded, small but decent apartments in Taipa start around US$400 monthly.

Coloâne

Though Coloâne is just a 15-minute drive from downtown Macau on the peninsula, it feels quite remote. Here you'll find quiet residential areas surrounded by trees, clean air, and beaches, as well as the Macau Golf and Country Club. What you won't find here is convenient public transportation or good shopping. The popular Hellene Garden has 1,600-square-foot three-bedroom apartments, some with sea views, typically starting around HK$10,000 (US$1,300) and up to HK$28,000 (US$3,600) for larger and more luxurious executive units. For those that prefer a house rather than an apartment, there are some villas here. Rents usually start around US$4,000 for a large four-bedroom house overlooking the sea.

DAILY LIFE

Macau can be either delightful or disappointing, depending on your expectations. If you are coming from the mainland and expecting just another Chinese city, you'll enjoy the unique cultural charms here. But if you're expecting a quaint old place brimming with history on every corner, you may

© BARBARA STROTHER

big dog and little shrine in Macau

be disappointed by the ways Macau is still very much a Chinese city—often dirty and in disrepair. Nevertheless, there is a growing community of expatriates in Macau who love their quirky new home.

Foreigners in Macau work in a number of fields, but the major employers are in tourism, especially the new casinos. In recent years Macau has had a shortage of workers in just about every field—health care, construction, education, you name it—and employers can't seem to hire enough people for the jobs. If, on the other hand, you're more inclined to be the boss than to have one, Macau's government has an easy "one stop" service for setting up a business that makes the process simple enough that you can get by without a lawyer.

Visas

People of most nationalities can enter Macau without any visa, although how long you can stay after that depends on where you're from. Most Europeans can stay up to 90 days; North Americans, 30 days. To stay and work in Macau long-term, you'll first need to land the job, and then you can apply for a work visa at any PRC embassy or consulate.

Finance

Although control of Macau reverted to China in 1999, the territory retained its own municipal government and its own currency, the pataca. One hundred avos make a pataca. The pataca's exchange rate is pegged to the Hong Kong dollar at an official rate of 1:1, although you'll lose about 3 percent when changing money. Hong Kong dollars can be spent in Macau, but you should exchange or spend all your pataca before leaving Macau because you can't spend them anywhere in Hong Kong or the mainland, except for a few generous shopkeepers in Zhuhai.

PRIME LIVING LOCATIONS

Expat Social Scene

Some say Macau's expat community is not as close-knit as you'll find on the mainland, perhaps because it is a tourist town and people tend to come and go with the tide. The luncheons and activities of the International Ladies Club of Macau is the best way to get connected if you're female, though their regular events such as cocktail parties, Easter egg hunts, and charity balls can be enjoyed by all. If you're looking for something else to do besides gambling, you won't have a huge range of entertainment in this laid-back place, though you will find culturally rich museums, pleasant parks, and a number of fine beaches, including a black-

The Macau Tower has the highest bungee jump in the world; daring expats can join their frequent jumper club.

sand beach on Coloâne where you can camp. Macau also has its own grand prix car race. Check the bimonthly English magazine *MacauTalk* to stay informed on upcoming local events such as festivals, flea markets, and art and cultural exhibits.

Health Care

For health care, Macau's doctors are highly qualified, and the Hope Medical Clinic is a highly regarded hospital with international standards. Hong Kong's medical facilities are another option if necessary.

Schools

For schooling options in Macau, the International School of Macau follows a Canadian curriculum for all grades. The School of the Nations has its roots in the Baha'i faith and is open to both Macanese and foreigners. A few international students also attend the Sheng Kung Hui primary school (a local Episcopalian school that teaches a U.K. curriculum) and the Sacred Heart Catholic School for girls.

© BARBARA STROTHER

Shopping

Expats will be able to find most of what they want and need in Macau, and for everything else, just hop over to Hong Kong. Though Macau doesn't yet have the international hypermarkets that are all over cities on the mainland, you'll still find imported goods. Macau has Watson's drugstores as well as a Park'n Shop supermarket; Gourmet Fine Foods in Taipa sells goodies like cheese and cold cuts.

GETTING AROUND

Because downtown Macau is so small, you can get to many places on foot, but there are plenty of buses and taxis that will get you around the whole SAR. Taxis aren't too expensive—a ride from the peninsula to the tip of Coloâne Island is only about HK$75 (US$10)—but it can be very difficult to find one available. Buses are cheap, and routes are posted with convenient photographs of the tourist spots where they stop, but they do not come as frequently as in Hong Kong or the mainland. Many of the casinos also run their own buses that stop at just a couple of key spots in Macau; these buses are always free but are only convenient if the casino is your origin point or destination.

PRIME LIVING LOCATIONS

© BARBARA STROTHER
church in the Largo do Senado, Macau's main square

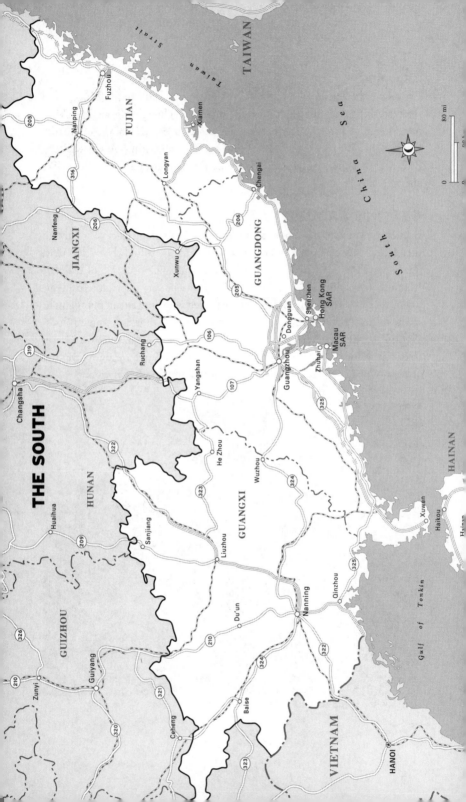

THE SOUTH

Southern China is a land of boomtowns and economic growth. The Pearl River Delta (PRD), one of the three key economic regions in China, is here. It's the world's workshop: 5 percent of the world's goods are produced here. And economic reform has created a huge amount of prosperity for its residents, some of the wealthiest in the nation. Guangzhou, Shenzhen, and Zhuhai are all key cities located in the PRD and are great spots for expat relocation. A fourth popular option for foreigners in the south but not located in the Pearl River region is the city of Xiamen in Fujian Province.

The cities of the Pearl River Delta share much in common, including the Cantonese language and cuisine as well as the ever-present influence of nearby Hong Kong. Xiamen, on the other hand, may not feel Hong Kong's presence as much, but it does feel Taiwan's, as its proximity to Taiwan draws wealthy Taiwanese who are looking to give back to their original homeland. None of the southern cities use Mandarin, neither in dialect nor in accent. And all are

© BARBARA STROTHER

very far from Beijing, both literally as well as figuratively, meaning that the local attitude towards rules and laws is that the iron hand of the Communist state doesn't always reach this far.

The Lay of the Land

The majority of prime expat locations in southern China are in Guangdong Province, lining the banks of the Pearl River as it flows into the South China Sea. Guangzhou is the northernmost of the bunch, followed by Shenzhen on the river's eastern bank and Zhuhai on its western bank. And then there's lone Xiamen, the only one of the bunch that lies far from the Pearl River, on the southeastern coast of Fujian Province.

CLIMATE

All of the Pearl River Delta cities share the same climate. Most of the year is pleasant and springlike with ever-blooming flowers and no real winter. Summers, on the other hand, are long, sticky, muggy, hot, and humid, especially in Guangzhou, which doesn't have the ocean breeze to cool the air. Typhoons and tropical storms regularly wreak havoc on these cities. Though Xiamen also experiences an occasional typhoon, its position between the mountains and the sea gives it one of the best climates in China—a land of eternal spring.

Guangzhou 广州

Guangzhou, the capital of Guangdong Province and home to over 10 million people, is best known in the West as Canton (though the name technically refers to its province). It occupies the strategic spot at the head of the Pearl River Delta where the east, west, and north rivers converge.

Guangzhou has been around for 2,000 years, serving as a pivotal port during the days of the Silk Road trade and again during the era of foreign concessions. Today Guangzhou is once again bustling with the activity of international trade, with 30 percent of the Fortune 500 companies represented within its borders. It shares a spot in the top four first-tier cities of the mainland, along with Shanghai, Beijing, and Shenzhen.

Cantonese cuisine is the most famous in all of China. The locals here believe that every part of every creature whose back faces the sun is good for eating (anyone for ox genitals or duck tongues?). The little plates of snacks at Cantonese dim sum restaurants are delicious and much more palatable for those who aren't fond of exotic foods.

All Americans adopting Chinese children must handle the paperwork in Guangzhou.

Guangzhou has a reputation for being a freewheeling city, fond of quoting "heaven is high, the emperor far away." Down here the laws are sometimes seen as merely recommendations. This place is also one of the few cities in China that has a reputation for thievery on its streets, though chances are you'll never experience crime firsthand. Fortunately Guangzhou's crime is very rarely violent, and it still feels much safer here than any big city in the United States.

The downsides to life in Guangzhou include the sooty pollution and the petty criminals. This place is also infamous for the aggressive local women looking for foreign companionship (wives, watch your husbands!).

WHERE TO LIVE

In Guangzhou, housing options include standard apartments and serviced apartments, luxury villas, and town houses. The expat housing scene can be divided into four key areas: downtown Guangzhou, Tianhe, Baiyun, and Zengcheng.

Downtown

Two adjacent districts on the north bank of the Pearl River, Yuexiu and Dongshan, blend into one to create downtown Guangzhou. This area is the birthplace of Guangzhou and has a history of over 2,000 years. It's everything you would expect of a city this big: active, busy, and with access to just about anything you

shopping in Guangzhou

© BARBARA STROTHER

PRIME LIVING LOCATIONS

could want (except for peace, quiet, and clean air). Downtown apartments range from places like Park View Place in Yuexiu and Eastern and Central Plazas in Dongshan, where rents start as low as $450 per month for a two-bedroom with less than 100 square meters, up to super-luxury four-bedroom apartments at Caesar's Palace that rent for $5,000 per month, with lots of options in between.

Er Sha Island, the largest island in the Pearl River, is also part of downtown. Er Sha is a fashionable enclave for foreign staff from local consulates and businesses. The elementary campus of the American International School Guangzhou is here, along with a handful of Western preschools. Er Sha has several housing complexes that are popular with expats, such as the New World Riverside Villas, where luxury villas with up to 600 square meters and six bedrooms rent in the $5,000–10,000 per month range.

SHAMIAN ISLAND 沙面岛

Shamian Island is a historic little place that used to be the stomping grounds of European traders. This genteel spot is a pleasant change of pace from the downtown Guangzhou commotion across the way, making it a nice place to wander among its old colonial European homes. Both Protestant and Catholic services in English are offered at the island's churches. The Qingping market nearby is a fascinating place, though if you can't stomach the idea of petting your food before it is slaughtered, you'll want to stay clear of the live animals section.

© BARBARA STROTHER

Shamian architecture

PRIME LIVING LOCATIONS

Baiyun

Baiyun District covers a huge mountainous area mostly to the north of the central city. The Nanhu (South Lake) National Tourism and Holiday Zone is here, with its heavily forested mountain park. The biggest draw of Baiyun is its natural environment and fresh air. Just a 15-minute (on average) driving commute to the central Guangzhou districts, Baiyun provides a chance to leave the city's intense activity behind yet still easily access it when you want it.

Baiyun has plenty of villas and upscale apartment complexes to choose from. Castle Hill Luxury Homes lives up to its name with five-bedroom 660-square-meter villas renting for around $8,000–10,000, as well as two- to four-bedroom apartments renting for around $1,500–2,000. If you're looking for something a little lighter on the wallet but still expat-friendly, Summer Palace has apartments in the $500–1,200 range.

Tianhe

Just east of the central downtown districts, the popular Tianhe District is a vibrant new commercial center studded with futuristic skyscrapers and glassy towers. If you're a shopaholic or a night owl, this metropolitan (and pricey) quarter is the best place to be. The Guangzhou Nanhu International School is located here. The eastern side of the district has a sizeable foreign community, with housing, bars, and restaurants that cater to expat wants and needs.

If you're in the market for a Tianhe apartment, you'll have tons of options, but fewer if you're in the market for a villa. Either way, you can drop a few bucks here. Apartments at places like the Eton Eighteen and the Greenery both start around $600 or $700 per month for a two-bedroom place; the Greenery also has duplexes as well as swimming, squash, and snooker. Villas like those at Pearl River Villa and Favorview Palace rent for $1,000–2,000 monthly.

Zengcheng

Zengcheng is technically a separate city, although it falls within the municipality of Guangzhou. It consists of the easternmost region of Guangzhou, just north of Dongguan city. Zengcheng may not have as many residential complexes as the others, but what it does have is impressively large and luxurious villas, such as the three-story homes at the gorgeous Jade Green Island with floor plans up to 500 square meters and mountain views. One of the Utahloy International Schools is here in Zengcheng, as well as the Economic and Technical Development Zone (ETDZ) with its multinational corporations. Many of the ETDZ employees live in the villas and town houses on the expansive grounds of the five-star Phoenix City Hotel. You can expect to pay, on average, $2,000–6,000 for villas in Zengcheng; luxury apartments run $1,000–3,000 per month.

DAILY LIFE

If you are interested in learning Cantonese or if you already speak it, this city is obviously a great choice. But if you are hoping to pick up good Mandarin skills while in China, you'll have a harder time here, since the Cantonese dialect is so deeply embedded in the society. As for English, not much is spoken, although you'll see it on road signs. It would be possible to get by here without Chinese language skills, but having at least a very basic knowledge will greatly enhance your experience.

Expat Social Scene

Guangzhou's expatriate community is enormous—bigger than Shanghai's or Beijing's—although the vast majority of foreign residents here are Asian. Most expats are in Guangzhou for business, with the usual teachers and students thrown into the mix, along with diplomatic types working at one of Guangzhou's several consulates.

Those with a spiritual bent will have their choice of English services, not just the typical Catholic and Protestant but also Mormon and Jewish. Expat sports groups gather informally for softball, soccer, basketball, rugby, bowling, and the like; others prefer to take advantage of Guangzhou's growing adventure sports like rock-climbing, caving, waterskiing, canoeing, paragliding, and hiking.

Expats will find most everything they need in Guangzhou, including tons of first-rate shopping, impressive and inexpensive restaurants of all types of cuisine, a vibrant bar scene, and both an SOS Clinic and a Can-Am Clinic for Western health care. The Guangzhou Women's International Club can help you get settled, and the U.S. Consulate can provide help if and when you need it.

Expat resources such as the English magazine *That's Guangzhou*, with its corresponding website, and the email newsletter XianzaiGuangdong (www. xianzai.com) can direct you to local events, and the *South China Morning Post* will keep you abreast of the daily news in English.

Schools

Guangzhou has quite a few international schools for expat families. The American International School Guangzhou (AISG) is the oldest school in town, with over 900 students between its elementary campus on Er Sha Island and the new campus for upper grades in the Science Park. The Utahloy International

School in Tianhe, another popular choice, is much more European in its focus. Other options include the British School of Guangzhou, the Guangzhou Nanhu International School, and Guangzhou Grace Academy, which is perhaps the most religious school in the mainland.

GETTING AROUND

Getting around central Guangzhou city is easy enough using the subway around downtown, and public buses reach every corner of the Guangzhou metro area. Expect public transportation to be crowded, however. Even if you live too far out to take advantage of the subway and find riding buses inconvenient, taxis are always a convenient solution. If you choose to live way out in the suburbs, having a car at your disposal (preferably with a driver) will make life easier, though cabs and buses serve all areas.

You can leave town for other Pearl River Delta locations via a short boat or train ride from Guangzhou, and Hong Kong is less than two hours away. And if living in China isn't adventurous enough for you, Guangzhou is arguably the best mainland city for exploring beyond China's borders, with flights to all major Asian destinations and beyond.

Shenzhen 深圳

There is a saying about Chinese cities: If you want to learn 5,000 years of history, go to Xi'an; 1,000 years, Beijing; 200 years, Shanghai; and 20 years, Shenzhen. This city was once just a fishing village with a border crossing to Hong Kong, but since it became the first Special Economic Zone (SEZ) in the 1980s, Shenzhen has taken off. It now ranks in the top four first-tier cities in China, along with Guangzhou, Shanghai, and Beijing, and has a boomtown population of 10.4 million people. It also boasts the highest per capita GDP of all major mainland cities, the richest city in China.

Shenzhen has gained the position of number-one Chinese city for quality of life. It's a very international city and a shopping mecca for rich and bored Hong Kong housewives. This was the first city in China to get its pollution under control, and it enjoys a reputation for having a clean and pretty seaside area. Real estate prices have skyrocketed in recent years, mostly due to the fact that they are running out of land to build on—the classic economics textbook example of supply not meeting demand.

Located on the southeastern tip of the Pearl River Estuary, Shenzhen is separated from Hong Kong by the Shenzhen River downtown and by Hong Kong Bay in Shekou, Shenzhen's satellite city to the west and the heart of its SEZ.

PRIME LIVING LOCATIONS

© BARBARA STROTHER

Pearl River Delta ships

WHERE TO LIVE

The prime expat housing in Shenzhen Municipality is divided into two parts; central Shenzhen city and the Nanshan District that includes the satellite city of Shekou and the Overseas Chinese Town. While central Shenzhen will give you access to all the downtown amenities as well as the border crossing to Hong Kong, expats with kids will most likely want to be in Nanshan, where all of the key international schools for Westerners are located.

Downtown Shenzhen

Central Shenzhen city is divided into two districts, Luohu and Futian. Luohu contains downtown Shenzhen proper and has the highest apartment rents of any district within Shenzhen Municipality. What you get for your money, though, is convenience and all the excitement of being in the middle of the city's hubbub. Dongmen pedestrian shopping street is here, as well as the main border crossing to Hong Kong. You'll find basic high-rise apartments renting for $500–1,000 per month.

Futian District lies to the west of Luohu and also contains a good chunk of the central city with all its conveniences. A little farther out in Futian, the resort area around Honey Lake (Xiangmihu) boasts fun spots like a water park, an amusement park, and an opera house, as well as a number of high-end residences that cater to expats. Futian's central apartments are a little cheaper than Luohu's, with basic apartments renting for as low as $300 up to modern high-quality apartments for $1,500. There are also a few luxury places where you can rent a four- or five-bedroom apartment overlooking the sea. If you'd prefer a villa, head to Honey Lake, where a five-bedroom home set in a botanical garden environment will put you out over $4,000 per month. Luxury apartments at Honey Lake rent for $1,000–2,000 for a three-bedroom place.

Nanshan District and Shekou
Nanshan District, roughly a 30-minute drive to the west of downtown Shenzhen, includes two key areas for both Western and Eastern expats: Shekou and the Overseas Chinese Town. Though Shekou technically refers to the central business district, the name is often used interchangeably with Nanshan district. Nanshan has tons of housing options, from convenient central apartments where you can literally run your errands, to a plethora of upscale villas, some in pleasant mountainside settings.

Shekou has traditionally been the primary hub for foreign residents. A prime location here may put you within walking distance of Sea World, where you won't find Shamu doing flips in a pool but you will find a landlocked ship-cum–entertainment complex with all kinds of international eateries.

Apartments are available both in central Shekou as well as at high-end residential complexes farther out into the mountainside areas. Rents start around $300 for a simple place but go as high as $2,000 or more for upscale spots. Nanshan's villas typically offer four- or five-bedroom layouts, most with two or three stories, and start around $3,000 per month, though some very prestigious places can go as high as $6,000–12,000 per month. A few places to consider include the sea-view apartments at Mont Orchid Garden, renting two or three bedrooms for $1,000–2,000, or Jingshan Villas, popular with foreigners because the Shekou International School is here. At the trendy and popular Coastal Rose Garden, $1,200 can rent you a three-bedroom, 170-square-meter high-rise apartment with a large balcony overlooking Hong Kong beyond the sea. From here you can easily walk to the nearby Starbucks and restaurants around Shekou Square, as well as the ferry terminal.

DAILY LIFE
Shenzhen's populace is a strong mix of peoples, both from other parts of China as well as foreigners and overseas Chinese, which all use Mandarin as the lingual common denominator. You'll still hear Cantonese here, but you can expect everyone to know and speak Mandarin. English, on the other hand, is spoken about as much as in the average big Chinese city (which is to say, not much at all).

edible art: sugary Chinese zodiac animals

© BARBARA STROTHER

The shopping is good in Shenzhen. A smattering of international grocery stores sell the expat holy grails—cheese, Mexican food, imported beer, and the like. Try US Grocers and Silver Palate in the same building as Park'n Shop Shekou. Of course, all the usual hypermarkets are always popular for everyday purchases, such as Carrefour, lots of Wal-Marts, Park'n Shop, Metro, Sam's Club, and Jusco. And then there's always the easy access to Hong Kong's limitless shopping options.

There's an SOS Medical Clinic in Shekou, and VIP services at the Beijing University Shenzhen Hospital and the Shenzhen People's Hospital. The quick commute to Hong Kong makes it easy to take advantage of Hong Kong's advanced health care facilities as well.

Expat Social Scene

Shenzhen has a lively expat scene and an even livelier night scene, with numerous dance clubs and Western-style bars where expats and locals party until the sun comes up. It's very multicultural, with a good mix of people—and restaurants—from all over the globe, including a couple of Brazilian barbecues as well as Moroccan and Indian food served in exotic settings.

If you find yourself in Shenzhen looking for a foreign friend, the sophisticated expat community here tends to gather based on common interests. Options include the Shekou Women's International Club, the Wine and Cheese Club,

Toastmasters, Shekou Hash running and drinking club, Mahjong for Ladies, and Mothers with Toddlers, to name a few. The Snake Pit, in Shekou, is a legendary sports and social club that has been serving the expat community for almost 20 years. Family activities include local theme parks, water parks, a safari garden, and even an indoor ski area (at the Windows of the World theme park) and horseback riding.

Expats here can stay well informed with a daily English-language newspaper, *Shenzhen Daily,* as well as *That's PRD* (Pearl River Delta). Several websites can help you to connect with others who share your interests in yoga or rugby, or to find out which restaurants are hosting holiday parties; these include www.shenzhenparty.com and www.shenzhenpeople.net.

Schools

Shenzhen has several international schools, though some are focused on Asian students. Top English schools include the Shekou International School, the oldest school serving all grades with a Western curriculum (WASC accredited); QSI Shekou, which follows its own curriculum; and the newest in Nanshan, the International School of Sino-Canada, which offers a Canadian diploma to graduates.

GETTING AROUND

Getting around Shenzhen is easy, especially since the traffic here isn't as bad as what you'll see in the most congested big cities. Most expats use the cheap taxis, though the public transportation network is efficient, and bikes are convenient for those who are centrally located. Shenzhen's subway system currently has two working lines, with three lines under construction, and there are plans to extend the system considerably throughout the Shenzhen-Shekou area. Excursions to other spots on the Pearl River can be made by boat, bus, or train. And for trips farther away, trains from Guangzhou or flights out of Hong Kong's International Airport (an easy ferry ride away) can get you to any destination you seek.

Zhuhai 珠海

They call Zhuhai the green city, and for more reasons than one. It's lush and green with forested mountains, it's environmentally green with low pollution, and it's green in light of the dollars that float around this place where the economy is blooming like its ever-present flowers. It's also green in terms of experience. Zhuhai is a new city, one of the first Special Economic Zones,

© BARBARA STROTHER

family fun in the sun on Zhuhai's islands and beaches

which in just 20 years has put what was once a sleepy fishing village on the economic map.

Located on the southwest tip of the Pearl River Delta, Zhuhai (pop. just 1.5 million) is consistently selected as one of the best cities in China for quality of life. What it lacks in ancient historical relics it makes up for in its modern urban planning: a pleasant and clean environment, wide boulevards, and a good transportation network with few traffic jams. Ferries connect Zhuhai to Hong Kong and the other Pearl River Delta cities, and it's just a simple walk across the border to the gambling grounds of Macau (the only place casinos are allowed in China). This seaside city has a pleasant springlike environment year-round, with sea breezes to cool down the summer heat and more than 145 islands within its boundaries. To top it off, Zhuhai is one of the cheapest cities in the Pearl River Delta, and for no better reason than that it is just less discovered by the world.

WHERE TO LIVE

Zhuhai has the cheapest housing of the prime Pearl River Delta cities. Three-bedroom apartments can run less than $300 per month, and you'll have plenty of choices in the $500–1,000 range; anything more puts you into the sweet lap of luxury. Here you'll find villas with beautiful surroundings close to beaches, or high-rise apartments with sparkling nighttime views of the city lights reflected on the sea. In Zhuhai you can expect to sit out on your balcony high above the bustling city below, propping your feet up on the intricate wrought-iron railing, sipping an ice-cold Tsingtao and gazing out at the wide blue yonder.

The three key districts for urban real estate in Zhuhai include Xiangzhou, Jida, and Gongbei. Jida and Gongbei tend to be the most expensive districts, due in part to the large number of ocean-view apartments they have along their seacoast. Zhuhai also has suburban areas with new villas and upscale apartment complexes, such as Nanping and Tangjia Districts.

Xiangzhou District

The Xiangzhou District is the central downtown area of the city along the banks of the Pearl River Estuary. It's a convenient location for the city's amenities. In Xiangzhou you can get a high-rise three-bedroom place, with 180-degree views of the ocean from the dining room and a matching view of downtown from the living room, for just $500 per month. Several apartment complexes here that are popular with foreigners include Haiwan Huayuan, with large four-bedroom apartments boasting great views of the sea as well as a handful of villas, and Phoenix Garden, a large complex with a pool, shops, and restaurants.

Jida District

Jida District is a central commerce area directly south of Xiangzhou, located at the corner where the Pearl River and the South China Sea meet. Jida boasts

© BARBARA STROTHER

Jida apartments on the beach

PRIME LIVING LOCATIONS

quiet residential areas and is just a bit more expensive than Xiangzhou. Here you can find both nice new apartments and sprawling five-bedroom villas, all convenient to shopping and restaurants.

Moving west along the coast on your way to Gongbei, you'll find plenty of sea-view complexes in the area where the two districts merge. High-rise apartments here rent for around $750–1,500 for two or three bedrooms; some boast two floors or on-site kids' fun rooms and fitness centers. The majority have gorgeous views of the sea. Inexpensive serviced apartments are available at the Nanhai Oil Hotel, where amenities include a variety of sporting activities, even lessons in tae kwon do and tennis for the kids.

Gongbei District

Farther down the coastline from Jida, Gongbei District is the land that borders Macau. This is a popular spot for people who work in Macau but prefer to live in the mainland, or those that want to frequent Macau's amenities, such as its beautiful historic cathedrals or its sparkly casinos. Within Gongbei you'll find Zhuhai's Bar Street, including the expat-popular Cohiba bar, along with lots of cheap shopping near the border. This district is also home to the QSI International School.

Most foreigners here choose central high-rise apartments with views of the mountains and the sea, though there are a few villas on offer, such as those at the Australian Garden, which also houses the QSI International School. A simple apartment in Gongbei can be rented for under $300, but for $2,000

Gongbei border with Macau

© BARBARA STROTHER

per month you can impress your friends with a luxury penthouse with amazing views of Macau and the great blue beyond.

Suburbs

The suburbs of Zhuhai, located west and north of the central city, are where you'll find new villa compounds and upscale low-rise apartments. Huafa New City in Nanping District is one of the most popular places in the city for foreigners and has a reputation for being one of the highest quality developers in the city (one-bedroom apartments rent for around $500, up to four bedrooms for around $1,500). Near the entertainment hub of Tangjia, the Mediterranean-style villas and apartments at Horizon Cove are a popular spot with a lake, green hills, outdoor pool, and easy access to the area's golf courses, racetracks, beaches, hot springs, and the new Zhuhai International School. Expect to pay up to $3,000 or more for a large home in this area; luxury apartments will rent closer to the $500–1,000 range.

DAILY LIFE

Zhuhai is a melting pot of Chinese that have come from all corners of the mainland in search of prime career positions in the top-rate businesses of its Special Economic Zone. Because of this, Zhuhai is uniquely more focused on speaking Mandarin as the lingua franca, unlike the typical Guangdong Province cities that are strongly Cantonese. If you want to master Mandarin but are interested in southern China, this city would be a good fit for you.

For shopping, Zhuhai has the typical international hypermarts, like Carrefour from France and Jusco from Japan, and typical Chinese department stores and malls. For medical and dental care, however, many foreigners prefer to go to the advanced facilities in nearby Hong Kong, though the local Chinese hospitals and clinics are sufficient.

Expat Social Scene

Zhuhai is adored by its growing foreign community. In fact, this city draws foreign residents working in other Pearl River Delta cities who prefer to live in Zhuhai's pleasant environment despite the commute. Zhuhai's foreign community enjoys a strong sense of connection. Like its local population, the foreign community here tends to be a melting pot of people from around the globe. Quite a few are here with their families, which adds to the sense of family-oriented community, though singles looking for action will find enough to keep them happy with Zhuhai's nightclub scene and bar street.

Expats of all ages can take pleasure in Zhuhai's aquatic sports, including waterskiing, boating, surfing, swimming, or working on killer tans and kingly sandcastles on its sandy beaches. Hikers will enjoy hiking trips into the nearby hills. And Zhuhai is a prime destination for golfers, who come here on the weekends from all over southern China and Hong Kong to play on Zhuhai's courses.

Schools

Zhuhai now has two international schools, QSI International School of Zhuhai and the new Zhuhai International School. Internationally accredited QSI is the older of the two schools and has a new campus in the Gongbei District. The Zhuhai International School has a bilingual focus and is surrounded by the natural environment of Qiao Island in Tangjia District.

GETTING AROUND

All parts of Zhuhai are easily navigable by taxi or bus, and bikes come in handy for shorter distances, though the city territory is quite spread out, with steep green hills that can block direct routes. Ferries and helicopters crisscross the Pearl River to the other cities nearby. Two projects in the works, a bridge that will connect Zhuhai with Hong Kong and a railway that will connect it with Guangzhou, will make it even easier to hop from one spot to another along the delta. For spots further away, some domestic cities can be reached through the Zhuhai airport, and the well-connected international airports at Hong Kong and Guangzhou are also a relatively easy option. Zhuhai is not served by trains at this time, but you can purchase tickets to depart from Guangzhou; a direct bus from Zhuhai to the Guangzhou train station (or direct to the airport) takes around 2 to 3 hours, depending on traffic.

Xiamen 厦门

Beautiful Xiamen, deep-water port and historic island playground of the rich and foreign, is considered to be one of China's cleanest and most pleasant cities. Here colonial past and modern China meet and mingle, and so do big-city business and tourist-town charms. With its agreeable climate year-round without the typical gray haze of most Chinese cities, and its fresh seafood, lovely beaches, and a nice variety of good restaurants and shopping, what's not to love?

Xiamen is well known by its old name, Amoy. This island city has been home to merchants and pirates through the ages. Its history is marked by endless port control struggles, in which the Dutch, British, French, German,

© BARBARA STROTHER

bird's-eye view of Xiamen

PRIME LIVING LOCATIONS

Japanese, and Portuguese all played their part. Gulangyu Island, located here, is still occupied by old colonial villas that reveal its flamboyant past.

Xiamen is situated on the southeastern coast of Fujian Province in an area protected by the mountains and the sea. Taiwan is just 100 miles eastward as the seagull flies, though Taiwan-owned Quemoy Island is a mere three miles from Xiamen. The people of Xiamen have a reputation for being lovers of life, not as caught up in business and money as the Shanghai or Guangzhou types. And Xiamen is small by Chinese standards—at 2 million, it's one of the smallest of China's prime expat cities. The cost of living in Xiamen is lower than most of the prime expat cities, but it's on the rise. Due to its location on the Taiwan straits, Xiamen appeals to Taiwanese investors and retirees looking for a cheap spot to spend their glory days, and the demand for real estate has driven the prices up in recent years.

WHERE TO LIVE

You shouldn't have any troubles finding a nice home in a city with an auspicious name like Xiamen (Gate of the Grand Mansion). Though housing prices have been rising dramatically in recent years, the market is still quite inexpensive compared to the high prices of the first-tier cities. Options range from luxury mountainside apartments or seaside villas renting for $3,000 or more per month to small and simple apartments renting as low as $200 per month.

The heart of Xiamen city lies on Xiamen Island, though the municipality

PRIME LIVING LOCATIONS

GULANGYU ISLAND 鼓浪嶼

Gulangyu is gloriously stuck in a bygone era, where scarlet bougainvillea climbs up colonial villas and music wafts from open windows in this little place long dubbed "piano island." Lying in the channel that separates Xiamen Island from the mainland, Gulangyu is accessed only by ferry. There are no vehicles on Gulangyu's cobblestone streets, though there are wooden handcarts used by its 20,000 residents. Many of the old colonial European homes here are in serious disrepair, which may awaken in you a remodeler's dream. While it is possible to buy one, fixing it up will prove both difficult and expensive in this place where hardware delivery trucks and concrete mixers don't ply the narrow hilly lanes. It is also possible to rent one of these homes (or more likely, part of one), but the quality is liable to be far below Western standards.

© BARBARA STROTHER

fixer-upper on Gulangyu Island

also includes Gulangyu Island and a large stretch of the mainland. Most expats live in central apartments within Xiamen Island's Siming and Huli Districts.

Siming District

After administrative redistricting a few years back, Kaiyuan District was folded into Siming, covering the southern two-thirds of Xiamen Island. For practical purposes, however, the areas are still often referred to by their original names. Traditional Siming, the southern tip of the island, includes the old city, the island's best beaches, and Xiamen University. Kaiyuan is the middle swath of the island; it's the vibrant new commercial district otherwise known as downtown and the place to be if you want an exciting nightlife, international restaurants, and easy access to great shopping venues.

The most recent housing development is along the island ring road, and this is the best place to find villas on the island. These places are further removed from the city's activity—which can be good or bad, depending on what kind of a lifestyle you're after. You can rent an apartment or a villa with great sea views and a short walk to the beach. Huge villas here rent for over $3,000; four- and five-bedroom apartments with great views go for around $1,000 and simpler places for half that.

The predominant hot spot for expat housing in Kaiyuan is the area around Yuan Dang Lake, with serviced apartments at places like the popular Marco Polo and Plaza Pacific. There's also a variety of upscale standard apartments in this vicinity. You can rent a large luxury apartment with a balcony as big as a second home for around $1,200.

Along the bay on Kaiyuan's western coastline is another popular spot. Some high-rise apartments here have spectacular views of the suspension bridge and the city lit up at night, such as the Guang Ming Da Xia, which rents two-bedroom apartments for around $300–500 per month. The Crowne Plaza Hotel here has a few high-end serviced apartments and boasts both panoramic views of Xiamen Bay and an easy walk to the Zhongshan Road shopping area.

In addition to these two areas, you'll find standard apartments in high-rises scattered throughout the district. An average three-bedroom apartment typically rents for $150–400; bump it up over $1,000 for a spacious five-bedroom apartment with luxury furnishings and imported appliances.

Huli District

Huli district comprises the northern third of the island, separated from downtown Xiamen by a mountain. Huli is home to one of largest central business districts in the city as well as the Gaoqi International Airport. The five-star Mandarin is here, offering both serviced apartments and villas with added perks such as bowling, indoor and outdoor pools, massages and a sauna, restaurants, and a coffee shop.

Villas in Huli rent for roughly $1,000–3,000 per month, and there are also plenty of standard apartments available, like those at the Long Men (Dragon Gate) World high-rise, where a top-floor three-bedroom apartment rents for around $500 per month.

DAILY LIFE

The name of the local dialect is Minnan. It's quite different from Mandarin and is actually closely related to the native Taiwanese language. Most everyone will know and speak Mandarin, however. There's not much English spoken here, so you'll most likely need to depend on Chinese friends to help out when in need.

For Western medical help, the Lifeline clinic has foreign doctors, and its pharmacy carries Western medications; the Zhongshan hospital also has a VIP ward for foreigners. Shopping should be easy, with the major hypermarkets such as Metro, Wal-Mart, and Trust-Mart.

Expat Social Scene

Xiamen is well loved by the people who live here. Expats come for a variety of reasons, from working with one of the large multinational companies here, such as Dell, General Electric, and Kodak, to studying at Xiamen University's Chinese-language program, reputedly one of the best in the nation.

The city's expat community is well connected. Xiamen International Christian Fellowship offers a way to meet other foreigners at their two services on Sundays and mid-week gatherings. Other expat groups tend to gather informally based on shared interests, like soccer or running. Singles will find plenty to do in the local nightlife scene.

As they say, big cities are good for fun and small cities are good for families, but small Xiamen is good for families that want to have fun. When school's

© BARBARA STROTHER

Xiamen University

out, you can head to the beaches (windsurfing and parasailing are available), hike along wooded paths, or splash around at the Xiamen Water World with its outdoor waterslides and pools. Or simply wander the peaceful and pretty Xiamen Botanical Gardens for some tranquil downtime.

There's an expat magazine in English, *What's On Xiamen* (with a matching website), that's handy for news on events, new restaurants, theaters showing the latest blockbusters in English, or shopping finds. You can pick one up at all the popular expat spots, like the Brazilian Barbecues and the Londoner bar. Or try the Marco Polo hotel, which often serves as the center of information and activity for the expat community.

Try to get your hands on Dr. Bill Brown's book, *Amoy Magic,* printed by the Xiamen University Press, for just about everything you ever wanted to know about Xiamen but didn't know who to ask.

Schools

The Xiamen International School is currently the only international school in Xiamen. XIS offers an American curriculum and International Baccalaureate programs for expat kids of all ages. The school is not located on Xiamen Island but in the Xinglin district across the causeway, but school bus transportation is available from all key areas of the city.

GETTING AROUND

Xiamen's taxis and buses are cheap, plentiful, and easy to catch; consult the how-to page on the *What's On Xiamen* website for bus routes. Getting out of town, however, is not quite as easy as getting around it. Fuzhou Province's mountainous terrain limits the possibilities for train travel, but if you plan to do your traveling by plane, the international airport here has flights to 90 destinations nationally and internationally, including spots in Malaysia, Indonesia, and the Philippines.

PRIME LIVING LOCATION

THE EAST

Eastern China is home to the Yangtze River Delta, one of China's three most important economic regions. The cities of this area in the shadows of Shanghai are one success story after another, enjoying a high level of prosperity. Several of China's best living locations for expats are here, including the cities of Nanjing, Suzhou, Hangzhou, and Ningbo. In each, business is booming, and foreign firms are moving in by the droves, bringing their expat jobs with them.

These smaller cities in the shadows of Shanghai tend to compare themselves with their glamorous neighbor, gloating about the unique charms and perks they have that Shanghai doesn't. Marco Polo spent a considerable amount of time here and lavished his highest praises on the cities in this region. Though times have changed since Polo's day, this area still enjoys the prosperity, charm, and innovative urban administration that first caught his attention.

© BARBARA STROTHER

© BARBARA STROTHER

Yangtze Bridge

The Lay of the Land

There are just two provinces covered in this region that butts up against Shanghai and the East China Sea. Nanjing and Suzhou are both situated within Jiangsu Province, to the north of Shanghai. Nanjing is located in the southwestern corner of the province on the banks of the mighty Yangtze River. Suzhou lies farther south, just a stone's throw from Shanghai.

Zhejiang Province, south of Jiangsu and southwest of Shanghai, is home to two important cities for expats. Hangzhou is the provincial capital and is located in the northern tip of the province where the Qiantang River meets Hangzhou Bay. Traveling east along the bay's shore you'll eventually run into the port city of Ningbo, where Hangzhou Bay folds into the East China Sea.

CLIMATE

Because all of the eastern cities are located within close proximity of each other, they share the same subtropical monsoon climate. They enjoy four distinct seasons, though the gray winter skies rarely produce snow. Summers are long and hot, sometimes insufferably so; July and August bring the monsoon rains.

Nanjing 南京

Throughout China's long and colorful history, Nanjing has often played a very significant role. Its name literally means "southern capital," and through the years this city has been the pivotal center of six consecutive dynasties as well as the Taiping Rebellion and later the Kuomingtang. When Nanjing fell during the Sino-Japanese war, the Japanese cruelly killed, raped, maimed, and pillaged in the city, an event indelibly seared into the nation's consciousness as the Rape of Nanking or the Nanjing Massacre.

Today Nanjing is a bustling provincial capital of 7 million, marked by rapid development that some compare to Shanghai's rise to prominence in the 1990s. Nanjing may never have quite the sophistication or glamour of Shanghai; on the other hand, it has kept more of its Chinese character, reflected in its ancient city wall that can still be seen in some of the oldest parts of town.

Nanjing's wooded hills turn red in autumn, which is the best time to wander their well-toured forest paths leading to historic sites and scenic viewpoints. Equally as vibrant, the cuisine is known for having a focus on color with simple seasonings. Nanjing salted duck is its most famous specialty; you can order just the head for a tasty appetizer.

© BARBARA STROTHER

Confucius Temple area

The cost of living in Nanjing is much cheaper than the larger and more glamorous cities, though as this place continues to rise in economic importance, so too will its cost of living. For now, the city can still be a bargain.

WHERE TO LIVE

Expat-quality housing can be found throughout Nanjing's seven key districts in a variety of price ranges. Downtown Nanjing's central districts are divided into four quadrants (Gulou to the northwest, Xuanwu to the northeast, Baixia to the southeast, and Jianye to the southwest) that meet at Xinjiekou, Nanjing's center of finance and

PRIME LIVING LOCATIONS

© BARBARA STROTHER

Nanjing highway

commerce. The remaining districts of Qixia, Jiangning, and Yuhuatai are all located on the outskirts of the city.

Central Districts

The center of Nanjing's business and leisure is the high-rise-studded Baixia District. Baixia encompasses the city's two key shopping areas, the Confucius Temple area in its south and the head of the Xinjiekou area in its northwest. Towering upscale apartment buildings near Xinjiekou, such as the Golden Eagle International Garden, rent for around $800–1,200 per month. Farther out, around Yue Ya Lake, you'll find a number of high-end residences. Luxury apartments with lake views typically start just under $1,000 per month, though small places without prime views can be had for half that. For $5,000 per month, you can get a sprawling European-style villa.

Gulou District is the oldest area of this ancient city. Here you'll find Nanjing University with its large contingent of foreign students, as well as nearby restaurants that cater to the student lifestyle. Gulou's Hunan Road is a busy shopping street with world-renowned boutiques and department stores. Apartments in Gulou tend to be smaller and cheaper than other districts, with small one-bedroom apartments, like those at Junlin International Mansion, renting for as little as $400 per month or less; larger three-bedroom apartments go for around $600–1,000 per month.

Xuanwu District is where the central urban areas mesh with the eastern hills. This area is predominantly wooded and hilly, encompassing the Zhongshan Hill

Scenic Area, with the famous mausoleum of Sun Yatsen as well as a couple of popular lakes. The luxury apartments and villas in Xuanwu cater to the international community, making this district popular with local expats. The Top Regent Garden has American-style villas as well as perks such as restaurants, a massage and beauty parlor, a fitness center, and an international kindergarten on the premises. Most places at Top Regent rent for $2,500–3,500, though they can go much higher, depending on the size. The Royal Garden was one of the first expat-oriented villa and apartment complexes in the city; apartments here rent for $1,000–3,000, including some serviced apartments.

Jianye District sees a lot of tourists due to its infamous Nanjing Massacre Memorial. Nanjing's new subway stops here, an important consideration for those who want to jet around the city easily. The real estate in Jianye is similar in modesty to Gulou, though it does have a few pricey upscale apartments such as the Vanke on the banks of Mochou Lake. Five-bedroom apartments at the Vanke rent for around $2,400, though smaller places can be had for around $1,000.

Outskirts

Of all the suburban districts, Qixia is the largest, wrapping around the northeastern corner of the central city. With the river along its northern edge, this district boasts over 70 ports and harbors. It gets its name from the Qixia mountain, an area rich in scenic spots and historic sites. The Nanjing International School is here, as well as several large Chinese universities. This district is in the midst of a residential building boom that will influence the flavor of this area in the coming years, as businesses such as supermarkets and restaurants follow the growing number of upper-class residents here. One of the most popular residence complexes in Qixia is Royal Family, which is near the international school and houses many of its teachers. Modern five-bedroom villas here rent for $3,000–4,000; large apartments range $700–2,000.

Yuhuatai, though on the outskirts of the city, isn't too far from Baixia's busy Confucius Temple area. Large and luxurious apartments in Yuhuatai rent for around $1,500–2,000 for 3–4 bedrooms, such as those at the Yulan Villas, located near the golf course.

Jiangning District is southeast of all the rest. There's not a whole lot to offer here right now, though this district is a key focus for future development. One option is the Green View Mandarin, with its scenic environment and amenities such as indoor and outdoor pools. Homes in Jiangning start around $1,000 monthly for a three-bedroom luxury apartment or town house, up to $4,500 for a four-bedroom house.

PRIME LIVING LOCATIONS

DAILY LIFE

Nanjing can feel like a sleepy city, but what one person calls sleepy another calls laid-back. Though it may be a less exciting choice as an expat destination, it is by no means a less viable option.

Nanjing's markets are full of bargains.

© BARBARA STROTHER

As for spending your cash here, Nanjing is big enough to have the key international chains. Retailers like Metro, Carrefour, Lotus, Wal-Mart, and the Foreign Goods Store, as well as the typical American fast food joints, will provide most of the foods and goods that foreigners crave. International restaurants serving cuisines from around the globe are scattered throughout the city. The back markets along the busy Confucius Temple area have unbelievably cheap bargains and name-brand knockoffs. Or skip the replicas and go for the real thing in the designer boutiques, department stores, and trendy malls along Hunan Road and the Xinjiekou area.

Foreigners have several options for quality health care in Nanjing. The AEA Nanjing Clinic is located on the first floor of the Nanjing Hilton Hotel on Zhong Shan Road and offers 24-hour care to SOS members. Along with international medical care, this multilingual clinic also has counseling services and TCM (traditional Chinese medicine) for those who are interested. There is also a VIP ward within the Jiangsu Province Hospital, a Global Doctors site, and more than 10 other hospitals scattered around the city can provide medical services in multiple languages for foreigners.

The local Nanjing dialect is one of the few dialects with quite a bit in common with standard Mandarin, similar to the difference between American English and British English. Basic Mandarin will get you by just fine and is highly recommended, since very little English is spoken here.

Expat Social Scene

Without the energy of Shanghai or the appealing charms of Suzhou and Hangzhou, Nanjing's expat community is somewhat less developed than other prime eastern cities, but it is growing.

The expat community here has a decent mix of nationalities and professions, including businesspeople, teachers, and a good-size foreign student population at Nanjing's universities. The small size of the community means you're likely to run into people you know.

For adults, an international soccer league, a rugby club, cricket games, and the Nanjing International Club are populated by many nationalities. The nightlife of Nanjing keeps singles hopping between a few good dance clubs and karaoke bars downtown. Hikers and mountain-bikers will have plenty of gorgeous green hills to keep them happy. For families, there's the indoor water park, a safari park, a wildlife park, fishing ponds, go-karts, or paintball, to name a few activities. Other local events and helpful living tips can be found in Nanjing's free English-language monthly, *Map Magazine*.

Schools

Nanjing has two key options for schooling expat kids. The Nanjing International School is the oldest and offers an International Baccalaureate program for all grades. The British School of Nanjing is a new school that does not yet cover high school, though at the speed it's growing, it probably won't be long before the curriculum is extended to all grades.

© BARBARA STROTHER

Rickshaws are a reminder of Nanjing's colorful history.

GETTING AROUND

Nanjing is relatively easy to navigate by bus, taxi, bike, or its new subway system. The new subway line runs from the Olympic Stadium in the southwestern part of the city through Xinjiekou and Gulou up to the main railway station. A second line connects at Xinjiekou. Getting in and out of the city is equally straightforward, with a 2.5-hour commute to Shanghai by bullet train and convenient overnight trains to Beijing and Xi'an. Nanjing's airport serves all key domestic destinations as well as other Asian hot spots such as Seoul and Singapore.

PRIME LIVING LOCATIONS

Suzhou 苏州

The city of Suzhou is synonymous with gardens, and we're not talking about rows of rutabagas or clumps of chrysanthemums. These are the grounds of the ancient wealthy, with paths that lead through swaying bamboo to aged pagodas, ponds graced by floating lotus leaves and darting golden koi, grotesque rock formations, and quirky fir trees that twist and curve in bonsai fashion. In addition to its gardens, Suzhou is also known for the canals this 2,500-year-old city was built on, making it the Venice of the Orient.

Modern-day Suzhou is again creating a name for itself with its urban design. This city has been recognized as a model of modern growth without disrupting its quaint old style. Suzhou's reputation for being a pleasant city (pop. 6 million) as well as an important center for industry is constantly drawing new international business, and the expats are following.

WHERE TO LIVE

Though cheaper than Shanghai, Suzhou's real estate is expensive for a city of this size, reflecting the influence of having one of the world's most expensive cities so close by. Suzhou's prime expat housing is predominantly located outside of the old city center in the two districts that flank it to the west and east: the Suzhou New District (SND) and the Suzhou Industrial Park (SIP). Which of these districts you choose will largely be determined by where your job is located.

Suzhou New District

The Suzhou New District (SND), west of downtown, is home to over 50 multinational corporations. Expat families in the SND can send their youngsters to the Etonhouse International School at the Suzhou Science and Technology Town in the north. The SND has plenty of housing choices, from villa complexes to luxury apartments, both standard and serviced. Most 2- or 3-bedroom apartments in the New

Suzhou's famous gardens are fun for young explorers.

© BARBARA STROTHER

District will put you out $600–1,000 per month depending on size and quality. The Regent on the Park hosts the Kinderland International Preschool on its premises, making it a great option for expat families with little *laowai*. Town houses at Regent rent for $1,500–3,000 for a 3- or 4-bedroom place. For serviced apartments in the SND, places like the Regalia rent luxury apartments in the $1,500–2,000 range.

Suzhou Industrial Park

The Suzhou Industrial Park (SIP), east of downtown, was developed as a joint project between the governments of China and Singapore, which is why the Suzhou Singapore International School was founded here. More than 50 of the world's top 500 multinational firms are represented within this district. Apartments in the SIP are quite plentiful; you'll have dozens of complexes to choose from in a wide range from around $400 per month to as high as $2,000 per month. In addition to apartments, the SIP also has several villa complexes. The Casa de Esplanade boasts that it has the only American-style houses in the city; sprawling luxury villas with 350–400 square meters rent for around $3,500 per month here. Less-expensive homes are available, such as those at Dushu Terrace and Han She ($1,200–2,500 for 3–5 bedrooms).

DAILY LIFE

Suzhou's proximity to Shanghai (less than an hour by train) provides an environment where expats can get a feel for a more realistically Chinese life while still having all of Shanghai's amenities at their fingertips.

Located on the Grand Canal just 80 kilometers west of Shanghai, Suzhou's softly toned local dialect is similar to Shanghai's. Suzhou's cuisine also mimics Shanghai's, placing the same emphasis on fresh seafood and vegetables with its own distinct dishes. But Shanghai's melting pot of residents from a variety of provinces promotes the use of Mandarin as the lingua franca, whereas in Suzhou the use of the local dialect is more prevalent. And the use of English is much less prevalent in Suzhou than in Shanghai; you'll want to work on your Mandarin if you're headed here.

The vast number of tourists that pour through this city has brought the businesses that cater to them (like high-end hotels with upscale restaurants and nice health club facilities), and expats living here can also take advantage of those amenities. The shopping is decent, with a few places like Carrefour and Auchon carrying imported foods, and plenty of (mostly fake) antiques and trinkets around the tourist sites.

For medical care, the Kowloon Hospital has both foreign doctors and

PRIME LIVING LOCATIONS

© BARBARA STROTHER

Warm and wonderfully aromatic, roasted chestnuts are a popular local snack.

foreign-trained ones, all of whom speak English. Or, like everything else you can't find here, you can simply go into Shanghai to meet your medical needs.

Expat Social Scene

Suzhou's expat community is somewhat small and largely Asian. Foreign residents here tend to socialize at local restaurants and in friends' homes, and head out to Shanghai if they really want something to *do*. Family activities in Suzhou revolve around simple pleasures like bowling, hanging out at the complex's pool, or an occasional day spent at the Suzhou Amusement Land and Water Park. Nearby Lake Taihu, China's third-largest lake, offers boating, swimming, fishing, and water-skiing. For information on other types of recreation, as well as English news and events, try the English-language magazines *More Suzhou* and *Open*. Shanghai's English magazines also often carry information about Suzhou.

Schools

Suzhou's foreign families have their choice of two international schools. The Suzhou Singapore International School has grown to over 1,500 students across all grades in their more than 10-year history. The Etonhouse International School is located on a new campus and has an enrollment cap of 500 students. Currently it offers only primary and middle school education.

GETTING AROUND

Getting around Suzhou is easy. Bikes are a pleasant way to wander along Suzhou's old canals; if you'd prefer not to break a sweat, hop in a three-wheeled pedicab and let someone else do the work for you. City buses ply the common routes; taxis are, as always, cheap and plentiful. The usual trains and domestic flights can be booked from here, plus you'll have Shanghai's airports and train stations to get you anywhere in China or beyond.

Hangzhou 杭州

Hanghzou is a great place to live. Of course, we might be a little biased, since it happens to be our favorite. But it's also been ranked number-one for business by *Forbes* magazine and is one of the most popular tourist destinations in China. It's home to Zhejiang University, the largest in the nation. But Hangzhou's greatest claim to fame is the beautiful West Lake, situated right in the central city, where it has been captivating visitors since the day Marco Polo first sang its praises.

When Polo visited here in the 13th century, this city was one of the most prosperous in the world, and quite possibly the most populous as well. Modern-day Hangzhou has retained that same prosperity, due in part to the 20 million visitors annually that come with tourist dollars to spend. In recent years the city has revamped its ancient culture street, rebuilt its Silk Museum, redesigned the parks and paths along the lake's edge, and made admission to many tourist sites free (which is *very* rare in China) to guarantee a never-ending flow of happy tourists.

Hangzhou's 6 million residents pride themselves on being much more laid-back than people in nearby Shanghai, where life is all about work and money. The presence of West Lake has made it part of the Hangzhou psyche to relax and hang out with friends at the end of the day, being peacefully rowed around

© BARBARA STROTHER
West Lake

THE MOST BEAUTIFUL WOMAN IN THE HISTORY OF CHINA

Of the four famous ancient Chinese beauties, the Zhejiang Province-native Xi Shi is considered the most beautiful woman of all time. These women are admired not just for their physical appearance but for the way they used it to serve their country. Xi Shi agreed to seduce the king of Wu, distracting him with her charms and convincing him to kill his top general, which brought about his defeat in the war. Today, West Lake in Hangzhou is nick-named after Xi Shi, with the claim that both hold the position as the most beautiful in China.

the lake on a Chinese gondola while munching on dried watermelon seeds and sipping Hangzhou's world-famous *Long Jin* (Dragon Well) tea. Along the lake's waterside paths and parks, musicians play traditional instruments, and a member of the crowd may sing along while old men practice tai chi and middle-aged women practice their jitterbug.

While the locals may not be as focused on success as Shanghaiers, they are no less successful. Hangzhou has a large and growing upper class. You'll feel their presence if you stop by one of the local malls, where suits in store windows carry $1,000 price tags. Unfortunately Hangzhou's real estate and cost of living have been growing along with its economy, and Hangzhou now has the fifth-highest housing costs in the mainland.

WHERE TO LIVE

Unlike many Chinese cities, the residential market in Hangzhou does not strictly follow its administrative districts. The three key housing areas include downtown Hangzhou, West Hangzhou, and along the banks of the Qiang-tang River to the south of the central city.

Downtown Hangzhou

Hangzhou's compact central city comprises two key districts, Shangcheng and Xiacheng. Shangcheng District, situated on the lake's eastern edge, is the heart of business and tourism in the city. Xiacheng District spreads north from the northeastern corner of the lake and is a key commercial area catering more to the well-off local population than to loaded tourists.

If you want to live in the middle of the most happening part of Hangzhou, pick a place in Shangcheng District. Here you'll find barhopping and inter-national eateries along Nanshan Street and Hubin Road, as well as the most popular stretch of West Lake's waterfront. This is a great spot for shopaholics, with fun night markets, classy department stores, small shops from the high-end to the unbelievably cheap, and a plethora of international goods of French megastore Carrefour, all within walking distance. As could be expected, this district is also quite a bit more expensive than those farther from the central activity. Luxury apartments, some with lake views and many within walking distance of key spots (all are within biking distance), rent for $1,500–3,000 per month for a 2- or 3-bedroom apartment.

The housing in Xiacheng District is cheaper and more varied than Shangcheng while still being convenient to the downtown hot spots. Xiacheng is home to Hangzhou's newest malls, filled with boutiques of the world's most famous designer names with price tags to match. The Wulin Road Women's Street is a female shopper's paradise; outdoor sports lovers can get gear and sign up for trips at the City Pack shop at Wulin Square. Plenty of Western eateries and upscale hotels are scattered around the area; you won't have to go far to get your cappuccino fix. Average apartments in this district typically rent for $500–1,500 per month, and there are tons to choose from.

West Hangzhou

The area typically referred to as West Hangzhou city is technically north-west of the central business district and the lake (the northern part of Xihu District). Important spots here include the main campus of Zhejiang University and the Yellow Dragon Stadium with its Trustmart megastore and

© BARBARA STROTHER

Hangzhou has always had a romantic reputation.

Tourist Center. There are just a few villas and town houses out this way, especially if you head to the westernmost edge. Apartments here are plentiful, however. Around the Yellow Dragon Stadium and Zhejiang University, rents typically run $600–2,000, many with amenities like swimming pools, restaurants, and fitness centers on the premises, such as the expat-popular Green Garden. The farther from the stadium and the university you go, the cheaper the rent.

PRIME LIVING LOCATIONS

A TASTE OF MEXICO IN HANGZHOU

AN INTERVIEW WITH ALEXANDER GARCIA

In 2005 Alexander Garcia came from Mexico to study Mandarin at Zhejiang University. After his program was complete, Alexander was hooked on the city of Hangzhou. With an educational background in computer science engineering, limited cooking abilities, and no restaurant experience, Alexander did the most logical thing to keep him in the city he loved: He opened a restaurant.

Pancho's Mexican Restaurant serves up real enchiladas, burritos, tacos, and more based on Alexander's mother's recipes. With a growing reputation among the local Chinese and a steady stream of foreigners, Pancho's does a brisk business as the only place in Hangzhou that you can get authentic Mexican food.

Alexander Garcia

© BARBARA STROTHER

What inspired you to open Pancho's?
We couldn't find any Mexican food here. Sometimes we would invite Chinese friends over and cook for them, and they would tell me I should open a restaurant. So I thought about it: *If I want to stay in China and be my own boss, then why not a restaurant?*

What is the typical Chinese response when they first try Mexican food?
They think it's weird at first. We have a lot of dishes with corn, and in the past when China had famine, all they got to eat was bread made from corn that the government gave them. For old people the corn tortillas remind them of a time when they were dying, when they had nothing else. The young people, though – they like it. For young people it's good. Originally foreigners made up 90 percent of the business at Pancho's, but now Chinese customers account for about 50 percent.

Qiangtang River Region

The Qiangtang River region covers territory along the river's northern bank in both Xihu and Jianggan Districts (known as Qianjiang New Town) as well as the up-and-coming Binjiang District, south of the Qiangtang River. This region is the predominant area for new housing developments. Though it's a little farther from the conveniences of the city, in exchange you'll get fresh air, quiet surroundings, and easy access to the Hangzhou

How have you found Chinese culture?
Are there many similarities with Mexico?
Mexican and Chinese people have a lot in common. Chinese people care a lot about family, and we do too; sons take care of their parents, and parents take care of the grandparents. And we are both very proud.

Guanxi is the same in Mexico. If you have friends, you have everything. If you don't know anybody, you've got nothing. In both Mexico and China relationships are not very straightforward. We both take time to get to the point. We invite someone to dinner because we want to talk about business, but we discuss everything except the business until the end when we say, "Oh, I wanted to tell you about such-and-such." And we drink together, and at the end we say, "Ah, by the way . . ."

What advice would you give to someone who
wanted to follow in your footsteps?
First, find somebody to help you – someone Chinese for sure, or somebody who knows somebody. If you're going to deal with the Chinese law by yourself, it's going to be crazy. Nowadays they respect international laws more than before, but still not much, so you need to find somebody to work with you. I have a Chinese business partner, and she helps me deal with the government and get cheaper prices. When I can't make things happen, she always knows a guy who knows a guy who knows this guy that can help. It's like this in China.

Second, work hard. That's it.

What do you like about what you're doing?
I like this city because it is similar to my hometown, Morelia, in Mexico. I like the way I feel here; it's like being at home. But my friends and the people that work here, that's what I like most. My Mexican friends here are my family. You are out of your country, and sometimes you get a little bit crazy without your loved ones from back home. Sometimes you just need someone to come and talk to you in your mother language.

Do you think you will be here a long time?
Yeah, that's what I want. That's the plan – 5, 10, or 20 years. But my parents don't like this idea.

PRIME LIVING LOCATIONS

International School in Binjiang. A 2–3 bedroom apartment with bird's-eye views of the river or the lush green hills typically rents for $800–1,500 per month, with all the usual amenities.

Villas in this region are plentiful. A Western-style home in Binjiang with 4 or 5 bedrooms can be rented fully furnished for $2,000–4,000 per month. West of Binjiang in the distant Zhijiang and Zhuangtang suburbs, giant homes with large lush yards rent for $4,000–6,000. A walk through some of these American-style neighborhoods will make you (and Toto) completely forget that you're not in Kansas anymore.

© BARBARA STROTHER

an old-fashioned puppet show along Hangzhou's ancient culture street

DAILY LIFE

You'll find most products you're looking for at the big retailers like TrustMart and Carrefour scattered around the city. Expats can head to the International Health Care Center and the North American International Hospital for their medical needs. For the things you can't find here, Shanghai is less than two hours away by train, bus, or private car.

The Hangzhou dialect is similar to Shanghai's, though Mandarin is widespread and typically spoken without a strong accent. Hangzhou has a fair amount of English spoken around the city to cater to its tourists, though like most places in China, English is not widely spoken outside of the tourist venues.

Expat Social Scene

There's plenty to do in Hangzhou when the sun goes down. Hangzhou's night markets are a fun place to barter for treasures like Chinese scrolls, antique trinkets, and tons of name-brand knockoffs. The numerous clubs and pubs along Nanshan Street are popular with expats and locals alike. You'll find a wide variety of restaurants featuring cuisine from around the world and around the country, especially in Hangzhou's upscale international hotels.

The Hangzhou International Fellowship holds nondenominational English services for expats at the Gulou Church as well as midweek Bible studies in homes around the city. Hangzhou also happens to have the largest church in China, the impressive Chong Yi Church; headphones are available for English translation.

Foreigners in Hangzhou will appreciate the resources of English magazines *In Touch Zhejiang* and *More Hangzhou* as well as the diminutive English newspaper *Hangzhou Weekly,* all of which offer news, events, and tips about the area.

Schools

The Hangzhou International School, sister school to the Shanghai Community International Schools, is currently the only school in Hangzhou dedicated to expat kids across all grades. Located in the southern Binjiang district of Hangzhou, their WASC-accredited curriculum is structured on the American system, including advanced placement courses where high school students can earn college credit.

PRIME LIVING LOCATIONS

© BARBARA STROTHER

Hangzhou street snacks: crabs

GETTING AROUND

Getting around Hangzhou is easy, with most of the key destinations conveniently located within the compact central business district. Local bus routes are easy to get to know, and there's even a bilingual bus schedule. Taxis are cheap and plentiful (except around 5 P.M., when the drivers' shifts change). Hangzhou is also currently constructing a subway system. And though hills decorate the area, the city itself is quite flat and easily navigable by bike. You can rent a bike at multiple spots around the city, especially by the lake. If you get a bike rental card, you won't pay for the bike rentals if you don't keep them for longer than a couple of hours at

students at Six Harmonies Pagoda, Hangzhou

© BARBARA STROTHER

a time, and they can be returned to any of the rental sites in the system.

Ningbo 宁波

Ningbo is a commercial city of 5 million located across the Hangzhou Bay from Shanghai Municipality, at the spot where the waters of the bay mingle with the waters of the East China Sea. This ancient port town had a long history of international trade throughout the centuries until it was eventually surpassed by neighboring Shanghai. Opened to foreign trade in the 1800s, little is left of its European concessions except a few cobblestone roads and its famous old Catholic church.

Today foreign enterprises are once again taking note of Ningbo, making business one of the main reasons why foreigners locate here. And with the new bridge connecting Ningbo to Shanghai, this little city is in a position to profit as wealthy Shanghai's new backyard.

Ningbo's watery position, with the bay, the sea, and numerous waterways that crisscross the urban landscape, has made its cuisine famous for fish and seafood. Famous dishes include yellow croaker, swimming crab, razor clam, and oysters from the East China Sea, typically cooked in a simple way that brings out their delicate flavors. The climate is mild; the air is clean; life can be good in Ningbo.

WHERE TO LIVE

Ningbo is divided into five key districts: Haishu, Jiangdong, Jiangbei, Beilun, and Yinzhou. Though most prime Chinese cities offer an equal number of choices between urban and suburban living, Ningbo doesn't yet fit this mold. The suburban districts of Beilun and Yinzhou are home to a number of large foreign companies as well as the AIAN international school in Beilun; however, the majority of expats live in one of the three central urban districts of Haishu, Jiangdong, and Jiangbei, trading short commutes for city conveniences. These three districts are divided by the rivers that meet in the city center; Jiangdong translates as "east of the river" and Jiangbei as "north of the river," with Haishu lying south and west of the other two.

Housing costs in Ningbo can be a bargain compared to the bigger cities, ranging from as low as a few hundred dollars for a small bachelor pad to under $2,000 for some villas and luxury apartments.

Haishu District

Haishu is the political, cultural, and commercial center of the city. Tian Yi Square is here as well as the two key residence complexes for expats, Century City and Central Garden, with hundreds of foreign families between them.

© BARBARA STROTHER

Ningbo is a port in the East China Sea.

Central Garden's 26-story skyscrapers and serviced apartments are popular among the young and/or single, while Century City's nine-story apartment towers offer ample space for kids to play in lush grounds and a landscaped pool area. Though rents rise with the apartment's size and floor level, both complexes start around $1,000 per month for a two-bedroom apartment, which is expensive by Ningbo standards. Haishu also has a few town houses farther from the city center, such as those at Tian Yi Jia Yuan, with rents around $3,000 per month.

Jiangbei District

Jiangbei District includes the ancient trade port area, with its version of Shanghai's Bund, the Laowaitan, now an entertainment area along the river. Here you'll find trendy restaurants popular with expats, with visions of its concession-era past in its cobblestone streets and the old Gothic church. High culture can be enjoyed at Jiangbei District's art venues and Grand Theatre.

Within Jiangbei there are both upscale apartments and modern villas where foreigners live, such as the Fangjing Garden with its picturesque canals and recreation center with an outdoor pool. Older villas (built 15 years ago) that may be due for a little renovation can be rented inexpensively at Fangjing Garden, though those that have undergone renovation will reflect it in their prices. Expect lease prices in the $1,700–3,000 range. Nearby, the International Village is much newer and equally popular with expats, with both apartments and villas available. Villas with 270–380 square meters rent for around $1,500 per month; three-bedroom apartments averaging 170 square meters rent for $600–1,200.

Jiangdong District

Jiangdong apartment residences tend to be just a little farther from the activity of the city center, roughly a 15-minute drive, though this area is more convenient for foreigners who will be working in the adjacent Beilun District. The Ningbo International School (NBIS) is also located here. Jiangdong has the highest concentration of 4- and 5-star international hotel chains in the city, as well as the widest selection of residential apartment towers and mixed complexes. Most apartments in Jiangdong rent for $800 to $1,500 per month, though there are some large and luxurious apartments that rent for $3,000 or more.

Beilun and Yinzhou Districts

If you prefer to get a little distance from the hectic central city, then Beilun or Yinzhou are a good location choice for you. Beilun offers the added convenience of the AIAN international school and the medical clinic for foreigners. Large modern town houses in these districts rent for $1,200–3,000; a quality three-bedroom apartment will put you out $600–1,200 per month. A good place to start your search is the East Lake Garden complex, which offers a combination of high-rise apartments, town houses, duplexes, and villas.

PUTUOSHAN ISLAND 普陀山岛

About 60 miles off the coast of Ningbo lies Putuoshan Island, a semitropical paradise that is one of China's four sacred Buddhist mountains. What you'll find on this little island, just 2 miles wide by 3.5 miles long, are numerous temples scattered throughout its lush green hills. What you won't find here is a lot of cars or commerce. A handful of minibuses shuttle visitors from temple sites to sandy beaches during daylight hours; otherwise, most transportation is on foot.

Putuoshan Island is a tranquil place for city-worn expats to escape the urban jungle. It's the closest beach to Shanghai (whose coastline is predominantly thick mud). From Ningbo you can reach Putuoshan by a quick but often rocky two-hour express ferry, where you can alternate between watching Hong Kong horror flicks on TV monitors and watching monks in holy Buddhist garb spewing their temple lunches. A steadier option is to take the overnight ferry, sleeping in bunks in shared quarters and waking to the sight of submarines surfacing outside your porthole.

a Buddhist ceremony on the beach in Putuoshan

© BARBARA STROTHER

PRIME LIVING LOCATIONS

DAILY LIFE

Of all the prime eastern cities, Ningbo has the lowest number of foreign residents and is not a tourist destination like the others. But this is exactly why some expats prefer this place to the flashier destinations like Shanghai, Hangzhou, and the rest. In Ningbo you can know and be known, rather than getting lost in the bigness of bigger cities.

As you would expect in a place without a large number of foreigners, you won't find much English here. Luckily, Mandarin has for the most part slowly supplanted the local Ningbo dialect, making communication no more difficult than just the regular frustrations of learning standard Chinese.

Ningbo is big enough to have plenty of top international brand stores, like Hugo Boss and Burberry, along with the less-heeled local department stores sharing space at the trendy Tian Yi Square in the center of town. Starbucks has several locations in the city; big retailers like Carrefour, Auchan, and Metro are convenient places to stock up on imported goods.

For international health facilities, try the Beilun Foreigners Medical Clinic inside the Ningbo Development Zone Hospital. Several local hospitals have also been designated as foreigner-friendly with English-speaking services, including the Ningbo No. 1 Hospital, Ningbo No. 2 Hospital, and the Ningbo Women and Children Hospital.

Expat Social Scene

The foreign community in Ningbo has a reputation for being friendly and laid-back. There's a good mix within the expat community, though this city tends to be a better spot for families than swinging singles. Ningbo has a handful of excellent restaurants and clubs, but as some would be quick to point out, it's no Shanghai. If that's important to you, however, the larger-than-life evening scene in Shanghai is close enough to do frequent weekends away to get your fix.

Several websites provide handy city information, such as www.helloningbo.com and www.ningboguide.com, both of which publish a print version of their online publication. The monthly English magazine *In Touch Zhejiang* supposedly covers Ningbo, although it predominantly focuses on Hangzhou. Check out www.ninbgoexpat.com for the latest news and events, including announcements of the chosen restaurant for the weekly Ningbo Expat Association gathering.

Schools

Ningbo's two premier international schools for expat kids are the Access International Academy Ningbo (AIAN) and the Ningbo International School (NBIS). AIAN, located in suburban Beilun district, teaches all grades with a global curriculum based on North American core standards. The Ningbo International School (NBIS) follows an Australian curriculum and has optional boarding facilities on its campus in the Jiandong District.

GETTING AROUND

The city is easy to get around on foot or by bike, or take a cheap and easy bus or taxi to spots farther afield. When you're ready to get out of town, Ningbo is about a 1.5-hour drive or train ride to Hangzhou and two hours to Shanghai with the new bridge. Ningbo's airport has flights to many domestic cities as well as a few other Asian destinations, and the nearby airports at Hangzhou and Shanghai are also an option. Better yet, Ningbo is the key launching point for ferries to Putuoshan Island, where you can spend a rejuvenating weekend rambling among its many Buddhist temples or relaxing on its subtropical beaches—some of the best beaches for hundreds of miles.

PRIME LIVING LOCATIONS

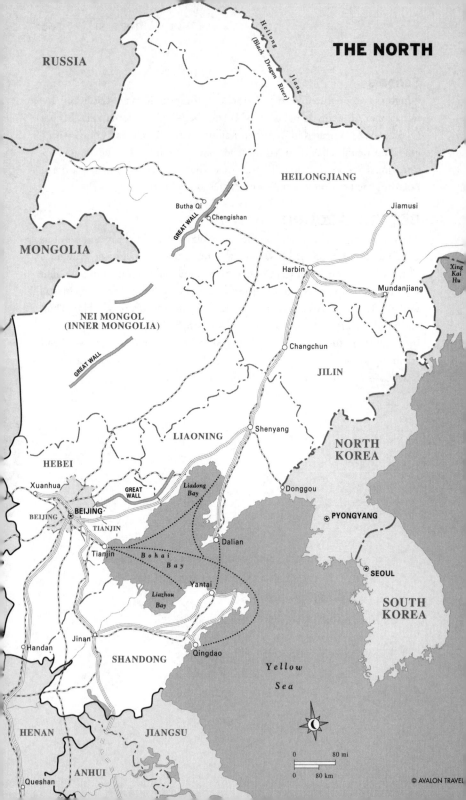

THE NORTH

RUSSIA

Heilong Jiang (Black Dragon River)

MONGOLIA

HEILONGJIANG

Butha Qi
GREAT WALL
Chengishan

Jiamusi

NEI MONGOL
(INNER MONGOLIA)

Harbin

Mundanjiang

Xing Kai Hu

GREAT WALL

Changchun

JILIN

LIAONING

Shenyang

NORTH
KOREA

HEBEI

Xuanhua

GREAT WALL

Liadong Bay

Donggou

BEIJING
BEIJING
TIANJIN

PYONGYANG

Tianjin

B o h a i   B a y

Dalian

Yantai

Liazhou Bay

SEOUL

Handan

Jinan

SHANDONG

Qingdao

SOUTH
KOREA

Yellow

Sea

HENAN

JIANGSU

ANHUI

Queshan

0   80 mi

0   80 km

© AVALON TRAVEL

THE NORTH

Rugged and rough around the edges, northern China is industrious and well adapted to surviving hardship. An extensive coastline gives this region several of the nation's most prominent ports and most popular seaside resorts. Their food is hearty and filling, designed to take the edge off the winter's bitter cold, and they produce the country's most famous wines and beers. In this region that surrounds Beijing, the local languages are merely slight variations of standard Mandarin, unlike other areas where local dialects are mutually unintelligible.

The northern port cities of Tianjin, Qingdao, and Dalian frequently make the "Most Livable Cities in China" lists. Dalian and Qingdao boast pretty beaches and clean environments, while Tianjin offers big-city amenities without all the buzz of nearby Beijing. All three are a part of the Bohai Rim Economic Zone, which competes with the cities of the Yangtze River Delta and the Pearl River Delta for top economic production. Shenyang, the only prime northern city that is neither a port nor part of the Bohai Rim, is a rising star

© BARBARA STROTHER

in the northeastern rust belt, a land tarnished by unemployment as the state-owned enterprises of this hearty industrial zone have been shut down for lack of profitability.

The Lay of the Land

Green hills and majestic mountains dot the terrain of northern China. Around the crescent shape of the Bohai Sea's coastline, Dalian lies at its northernmost tip, Tianjin right in its middle, and the city of Yantai at its southern tip, followed by Qingdao on the south side of the Shandong Peninsula. The provinces to the northeast of Beijing are collectively known as Dongbei (literally, northeast), home to both Shenyang and the tourist-popular Harbin city with its strong Russian influences.

CLIMATE

When it comes to climate, northern China can be divided into two camps. Cities that are located on the edge of the ocean like Dalian, Qingdao, and Yantai enjoy milder weather patterns throughout the year. But cities that are located farther away from the weather-calming effects of the Pacific Ocean endure extreme climate changes, with hot summers giving way to bitter cold and snowy winters.

© BARBARA STROTHER

Northerners have a reputation of being tough and hardy individuals.

Tianjin 天津

Tianjin (pop. 11 million) is the third-largest city in China and one of the four independent municipalities. A sprawling commercial city, Tianjin has been described as simultaneously "gritty" and "vibrant," and as the largest city nobody's heard of. Its prosperity and its reputation have always been linked with Beijing, its importance often overlooked in light of its famous neighbor. Just down the Hai River from Beijing lies Tianjin's central city; farther down, the river meets the Bohai Sea at the busy port of Tanggu.

With a history similar to Shanghai's, Tianjin was once teeming with foreigners building up their colonial concessions, doing businesses in imposing banks, and worshipping in fancy cathedrals of stained glass. A walk around the city reveals ornate European villas, churches, banks, and shops playing peek-a-boo among towering modern glass skyscrapers. For a glimpse into its non-European history, Tianjin's famous antiques market is located in what was once, ironically, "Chinatown," now an area of winding *hutong* streets lined with "antiques" (buyer beware).

Tianjin's Economic Development Area (TEDA) is one of the best-managed in the country, and it has brought in well over 3,000 foreign corporations, including giants like Motorola and Nestlé. Consequently, the expat community here has plenty of international business types, as well as a good mix of the typical English teachers, foreign students, and the like.

Tianjin enjoys a climate that is temperate and seasonal. January brings below-freezing temperatures, and July brings a muggy monsoon season, but spring and fall are pleasantly filled with cloudless skies. While many Chinese cities may make you exclaim, "It's nice to visit, but I wouldn't want to live here," Tianjin is just the opposite—there's not much here to keep a tourist busy for long, but it's a good place to raise a family.

WHERE TO LIVE

The first step to finding a home in Tianjin begins with determining whether you need to be in the city proper or within TEDA. TEDA is located 45 kilometers southeast of downtown Tianjin. The two areas are connected by several freeways and the subway, making it possible to commute between the two, but most people prefer to focus their attention on one or the other. To be in the heart of Tianjin is to have all the city's conveniences, history, and entertainment venues at hand. Easy access to the train station makes for quick getaways, and being closer to Beijing may prove to be convenient for those whose jobs require frequent trips to the capital. TEDA, on the other hand, is where many of the foreign businesses are located. TEDA also offers a choice of international schools and a greater variety of upscale housing complexes.

Tianjin City

Within the city of Tianjin proper, monthly apartment rentals range from $250 for a basic 1- or 2-bedroom up to $1,500 for an upscale and spacious place with added amenities like a health club, restaurants, and swimming pools. Serviced apartments at luxury hotels range $1,000–7,000 per month and offer the perks of hotel living (such as never having to make your bed again) without the space limitations

© BARBARA STROTHER

Yams freshly baked in a drum barrel will warm you nicely on a chilly winter day.

of a hotel room. Tianjin city has fewer villas to offer than TEDA; the few here typically rent for $2,500–6,000. Within Tianjin city the key areas for expats include Heping, Nankai, and Hexi Districts.

The densely populated central Heping District is Tianjin's political and economic center. Home to the antiques market and dotted with old European architecture, Heping is a mix of the old and the new, Tianjin's history and its future. Located in Heping, the Wudadao area is a residential area of the old British and French concessions with homes from the 1920s and 1930s that were required to be built without so much as a hint of Chinese architecture. There are plenty of housing complexes scattered around this district. The Somerset Olympic Towers is popular with foreign families with its on-site preschool, bus service to the nearby international schools, an indoor pool, a gym, and a rooftop garden. Serviced apartments here range from simple one-bedroom suites to four-bedroom penthouses.

The Nankai District is Tianjin's cultural and educational center, southwest of the central city and home to two prominent universities as well as the Tianjin International School. This is the site of Tianjin's birthplace, as seen in its ancient city gate and drum tower, as well as its Culture Street, a new reproduction of its ancient past. Popular housing options for foreigners in Nankai are focused on serviced apartments. At the TEDA International Club, residents have access to the club's restaurants, nightclub, indoor ice-skating rink, bowling alley, archery, tennis courts, swimming pool, and sauna.

Hexi District to the south was formerly a German colony and still boasts some Bavarian architecture. The You Yi Road bar area is located here, as well as the Sheraton, where elegant 2- to 4-bedroom serviced apartments come with access to the all-day buffet, pools and sauna, disco, massage center, tennis courts, gym, business facilities, and restaurants. Other options include City House's cozy town houses, the Rego Garden, and any number of towering residential skyscrapers that will give you a dizzying bird's-eye view of the city.

TEDA

The TEDA housing market is developing briskly. If you're in the market for a nice house with your own yard, you'll most likely end up in one of TEDA's villa complexes. Both the International School of Tianjin and the TEDA international school are located here.

TEDA has an abundance of classy low-rise residential apartment buildings and townhomes for lease. Most villas and town houses in TEDA rent between $1,500 and $4,000, though some large and luxurious homes rent as high as $8,000 per month. If all of this is beyond your budget, there are cheaper apartments available that cater more to the locals than to the wealthy foreign population that lives here. It is possible to find a nice but small two-bedroom apartment in TEDA for less than $200 per month.

DAILY LIFE

One of Tianjin's biggest appeals is that for a large city with so many Western amenities, you'll get a more "Chinese" experience here than in cities like Shanghai or Beijing. That is what expats love about the place—its own blend of quirkiness—and it's not uncommon to meet foreigners who have lived here, happily, for 5 or 10 years or more.

With plenty of international retailers like Carrefour and Wal-Mart, Starbucks galore, and American restaurants like TGI Friday's, Tianjin's foreigners are able to find most of the things they crave here. The local dialect is easy, being very similar to standard Mandarin (which is a good thing, since not much English is spoken here).

Tianjin also has its own SOS health clinic for foreigners, the AEA Tianjin International Clinic located within the Tianjin Sheraton Hotel in Hexi District.

Expat Social Scene

Tianjin's foreign community feels smaller than it really is. It won't take long hanging out in expat bars before you'll start to recognize familiar faces. If you're looking to join in the expat bar scene, Cosy's, Broadies, and Alibaba's have their own group of regulars, and the joints along the You Yi Lu bar street all make the list. Sports lovers can be found at the Upper Deck Bar for large-screen showings of sporting events. Many expats also take advantage of the weekly worship at the International Christian Fellowship.

© BARBARA STROTHER

Tianjin's antique market is loaded with quirky finds.

For community events, check out the local expat magazine *Jin,* found at popular restaurants and bars or online at www.expatriatejin.com. Additionally, the Tianjin International Community Center and the American Women's Association are two organizations that can help you get settled in to your new community here.

Schools

Tianjin has four international schools to choose from. Both the TEDA International School and the Tianjin International School (TIS) follow a North American curriculum, though TIS has a Christian focus. Tuition at the TEDA International School is financially subsidized by the TEDA administration, but you must reside in TEDA to attend. The International School Tianjin offers an International Baccalaureate program; the Tianjing Rego International School offers the only British curriculum in the city.

GETTING AROUND

Although the city is quite spread out, it's easy enough to get around by taxi, bus, or the Tianjin subway. The subway system here includes one of the oldest subway lines in the nation, though much of it has been recently rebuilt and more lines are planned to add to the current ones. The light-rail Binhai Line conveniently connects TEDA with downtown Tianjin.

Qingdao 青岛

Ah, life in Qingdao—a laid-back time of good beaches and good beer. Though known domestically for its golden sands and deep clear waters, its bigger claim to fame is the world-famous Tsingtao beer (Tsingtao being the old way of spelling Qingdao). With over 100 years in the business, the brewery industry here has set the tone for the city. Pubs dot the landscape, and every August millions of tourists from around the world descend on Qingdao to enjoy drinking games, contests, and a rather joyful parade at the Annual Beer Festival.

It was the Germans who started all this beer business in Qingdao. When the city served as a German colony, the Germans turned a sleepy fishing village into the bustling port that Qingdao still is today. Quite a bit of the European colonial architecture remains, giving a quaint aura to this city of 8 million.

Though its name literally translates as "green island," Qingdao is actually located on a peninsula that juts southward into the Yellow Sea. The quaint historic part of town lies in the west, while the eastern districts are dotted with modern high-rises, upscale shopping venues, and vibrant nightlife. Farther out, suburban areas boast resort-like grounds. All along the southern coastline you'll find picturesque bays and sandy beaches. Qingdao's temperate marine climate has helped to establish it as a resort destination, with four distinct and pleasant seasons. This place well deserves its green name—it's one of China's greenest cities due to an abundance of trees and grassy areas that decorate the city. You'll also find plenty of cheap shopping and cheap food (including tons of wonderfully fresh seafood) in Qingdao.

Qingdao may not be overly cosmopolitan, and if you want a highly cultured life, you should look elsewhere. But if you're into laid-back living, hanging out at the beaches and the pubs with a few good friends, Qingdao may just be the place for you.

© KEVIN SELDOMRIDGE
vestiges of colonialism in Qingdao

WHERE TO LIVE

Qingdao expats can be found scattered throughout the city's seven districts, though most locate on the east side of the city along the shore in the Shinan (literally, southwest) District, which includes the central city; or the Laoshan District, which spreads southeast along the coast. Downtown Qingdao used to be the center of town, bordering the old European neighborhood of Badaguan, but the city has purposefully been moving its central business district to the east.

Options for housing in Qingdao include numerous modern apartments and a fair number of villa complexes, all of which typically advertise whether they have a sea view and how long the walk is to the nearest beach. Huge luxury villas can rent for upwards of $8,000 per month, though a very basic local apartment can run $250 monthly, and there are lots of options in between.

Shinan District

Shinan District is the tourist magnet of the city. Including downtown proper and all of the major hotels, the famous Bavarian villas of Badaguan, a number of the city's most popular beaches, the Qingdao MTI International School, the Qingdao American International School, and Qingdao's universities, Shinan is the place to be if you are looking for a convenient location. There are just a handful of villas to rent in this district, though the choices among apartments are plentiful. Sky-piercing high-rise residential buildings scattered throughout the district offer apartments for a wide range of budgets; expect to pay around $400 for an average two bedroom up to $2,500 or more for a sprawling five-bedroom penthouse that overlooks the sea. Beer enthusiasts might get a kick out of living at the huge Pacific Center, which offers apartments with great views for $650–1,000 per month in a complex that includes a shopping center, a swimming pool, tennis courts, a dancing room, and the international headquarters of Tsingtao Beer.

Laoshan District

If you are in the market for a villa, you'll more than likely end up in Laoshan District. Within the district lies the Shilaoren National Tourist Resort, which includes numerous villa and luxury apartment complexes, beaches, the Qingdao No. 1 International School Shandong, an amusement park, a marine sightseeing district, and two golf courses. Most luxury villas have sea views, are a close walk to the shore, and have their own "garden" (lawn); both apartment and villa dwellers in these complexes share the use of indoor swimming pools, tennis courts, restaurants, or other amenities. The expat-popular town

© BARBARA STROTHER

Qingdao is known for its fresh seafood, like this freshly grilled spicy squid-on-a-stick.

houses of Eldo View Garden face the sea; five-bedroom homes here rent in the $4,000–5,000 range.

A second area within Laoshan District is the Economic and Technical Development Zone. Housing options in this area mostly consist of modern apartment complexes with mountain and sea views; rents run about $500 for a 2- or 3-bedroom. These places are especially convenient for those who will be working within this zone, and most offer amenities such as swimming pools and tennis courts.

DAILY LIFE

Expats will find that Qingdao has most of what they will need to live a comfortable lifestyle.

The Qingdao Municipal Hospital, the official medical facility for the 2008 Olympics Sailing Regatta in Qingdao, has been developed into a first-class health center for foreigners as well as local citizens. Another option in health care for foreigners is the Korean-run Qingdao Severance Hospital, which was created to cater to foreigners (especially Korean expats) and wealthy Chinese.

The Qingdao dialect is mostly just a slightly accented version of standard Mandarin. As a result, some find Qingdao a good place to study the language. On the other hand, not much English is spoken here outside of the establishments that cater to Qingdao's large tourist crowd.

Expat Social Scene

The Qingdao expat community is quite diverse, with a large contingent of Koreans. Some come to work in one of the hundreds of foreign companies within the economic development zone; some come to teach at local schools. The foreign community here is quite active, and residents boast it's the closest-knit expat community in China. To get connected and find out what's going on in the city, pick up a copy of *Redstar* magazine or check out the English-language websites www.qingdaoexpat.com and www.thatsqingdao.com.

Schools

Qingdao currently has four key international schools for English-speaking expat kids. The Qingdao MTI International School is the oldest and most established; it follows an American curriculum with a Christian emphasis. The Qingdao No. 1 International School Shandong (QISS) offers Western-style (and accredited) education in a government-run school, and the Yew-Chung International School (YCIS) incorporates both Eastern and Western approaches to education. The Qingdao American International School (QAIS) is the latest newcomer to the city's educational scene.

GETTING AROUND

Qingdao is easy to navigate due to its compact location sandwiched between the mountains and the sea. Unless you choose to locate in the suburbs, getting around by foot, bike, taxi, or bus will all be cheap, easy, and quick. In the suburbs some public buses and taxis are available to take you around.

Dalian 大连

Dalian is the crown jewel of Dongbei, the diamond stud in the old rust belt. It is home to 6 million people and the largest community of expats north of Beijing. The people who live here love it, thanks to its clean streets, green parks, beautiful bays, sandy beaches, and spicy squid-on-a-stick, a delicious though chewy treat. It's been rated the number-two most livable city in China, and the residents wonder why it didn't get a higher rating. The downside to Dalian's prosperous economic development is its rising prices. While still cheaper than Shanghai and Beijing, the cost of living is more than what you would expect for a city of this size, though some would argue that it is well worth it.

Situated at the southern end of the Laiodong Peninsula, Dalian straddles the Bohai Bay and the Yellow Sea. Winters don't get too bad here—except for the Chicago-like winds—and summers stay mostly pleasant.

© BARBARA STROTHER

Dalian's local restaurants have strong Japanese and Korean influences.

This city was once controlled by the Russians, taken over by the Japanese, returned to Russian hands, and then reverted to Chinese control in the 1950s. Both foreign cultures left their mark in the architecture that lends this place its charm. Today, Japanese and Koreans wield great influence in Dalian's business, with the happy result of numerous Japanese and Korean restaurants to cater to their presence here. In fact, Dalian is full of great restaurants with flavors spanning China and the globe, including plenty of spots where the expats hang. The bar district along Chang Jiang Road downtown is a good place to start if you're looking to join the fun.

WHERE TO LIVE

Foreigner-friendly housing can be found scattered throughout Dalian's four key areas: Xigang, Zhongshan, Jinzhou, and Lushun.

Xigang District

Xigang District in central Dalian is the heart of the city's business and tourism. Top-notch shopping venues and acclaimed international restaurants mix with modern skyscrapers. This district is also home to the old European-style villas surprisingly built by the Japanese. The University of Foreign Languages is also in Xigang District, south of the city center, as are the coffee shops and pubs that cater to its students.

Residential high-rise towers dot the urban landscape, offering modern and spacious apartments with bird's-eye views to the city below and convenient access on foot around this city that is known as a great place to walk. Expect to spend $300–800 per month in rent here for a nice but average apartment. If you're in the market for something large and luxurious, a four-bedroom apartment with grand views of the city below will rent for around $2,400 a month.

Farther south, the Fujiazhuang resort area has several high-end hotels that have luxury villas available to rent by the night, month, or year, like the Hai Huan Villas, located on the side of the mountain overlooking the sea, or the gorgeous Furama Nanshan Garden Hotel, set in a lush environment reminiscent of Japanese gardens.

Zhongshan District

Zhongshan District, in the southeastern corner of Dalian, boasts popular beaches and a myriad of tourist attractions, including an amusement park and China's largest aquarium. The Dalian Maple Leaf Foreign Nationals School for elementary and middle school grades is located here, as well as several hospitals with VIP wards for foreigners. Within this district there are several serviced apartments that are popular with business expats, such as the Ascott Somerset Harbour Court, the Shangri-La Century Tower, and the Hilton. For those without corporate budgets, a standard two-bedroom apartment within walking distance of the central business district will cost around $400–500 per month.

Jinzhou and Lushun Districts

Jinzhou is Dalian's main economic district. With an eager focus on foreign investment, this area prides itself on being a place that is becoming increasingly foreigner-oriented. With the new villa housing options going up around the district, kids can have their own bedrooms and a yard to play in. Outdoors lovers will enjoy Daheishan Mountain, the highest peak on the peninsula and a great place to get away from the hustle and bustle of the commerce below. Two-bedroom apartments can be rented here for around $500–600.

Lushun District is home to great swimming, fishing, hiking, camping, boating, and island-hopping, with some 700 islands along the coast. Nearby Jin Shi Tan (Golden Pebble) National Holiday Resort, 60 kilometers to the north of the central city, is Dalian's "back garden." Here you'll find the Maple Leaf International School Senior High Campus, the Dalian American International School, golf and hunting clubs, and the Golden Pebble Beach that gives this area its name. New housing complexes are currently being developed here, like the Campus Village residential complex conveniently located next to the American International School.

DAILY LIFE

The locals are used to seeing foreigners ramble along their city streets, which means they are less likely to stare and point and treat you like an odd scientific discovery. The flip side to this local exposure to foreigners is that the culture of Dalian is no longer as Chinese as it once was, having become something of a melting pot.

Dalian shares the same language base as Qingdao, a slight variation of standard Mandarin, which makes it a good option for those who want to master Chinese. On the other hand, there's not much English spoken here; Japanese is the language du jour in Dalian.

Western goods are somewhat easy to find, thanks to the city's big-box retailers such as Carrefour, Wal-Mart, and Metro. VIP hospital wards that care for foreigners can be found in Zhongshan at the Dalian Friendship Hospital, the Dalian Railway Hospital, and the First Affiliated Hospital of Dalian Medical University Part II (let's hope you won't have to sputter out that long name in an emergency).

Expat Social Scene

Dalian's expat community is predominantly Japanese and secondarily Korean, with a few Westerners and others thrown into the mix. Unfortunately, Dalian's biggest disadvantage has been that its expat community is not very tightly knit. But the city's new English-language magazine, *Focus Dalian,* should help bring its expats together.

Dalian has plenty of recreation to offer the whole family: Build sandcastles at the beach, check out the 400 crocs at the Crocodile Garden, see the underwater world of Dalian's two aquariums, go hiking or fishing or island-hopping, or just relax at one of the city's many green parks. Golf heaven can be found at the Golden Pebble Golf Course, with three fairways that rank in the top 100 worldwide, all picturesquely located along the edge of dramatic seaside cliffs.

Schools

Dalian's school choices for foreigners include the Dalian American International School, offering an American curriculum to kids of all ages, and the Dalian Maple Leaf International School, a Sino-Canadian joint venture split into two campuses for a Foreign Nationals school up to grade 9 and an

International School for grades 10 through 12. Maple Leaf students graduate with both Chinese and Canadian diplomas.

GETTING AROUND

Dalian has its own quirky modes of transportation. It's one of the three cities in mainland China that still have colonial-era trams, and its position on the sea means ferries can carry you to half a dozen Chinese cities around the Bohai Sea as well as to Korea. A light-rail train connects downtown Dalian to its northern suburbs. Of course the typically numerous taxis and city buses of any Chinese city are ubiquitous here. To venture beyond the city, Dalian's international airport connects with several Asian cities, especially convenient to Korea and Japan, as well as all major airports within China. Dalian is served by trains as well, though due to its location on the peninsula, the routes must go north before they can head out to other parts of the nation.

Shenyang 沈阳

Shenyang, Laioning's provincial capital of 7 million residents, is at the heart of China's efforts to revitalize the northeastern Rust Belt. Centrally located about 100 miles inland from the Bohai Sea, Shenyang's winters are long and cold, averaging a January high of just 10°F but dropping as low as 30°F. Here the white winter snow quickly turns black from dirt and pollution. Local expats claim the best way to ward off the winter blahs is to schedule regular activities out. Luckily there are plenty of winter sports here to combat cabin fever, such as the nearby Qi Pan Shan ski resort. The fall and the spring are pleasant, though, other than the occasional sandstorms, and summers are plenty hot but without the stifling humidity of most other key Chinese cities.

Shenyang's 2,300-year history as a city reached its climax when it was the capital of the Qing Dynasty in the 1600s, leaving behind the city's most impressive attraction, the Imperial Palace. The Russians and Japanese both came and went in various war occupations, and SOEs (state-owned enterprises) did the same, bringing industrial prosperity to the area for a short time before the poorly run companies crumbled. Now with foreign investment and government commitment to revitalization, Shenyang is finally building a position for itself that will last. Throughout the city, old industrial districts are giving way to modern residential developments, upscale boutiques, and luxury hotels. Shenyang is also establishing itself as the commercial and financial center of the entire northeast, like a small-scale version of Shanghai's transformation in the 1990s. You may just find the real China you've been looking for in this unspoiled northern city.

WHERE TO LIVE

Shenyang's cost of living is low, and it's possible to get by here on the cheap if you live like the locals. On the other hand, in recent years Shenyang has experienced the highest inflation in housing prices anywhere in the mainland. Upscale villas and luxury apartments will be cheaper than in Beijing or Shanghai—but cheaper is not the same as cheap.

Heping District

traditional door knockers and masks for sale at a local shop

© BARBARA STROTHER

The downtown Heping District is convenient to all that the city has to offer. If you like the buzz of city life, the neon lights at night, the energy that comes with the nonstop activity of the big city, you'll enjoy downtown Shenyang. The U.S. consulate is located here, as well as most of the Western hotels that host the popular pubs and restaurants of the city.

Most foreigners living in central Heping rent a serviced apartment at one of the luxury hotels. The five-star Intercontinental Hotel's serviced apartments have long been a favorite, with their modern Western kitchens, indoor tennis courts, swimming pool, and indoor golf driving range, as well as the nearby Mulligan's Irish Bar, where expats tend to congregate. For a nonhotel option, the New World Garden Villas has apartments and villas that rent for $750–1,000 for an apartment or around $3,800–4,500 for a spacious four-bedroom villa.

Hunnan Development Zone

On the southern edge of the city is Shenyang's hope of economic salvation, the Hunnan Development Zone, a top priority in the government's plans to bring economic growth to Shenyang. This area is where the long-term foreign residents first started to settle in Shenyang. Though on the edge of the city, Hunnan feels more like a part of the town than a suburb, and the commute time to downtown is only about a 15-minute drive. For serviced apartments, the Marriott offers an indoor pool, a health club, and Shenyang's top Japanese restaurant conveniently located next to the Foreign Joint Venture office. Or try the Sheraton, with condominium-style apartments and multiple restaurants and bars, including Mezza, serving more than 100 different beers.

Across the street from the Marriott and Sheraton is Riverside Gardens, a large complex of villas and apartments that includes an imported-foods market, a health club and tennis courts, a playground, and the International Club of Shenyang with its social activities. There are over 1,000 families living in Riverside Gardens; almost a third of them are from foreign countries.

HAPPY IN HARBIN?

Poetically named after the Black Dragon River, Heilongjiang Province's snow-covered peaks and white glaciers resemble the northern Canadian wilderness. At the mention of this northernmost Chinese province or its famous city, Harbin (哈尔滨), the first three words that come to mind are cold, cold, and cold. A winter night here sees the temperature drop to a mind- and body-numbing 20°F.

In spite of its frigid climate, winter brings the greatest number of visitors to the area for Harbin's Ice Lantern Festival. If the cold doesn't take your breath away, the intricately carved and lighted giant ice sculptures will.

Harbin is also known for its strong Russian influence, and Harbin's cobblestone streets, onion domes, and ornate Russian architecture all lend a distinctly Russian elegance to the

© KEVIN SELDOMRIDGE

There's nothing like a refreshing swim in January!

Apartments rent for $1,200–2,500, or double that for huge two-story apartments. Furnished villas have 3–5 bedrooms with 200–320 square meters and rent for $3,000–5,000 per month.

Shenhe District

The Shenhe District to the east of downtown showcases Shenyang's history in its Imperial Palace and ancient culture street as well as Shenyang's modern enterprise. This is Shenyang's financial and commercial district. Here you'll find the north railway station and next to it the Gloria Plaza Hotel's serviced apartments. Other housing options in the district include elegant

PRIME LIVING LOCATIONS

city. Here you can dine on Russian breads, vodka, and caviar in restaurants with the gilded columns of a bygone era. Or wrap up tight in a Siberian fur and hit the cobbled pedestrian shopping district along Zhongyan Lu, where trendy cafés and upscale boutiques with preserved Russian facades offer a pleasant place to while away a chilly afternoon.

Harbin offers plenty of hotels, restaurants, bars, and shops that appeal to overnight visitors – but little to offer the long-term foreign resident. Without international schools or Western medical facilities and little imported food beyond that which caters to the Russian population, Harbin lacks the basic Western amenities that most internationals want. Although the winters can be beautiful, the cold and the early-setting sun force many to stay isolated in their homes. The summer reveals a shabby image of the city. The countryside may be like northern Canada, but the city has been likened to Detroit – not the best option for an expat with a family, or anyone that struggles with Seasonal Affective Disorder, for that matter. However, after suf-

© KEVIN SELDOMRIDGE

Russian architecture in Harbin

fering for years from the effects of Russia's economic woes, Harbin is finally on the upswing, enjoying a relatively high standard of living with a cost of living that's just a quarter of Shanghai's or Beijing's. It may be just a few years before Harbin develops into a decent destination for thick-blooded foreigners.

luxury apartments at the five-star Kempinski Hotel, popular among German expatriates, and the five-star Hua Fu Tiandi (Rich Gate) plaza, an office and residential complex with apartments ranging from 1-bedrooms for less than $500 up to 5-bedrooms for $3,000.

Dongling District

Southwestern Dongling District is home to many of Shenyang's foreign families. For those that don't mind being far from town (about a 20-minute drive just to the edge of the city), there are several high-end villa complexes available here, including the Civic Moon, popular with diplomatic families from the local consulates. Civic Moon also offers apartments for those that don't need the space of a villa, as well as tennis courts, an indoor pool, two restaurants, a store, and regular shuttles to downtown. The Shenyang International School is also located within this district, making this area a prime option for those with school-age children.

DAILY LIFE

Shenyang has a small variety of typical international restaurants, and imported products can be picked up at the usual Carrefour, Wal-Mart, PriceSmart, and Metro, along with the Riverside Garden Supermarket and Civic Moon convenience stores. Shenyang is also home to a foreign medical clinic run by Global Doctors.

The Shenyang dialect is a variation of standard Mandarin that is often used in Chinese humor to depict charming simpletons. Mandarin students should find it easy to understand (if you can ever call Mandarin easy). English is almost nonexistent; make sure you've got a sturdy pocket phrasebook because you'll want to keep it with you always.

Expat Social Scene

Expats who spent time here in the past tend to refer to the city as a hardship post, but current residents say that morale is high among foreigners and that things are getting better all the time. Shenyang is finally becoming a place that an expat can comfortably call home. And the number of expats who are calling Shenyang home is steadily growing, as they come to work at the consulates or at one of the many foreign businesses such as GM, Boeing, and Coca-Cola.

DINING ON DOG MEAT

Dog is a signature food of the northeast, a culinary custom imported from nearby Korea. Its popularity here is due in part to the belief that eating dog will keep you warm in the winter. You'll recognize it in your hot-pot by its slightly green tint. A "three-dog night" takes on a whole new meaning up here!

The presence of a U.S. consulate here means you'll have help available when you need it. The International Club of Shenyang is a good place to tap into the tight-knit Shenyang expat community, or try the Scottish Bar at the Holiday Inn. And although Shenyang doesn't yet have a glossy English magazine, the Liaoning Gateway online newsletter (www.liaoninggateway.com) will clue you in to life in the city and surrounding province. Expats can also attend English mass at the beautiful Shenyang City Catholic Cathedral.

Schools

The Shenyang International School is the only one in the city for English speakers where classes are taught by expatriates. The school teaches an American curriculum within a Christian worldview for students of all grades on a new campus south of the city in the Dongling District.

GETTING AROUND

Shenyang's sprawl is easily traversed by cheap taxis and public buses, and when the new subway system is fully functional it will be easier still. If you're looking to go farther afield, express trains run from Shenyang's train stations northwest to Harbin and southeast to Beijing and beyond. Flights from Shenyang's international airport can carry you off to all corners of China as well as on easy jaunts to Korea and Japan.

PRIME LIVING LOCATIONS

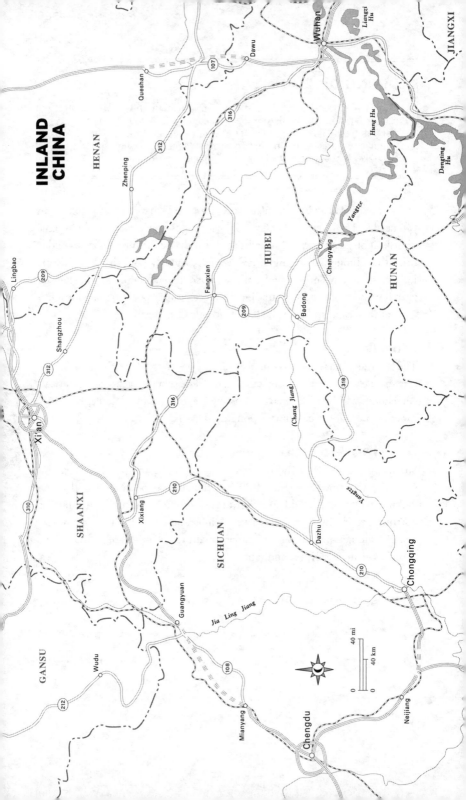

INLAND CHINA

The interior, the hinterlands, the middle of the Middle Kingdom: No matter what you call it, this is the *real* China. The inland region covers the greatest expanse of territory and draws the greatest number of tourists to explore its rich history, culture, and natural scenery. Even people who know very little about China are acquainted with the things that make the inland famous, such as its spicy Sichuan (Szechuan) food, its ancient terra-cotta warriors, and its controversial Three Gorges dam.

This region is the geographic center of the nation, but it's definitely not the economic center. Without a first-tier city or an economic region on par with the Yangtze Delta or the Pearl River Delta, this area has traditionally had less reason to draw foreign businesses, though that trend is starting to change. With a determined commitment to bring interior China up to speed with the development along the coast, the government is continuously advancing the infrastructure and amenities of its inland cities to make them more appealing to foreign firms.

© BARBARA STROTHER

The expats who've chosen to live in one of the hinterland cities are often in search of a more authentic Chinese experience. Small pockets of foreigners live and work in a vast number of places spread across this grand region, though the three cities that are the most foreigner-friendly are Wuhan, Chengdu, and Xi'an.

The Lay of the Land

The cities of Wuhan, Chongqing, and Chengdu are all situated within the Yangtze River Valley (though Chengdu actually lies a bit north of the river). Wuhan is the easternmost city, 600 miles upstream from Shanghai, while Chengdu is the westernmost, over 1,000 miles from Shanghai as the crested ibis flies. Xi'an lays a little farther north near another important Chinese waterway, the Yellow River, and Kunming is located in the colorful southwest.

CLIMATE

Due to the vast distances and the differences in terrain, the climates of the individual interior cities can vary quite a bit. The one thing most share, though, is four strongly distinct seasons, including chilly winters with occasional snow and intensely hot summers that are all the hotter here, away from the cooling effect of the ocean. Kunming is the exception with wonderfully springlike temperatures year-round.

Wuhan 武汉

Wuhan, capital of Hubei Province and home to roughly 9 million people, is a combination of what were once three separate cities: Hankou, Wuchang, and Hanyang. This city's heartland position and its strong industry and commerce have garnered it the nickname of China's Chicago. It's famous for being the hottest of China's three furnaces; summers here are spent going from one air-conditioned space to another in an effort to avoid the breath-sucking intensity of the heat.

Wuhan has a colorful past. During concession-era times, Hankou was forced to open its Yangtze River port to foreigners and became a key center of missionary activity; today a handful of the old European buildings are still in use here. Wuchang, a capital city in A.D. 220, was also the spot where Sun Yatsen led the famous Wuchang Uprising that ended dynastic rule in China.

With the Yangtze River flowing through its center and more than a hundred lakes, Wuhan is a watery town famous for its fish dishes. Tourists pour

© JEFF CULP

Wuhan's famous Yellow Crane Tower

through here on their way to embark on a Three Gorges river cruise. Though the city has just a handful of interesting tourist sites, the surrounding area has popular excursions worthy of day trips or short weekend adventures.

WHERE TO LIVE

Wuhan's real estate is divided into Hankou, Wuchang, and Hanyang, the original three towns. Most newcomers to Wuhan will want to live as close to their work as possible because it can take hours to get from one corner of the city to another.

THE MIGHTY YANGTZE

The Yangtze is China's longest river and the third largest in the world, after the Amazon and the Nile. The river made the pages of Communist history for Chairman Mao's famous cross-river swims, a ploy to disprove rumors of his failing health. It's also home to the few remaining Chinese river dolphins, a unique freshwater breed that is tragically losing its battle against the big ships and the fishing nets.

When most of the world thinks of the Yangtze, the Three Gorges Dam project comes to mind. The new dam is the world's largest hydroelectric project, and its construction has brought considerable criticism. The dam displaced over 1 million residents, submerged over 1,000 archaeological sites, and tainted the splendor of the gorges, all in the name of progress.

© JEFF CULP

a bird's-eye view of Wuhan, a sprawling metropolis

Hankou

Hankou, the northwestern piece of the Wuhan puzzle, is a fusion of the old and the new. Here you'll find the city's historic shopping streets, the best hospitals equipped to handle foreigners, and old colonial churches that are active once again. If you like being in the heart of a city's activity and convenient to its businesses, international restaurants, and trendy bars, you'll enjoy Hankou.

This district is home to serviced apartments popular with the business crowd. The centrally located Best Western C-Bank Hotel has executive apartments for around $2,300 per month; the Swiss-Belhotel has one or two bedroom rentals in the $2,600–3,600 range. Hankou also has plenty of standard apartments in modern new high-rises that typically rent for around $400–500 for a simple place up to $2,000 for an upscale apartment. If you're looking for a quiet villa neighborhood, you'll find a variety out toward the airport and the golf course. Most villas and townhomes in Hankou rent for $1,500–3,000 per month.

Wuchang

Wuchang, on the eastern bank of the Yangtze, is home to the picturesque East Lake, the largest urban lake in China and the sister of Hangzhou's famous West Lake. Near the East Lake you'll find several key Wuhan spots, such as the East Lake Development Zone with its many foreign businesses and the impressive Wuhan University. Because most of the city's universities are in Wuchang, this is where foreign students and foreign teachers tend to live. The area by the lake and the universities is a pleasant spot for walking or jogging along the lake's edge past traditional pavilions and Chinese landscapes.

Luxury apartments in the central-city area of Wuchang rent for around $700–1,200 and come with amenities like indoor pools and fitness centers. Apartments by the universities or the lake can be had for under $500 per month, or considerably less if you don't mind forgoing modern amenities for simplicity. Villas or town houses here start around $1,500 per month; some come with nice views of Wuchang's lakes and rivers.

Hanyang

Hanyang, in the southwestern corner of the city, is the quietest of the three districts. The Economic Development Zone here is home to several multinational corporations, including Coca Cola and the French joint venture Citroën as well as a significant French community. The Wuhan Yangtze International School is also here. Hanyang has villa options starting around $1,000 but going as high as $4,000 for a four-bedroom luxury home. Apartment prices and availability are similar to the other districts; expect to pay just a couple of hundred dollars for a basic place up to $1,200 for a nice 2- or 3-bedroom at a foreigner-friendly complex like Southern Paradise or Golden Harbor.

DAILY LIFE

Compared to cities like Shanghai and Beijing, Wuhan's expats consider this place the "real China." Wuhan has fewer places to hide yourself away and forget for a moment that you are living in China when those moments of culture shock or homesickness hit. Few describe Wuhan as charming, but the expat life here can be pleasant enough.

The locals speak a dialect of standard Mandarin that once competed with Beijing to be the national language. If you already know some Mandarin, you shouldn't have a problem communicating here. If you don't, consider enrolling in one of the top-notch language programs at Wuhan's universities. Little English is spoken in this city.

For daily purchases, Wuhan's multiple international retailers include American chains Wal-Mart and PriceSmart, the German Metro, the British B&Q, and several French Carrefour stores. There are also quite a few department-store malls with a growing variety of world brands.

PRIME LIVING LOCATIONS

Expat Social Scene

Foreigners move here for a variety of reasons, from teaching English to managing multinational operations and everything in between. Though there is currently no English magazine, expats here will find the website www.wuhantime.com to be good source for local information. If you're craving a break from Chinese food, Wuhan has a decent number of international restaurants and bars, such as the expat-popular Blue Sky Café in Hankou and Aloha Diner in Hanyang. For nightlife, you'll find plenty of discos, pubs, and clubs scattered around the city. At the Jianghan Lu pedestrian street, you can dine on Brazilian barbeque or Thai food in the midst of shops set in old European buildings.

The Aloha Diner in Hanyang is popular among expats.

© ERNESTO GUTIERREZ

Schools

Expat families have a couple of options for English education in Wuhan. The Wuhan Yangtze International School teaches an American curriculum for kindergarten through 12th grade based on Christian principles. Their location on the campus of a local Chinese school gives students access to amenities such as playgrounds and sports fields. The Wuhan Maple Leaf Foreign Nationals School offers a Canadian curriculum through 9th grade on a picturesque campus around a lake. Upper high school grades have a separate program at the Wuhan Maple Leaf International School, which is open to both Chinese and foreign students and offers a full boarding option.

GETTING AROUND

Due to its central location Wuhan is an important railway junction, making it cheap and easy to hop a train headed out of town; or venture out by overnight boat, traveling upriver to Chongqing or downriver to Nanjing or Shanghai. Easy flights from Wuhan reach every corner of China.

Within the city, however, navigation is not so easy, since the city is absolutely huge and crossed by a complex network of waterways. You'll find the ubiquitous Chinese taxis and public buses that access every neighborhood throughout the city, albeit slowly. Wuhan's subway system is just a couple of years old and currently only makes stops within Hankou along a light-rail line, but several other lines that will connect the three major parts of the city are under construction. And by the way, if a taxi refuses you, don't take it personally: It's probably just not their appointed day to cross over the bridges, a system used to reduce traffic congestion.

Chengdu 成都

Chengdu, the ancient capital of spicy Sichuan Province and home to around 10 million urban residents, is known for its icons: teahouses, hot peppers, and pandas. In Chengdu they know how to take it easy, spending lazy afternoons at tranquil riverside teahouses or long evenings eating fiery Sichuan hot-pot with friends. Even the sleepy pandas of the Sichuan bamboo forests reflect this unhurried life. The Panda Research Center near Chengdu is one of the best places in the world to observe giant pandas . . . when they're not sleeping.

The people and the pandas may be relaxed, but the local economy is not. Chengdu serves as a key regional center for the transportation and infrastructure that is drawing a growing number of foreign businesses this far west, including Intel, Siemens, and Motorola. This position as a prosperous commercial center is nothing new to this ancient city. In fact, Chengdu was the

PRIME LIVING LOCATIONS

© BARBARA STROTHER

one of Chengdu's laidback residents

first to introduce paper money, to the fascination of the young Marco Polo, who traveled with heavy pockets of metal coins. Today in Chengdu you can spend all your paper money on something special from Gucci or Cartier, Buick or Audi.

Impressions of Chengdu differ. On the one hand, it's a long way from the vibrant expat life of the coastal cities; on the other hand, it's very affordable and offers incredible travel opportunities to some of China's most exotic and scenic spots located nearby. Some see the city as dusty, noisy, busy, and gloomily overcast; a place where you can taste the pollution in the air. Some see it as a place full of vitality and vigor and fascinating culture. Though there's nothing to be done about the weather, Chengdu is working on cleaning up its polluted image, thanks in part to the strong voice (and tourist dollars) of the foreigners who come through here on their way to the pristine natural environments nearby.

Chengdu is a popular resting spot for travelers on their way to the minority

THE CHONGQING CHALLENGE

Chongqing (重庆, a.k.a. Chung-king) has an urban population of 9.2 million and a total population of more than 31 million within its municipal borders, one of the most populated places in the world. This hilly city on the Yangtze River, long popular as the Western gateway to the Three Gorges, is one of the four independent municipalities that answer directly to the central government. It's so hilly here that no one rides a bicycle – as unfathomable for China as an American city without a McDonald's. With a place this big and well known, you may wonder why it's not included as a prime living location. The truth is, Chongqing is on the verge of greatness, but it's not there yet.

On the one hand, foreign businesses are moving into Chongqing, new upscale housing areas are being built, and there is a new international school. On the other hand, that international school is still small, and many of those residential areas are still in the design and construction stages. The expat community in Chongqing is quite small, and some are less than thrilled to be in this polluted metropolis, nicknamed one of the furnaces of China. There are very few resources for foreigners here – no glossy English magazines, no good expat websites announcing clubs and events.

But the central government is dedicated to turning Chongqing into a first-class city and a key commercial center. They're turning out crooked officials and polluting factories, and building infrastructure to support foreign business. They're aggressively seeking the foreign investment that will turn this town around. With all this new development in the works, Chongqing may just be on the threshold of becoming the kind of place expats would be proud to call their home away from home.

© BARBARA STROTHER

Chairman Mao still stands over the center of downtown Chengdu.

villages, holy mountains, and incredible scenery beyond the city's borders. From Chengdu you can journey out to the tallest cliff-carved Buddha carving in the world at Leshan, or to the turquoise lakes and waterfalls of Jiuzhaigou, labeled by the United Nations as one of the greatest natural legacies in the world. Chengdu is also the main gateway to Tibet; most tourists hook up with their requisite official tour group here before flying in to Lhasa.

With a 2,000-year history, Chengdu has its share of historic spots as well as its own flavor of Chinese high culture with the Sichuan opera, a visual feast filled with humor and stage tricks. The Tibetan community contributes a certain flavor to the city as well, with their minority shops and colorful traditional dance shows.

WHERE TO LIVE

Foreigners heading to Chengdu will want to consider one of the three prime housing areas: the city center, south city, and the northwestern high-tech zone. Most Chengdu expats rent apartments, though there are a growing number of villas and town houses available.

City Center

If you like the vigor and vitality of being in the energetic core of a city, living downtown will give you easy access to all the city's shopping and entertainment

PRIME LIVING LOCATIONS

venues, including the fashionable Chunqi Lu pedestrian street, the Chengdu stadium, the foreign-language bookstore, and tons of great restaurants. The main (Huaxi) campus of Sichuan University is also located here inside the first ring road. With all the high-end international hotels and popular backpacker hostels around, downtown is always jumping with a diverse tourist crowd. An average high-rise apartment with a good location will rent for around $500 per month.

South City

The Wuhou District, directly south of the city center, is the most popular spot for foreigners to live. This upscale area is also a busy shopping and business district and home to one of Chengdu's two high-tech zones. The U.S. Consulate is here, as well as the Shamrock Irish pub, one of the best places for expats to find out what's going down in the 'Du. Both Meishi International School and the QSI Chengdu School are located in this district, and Sichuan University's large new campus is in the far south beyond the third ring road.

Within the South City area a growing number of upscale villa complexes, such as the American Garden complex, where the QSI International School is located,

Sichuan University, Chengdu

Shamrock Pub, a favorite gathering spot for Chengdu expats

© BARBARA STROTHER

© BARBARA STROTHER

or the sprawling high-end Luxe Hills. Orchard Villas is a popular option for foreigners with a choice of an apartment ($1,200–3,000), a town house ($2,500–4,500), or a villa (200–400 square meters, $3,000–6,500). If all this is beyond your budget, try a place that doesn't cater to expats. A modern local apartment with a couple of bedrooms and decent—but not sprawling—space will rent for just $250–750 per month.

Northwest City High-Tech Zone

Though the South City area has traditionally been the spot for foreigners, the trend is moving to the northwest into the High-Tech Zone of the Qingyang (green goat) and Jinniu (golden cow) Districts. This is the location of Intel's new facility, as well as Chengdu International School's beautiful new campus.

You'll find many new complexes to choose from, with more on the way. The Peninsula, which has the reputation for being one of the best in the city (with the highest rents to match), has large 3- and 4-bedroom apartments for $1,000–4,000 per month and huge 355-square-meter town houses for $6,000–9,000. If you can forgo all the bells and whistles, it's still possible to find inexpensive housing in the northwestern districts. Two-bedroom apartments rent for around $300 at more modest complexes.

© BARBARA STROTHER

shopping advice (that you'd better take!) in Chengdu

DAILY LIFE

Expats will find most of their daily shopping needs met in Chengdu at all the usual hypermarkets, including Metro, Wal-Mart, and Carrefour. Sabrina's Country Store carries rare imported goodies like Reese's Peanut Butter Cups, Pop-Tarts, and Doritos (you don't know just how good these things will sound until you've gone without them for a while). For health needs, Global Doctors is located here, as is Parkway Health, and the Sichuan International Medical Center has a foreigners clinic.

The language of the locals is a Sichuan dialect. Though all official business is run in Mandarin,

PRIME LIVING LOCATIONS

the heavy accent can be quite difficult to understand, and you may run into elderly people and villagers who don't speak Mandarin at all. On top of that, hardly anybody here speaks much English. The good news is you'll be really good at charades after living in Chengdu.

Expat Social Scene

Unusual for a place so far from the populated coast, Chengdu has a burgeoning expat scene. The majority of Westerners here are associated with education (English teachers, international-school teachers, and foreign exchange students), although the community of business-related expats is growing. With a significant number of Tibetans here, Chengdu is also a great place to be exposed to their culture and language without giving up the big-city amenities.

There are a few consulates here, including one of just four American consulates in the country, as well as the China headquarters for the Peace Corps. But despite its quick growth, the foreign community is still much smaller than in the big east coast cities, and on occasion foreigners heading this far out may still get watched like an odd zoo animal. Chengdu's expat scene is slowly becoming more sophisticated as well, with a growing number of English websites and magazines such as *More Chengdu* and *Chengdoo*.

Visit Shamrock Pub's website, www.shamrockinchengdu.com, for info on local events and clubs.

When you need a break from the local mouth-blistering Sichuan cuisine, you'll have a small choice of international restaurants, including Thai, German, French, Japanese, and even American home cooking at Grandma's Kitchen. And when homesickness hits, you can hang out with the other expats at Peter's Tex-Mex Grill and wallow in self-pity over one of their famous gooey cinnamon rolls.

Schools

Expat families have three international schools to choose from, all of which offer an American curriculum

© BARBARA STROTHER

Hop a local ride to the expat-popular Peter's Tex-Mex Grill.

© BARBARA STROTHER

Spicy food, local beer, outdoor dining: Life is good in Chengdu.

and cover all grades. The Chengdu International School (CDIS) is a Christian school located in northwestern Chengdu and has an excellent reputation even among its nonreligious families. The Chengdu QSI School has a new campus located south of the third ring road at the American Garden housing complex. Chengdu Meishi International School offers a bilingual program as part of a private Chinese boarding school on an impressive 50-acre campus south of the city.

GETTING AROUND

Downtown Chengdu is relatively compact and easy to navigate on foot or by bike, and taxis are always a cheap and easy way to get around. The public bus system is extensive and covers all areas of the city, and an efficient tourist bus system runs among Chengdu's numerous famous places. If you can decipher the routes and you don't mind crowds, public buses are always a cheap way to get around.

As for getting out of town, in addition to the buses and trains that will take you to exotic and primitive locales, the Chengdu airport has service to all major Chinese cities as well as a few foreign ones. Should you choose to live here, you will want to get out of town regularly—just to see the sun. The combination of the climate (high humidity), geography (surrounded by mountains), and pollution result in a Chengdu sky that is almost always overcast.

Xi'an 西安

The most famous of all inland cities, Xi'an hosts more than 20 million tourists each year traipsing through to see the famous terra-cotta warriors. Xi'an is the gateway to the ancient Silk Road and home to a strong Muslim community. If you're into ancient history and archaeology, this is the best place for you. It was the largest city in the world back in the first century, on par with Rome, Athens, and Cairo as an ancient metropolis. The number and

PRIME LIVING LOCATIONS

PRIME LIVING LOCATIONS

quality of its historic sites are un-rivaled in China.

But this city isn't just about its past. Xi'an is the center of China's aviation and space-flight technology and satellite monitoring. And with over 3,000 research institutions, Xi'an regularly produces significant scientific achievements. It's home to an increasing number of multinational operations, including GM, Volvo, Rolls Royce, and Siemens.

Situated within central Shaanxi Province where the Guangzhong plain meets the Qinling Mountains, 8 million people call the city of Xi'an home. The winters here are chilly, though not as intense as in northern locations, and Xi'an gets a small amount of snow. Xi'an also gets frequent thunderstorms and rain, especially in summers, which are toasty but generally a little cooler than in other major cities.

The layout of Xi'an revolves around its ancient city wall, the best-preserved in China. Directions are often given based on the nearest city gate and whether it's inside or outside the wall. The city's ancient streets are laid out on a square grid marked by the South, North, East, and West Boulevards, with the Bell Tower at the city center.

This city's cuisine has strong Muslim influences, and you'll find plenty of yummy *yang-rou chuan* (lamb kebab) vendors on its dusty

The layout of Xi'an revolves around its ancient city wall.

a few of Emperor Qin's terra-cotta warriors

© BARBARA STROTHER

© BARBARA STROTHER

Welcome to Islamic Street, the Muslim quarter of Xi'an.

PRIME LIVING LOCATIONS

streets. One of the most famous Xi'an dishes is *yang-rou paomo,* a lamb-based soup that is poured over broken pieces of flat bread. The Muslim restaurants are festive places, often with Middle Eastern–style dancing and music; you'll know them by their blue lanterns hanging outside instead of the traditional red. You can also indulge at one of the city's nighttime food street markets.

Between the precipitation and pollution, you won't see too many blue skies in Xi'an. But if you can put up with the environment, one of the best perks of living here is the money you can save. Xi'an is one of the cheapest of all the provincial capitals. You can get by here on as little as $250 per month if you don't mind making a few sacrifices. Perhaps the biggest drawbacks to life in Xi'an are the pollution and the few conniving locals who will only see dollar signs when they look at you. Any city with this many wealthy tourists tends to inspire a little greedy manipulation by its less-upstanding residents. And despite its growing expat community and large tourism industry, Xi'an does not have the sophistication of cities like Beijing or Shanghai, which for some foreigners is exactly what they love about it.

WHERE TO LIVE

If you're looking for a place to call home in Xi'an, you'll want to be in one of three key areas: central downtown, south of downtown in the High-Tech Zone, or north of the city center in the Economic and Technology Development Zone.

Downtown

Downtown Xi'an is divided between two districts, Beilin and Lianhu. The vibrant Beilin District comprises the core downtown area within the city wall and some territory east and south of it. Beilin has more than its fair share of ancient sites, but it's modern as well, home to upscale malls, high-end hotels, and 17 universities. Lianhu starts inside the city's west wall and extends to

the Hua Qing Hot Springs near Xi'an, where emperors bathed

the second ring road; there's much less here in terms of tourist sites or trendy spots, but it's still quite convenient to the downtown hot spots.

The downtown housing is predominantly focused on apartment towers just steps away from the buzz of the central city. A small but upscale 1- or 2-bedroom place can be rented for as little as $250–500. The area outside the east gate of the city wall has several luxury apartments; expect to pay $300–800 per month for a 2- or 3-bedroom unit. Downtown Xi'an also has a few hotels that offer serviced apartments, such as the centrally located Citadines, where one-bedroom apartments rent for a little over $2,000 monthly.

South Xi'an

Moving south from downtown you'll find the Xi'an High-Tech Zone as well as the Qujiang Tourism and Holiday Resort Zone, which overlap with two districts, Yanta and Chang'an. This southern area will be your best location option if you plan work in the High-Tech Zone or send your kids to its international school. The School of Chinese Studies of the Foreign Language University is also here, drawing international students. If you're in the market for a villa or a town house, this is the best place to look.

South Xi'an, especially Yanta District, has been developed into a new center for the city's commerce and tourism with the highest number of foreign firms in the city. Though you'll occasionally run across sprawling luxury apartments that rent for as high as $1,500, standard two-bedroom apartments here typically rent for $250–400. The Ziwei Garden is huge, attractive, and popular; apartments rent for $350–500 for 2–4 bedrooms, and they do have a few houses as well for around $1,500 per month. Villas in South Xi'an cover a range of styles and sizes renting for $1,000–3,000; within the High-Tech Zone you can find a few town houses for under $1,000 per month.

North Xi'an

Starting at the north city gate, the Weiyang District is home to the Xi'an ETDZ (Economic and Technology Development Zone) as well as major multinational corporations like Siemens, Coca-Cola, and Rolls Royce. Apartments here start around $200, and you can get a large four-bedroom apartment for as little as $400–500. There are a few villa complexes here with typical rentals under $2,000, though the majority of villas are located in the south.

DAILY LIFE

In addition to official Mandarin, the locals communicate in the Shaanxi dialect. Fortunately this dialect is just a slight variation from standard Mandarin, so students of Chinese will not be as troubled by communication issues here as much as in places with dialects that are more difficult. In the areas of the city that are exposed to masses of foreign visitors, you'll find a decent amount of English for an inland city, though don't expect much English outside the tourist sites.

As for shopping, Dong Dajie (East Avenue) has a variety of name-brand shops, and designer labels can be bought for a high price at the Century Ginwa department store. Cheap knockoffs are on offer at the various street markets around town. Imported goods are much harder to get here than in cities with more significant expat populations, though Xi'an does have the typical Watsons drugstores and hypermarts like Lotus, TrustMart, and Carrefour.

If you find yourself in a medical emergency in Xi'an, there are a couple of foreign doctors in town, and the Chang'an hospital has a national reputation for having advanced facilities for a Chinese hospital.

Expat Social Scene

Xi'an's expat community is by no means large, but it is growing. If you're looking for the local expats, you might find them playing snooker at Chaplin's Bar in the Bell Tower Hotel or partying on the bar street near Nan Dajie (South Avenue). The China Grooves website (www.chinagrooves.com) keeps foreigners clued in to the city vibe, as does their English-language magazine, *Grooves*. The Xi'an Foreign Language University has a school of Chinese studies that draws international students from around the globe.

Some expats attend the large Catholic church in town; there are also Protestant expat groups that meet casually. For fine cuisine, Xi'an has Portuguese,

PRIME LIVING LOCATIONS

French, Thai, and Japanese restaurants, among others. Of course, you'll also find the ubiquitous American chains of KFC, Pizza Hut, McDonald's, Starbucks, and the like.

When you need a little break from the stresses of life, you won't have to go too far out of town to find a spot to relax. Try one of the golf courses in the suburbs, or go for a foot soak in the misty hot waters of the Tang Dynasty–style Hua Qing Hot Spring Palace, where emperors bathed for centuries. Several nearby mountains provide ample opportunity for good hikes; thrill seekers may be drawn to defy death at Mt. Huashan, China's most dangerous climb.

Schools

The Xi'an Hi-Tech International School (XHIS), located in the southwest part of the city, teaches a Canadian curriculum and covers all grades. The Xi'an International School (XIS) is a new entrant to the city. The Xi'an BO-AI International School, a Chinese boarding school with an intensive Mandarin program for foreign students, is located in the North ETDZ.

GETTING AROUND

Getting around Xi'an is not too complicated, with its efficient and extensive bus system that covers the whole city. Most public buses stop at the key city landmarks (the four gates, the bell tower, or the small or big goose pagoda), making it easy to get your bearings if you feel lost. Biking is a great way to get around the city, and you can even bike on top of the city wall (rentals available at the south and west gates). Xi'an taxis are cheap and plentiful, but be aware that in order to keep traffic down, taxis have limitations as to when they can drive into the city center. The city has been trying for years to create a viable plan for building a subway, but the possibility of disturbing ancient relics buried beneath the city has slowed the process.

You can ride a pedicab along Xi'an's wall.

RESOURCES

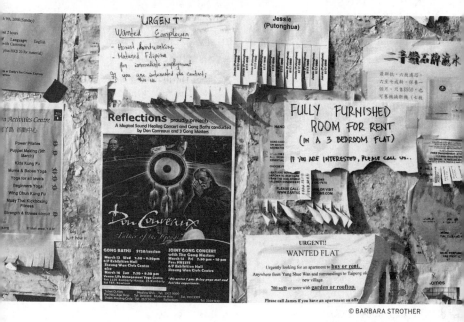

© BARBARA STROTHER

Embassies and Consulates

IN THE UNITED STATES

States not mentioned in one of the consular districts below come under the jurisdiction of the embassy in Washington, D.C.

THE EMBASSY OF THE PEOPLE'S REPUBLIC OF CHINA IN THE UNITED STATES

2201 Wisconsin Ave. NW
Washington, DC 20007
tel. 202/338-6688 or 202/588-9760
fax 202/588-9760
www.chinaembassy.org

THE PRC CONSULATE IN SAN FRANCISCO

1450 Laguna St.
San Francisco, CA 94115
tel. 415/674-2900
fax 415/563-0494
www.chinaconsulatesf.org
Districts: Alaska, Nevada, Northern California, Oregon, Washington

THE PRC CONSULATE IN LOS ANGELES

443 Shatto Pl.
Los Angeles, CA 90020
tel. 213/807-8088
fax 213/380-1961
www.chinaconsulatela.org
Districts: Arizona, Hawaii, New Mexico, Southern California

THE PRC CONSULATE IN HOUSTON

3417 Montrose Blvd.
Houston, TX 77006
tel. 713/524-4311
fax 713/524-7656
www.chinahouston.org
Districts: Alabama, Arkansas, Florida, Georgia, Louisiana, Mississippi, Oklahoma, Texas

THE PRC CONSULATE IN CHICAGO

100 W. Erie St.
Chicago, IL 60610
tel. 312/803-0098
fax 312/803-0122
www.chinaconsulatechicago.org
Districts: Colorado, Illinois, Indiana, Iowa, Kansas, Michigan, Minnesota, Missouri, Wisconsin

THE PRC CONSULATE IN NEW YORK CITY

520 12th Ave.
New York, NY 10036
tel. 212/868-7752
fax 212/502-0245
www.nyconsulate.prchina.org
Districts: Connecticut, Maine, Massachusetts, New Hampshire, New Jersey, New York, Ohio, Pennsylvania, Rhode Island, Vermont

IN CANADA

THE EMBASSY OF THE PRC IN CANADA

515 St. Patrick St.
Ottawa, ON K1N 5H3
tel. 613/789-9608
fax 613/789-1414
www.chinaembassycanada.org

IN GREAT BRITAIN

THE EMBASSY OF THE PRC IN THE UNITED KINGDOM

49-51 Portland Pl.
London W1B 1JL
tel. 020/7299-4049
fax 020/7436-9178
www.chineseembassy.org.uk

IN AUSTRALIA

THE EMBASSY OF THE PRC IN AUSTRALIA

15 Coronation Dr.
Yarralumla, ACT 2600
tel. 02/6273-4783 or 02/6273-7443
fax 02/6273-9615
http://au.chinaembassy.org

IN CHINA
United States
U.S. EMBASSY
Xiu Shui Bei Jie 3
Beijing
tel. 10/6532-4153
http://beijing.usembassychina.org.cn

U.S. CONSULATE CHENGDU
4 Lingshiguan Rd.
Chengdu
tel. 28/8558-3992 or 28/8558-9642
fax 28/8558-3520
www.usembassychina.org.cn/chengdu

U.S. CONSULATE GUANGZHOU
1 Shamian St. South
Guangzhou
tel. 20/8121-8000
fax 20/8121-9001
www.usembassychina.org.cn/guangzhou

U.S. CONSULATE HONG KONG
26 Garden Rd.
Central, Hong Kong
tel. 852/2523-9011
fax 852/2845-4845
http://HongKong.usconsulate.gov

U.S. CONSULATE SHANGHAI
1469 Huai Hai Zhong Lu
Shanghai

tel. 21/6433-6880
fax 21/6433-4122
www.usembassychina.org.cn/shanghai

U.S. CONSULATE SHENYANG
52 14th Wei Rd.
Heping District, Shenyang
tel. 24/2322-0848
fax 24/2322-2374
http://shenyang.usconsulate.gov

Canada, Great Britain, and Australia
CANADIAN EMBASSY
19 Dongzhimenwai Dajie
Chao Yang District, Beijing
tel. 10/6532-3536
fax 10/6532-1684
www.beijing.gc.ca/beijing/en/

BRITISH EMBASSY
Floor 21, North Tower, Kerry Centre
1 Guanghualu
Beijing
tel. 10/8529-6600
fax 10/8529-6081
www.uk.cn/bj/

AUSTRALIAN EMBASSY
21 Dongzhimenwai Dajie
Beijing
tel. 10/5140 4111
fax 10/5140 4230
www.austemb.org.cn/indexe.htm

Planning Your Fact-Finding Trip

RESOURCES

GUIDED TOURS
BIKE CHINA
www.bikechina.com
Bike China offers private and custom
bicycle tours.

CHINA SPREE
www.chinaspree.com
This company offers set itineraries as
well as custom trips throughout China.

TRAVEL CHINA GUIDE
www.travelchinaguide.com
This online travel agency offers tours

plus a wealth of travel and expat
information.

ACCOMMODATION OPTIONS
Hostels
HOSTEL WORLD
www.hostelworld.com
Hostels and budget hotels are listed
on this booking site, including handy
reviews and photos.

Making the Move

LIVING IN CHINA
CHINA BLOG LIST
www.chinabloglist.org
Links to hundreds of blogs about China.

CHINA EXPAT
www.chinaexpat.com
Offers advice and information on
China's top 50 cities.

EXPATEXCHANGE
www.expatexchange.com
A general guide to expat living
worldwide, including in China.

INTERNATIONAL MOVING COMPANIES
CROWN RELOCATIONS
www.crownrelocations.com

INTERNATIONALMOVERS.COM
www.internationalmovers.com
Provides quotes from multiple
companies.

Language and Education

MANDARIN LANGUAGE PROGRAMS
Beijing
BEIJING FOREIGN STUDIES UNIVERSITY
2 Xisanhuan Beilu
Haidian District, Beijing
tel. 10/6891-6549
www.bfsu.edu.cn

BEIJING LANGUAGE AND CULTURE UNIVERSITY
15 Xueyuan Rd.
Haidian District, Beijing
tel. 10/8230-3923
fax 10/8230-3923
www.blcu.edu.cn

GLOBAL EXCHANGE CENTER
229 Beisihuan Zhonglu
Hai Tai Plaza, Suite 1215
Beijing
tel. 10/6231-5029
fax 10/6231-5029
www.glexchange.net

INTERNATIONAL CULTURAL EXCHANGE CENTER (BEIJING)
Beijing University of Posts and
   Telecommunications
10 Xitucheng Rd.
Haidian District, Beijing
tel. 10/6228-2797
fax 10/6228-2797
www.icec.cn

Shanghai
MODERN MANDARIN
Room 510, Ruijin Business Center
96 Zhaojiabang Rd.
Shanghai
tel. 21/6437-4808
fax 21/6437-6938
www.modernmandarin.com

Hong Kong
NEW CONCEPT MANDARIN
2nd Floor, Beautiful Group Tower
74-77 Connaught Rd.
Central, Hong Kong
tel. 852/2850-4332
www.newconceptmandarin.com
This language center has options for
online, classroom, and immersion
learning.

ONLINE LANGUAGE TOOLS
CHINESE POD
www.chinesepod.com
At this site you can download MP3 audio lessons for free.

MANDARIN TOOLS
www.mandarintools.com
Offers a downloadable dictionary and a whole lot more.

UNIVERSITY INFORMATION
PRC GOVERNMENT SCHOLARSHIPS
www.ebeijing.gov.cn
Get the lowdown on scholarships and study visas.

Beijing
BEIJING UNIVERSITY
International Student Affairs
1st Floor, South Pavilion
Beijing
tel. 10/6275-1246
fax 10/6275-1240
www.pku.edu.cn

QINGHUA UNIVERSITY, BEIJING
Tsinghua University
Beijing
tel. 10/6278-5001
www.tsinghua.edu.cn

Shanghai
CHINA EUROPE INTERNATIONAL BUSINESS SCHOOL, SHANGHAI
699 Hongfeng Rd.
Pudong, Shanghai
tel. 21/2890-5890
fax 21/2890-5678
www.ceibs.edu

FUDAN UNIVERSITY, SHANGHAI
Foreign Students Office
Fudan University
220 Han Dan Rd.
Shanghai
tel. 21/6511-7628
fax 21/6511-7298
www.fudan.edu.cn

SHANGHAI JIAO TONG UNIVERSITY
School of International Education
1954 Hua Shan Rd.
Shanghai
tel. 21/6282-1079
fax 21/6281-7613
www.sjtu.edu.cn

Hangzhou
ZHEJIANG UNIVERSITY
Hangzhou
tel. 571/8795-1717
fax 571/8795-1755
www.zju.edu.cn

Health

GENERAL
ENGLISH-CHINESE MEDICAL DICTIONARY
www.esaurus.org

U.S. CENTERS FOR DISEASE CONTROL
www.cdc.gov

WORLD HEALTH ORGANIZATION
www.WHO.org

HEALTH INSURANCE
MEDAIRE
www.medaire.com
Global Doctor insurance

SOS
www.internationalsos.com

HOSPITALS AND CLINICS
THE U.S. EMBASSY LIST OF HOSPITALS IN CHINA
http//Beijing.usembassychina.org.cn/
    medical_information.html

GLOBALDOCTOR
tel. 10/8456-9191
www.globaldoctor.com.au

EMERGENCY PHONE NUMBERS
Emergency: tel. 999
Ambulance: tel. 120
Fire: tel. 119
Police: tel. 110

Employment

BUSINESS
CHINA JOB
www.chinajob.com
Listings of jobs in teaching and business.

JOBS IN CHINA
http://english.jobchina.net
Job postings for teaching, business, and high-tech.

MONSTER
www.monster.com
This very large, U.S.-based job website lists thousands of international jobs.

ZHAOPIN
www.zhaopin.com
Hundreds of Chinese companies post their jobs on this website.

TEACHING ENGLISH
ESL TEACHERS BOARD
www.ESLteachersboard.com
Schools post their teaching jobs here, and teachers upload their résumés.

PEACE CORPS
www.peacecorps.gov

TEACHING AT INTERNATIONAL SCHOOLS
THE INTERNATIONAL EDUCATOR
www.tieonline.com
The number-one international school magazine is now online.

Finance

LEGAL CONSULTING
BOSTON CONSULTING GROUP
www.bcg.com.cn
Exceptional business consulting services.

LEHMAN LEE & XU LAW FIRM
10-2 Liangmaqiao Diplomatic Compound
22 Dongfang East Rd.
Chaoyang District, Beijing
tel. 10/8532-1919
fax 10/8532-1999
www.lehmanlaw.com
Legal, tax, and business consulting.

PRICEWATERHOUSECOOPERS
26th Floor, Office Tower A
Beijing Fortune Plaza
7 Dongsanhuan Zhong Rd.
Chaoyang District, Beijing
tel. 10/6533-8888
fax 10/6533-8800
www.pwchk.com/home/eng
Tax consulting from one of the best.

INTERNATIONAL BANKS
CITIBANK
www.citigroup.com

CITIC SECURITIES (BROKERAGE)
www.citiccapital.com

HSBC INTERNATIONAL BANK
www.hsbc.com

STANDARD CHARTERED BANK
www.standardchartered.com.cn

Communications

MEDIA
***CHINA DAILY* ONLINE**
www.chinadaily.com.cn

INTERNATIONAL HERALD TRIBUNE
www.iht.com

SOUTH CHINA MORNING POST
www.scmp.com

TELEPHONE
CHINA TELECOM
www.chinatelecom.com.cn
The large state-run phone company in China.

EXPRESS MAIL SERVICES
CHINA POST
www.chinapost.gov.cn

DHL (CHINA)
www.cn.dhl.com

FEDEX (CHINA)
www.fedex.com/cn_english

UPS (CHINA)
www.ups.com/content/cn/en/index.jsx

Travel and Transportation

BY AIR
AIR CHINA
www.airchina.com.cn

CHINA EASTERN AIRLINES
www.ceair.com

CHINA SOUTHERN AIRLINES
www.csair.com

HELICOPTER ROUTES IN THE PEARL RIVER DELTA
www.helihongkong.com

Nonaffiliated Airline Reservation Sites
C TRIP
www.english.ctrip.com

ELONG TRAVEL
www.elong.net

BY TRAIN
TRAVEL CHINA GUIDE TRAIN SCHEDULE
www.travelchinaguide.com/chinatrains

BY BOAT
PEARL RIVER DELTA FERRY ROUTES
www.turbojet.com.hk

RESOURCES

Housing Considerations

CENTURY 21 REAL ESTATE, CHINA
www.century21cn.com/english
U.S.-based real estate company now
operating in China.

EXPATRIATES.COM
www.expatriates.com
Online classifieds for housing, jobs, and
more.

5I5J ("I LOVE MY HOME")
www.5i5j.com
Online Chinese real estate site with
some English.

CHINA REAL ESTATE
www.chinarealestate.cn
Has property listings for most of the
cities covered in this book.

MOVE AND STAY
www.moveandstay.com
Lists serviced apartments for executives
in several Chinese cities.

SANTAFE RELOCATIONS
www.santaferelo.com
Provides total relocation management,
including all aspects of the home search.

Prime Living Locations

BEIJING

General
BEJING CITY GOVERNMENT
www.ebeijing.gov.cn

ALLO' EXPAT BEIJING
www.beijing.alloexpat.com
Online community for Beijing expats.

Housing
BEIJING REAL ESTATE
406 BaiYan Building
238 North 4th Ring Middle Rd.
Haidian District, Beijing
tel. 10/8231-8640
fax 10/8231-8740
info@beijingrealestate.com
www.beijingrealestate.com

CENTURY 21 REAL ESTATE
1725 Hanwei Plaza
7 Guanghua Rd.
Chaoyang District, Beijing
tel. 10/6561-7788
www.century21cn.com/english

Media
BEIJING REVIEW
www.bjreview.com.cn

THAT'S BEIJING
www.thatsbj.com

Medical
BEIJING UNITED FAMILY HOSPITAL
2 Jiang Tai Lu
Chaoyang District, Beijing
tel. 10/6433-3960
emergency tel. 10/6433-2345

**SOS BEIJING 24-HOUR
MEDICAL HOTLINE**
tel. 10/6462-9100

Organizations
**AMERICAN CHAMBER
OF COMMERCE**
www.amchamchina.org.cn

**CHINA-AUSTRALIA
CHAMBER OF COMMERCE**
www.austcham.org

International Schools
**BEIJING BISS
INTERNATIONAL SCHOOL**
17, Area 4, Anzhen Xi Li
Chaoyang District, Beijing
tel. 10/6443-3151
fax 10/6443-3156
www.biss.com.cn

RESOURCES

INTERNATIONAL MONTESSORI SCHOOL OF BEIJING
China World Trade Center, North Lodge
1 Jian Guo Men Wai Ave.
Beijing
tel. 10/6505-3869
fax 10/6505-1237
www.montessoribeijing.com

THE INTERNATIONAL SCHOOL OF BEIJING
10 An Hua St.
Shunyi District, Beijing
Tel. 10/8046-2007
www.isb.bj.edu.cn

WESTERN ACADEMY OF BEIJING
10 Lai Guang Ying Dong Lu
Chaoyang District, Beijing
tel. 10/8456-4155
fax 10/6432-2440
www.wab.edu

YEW CHUNG INTERNATIONAL SCHOOL OF BEIJING
Honglingjin Park
5 Houbalizhuang
Chaoyang District, Beijing
tel. 10/8583-3731
fax 10/8583-2734
www.ycef.com

SHANGHAI

General
CITY GOVERNMENT WEBSITE
www.shanghai.gov.cn

ALLO' EXPAT SHANGHAI
www.shanghai.alloexpat.com
Online community for Shanghai expats.

SHANGHAI EXPAT
www.shanghaiexpat.com
Another online community catering to Shanghai expats.

LIFELINE SHANGHAI
tel. 21/6279-8990
This free hotline offers community information and emotional support.

Housing
SHANGHAI METROPOLIS REAL ESTATE AGENCY
www.metropolissh.com
tel. 21/1391-651-2856
High-end real estate agency catering to expats.

SHANGHAI PROPERTIES
www.shanghaiprops.com
By and for foreigners.

SPACE INTERNATIONAL
www.space.sh.cn
Real estate agency specializing in luxury properties.

Media
SHANGHAI DAILY NEWSPAPER
www.shanghaidaily.com

THAT'S SHANGHAI MAGAZINE
http://shanghai.asiaxpat.com

Medical
SOS SHANGHAI 24-HOUR MEDICAL HOTLINE
tel. 21/6295-0099

PARKWAY MEDICAL CENTERS
24-hour Healthline
Tel. 21/6445-5999
www.parkwayhealth.cn

Organizations
AMERICAN CHAMBER OF COMMERCE
www.amchamchina.org.cn

BRITISH CHAMBER OF COMMERCE
www.britcham.org

International Schools
CONCORDIA INTERNATIONAL SCHOOL SHANGHAI
999 Ming Yue Rd., Jinqiao
Pudong, Shanghai
tel. 21/5899-0380
fax 21/5899-1685
www.ciss.com.cn

RESOURCES

DULWICH COLLEGE INTERNATIONAL SCHOOL
222 Lan An Lu, Jinqiao
Pudong, Shanghai
tel. 21/5899-9910
fax 21/5899-9810
www.dulwichshanghai.cn

SHANGHAI AMERICAN SCHOOL, EAST CAMPUS
Shanghai Links Executive Community
1600 Ling Bai Lu
San Jia Gang, Pudong, Shanghai
tel. 21/6221-1445
fax 21/5897-0011
www.saschina.org

SHANGHAI AMERICAN SCHOOL, WEST CAMPUS
258 Jin Feng Rd.
Zhudi Town, Minhang, Shanghai
tel. 21/6221-1445
fax 21/6221-1269
www.saschina.org

SHANGHAI PINGHE BILINGUAL SCHOOL
261 Huang Yang Rd., Jinqiao
Pudong, Shanghai
tel. 21/5031-0417
fax 21/5854-1617
www.shphschool.com
A top private Chinese school with a bilingual curriculum.

YEW CHUNG INTERNATIONAL SCHOOL OF SHANGHAI
11 Shui Cheng Rd.
Hongqiao, Shanghai
tel. 21/6242-3243
fax 21/6242-7331
www.ycissh.com

HONG KONG

General
HONG KONG GOVERNMENT
www.info.gov.hk

ASIA EXPAT HONG KONG
http://hongkong.asiaxpat.com/
General city guide to Hong Kong covering real estate, jobs, lifestyle, etc.

Housing
852 REAL ESTATE, HONG KONG
www.852realestate.com

HOUSE HUNTERS, HONG KONG
Unit B, 7th Floor, Wyndham Place
40-44 Wyndham St.
Central, Hong Kong
tel. 852/2869-1001
www.househunters.com.hk

Media
BC MAGAZINE
www.bcmagazine.net

SOUTH CHINA MORNING POST
www.scmp.com

THE STANDARD
www.thestandard.com.hk

Medical
BAPTIST HOSPITAL
223 Waterloo Rd.
Kowloon Tong, Kowloon, Hong Kong
tel. 852/2339-8888

HONG KONG ADVENTIST HOSPITAL
40 Stubbs Rd.
Wanchai, Hong Kong
tel. 852/2835-0578

SOS HONG KONG 24-HOUR MEDICAL HOTLINE
tel. 852/2528-9900

Organizations
AMERICAN CHAMBER OF COMMERCE
www.amcham.org.hk/home

AUSTRALIAN CHAMBER OF COMMERCE
www.austcham.com.hk

CANADIAN CHAMBER OF COMMERCE
www.cancham.org

International Schools

AMERICAN INTERNATIONAL SCHOOL
125 Waterloo Rd.
Kowloon Tong, Kowloon, Hong Kong
tel. 852/2336-3812
fax 852/2336-5276
www.ais.edu.hk

AUSTRALIAN INTERNATIONAL SCHOOL HONG KONG
3A Norfolk Rd.
Kowloon Tong, Kowloon, Hong Kong
tel. 852/2304-6078
fax 852/2304-6077
www.aishk.edu.hk

BRITISH SOUTH ISLAND SCHOOL
50 Nam Fung Rd.
Aberdeen, Hong Kong
tel. 852/2555-9313
fax 852/2553-8811
www.sis.edu.hk

CANADIAN INTERNATIONAL SCHOOL
36 Nam Long Shan Rd.
Aberdeen, Hong Kong
tel. 852/2525-9133
fax 852/2525-7579
www.cdnis.edu.hk

CLEARWATER BAY SCHOOL
Lot 235, DD229
Clearwater Bay Rd.
Kowloon, Hong Kong
tel. 852/2358-3221
fax 852/2358-3246
www.cwbs.edu.hk

CONCORDIA INTERNATIONAL SCHOOL
68 Begonia Rd.
Yau Yat Chuen
Kowloon, Hong Kong
tel. 852/2789-9890
fax 852/2392-8820
www.cihs.edu.hk

DISCOVERY BAY INTERNATIONAL SCHOOL
Discovery Bay
Lantau Island, Hong Kong
tel. 852/2987-7331
fax 852/2987-7076
www.dbis.edu.hk

HONG KONG INTERNATIONAL SCHOOL
1 Red Hill Rd.
Tai Tam, Hong Kong
tel. 852/2812-5000
fax 852/2812-0669
www.hkis.edu.hk

INTERNATIONAL CHRISTIAN SCHOOL
45 Grampian Rd.
Kowloon City, Kowloon, Hong Kong
tel. 852/2338-9606
www.ics.edu.hk

PEAK SCHOOL
20 Plunketts Rd.
The Peak, Hong Kong
tel. 852/2849-7211
fax 852/2849-7151
www.ps.edu.hk

WEST ISLAND SCHOOL
250 Victoria Rd.
Pokfulam, Hong Kong
tel. 852/2819-1962
fax 852/2816-7257
www.wis.edu.hk

YEW CHUNG INTERNATIONAL SCHOOL OF HONG KONG
3 To Fuk Rd.
Kowloon Tong, Kowloon, Hong Kong
tel. 852/2336-3443
fax 852/2337-5370
www.ycishk.com

MACAU

General
MACAU GOVERNMENT
www.cityguide.gov.mo

Media
MACAUTALK
www.ismaychina.com

Medical
HOPE MEDICAL CLINIC, MACAU
Fu Wah Court, 1-D
26 Ave. de Sidonio Pais, 1/F
Macau
tel. 853/2858-9000
www.hopemacau.com

RESOURCES

Organizations
**INTERNATIONAL
LADIES CLUB OF MACAO**
www.ilcm.org.mo

International Schools
INTERNATIONAL SCHOOL OF MACAU
Macau University of Science and Technology
 (Block E)
Avenida Wai Long
Taipa, Macau
tel. 853/2853-3700
fax 853/2853-3702
www.tis.edu.mo

THE SCHOOL OF THE NATIONS
Rua de Luis G. Gomes
No. 136, Edf. Lei San, 4
Andar, Macau
tel. 853/2870-1759
fax 853/2870-1724
www.schoolofthenations.com

THE SOUTH

Guangdong Province Media
GUANGDONG PROVINCE NEWS
www.newsgd.com

XIANZAI GUANGDONG E-ZINE
www.xianzai.com.cn

Guangzhou
JRE REAL ESTATE, GUANGZHOU
Rm. 2108, Dongshan Plaza
69 Xianlie Zhong Lu
Guangzhou
tel. 20/2237-1226 or 20/2237-1228
www.joannarealestate.com.cn/guangzhou

THAT'S GUANGZHOU MAGAZINE
www.thatsgz.com

**GUANGZHOU WOMEN'S
INTERNATIONAL CLUB**
www.gwic.org

**AMERICAN INTERNATIONAL
SCHOOL OF GUANGZHOU**
3 Yan Yu St. South, Ersha Island
Yuexiu District, Guangzhou
tel. 20/8735-3392
fax 20/8735-3339
www.aisgz.edu.cn

GUANGZHOU GRACE ACADEMY
Riverside Garden
Guangzhou
tel. 20/8450-0180
fax 20/8450-0190
www.grace.gd.edu.cn

**GUANGZHOU NANHU
INTERNATIONAL SCHOOL**
55 Huayang St.
Tianhe District, Guangzhou
tel. 20/3886-6952
fax 20/3886-3680
www.gnischina.com

**UTAHLOY INTERNATIONAL
SCHOOL, GUANGZHOU**
6km Sha Tai Highway
Jin Bao Gang
Tong He, Guangzhou
tel. 20/8720-2019
fax 20/8704-4296
www.utahloy.com

**UTAHLOY INTERNATIONAL
SCHOOL, ZENG CHENG**
San Jiang Town
Zeng Cheng City
tel. 20/8291-3201
www.utahloy.com

Shenzhen
SHENZHEN PARTY
www.shenzhenparty.com
Offers a guide to parties and events in
Shenzhen.

SHENZHEN PEOPLE
www.shenzhenpeople.net
A general guide to Shenzhen.

**SHENZHEN WOMEN'S
INTERNATIONAL CLUB**
www.swiconline.com

**INTERNATIONAL SCHOOL OF
SINO-CANADA, SHENZHEN**
166 Nanguang Rd.
Nanshan District, Shenzhen
tel. 755/2666-1000
fax 755/2645-4090
www.issc.com.cn

RESOURCES

QSI INTERNATIONAL SCHOOL SHEKOU
8 Tai Zi Rd.
Shekou, Shenzhen
tel. 755/2667-6031
fax 755/2667-6030
www.qsi.org/SHK_HOME

SHEKOU INTERNATIONAL SCHOOL
Jing Shan Villas, Nan Hai Rd.
Shenzhen
tel. 755/2669-3669
fax 755/2667-4099
www.sis.org.cn

Zhuhai
QSI INTERNATIONAL SCHOOL OF ZHUHAI
#2001 Jiuzhou Dadao West, Bldg. 2B
Gongbei, Zhuhai
tel. 756/815-6134
www.qsi.org/zhu_home

Xiamen
AMOY MAGIC
www.amoymagic.com
A guide to Xiamen and Fujian province.

***WHAT'S ON XIAMEN* MAGAZINE**
www.WhatsOnXiamen.com

XIAMEN INTERNATIONAL SCHOOL
Jiu Tian Hu
Xinglin, Xiamen
tel. 592/625-6581
fax 592/625-6584
www.xischina.com

THE EAST
Nanjing
JRE REAL ESTATE, NANJING
Rm. A4, 11th Floor, Golden Eagle International
    Plaza
89 Hanzhong Rd.
Nanjing
tel. 25/8695-2966 or 25/8695-2988
www.joannarealestate.com.cn/nanjing

JUEE REAL ESTATE, NANJING
tel. 25/8464-2822
www.juee.com/en

AEA NANJING HEALTH CLINIC
Hilton Hotel
319 Zhongshan East Rd.
Nanjing
tel. 25/480-2842

JIANGSU PROVINCE HOSPITAL VIP CLINIC
300 Guangzhou Rd.
Nanjing
tel. 25/8371-8836

NANJING INTERNATIONAL SCHOOL
8 Xue Heng Road
Xian Lin College and University Town
Qi Xia District, Nanjing
tel. 25/8589-9111
fax 25/8589-9222
www.nanjingschool.com

Suzhou
JRE REAL ESTATE, SUZHOU
Rm. 812, Century Financial Tower No. 1
Su Hua Rd.
Suzhou Industrial Park, Suzhou
tel. 12/6761-9816 or 12/6761-9826
www.joannarealestate.com.cn/suzhou

SUZHOU ETONHOUSE INTERNATIONAL SCHOOL
102 Kefa Rd.
Suzhou Science and Technology Town,
    Suzhou
tel. 512/6825-5666
fax 512/6825-5939
www.etonhousesz.com

SUZHOU SINGAPORE INTERNATIONAL SCHOOL
208 Zhong Nan Jie
Suzhou Industrial Park, Jiangsu
tel. 512/6258-0388
fax 512/6258-6388
www.ssissuzhou.net

Hangzhou
HANGZHOU MAOS REAL ESTATE
www.hangzhourelocation.com

HANGZHOU EXPAT
www.HangzhouExpat.com
Online expat guide to the city.

IN TOUCH ZHEJIANG MAGAZINE
www.intouchzhejiang.com
Covers Zhejiang Province, which includes both Hangzhou and Ningbo, but the focus is primarily on Hangzhou.

HANGZHOU INTERNATIONAL SCHOOL
80 Dongxin St.
Bin Jiang District, Hangzhou
tel. 571/8669-0045
fax 571/8669-0044
www.scischina.org/hangzhou

Ningbo
NINGBO EXPAT ASSOCIATION
www.NingboExpat.com

NINGBO GUIDE
www.ningboGuide.com

ACCESS INTERNATIONAL ACADEMY NINGBO
1 Ai Xue Rd.
Beilun District, Ningbo
tel. 574/8686-9999
www.aian.org.cn

THE NORTH

Tianjin
E-SMART TIANJIN
www.esmart.com.cn
Tianjin real estate and city guide.

JIN MAGAZINE
www.expatriatejin.com

TIANJIN EXPATS COMMUNITY WEBSITE
www.tianjinexpats.net

TIANJIN SOS INTERNATIONAL CLINIC
Sheraton Tianjin Hotel
Zijinshan Rd.
Hexi District, Tianjin
tel. 22/2352-0143
fax 22/2352-0145

INTERNATIONAL SCHOOL TIANJIN
Weishan Rd. (Shuanggang)
Jinnan District, Tianjin
tel. 22/2859-2001
fax 22/2859-2007
www.istianjin.org

TEDA INTERNATIONAL SCHOOL
72 Third Ave.
TEDA, Tianjin
tel. 22/6622-6158
fax 22/6200-1818
www.tedainternationalschool.net

TIANJIN INTERNATIONAL SCHOOL
1 Meiyuan Rd.
Tianjin New Technological and Industrial Garden
Nan Kai District, Tianjin
tel. 22/8371-0900
fax 22/8371-4035
www.tiseagles.com

TIANJIN REGO INTERNATIONAL SCHOOL
38 Huan Dao Dong Rd.
Mei Jiang Nan Residence Zone, Tianjin
tel. 22/8816-1180
fax 22/8816-1190
www.regoschool.org

Qingdao
J&M REALTY
Qingdao World Trade Centre
Building B, Shop 204B
6 Hong Kong Middle Rd.
Qingdao
tel. 532/8388-9232
fax 532/8591-9859
www.jmrealtyco.com

RED STAR MAGAZINE
www.MyRedStar.com

QINGDAO NO.1 INTERNATIONAL SCHOOL SHANDONG (QISS)
70 Songling Rd.
Qingdao
tel. 532/8890-9801
fax 532/8890-8876
www.qiss.org

QINGDAO MTI INTERNATIONAL SCHOOL
Baishan Xue Xiao
Laoshan District, Qingdao
tel. 532/8881-5668
fax 532/8881-6792
www.qmischina.com

YEW CHUNG INTERNATIONAL SCHOOL, QINGDAO
Admissions address:
Ste. 2106
36 Xianggang Zhong Lu
Qingdao
tel. 532/8687-1122
fax 532/8687-0099
www.ycisqd.com

Dalian
XIANZAI DALIAN E-ZINE
www.xianzai.com.cn

MAPLE LEAF (INTERNATIONAL SCHOOL)
78 Caiyun Rd.
Xigang, Dalian
tel. 411/8433-2821
fax 411/8433-0737
www.mapleleaf.net.cn

Shenyang
LIAONING GATEWAY ONLINE NEWSLETTER
www.liaoninggateway.com

GLOBAL DOCTORS SHENYANG 24-HOUR MEDICAL HOTLINE
tel. 24/2433-0678

SHENYANG INTERNATIONAL SCHOOL
55 Zusheng Rd.
Minzu Economic Development Zone,
  Dongling District
Shenyang
tel. 24/8912-1177
fax 24/8981-7456
www.syistigers.com

INLAND

Wuhan
OFFICIAL WUHAN GOVERNMENT WEBSITE
http://english.wh.gov.cn

WUHAN TIME EXPAT PORTAL
www.wuhantime.com
City guide to Wuhan for expats.

WUHAN YANGTZE INTERNATIONAL SCHOOL
San Jiao Hu Xiao Xue
Wuhan Economic and Development Zone,
  Wuhan
tel. 27/8423-8713
fax 27/8423-8726
www.wuhanschool.com

Chengdu
OFFICIAL CHENGDU GOVERNMENT WEBSITE
www1.chengdu.gov.cn/echengdu

SHAMROCK PUB, CHENGDU
www.ShamrockInChengdu.com

GLOBAL DOCTORS CHENGDU 24-HOUR MEDICAL HOTLINE
tel. 28/8522-6058

CHENGDU INTERNATIONAL SCHOOL
399 Shuxi Lu
Zhong Hai International Community, Chengdu
tel. 28/8608-1162
fax 28/8759-2265
www.iscchengdu.org

QSI INTERNATIONAL SCHOOL, CHENGDU
American Garden #188, South 3rd Ring Road
Chengdu
tel. 28/8511-3853
fax 28/8519-8393
www.qsiweb.org/cdu

Xi'an
XI'AN EXPAT
www.toureasy.net/expat

XI'AN HI-TECH INTERNATIONAL SCHOOL (XHIS)
New Industrial Park of Xi'an Hi-Tech Zone
Xi'an
tel. 29/8408-1323
fax 29/8569-1659
www.etonhousexian.com

RESOURCES

Glossary

amah Cantonese for domestic helper or auntie; same as *ayi* in Mandarin

ayi domestic helper, literally "auntie"

bagua an octagonal diagram used in Taoism and feng shui; literally "eight symbols"

Chinglish awkward, often humorous, translations of Chinese into English

dizi traditional Chinese flute

erhu traditional Chinese violin; literally "two strings"

feng shui mystical belief that architectural layout is related to qi; literally "wind and water"

guanxi connections through relationships; literally "closed system"

gwailo Cantonese for foreigner or foreign devil; literally "ghost person"

hutong traditional alley in Beijing

jiao 1/10th of a yuan; literally "horn"

junk fishing boat with square sails

kowtow to bow down; literally "to knock your head (on the ground)"

kuai slang for money; literally "a piece"

lama Buddhist holy man

laowai foreigner; literally "old outsider"

mahjong game played with engraved tiles

nai nai grandma

pedicab three-wheeled bicycle taxi

pinyin system of writing Chinese words in Roman letters

pipa stringed musical instrument

PRC People's Republic of China, the mainland

PSB Public Security Bureau, the Chinese government offices responsible for policing, immigration, and other public oversight

putonghua the official Mandarin language; literally "common language"

qi energy, power, or life force

qi gong exercise to channel qi into your life

qipao sleek traditional Chinese woman's dress

renminbi Chinese currency; literally "the people's money"

ROC Republic of China, Taiwan

SAR Special Administrative Region (Hong Kong and Macau)

shikoumen Shanghai's old style houses; literally "stone doorway"

siheyuan Beijing's courtyard homes in *hutong* neighborhoods

tai chi graceful exercise related to martial arts

Tao the way of nature, guiding principle for Taoists; literally "path"

Uighur ethnic group from the northwest

VoIP voice over Internet Protocol, using the Internet to make telephone calls

yin and yang opposite forces in the universe such as positive and negative, light and dark, female and male

yuan the PRC currency unit

Phrasebook

Chinese translations by Alex Chen

PRONUNCIATION

When a Chinese word is written in pinyin, the diacritic marks above the vowels tell the speaker which of the five tones to use when pronouncing the word. The first tone is called the flat tone, and it sounds a little high-pitched, like a man trying to imitate a female voice. The second tone is called rising because the pitch rises at the end of the syllable, such as when a person says "yes?" in response to a knock on the door. The third tone is the difficult tone that falls then rises, like when a person hears an unbelievable bit of gossip and responds "what?" The fourth tone is the falling tone, which sounds like you are impatient or angry. The fifth tone is a relaxed pronunciation and is mostly reserved for the last word of a sentence.

NUMBERS

ENGLISH	PINYIN	CHINESE
one	yī	一
two	èr	二
three	sān	三
four	sì	四
five	wǔ	五
six	liù	六
seven	qī	七
eight	bā	八
nine	jiǔ	九
10	shí	十
50	wǔ shí	五十
100	yì bǎi	一百
500	wú bǎi	五百
1,000	yì qiān	一千
5,000	wǔ qiān	五千
10,000	wàn	万
100,000	shí wàn	十万
500,000	wǔ shí wàn	五十万
1,000,000	yì bǎi wàn	一百万

DAYS OF THE WEEK

ENGLISH	PINYIN	CHINESE
Sunday	xīng qī tiān / xīng qī rì	星期天 / 星期日
Monday	xīng qī yī	星期一
Tuesday	xīng qī èr	星期二
Wednesday	xīng qī sān	星期三
Thursday	xīng qī sì	星期四
Friday	xīng qī wǔ	星期五
Saturday	xīng qī liù	星期六

RESOURCES

RESOURCES

TIME

ENGLISH	PINYIN	CHINESE
today	jīn tiān	今天
yesterday	zuó tiān	昨天
tomorrow	míng tiān	明天
the day before yesterday	qián tiān	前天
the day after tomorrow	hòu tiān	后天
this week	zhè zhōu / zhè xīng qī	这周 / 这星期
last week	shàng zhōu / shàng xīng qī	上周 / 上星期
next week	xià zhōu / xià xīng qī	下周 / 下星期
this morning	jīn tiān zǎo shàng	今天早上
this afternoon	jīn tiān xià wǔ	今天下午
this evening	jīn tiān wǎn shàng	今天晚上
tonight	jīn tiān wǎn shàng	今天晚上
last night	zuó tiān wǎn shàng	昨天晚上
one month	yí gè yuè	一个月
six months	liù gè yuè	六个月
late	wǎn	晚
early	zǎo	早
soon	bù jǔ / mǎ shàng	不久 / 马上
later on	yǐ hòu	以后
now	xiàn zài	现在
second	miǎo	秒
minute	fēn zhōng	分钟
one minute	yì fēn zhōng	一分钟
five minutes	wǔ fēn zhōng	五分钟
quarter of an hour	yí kè zhōng	一刻钟
half an hour	bàn xiǎo shí	半小时
that day	nà tiān	那天
every day	měi tiān	每天
all day	zhěng tiān	整天

USEFUL WORDS AND PHRASES

ENGLISH	PINYIN	CHINESE
Hello.	ní hǎo	你好
good morning	zǎo shàng hǎo	早上好
good afternoon	xià wǔ hǎo	下午好
good evening	wǎn shàng hǎo	晚上好
How are you?	ní hǎo ma?	你好吗?
fine	bú cuò	不错
And you?	nǐ ne?	你呢?
so-so	yì bān	一般
thank you	xiè xie	谢谢
thank you very much	duō xiè	多谢
You're welcome.	bú kè qì	不客气
It's nothing.	méi shén me	没什么

ENGLISH	PINYIN	CHINESE
yes (correct)	duì	对
no (incorrect)	cuò	错
is	shì	是
isn't	bú shì	不是
I don't know.	wǒ bù zhī dào	我不知道
please	qǐng	请
nice to meet you	hěn gāo xìng rèn shì nǐ	很高兴认识你
I'm sorry.	bù hǎo yì sī	不好意思
good–bye/see you later	zài jiàn	再见
more	gèng duō	更多
less	gèng shǎo	更少
a little	yì diǎn	一点
a lot	hěn duō	很多
big	dà	大
small	xiǎo	小
good	hǎo	好
better	gèng hǎo	更好
best	zuì hǎo	最好
bad	huài	坏
quick, fast	kuai	快
slow	màn	慢
easy	róng yì	容易
difficult	nán	难
he	tā	他
she	tā	她
it	tā	它
I don't speak Chinese well.	wǒ de zhōng wén bú tài hǎo	我的中文不太好
I don't understand.	wǒ bù míng bai	我不明白

SHOPPING

ENGLISH	PINYIN	CHINESE
I need...	wǒ yào	我要
I want...	wǒ yào	我要
How much? (quantity)	duō shǎo?	多少?
How much? (money)	duō shǎo qián?	多少钱?
May I see...	wǒ néng kàn kàn...	我能看看...
this one	zhè gè	这个
that one	nà gè	那个
expensive	guì	贵
cheap	pián yi	便宜
too much (quantity)	tài duō	太多
too much (money)	tài guì	太贵
can you go cheaper?	pián yi diǎn	便宜点

GETTING AROUND

ENGLISH	PINYIN	CHINESE
north	běi	北
south	něn	南
east	dōng	东
west	xī	西
central	zhōng	中
taxi	chū zū chē	出租车
go straight/keep going	zhí zǒu	直走
the right side	yòu biān	右边
turn right	yòu zhuǎn	右转
the left side	zuǒ biān	左边
turn left	zuǒ zhuǎn	左转
Stop!/Stop here!	tíng	停
the next street	xià tiáo jiē	下条街
Please slow down a little.	màn yì diǎn	慢一点
Hurry up a little.	kuài yì diǎn	快一点
here	zhè lǐ	这里
there	nà lǐ	那里
OK, good	xíng, hǎo	行, 好
How much do I owe you?	duō shǎo qián ?	多少钱?

HEALTH

ENGLISH	PINYIN	CHINESE
Help me please.	qǐng bāng bāng wǒ	请帮帮我
I am sick.	wǒ shēng bìng le	我生病了
pain	téng	疼
itch	yǎng	痒
lump	zhǒng zhàng / zhǒng kuài	肿胀 / 肿块
sore	suān tòng	酸痛
rash	zhěn	疹
fever	fā shāo	发烧
mucous	nián yè	粘液
discharge	pái chū	排出
pus	nóng	脓
blood	xiě	血
stomach ache	dù zi tong	肚子痛
vomiting	ǒu tù	呕吐
diarrhea	fù xiè	腹泻
constipation	biàn mì	便秘
feces/to defecate	dà biàn	大便
urine/to urinate	xiǎo biàn	小便
drugstore	yào diàn	药店
medicine	yào	药
pill, tablet	yào piàn	药片
diarrhea medicine	zhǐ xiè yào	止泻药
antacid	jiě suān yào	解酸药
cold medicine	gǎn mào yào	感冒药

RESOURCES

ENGLISH	PINYIN	CHINESE
anti-inflammatory medicine	xiāo yán yào	消炎药
pain reliever	zhǐ tòng yào	止痛药
anti-nausea medicine	zhì ě xīn de yào	治恶心的药
antihistamine	kàng zǔ ān	抗组胺
cortisone	shèn shàng xiàn pí zhǐ sù	肾上腺皮质素
anti-fungal	shā zhēn jūn jì	杀真菌剂
analgesic cream	zhǐ tòng gāo	止痛膏
antibiotic	kàng shēng sù	抗生素
Viagra	wēi ěr gāng (kàng yáng wěi / zhì liáo bó qǐ shī tiáo)	威而刚 （抗阳痿 / 治疗勃起失调）
Prozac	bǎi yōu jiě (zhì liáo yōu yù de yào jì)	百忧解 （治疗忧郁的药剂）
birth control pills	bì yùn yào	避孕药
condom	bì yùn tào	避孕套
period	yuè jīng	月经
pad	wèi shēng jīn	卫生巾
tampon	wèi shēng mián tiáo	卫生棉条
gynecologist	fù kē zhuān jiā	妇科专家

Chinese Measurements

SHOES AND CLOTHING

Women's Clothing

U.S.:	3/4	5/6	7/8	9/10	11/12	13/14
China:	34	36	38	40	42	44

Women's Shoes

U.S.:	5	6	7	8	9	10
China:	36	37	38	39	40	41

Men's Suits/Coats

U.S.:	34	36	38	40	42	44	46	48
China:	44	46	48	50	52	54	56	58

Men's Shirts

U.S.:	14½	15	15½	16	16½	17	17½	18
China:	37	38	39	41	42	43	44	45

Men's Shoes

U.S.:	7	8	9	10	11	12	13
China:	41	42	43	44	46	47	48

Children's Clothing

U.S.:	3	4	5	6	6x
China:	98	104	110	116	122

Children's Shoes

U.S.:	8	9	10	11	12	13	1	2	3
China:	24	25	27	28	29	30	32	33	34

OTHER CHINESE MEASURES

Long distances are measured in *li;* 1 *li* equals 0.311 miles.

Acreage is measured in *mu;* 1 *mu* equals 0.1647 acres.

Small weights, such as for buying produce or dry goods, are measured in *jin;* 1 *jin* equals 1.102 pounds; *ban jin* (half a *jin*) equals 0.551 pounds.

Numbers over 1,000 are measured in *wan,* which means 10,000. For example, 40 *wan* equals 400,000.

Discounts *(da zhe)* are expressed in the percentage you pay, not the percentage the item is reduced. For example, a sale for 30 percent off will have signs displaying "70."

Suggested Reading

BUSINESS AND ECONOMICS

Chan, John. *China Streetsmart: What You Must Know to be Effective and Profitable in China*. Jurong: Prentice Hall, 2003. Practical advice for international business.

Chang, Leslie T. *Factory Girls: From Village to City in a Changing China*. New York: Spiegel & Grau, 2008. The plight of the modern Chinese worker, with a focus on what life is like for women in China.

The China Business Handbook. London: Alain Charles, 2008. Updated annually, this book will keep you up-to-date on the business trends and new regulations for foreign firms and includes a business outlook for each province.

Fernandez, Juan Antonio and Laurie Underwood. *China CEO: Voices of Experience from 20 International Business Leaders*. Singapore: John Wiley & Sons, 2006.

Fernandez, Juan Antonio and Laurie Underwood. *China Entrepreneur: Voices of Experience from 40 International Business Pioneers*. Singapore: John Wiley & Sons, 2009.

Fishman, Ted. *China, Inc.: How the Rise of the Next Superpower Challenges America and the World* New York: Scribner, 2005. Explores China's growing economic prominence and what it means for the future.

Menges, Constantine C. *China: The Gathering Threat*. Nashville: Nelson Current, 2005. A worrisome look at how China's growth might negatively impact the West.

Shenkar, Oded. *The Chinese Century*. Upper Saddle River, NJ: Wharton School, 2005. The 21st century belongs to China, so we're told.

HISTORY AND POLITICS

Collis, Maurice. *Foreign Mud*. New Directions, 2002. A history of the opium trade.

Ebrey, Patricia Buckley. *Illustrated History of China*. London: Cambridge University Press, 1996. An extremely thorough and well-researched history that includes many insights not included in other similar books, such as the topic of the status of women throughout China's history.

Needham, Joseph, and Robert K. G. Temple. *The Genius of China*. London: Prion, 1998. This book shows how the Chinese were often well ahead of the West on many important scientific and societal advances.

Snow, Edgar. *Red Star over China*. New York: Grove, 1968. A firsthand biography of Mao by a Western journalist who traveled through China before the revolution.

Starr, John Bryan. *Understanding China: A Guide to China's Economy, History, and Political Culture*. New York: Hill and Wang, 1997. A broad overview and background introduction to China.

CULTURE

Schneiter, Fred, and Larry Feign. *Getting Along with the Chinese*. Hong Kong: Asia 2000, 2000. One of the best guides to understanding Chinese values, thinking, and customs.

Seligman, Scott. *Chinese Business Etiquette: A Guide to Protocol, Manners, and Culture in the People's Republic of China*. New York: Grand Central, 1999.

RESOURCES

Wilkinson, Kenneth. *Chinese Language, Life & Culture.* London: Teach Yourself Books, 2002. If you only bought one general book about China, this would be a good one.

FICTION

Buck, Pearl S. *The Good Earth.* New York: Pocket, 1994. A well-loved classic about a Chinese farmer and his family.

Tan, Amy. *The Joy Luck Club.* New York: Ivy Books, 1990. The tale of four Chinese mothers and their Americanized daughters.

Terada, Katsuya. *The Monkey King.* Milwaukie, OR: Dark Horse, 2005. An eccentric Hong Kong family in the 1950s.

Theroux, Paul. *Kowloon Tong.* New York: Mariner Books, 1998. A story of greed set during the handover of Hong Kong.

MEMOIR

Chang, Jung. *Wild Swans: Three Daughters of China.* New York: Touchstone, 2003. The moving memoirs of three generations of women interwoven with the history of the rise of communism.

Chen, Da. *Colors of the Mountain.* New York: Anchor, 2001. The struggles of growing up in rural Fujian province as a member of the despised landlord class.

Chen, Da. *Sounds of the River.* New York: Harper Perennial, 2003. Moving from the Chinese countryside to attend college in big city Beijing.

Clissold, Tim. *Mr. China, a Memoir.* New York: Collins, 2005. The tales of a British businessman as he struggled to meet the challenges of investing in China.

DeWoskin, Rachel. *Foreign Babes in Beijing: Behind the Scenes of a New China.* New York: W. W. Norton, 2005. The true account of an American woman in Beijing who finds unexpected fame as the star of a steamy soap opera.

Dunlop, Fuchsia. *Shark's Fin and Sichuan Pepper: A Sweet-Sour Memoir of Eating in China.* New York: W. W. Norton, 2008. Entertaining and enlightening tales of learning the intricacies of Chinese cuisine from one of the foremost experts on the subject.

Faison, Seth. *South of the Clouds: Exploring the Hidden Realms of China.* New York: St. Martin's, 2004. An intimate look at China based on 15 years as a student and journalist in the Middle Kingdom.

Hessler, Peter. *Oracle Bones: A Journey Through Time in China.* New York: Harper Perennial, 2006. Interwoven tales of the author's experiences in China and the Chinese individuals who have made an impression on him.

Hessler, Peter. *River Town: Two Years on the Yangtze.* New York: Harper Perennial, 2002. The tales of a Peace Corps volunteer.

Troost, J. Maarten. *Lost on Planet China: The Strange and True Story of One Man's Attempt to Understand the World's Most Mystifying Nation, or How He Became Comfortable Eating Live Squid.* New York: Broadway Books, 2008. Witty travel memoir.

LANGUAGE

Harbaugh, Rick. *Chinese Characters: A Genealogy and Dictionary.* New Haven, CT: Yale University Press, 1998.

Ho, Yong. *Chinese-English Frequency Dictionary,* New York: Hippocrene, 2003. The 500 most common Chinese words.

Peng, Tan Huay, and Huoping Chen. *Fun with Chinese Characters (Vols. 1–4.)* Singapore: Federal Publications, 1988. An amusing way to see the pictographs embedded in Chinese characters and radicals.

McNaughton, William. *Reading & Writing Chinese*. North Clarendon, VT: Tuttle, 2005.

CHILDREN'S BOOKS

Buck, Pearl S. *The Man Who Changed China: The Story of Sun Yat-sen*. New York: Random House, 1953. For grades 7–9.

Haskins, James, and Dennis Hockerman. *Count Your Way Through China*. Minneapolis: Carolrhoda, 1988. An introduction to China through Chinese characters for numbers 1–10. Best for those under 6, although the reading level is higher.

Lee, Huy Voun. *At the Beach*. New York: Henry Holt, 1994. A story about learning Chinese characters by writing in the sand. Ages 4–10.

McMahon, Patricia. *Six Words, Many Turtles, and Three Days in Hong Kong*. Boston: Houghton Mifflin, 1997. A true account of the daily life of an eight-year-old girl who lives in Hong Kong. For elementary grades.

So, Sungwan. *C Is for China*. Parsippany, NJ: Silver, 1997. An alphabetical photo book about China's people and history for 4–8-year-olds.

TRAVEL

Eyewitness Travel Guides China. London: DK, 2008.

Fodor's Exploring China. New York: Fodor's Travel, 2007.

Harper, Damian. *National Geographic Traveler China*. Washington, DC: National Geographic, 2007. A beautifully illustrated guide with an emphasis on historical and cultural sites.

Harper, Damian, et al. *Lonely Planet China*. Melbourne: Lonely Planet, 2007. Although this LP guide often gets complaints for missing or inaccurate information, it's still the most comprehensive China travel guide and a favorite among budget travelers.

Lewis, Simon, David Leffman, and Rough Guides. *The Rough Guide to China*. London: Rough Guides, 2008.

Stone, Andrew. *Lonely Planet Hong Kong & Macau*. Melbourne: Lonely Planet, 2008.

City Guides

Brown, Jules. *The Rough Guide to Hong Kong & Macau*. London: Rough Guides, 2008.

Harper, Damian. *Lonely Planet Beijing*. Melbourne: Lonely Planet, 2007.

Harper, Damian. *Lonely Planet Shanghai*. Melbourne: Lonely Planet, 2008.

Iveson, Helena. *Moon Beijing and Shanghai*. Berkeley, CA: Avalon Travel, 2008.

Lewis, Simon. *The Rough Guide to Beijing*. London: Rough Guides, 2008.

Pillsbury, Adam. *The Insider's Guide to Beijing*. Beijing: True Run Media. Published annually.

Stephens, Cindy Miller. *Hong Kong for Kids: A Parent's Guide*. Hong Kong: SCMP, 2007.

Urbanatomy Shanghai. Tianjin: Nankai University Press. Published annually.

RESOURCES

Suggested Films

Beijing Bicycle. Directed by Xiaoshuai Wang. 113 min. Sony Pictures, 2002. A coming-of-age story of Beijing boys as they proudly express themselves through bicycle tricks.

The Blue Kite. Directed by Tian Yi. 140 min. Kino, 2003. Beijing courtyard living during the 1950s and 1960s against the political backdrop of Maoism and the Cultural Revolution.

Crouching Tiger, Hidden Dragon. Directed by Ang Lee. 120 min. Sony Pictures, 2001. The quest to retrieve a mythic sword, complete with all the glorious special effects of Chinese martial arts films.

Eat Drink Man Woman. Directed by Ang Lee. 124 min. MGM, 2002. Set in Taiwan, this movie uses amazing cooking imagery as a metaphor for the way traditional family values are giving way to modern life.

The Joy Luck Club. Directed by Wayne Wang. 139 min. Buena Vista, 2002. An excellent adaptation of Amy Tan's 1990 novel of the same name.

The King of Masks. Directed by Wu Tian Ming. 101 min. Sony Pictures, 1999. A heartwarming tale of a stubborn old Sichuan street performer who desperately wants a male heir.

The Last Emperor. Directed by Bernardo Bertolucci. 218 min. Live/Artisan, 1999. A beautifully artistic film about the story of Pu Yi, the last emperor of China.

Mission Impossible: III. Directed by J. J. Abrams. 126 min. Paramount, 2006. Action-adventure flick partly set in Shanghai and filmed in nearby river town Xitang.

The Mummy: Tomb of the Dragon Emperor. Directed by Rob Cohen. 112 min. Universal, 2008. The terra-cotta warriors come to life to fight a final battle.

Not One Less. Directed by Yimou Zhang.

106 min. Sony Pictures, 2000. A touching story about a tiny school in the countryside.

Shanghai Kiss. Directed by Kern Konwiser. 106 min. Anchor Bay, 2007. A quirky and charming tale of a Chinese American returning to his homeland featuring Hayden Panettiere of the *Heroes* TV show.

Shanghai Knights. Directed by David Dobkin. 114 min. Walt Disney, 2003. In the sequel to *Shanghai Noon,* Chan and Wilson are at it again in this madcap comedy set in London.

Shanghai Noon. Directed by Tom Dey. 110 min. Walt Disney, 2000. A hilarious western starring Jacky Chan as a Chinese palace guard who travels to the United States and partners with a cowboy played by Owen Wilson.

To Live. Directed by Yimou Zhang. 132 min. MGM, 2003. Touching fictional history of one couple's life set during the years of the Cultural Revolution.

FAMILY FILMS

The Amazing Panda Adventure. Directed by Christopher Cain. 84 min. Warner Brothers, 1995. Set and filmed in Chengdu; an American boy and a Chinese girl try to save a panda from poachers.

Big Bird in China. Directed by Jon Stone. 75 min. Sony Wonder, 2004. Big Bird makes new friends and learns about China on a short trip to the Middle Kingdom.

Kung Fu Panda. Directed by Mark Osborne. 92 min. Dreamworks, 2008. A graceless panda tries to become a kung fu master. Animated.

Mulan. Directed by Tony Bancroft. 88 min. Walt Disney, 1999. The Chinese folk tale of a young woman who disguises herself as a man in order to join the army. Animated.

Index

www.moon.com

DESTINATIONS | ACTIVITIES | BLOGS | MAPS | BOOKS

MOON.COM is all new, and ready to help plan your next trip! Filled with fresh trip ideas and strategies, author interviews, informative blogs, a detailed map library, and descriptions of all the Moon guidebooks, Moon.com is all you need to get out and explore the world—or even places in your own backyard. As always, when you travel with Moon, expect an experience that is uncommon and truly unique.

MAP SYMBOLS

▦ Expressway	○ City/Town	✗ Airfield	≜ Archaeological Site
═══ Primary Road	◉ State Capital	✈ Airport	♟ Church
═══ Secondary Road			▮ Gas Station
▪▪▪▪ Unpaved Road	✪ National Capital	▲ Mountain	▦ Mangrove
▪▪▪▪▪▪ Ferry	★ Point of Interest	♠♠ Park	▦ Reef
▪━▪━▪ Railroad	▪ Other Location	⛷ Skiing Area	▦ Swamp

CONVERSION TABLES

$°C = (°F - 32) / 1.8$
$°F = (°C \times 1.8) + 32$
1 inch = 2.54 centimeters (cm)
1 foot = 0.304 meters (m)
1 yard = 0.914 meters
1 mile = 1.6093 kilometers (km)
1 km = 0.6214 miles
1 fathom = 1.8288 m
1 chain = 20.1168 m
1 furlong = 201.168 m
1 acre = 0.4047 hectares
1 sq km = 100 hectares
1 sq mile = 2.59 square km
1 ounce = 28.35 grams
1 pound = 0.4536 kilograms
1 short ton = 0.90718 metric ton
1 short ton = 2,000 pounds
1 long ton = 1.016 metric tons
1 long ton = 2,240 pounds
1 metric ton = 1,000 kilograms
1 quart = 0.94635 liters
1 US gallon = 3.7854 liters
1 Imperial gallon = 4.5459 liters
1 nautical mile = 1.852 km

MOON LIVING ABROAD IN CHINA

Avalon Travel
a member of the Perseus Books Group
1700 Fourth Street
Berkeley, CA 94710, USA
www.moon.com

Editors: Annie Blakley, Tiffany Watson
Series Manager: Elizabeth Hansen
Copy Editor: Christopher Church
Graphics Coordinator: Elizabeth Jang
Production Coordinator: Elizabeth Jang
Cover Designer: Elizabeth Jang
Map Editor: Albert Angulo
Cartographers: Chris Markiewicz, Kat Bennett
Indexer: Judy Hunt

ISBN-13: 978-1-59880-169-9
ISSN: 1932-5215

Printing History
1st Edition – 2006
2nd Edition – October 2009
5 4 3 2 1

Text © 2009 by Barbara and Stuart Strother.
Maps © 2009 by Avalon Travel.
All rights reserved.

Some photos and illustrations are used by permission and are the property of the original copyright owners.

Front cover photo: neon lights along Nanjing Lu; © Greg Elms / Lonely Planet Images

Title page photo: Hong Kong temple cat © Barbara Strother

Printed in Canada by Friesens

Interior color photos: page 4: junk in Hong Kong harbor; page 6 (thumbnail): lanterns decorate a mountain lodge near the Great Wall at Mutianyu; (lower left): stone lion in Hangzhou; page 6-7 (middle): Chinese knot embroidery in Shanghai; page 7 (upper left): sampan in Aberdeen, Hong Kong; (upper right): trinkets for sale at the Forbidden City in Beijing; (lower right): terra cotta warriors in Xi'an; page 8: (upper left): dog and scooter in Xi'an; (upper right): giant Buddha in Leshan. All photos © Barbara Strother

Moon Living Abroad and the Moon logo are the property of Avalon Travel Publishing. All other marks and logos depicted are the property of the original owners. All rights reserved. No part of this book may be translated or reproduced in any form, except brief extracts by a reviewer for the purpose of a review, without written permission of the copyright owner.

Although every effort was made to ensure that the information was correct at the time of going to press, the author and publisher do not assume and hereby disclaim any liability to any party for any loss or damage caused by errors, omissions, or any potential travel disruption due to labor or financial difficulty, whether such errors or omissions result from negligence, accident, or any other cause.

KEEPING CURRENT

Although we strive to produce the most up-to-date guidebook that we possibly can, change is unavoidable. Between the time this book goes to print and the time you read it, the cost of goods and services may have increased, and a handful of the businesses noted in these pages will undoubtedly move, alter their prices, or close their doors forever. Exchange rates fluctuate – sometimes dramatically – on a daily basis. Federal and local legal requirements and restrictions are also subject to change, so be sure to check with the appropriate authorities before making the move. If you see anything in this book that needs updating, clarification, or correction, please drop us a line. Send your comments via email to feedback@moon.com, or write to the address above.